Kubernetes A Complete DevOps Cookbook

Build and manage your applications, orchestrate containers, and deploy cloud-native services

Murat Karslioglu

BIRMINGHAM - MUMBAI

Kubernetes A Complete DevOps Cookbook

Copyright © 2020 Packt Publishing

Commissioning Editor: Vijin Boricha
Acquisition Editor: Meeta Rajani
Content Development Editor: Alokita Amanna
Senior Editor: Rahul Dsouza
Technical Editor: Dinesh Pawar
Copy Editor: Safis Editing
Project Coordinator: Neil Dmello
Proofreader: Safis Editing
Indexer: Priyanka Dhadke
Production Designer: Deepika Naik

First published: March 2020

Production reference: 1130320

Published by Packt Publishing Ltd.
Livery Place
35 Livery Street
Birmingham
B3 2PB, UK.

ISBN 978-1-83882-804-2

www.packt.com

To my wife, Svetlana, for being my loving partner throughout our joint life journey.
And to my incredible daughters, Melissa and Aylin, for making world a brighter place.
Never stop reaching for your dreams...

Packt>

Contributors

About the author

Murat Karslioglu is a distinguished technologist with years of experience in the Agile and DevOps methodologies. Murat is currently a VP of Product at MayaData, a start-up building a data agility platform for stateful applications, and a maintainer of open source projects, namely OpenEBS and Litmus. In his free time, Murat is busy writing practical articles about DevOps best practices, CI/CD, Kubernetes, and running stateful applications on popular Kubernetes platforms on his blog, *Containerized Me*. Murat also runs a cloud-native news curator site, *The Containerized Today*, where he regularly publishes updates on the Kubernetes ecosystem.

> *I want to thank my wife, Svetlana, and the rest of my family for their continuous support, patience, and encouragement throughout the whole tedious process of book-writing.*

About the reviewer

Scott Surovich, CKA, CKAD, Mirantis MKP, (New Google Certification) is the container engineering lead for a G-SIFI global bank where he is focused on global design and standards for Kubernetes on-premises clusters. An evangelist for containers and Kubernetes, he has presented GKE networking in the enterprise at Google Next and multi-tenant Kubernetes clusters in the enterprise at Kubecon. He is an active member of the CNCF's Financial Services working group, he worked with the Kubernetes multi-tenancy working group, and he has been a developer advocate for Tremolo Security's OIDC provider, OpenUnison. Recently, he also achieved the Google Cloud Certified Fellow: Hybrid Multi-Cloud certification.

Packt is searching for authors like you

If you're interested in becoming an author for Packt, please visit `authors.packtpub.com` and apply today. We have worked with thousands of developers and tech professionals, just like you, to help them share their insight with the global tech community. You can make a general application, apply for a specific hot topic that we are recruiting an author for, or submit your own idea.

Table of Contents

Preface   1

Chapter 1: Building Production-Ready Kubernetes Clusters   7
  Technical requirements   7
  Configuring a Kubernetes cluster on Amazon Web Services   8
    Getting ready   8
    How to do it...   9
      Installing the command-line tools to configure AWS services   9
      Installing kops to provision a Kubernetes cluster   10
      Provisioning a Kubernetes cluster on Amazon EC2   10
      Provisioning a managed Kubernetes cluster on Amazon EKS   12
    How it works...   13
    There's more...   14
      Using the AWS Shell   14
      Using a gossip-based cluster   15
      Using different regions for an S3 bucket   15
      Editing the cluster configuration   16
      Deleting your cluster   16
      Provisioning an EKS cluster using the Amazon EKS Management Console   16
      Deploying Kubernetes Dashboard   17
    See also   19
  Configuring a Kubernetes cluster on Google Cloud Platform   20
    Getting ready   20
    How to do it...   20
      Installing the command-line tools to configure GCP services   21
      Provisioning a managed Kubernetes cluster on GKE   22
      Connecting to Google Kubernetes Engine (GKE) clusters   22
    How it works...   22
    There's more...   23
      Using Google Cloud Shell   23
      Deploying with a custom network configuration   24
      Deleting your cluster   25
      Viewing the Workloads dashboard   25
    See also   25
  Configuring a Kubernetes cluster on Microsoft Azure   25
    Getting ready   25
    How to do it...   26
      Installing the command-line tools to configure Azure services   26
      Provisioning a managed Kubernetes cluster on AKS   27
      Connecting to AKS clusters   27
    How it works...   28
    There's more...   28

Deleting your cluster   29
Viewing Kubernetes Dashboard   29
See also   29
Configuring a Kubernetes cluster on Alibaba Cloud   30
Getting ready   30
How to do it…   31
Installing the command-line tools to configure Alibaba Cloud services   31
Provisioning a highly available Kubernetes cluster on Alibaba Cloud   32
Connecting to Alibaba Container Service clusters   34
How it works…   35
There's more…   37
Configuring and managing Kubernetes clusters with Rancher   37
Getting ready   38
How to do it…   38
Installing Rancher Server   38
Deploying a Kubernetes cluster   39
Importing an existing cluster   40
Enabling cluster and node providers   42
How it works…   43
There's more…   43
Bind mounting a host volume to keep data   43
Keeping user volumes persistent   44
Running Rancher on the same Kubernetes nodes   44
See also   45
Configuring Red Hat OpenShift   45
Getting ready   45
How to do it…   45
Downloading OpenShift binaries   46
Provisioning an OpenShift cluster   46
Connecting to OpenShift clusters   47
How it works…   48
There's more…   48
Deleting your cluster   49
See also   49
Configuring a Kubernetes cluster using Ansible   49
Getting ready   49
How to do it…   50
Installing Ansible   50
Provisioning a Kubernetes cluster using an Ansible playbook   50
Connecting to the Kubernetes cluster   51
See also   52
Troubleshooting installation issues   52
How to do it…   52
How it works…   53
There's more…   54
Setting log levels   54
See also   55

Chapter 2: Operating Applications on Kubernetes   57
  Technical requirements   57
  Deploying workloads using YAML files   58
    Getting ready   58
    How to do it...   58
      Creating a Deployment   58
      Verifying a Deployment   59
      Editing a Deployment   60
      Rolling back a deployment   62
      Deleting a Deployment   63
    How it works...   63
    See also   64
  Deploying workloads using Kustomize   64
    Getting ready   64
    How to do it...   64
      Validating the Kubernetes cluster version   65
      Generating Kubernetes resources from files   65
      Creating a base for a development and production Deployment   67
    How it works...   70
    See also   71
  Deploying workloads using Helm charts   71
    Getting ready   71
    How to do it...   71
      Installing Helm 2.x   72
      Installing an application using Helm charts 73
      Searching for an application in Helm repositories   74
      Upgrading an application using Helm   75
      Rolling back an application using Helm   76
      Deleting an application using Helm   77
      Adding new Helm repositories   77
      Building a Helm chart   79
    How it works...   80
    See also   81
  Deploying and operating applications using Kubernetes operators 81
    Getting ready   81
    How to do it...   82
      Installing KUDO and the KUDO kubectl plugin 82
      Installing the Apache Kafka Operator using KUDO   83
      Installing Operator Lifecycle Manager   84
      Installing the Zalando PostgreSQL Operator   84
    See also   85
  Deploying and managing the life cycle of Jenkins X   86
    Getting ready   86
    How to do it...   87
      Installing the Jenkins X CLI   87
      Creating a Jenkins X Kubernetes cluster   88
      Verifying Jenkins X components   89

Switching Kubernetes clusters | 90
Validating cluster conformance | 91
How it works... | 91
There's more... | 92
Importing an application | 92
Upgrading a Jenkins X application | 92
Deleting a Jenkins X Kubernetes cluster | 93
See also | 93
Deploying and managing the life cycle of GitLab | 94
Getting ready | 94
How to do it... | 94
Installing GitLab using Helm | 95
Connecting to the GitLab dashboard | 96
Creating the first GitLab user | 96
Upgrading GitLab | 97
How it works... | 98
There's more... | 99
Using your own wildcard certificate | 99
Using autogenerated self-signed certificates | 99
Enabling the GitLab Operator | 100
Deleting GitLab | 100
See also | 101
Chapter 3: Building CI/CD Pipelines | 103
Technical requirements | 103
Creating a CI/CD pipeline in Jenkins X | 104
Getting ready | 104
How to do it... | 104
Connecting to Jenkins Pipeline Console | 104
Importing an application as a pipeline | 106
Checking application status | 107
Promoting an application to production | 108
Creating a pipeline using a QuickStart application | 109
How it works... | 110
Creating a CI/CD pipeline in GitLab | 111
Getting ready | 111
How to do it... | 112
Creating a project using templates | 112
Importing an existing project from GitHub | 114
Enabling Auto DevOps | 117
Enabling Kubernetes cluster integration | 119
Creating a pipeline using Auto DevOps | 122
Incrementally rolling out applications to production | 124
How it works... | 126
There's more... | 127
GitLab Web IDE | 127
Monitoring environments | 128
See also | 130

Creating a CI/CD pipeline in CircleCI   130
  Getting ready   130
  How to do it...   131
    Getting started with CircleCI   131
    Deploying changes to a Kubernetes cluster on EKS   132
  How it works...   133
  See also   134
Setting up a CI/CD pipeline using GitHub Actions   134
  Getting ready   135
  How to do it...   135
    Creating a workflow file   135
    Creating a basic Docker build workflow   137
    Building and publishing images to Docker Registry   138
    Adding a workflow status badge   139
  See also   140
Setting up a CI/CD pipeline on Amazon Web Services   140
  Getting ready   140
  How to do it...   140
    Creating an AWS CodeCommit code repository   141
    Building projects with AWS CodeBuild   145
    Creating an AWS CodeDeploy deployment   150
    Building a pipeline with AWS CodePipeline   150
  How it works...   153
  See also   154
Setting up a CI/CD pipeline with Spinnaker on Google Cloud Build   154
  Getting ready   154
  How to do it...   155
    Installing and configuring the Spin CLI   155
    Configuring a service account for the CI/CD   156
    Configuring events to trigger a pipeline   157
    Deploying Spinnaker using Helm   158
    Creating a Google Cloud Source code repository   159
    Building projects with Google Cloud Build   161
    Configuring a Spinnaker pipeline   164
    Rolling out an application to production   164
  See also   168
Setting up a CI/CD pipeline on Azure DevOps   168
  Getting ready   168
  How to do it...   168
    Getting started with Azure DevOps   169
    Configuring Azure Pipelines   170
    Deploying changes to an AKS cluster   174
  How it works...   178
  See also   179

Chapter 4: Automating Tests in DevOps   181
Technical requirements   181

Building event-driven automation with StackStorm   182
  Getting ready   182
  How to do it…   182
    Installing StackStorm   182
    Accessing the StackStorm UI   183
    Using the st2 CLI   185
    Defining a rule   186
    Deploying a rule   188
  See also   189
Automating tests with the Litmus framework   189
  Getting ready   189
  How to do it…   190
    Installing the Litmus Operator   190
    Using Chaos Charts for Kubernetes   191
    Creating a pod deletion chaos experiment   193
    Reviewing chaos experiment results   195
    Viewing chaos experiment logs   196
  How it works…   197
  See also   198
Automating Chaos Engineering with Gremlin   198
  Getting ready   198
  How to do it…   198
    Setting up Gremlin credentials   199
    Installing Gremlin on Kubernetes   200
    Creating a CPU attack against a Kubernetes worker 201
    Creating a node shutdown attack against a Kubernetes worker 205
    Running predefined scenario-based attacks   208
    Deleting Gremlin from your cluster   209
  How it works…   210
  See also   210
Automating your code review with Codacy   210
  Getting ready   210
  How to do it…   210
    Accessing the Project Dashboard   211
    Reviewing commits and PRs   213
    Viewing issues by category   215
    Adding a Codacy badge to your repository   217
  See also   218
Detecting bugs and anti-patterns with SonarQube   218
  Getting ready   218
  How to do it…   219
    Installing SonarQube using Helm   219
    Accessing the SonarQube Dashboard   220
    Creating a new user and tokens   222
    Enabling quality profiles   224
    Adding a project   227
    Reviewing a project's quality   229
    Adding marketplace plugins   230

Deleting SonarQube from your cluster 232
How it works... 232
See also 232
Detecting license compliance issues with FOSSA 233
Getting ready 233
How to do it... 233
Adding projects to FOSSA 234
Triaging licensing issues 236
Adding a FOSSA badge to your project 238
Chapter 5: Preparing for Stateful Workloads 241
Technical requirements 241
Managing Amazon EBS volumes in Kubernetes 242
Getting ready 242
How to do it... 242
Creating an EBS storage class 243
Changing the default storage class 244
Using EBS volumes for persistent storage 245
Using EBS storage classes to dynamically create persistent volumes 246
Deleting EBS persistent volumes 248
Installing the EBS CSI driver to manage EBS volumes 250
See also 252
Managing GCE PD volumes in Kubernetes 253
Getting ready 253
How to do it... 253
Creating a GCE persistent disk storage class 254
Changing the default storage class 255
Using GCE PD volumes for persistent storage 257
Using GCE PD storage classes to create dynamic persistent volumes 259
Deleting GCE PD persistent volumes 260
Installing the GCP Compute PD CSI driver to manage PD volumes 261
How it works... 263
See also 264
Managing Azure Disk volumes in Kubernetes 264
Getting ready 264
How to do it... 264
Creating an Azure Disk storage class 265
Changing the default storage class to ZRS 266
Using Azure Disk storage classes to create dynamic PVs 267
Deleting Azure Disk persistent volumes 268
Installing the Azure Disk CSI driver 269
See also 271
Configuring and managing persistent storage using Rook 271
Getting ready 272
How to do it... 272
Installing a Ceph provider using Rook 272
Creating a Ceph cluster 273
Verifying a Ceph cluster's health 273

Create a Ceph block storage class 274
Using a Ceph block storage class to create dynamic PVs 276
See also 277
Configuring and managing persistent storage using OpenEBS 277
Getting ready 278
How to do it... 278
Installing iSCSI client prerequisites 278
Installing OpenEBS 279
Using ephemeral storage to create persistent volumes 279
Creating storage pools 281
Creating OpenEBS storage classes 282
Using an OpenEBS storage class to create dynamic PVs 284
How it works... 285
See also 286
Setting up NFS for shared storage on Kubernetes 286
Getting ready 286
How to do it... 286
Installing NFS prerequisites 287
Installing an NFS provider using a Rook NFS operator 287
Using a Rook NFS operator storage class to create dynamic NFS PVs 289
Installing an NFS provisioner using OpenEBS 290
Using the OpenEBS NFS provisioner storage class to create dynamic NFS PVs 290
See also 291
Troubleshooting storage issues 291
Getting ready 291
How to do it... 292
Persistent volumes in the pending state 292
A PV is stuck once a PVC has been deleted 293

Chapter 6: Disaster Recovery and Backup 295
Technical requirements 295
Configuring and managing S3 object storage using MinIO 296
Getting ready 296
How to do it... 296
Creating a deployment YAML manifest 297
Creating a MinIO S3 service 298
Accessing the MinIO web user interface 299
How it works... 300
See also 301
Managing Kubernetes Volume Snapshots and restore 301
Getting ready 301
How to do it... 302
Enabling feature gates 302
Creating a volume snapshot via CSI 302
Restoring a volume from a snapshot via CSI 304
Cloning a volume via CSI 306
How it works... 306

See also 307
Application backup and recovery using Velero 307
Getting ready 308
How to do it... 308
Installing Velero 309
Backing up an application 310
Restoring an application 312
Creating a scheduled backup 312
Taking a backup of an entire namespace 313
Viewing backups with MinIO 314
Deleting backups and schedules 315
How it works... 316
See also 316
Application backup and recovery using Kasten 316
Getting ready 317
How to do it... 317
Installing Kasten 317
Accessing the Kasten Dashboard 319
Backing up an application 320
Restoring an application 324
How it works... 326
See also 326
Cross-cloud application migration 326
Getting ready 327
How to do it... 327
Creating an export profile in Kasten 327
Exporting a restore point in Kasten 328
Creating an import profile in Kasten 330
Migrating an application in Kasten 330
Importing clusters into OpenEBS Director 332
Migrating an application in OpenEBS Director 335
See also 338

Chapter 7: Scaling and Upgrading Applications 339
Technical requirements 339
Scaling applications on Kubernetes 340
Getting ready 340
How to do it... 340
Validating the installation of Metrics Server 340
Manually scaling an application 341
Autoscaling applications using a Horizontal Pod Autoscaler 343
How it works... 346
See also 347
Assigning applications to nodes 347
Getting ready 347
How to do it... 347
Labeling nodes 348

Assigning pods to nodes using nodeSelector 349
Assigning pods to nodes using node and inter-pod Affinity 351
How it works... 355
See also 357
Creating an external load balancer 357
Getting ready 358
How to do it... 358
Creating an external cloud load balancer 358
Finding the external address of the service 360
How it works... 361
See also 361
Creating an ingress service and service mesh using Istio 362
Getting ready 362
How to do it... 362
Installing Istio using Helm 363
Verifying the installation 363
Creating an ingress gateway 365
How it works... 366
There's more... 367
Deleting Istio 367
See also 367
Creating an ingress service and service mesh using Linkerd 368
Getting ready 368
How to do it... 368
Installing the Linkerd CLI 369
Installing Linkerd 369
Verifying a Linkerd deployment 370
Adding Linkerd to a service 370
There's more... 371
Accessing the dashboard 371
Deleting Linkerd 372
See also 372
Auto-healing pods in Kubernetes 373
Getting ready 373
How to do it... 373
Testing self-healing pods 373
Adding liveness probes to pods 374
How it works... 376
See also 376
Managing upgrades through blue/green deployments 377
Getting ready 377
How to do it... 377
Creating the blue deployment 378
Creating the green deployment 379
Switching traffic from blue to green 379
See also 380

Chapter 8: Observability and Monitoring on Kubernetes   381
  Technical requirements   381
  Monitoring in Kubernetes   382
    Getting ready   382
    How to do it...   382
      Adding metrics using Kubernetes Metrics Server   383
      Monitoring metrics using the CLI   383
      Monitoring metrics using Kubernetes Dashboard   384
      Monitoring node health   387
    See also   388
  Inspecting containers   388
    Getting ready   388
    How to do it...   389
      Inspecting pods in Pending status   389
      Inspecting pods in ImagePullBackOff status   391
      Inspecting pods in CrashLoopBackOff status   393
    See also   395
  Monitoring using Amazon CloudWatch   395
    Getting ready   396
    How to do it...   396
      Enabling Webhook authorization mode   396
      Installing Container Insights Agents for Amazon EKS   399
      Viewing Container Insights metrics   400
    See also   404
  Monitoring using Google Stackdriver   404
    Getting ready   405
    How to do it...   405
      Installing Stackdriver Kubernetes Engine Monitoring support for GKE   405
      Configuring a workspace on Stackdriver   406
      Monitoring GKE metrics using Stackdriver   409
    See also   414
  Monitoring using Azure Monitor   415
    Getting ready   415
    How to do it...   415
      Enabling Azure Monitor support for AKS using the CLI   415
      Monitoring AKS performance metrics using Azure Monitor   416
      Viewing live logs using Azure Monitor   422
    See also   428
  Monitoring Kubernetes using Prometheus and Grafana   429
    Getting ready   429
    How to do it...   429
      Deploying Prometheus using Helm charts   429
      Monitoring metrics using Grafana dashboards   430
      Adding a Grafana dashboard to monitor applications   435
    See also   439
  Monitoring and performance analysis using Sysdig   440

Getting ready 440
How to do it… 440
    Installing the Sysdig agent 440
    Analyzing application performance 443
See also 447
Managing the cost of resources using Kubecost 447
Getting ready 448
How to do it… 448
    Installing Kubecost 448
    Accessing the Kubecost dashboard 449
    Monitoring Kubernetes resource cost allocation 451
See also 455

Chapter 9: Securing Applications and Clusters 457
Technical requirements 457
Using RBAC to harden cluster security 458
Getting ready 458
How to do it… 458
    Viewing the default Roles 459
    Creating user accounts 460
    Creating Roles and RoleBindings 462
    Testing the RBAC rules 464
How it works… 464
See also 465
Configuring Pod Security Policies 465
Getting ready 466
How to do it… 466
    Enabling PSPs on EKS 466
    Enabling PSPs on GKE 467
    Enabling PodSecurityPolicy on AKS 468
    Creating a restricted PSPs 469
There's more… 470
    Restricting pods to access certain volume types 470
    Using Kubernetes PodSecurityPolicy advisor 472
See also 472
Using Kubernetes CIS Benchmark for security auditing 473
Getting ready 473
How to do it… 473
    Running kube-bench on Kubernetes 474
    Running kube-bench on managed Kubernetes services 477
    Running kube-bench on OpenShift 479
How it works… 480
See also 480
Building DevSecOps into the pipeline using Aqua Security 481
Getting ready 481
How to do it… 482
    Scanning images using Trivy 482

Building vulnerability scanning into GitLab 484
Building vulnerability scanning into CircleCI 485
See also 487
Monitoring suspicious application activities using Falco 488
Getting ready 488
How to do it... 488
Installing Falco on Kubernetes 488
Detecting anomalies using Falco 490
Defining custom rules 491
How it works... 493
See also 494
Securing credentials using HashiCorp Vault 494
Getting ready 495
How to do it... 495
Installing Vault on Kubernetes 495
Accessing the Vault UI 497
Storing credentials on Vault 499
See also 501

Chapter 10: Logging with Kubernetes 503
Technical requirements 503
Accessing Kubernetes logs locally 504
Getting ready 504
How to do it... 504
Accessing logs through Kubernetes 504
Debugging services locally using Telepresence 507
How it works... 509
See also 510
Accessing application-specific logs 510
Getting ready 510
How to do it... 511
Getting shell access in a container 511
Accessing PostgreSQL logs inside a container 512
Building centralized logging in Kubernetes using the EFK stack 513
Getting ready 514
How to do it... 514
Deploying Elasticsearch Operator 514
Requesting the Elasticsearch endpoint 516
Deploying Kibana 516
Aggregating logs with Fluent Bit 517
Accessing Kubernetes logs on Kibana 518
See also 524
Logging Kubernetes using Google Stackdriver 525
Getting ready 525
How to do it... 525
Installing Stackdriver Kubernetes Engine Monitoring support for GKE 526
Viewing GKE logs using Stackdriver 528

See also   531
Using a managed Kubernetes logging service   532
Getting ready   532
How to do it...   532
Connecting clusters to Director Online   532
Accessing logs using Director Online   536
Logging for your Jenkins CI/CD environment   537
Getting ready   538
How to do it...   538
Installing the Fluentd plugin   538
Streaming Jenkins logs to Elasticsearch using Fluentd   540
There's more...   541
Installing the Logstash plugin   541
Streaming Jenkins logs to Elasticsearch using Logstash   543
See also   544

Other Books You May Enjoy   545

Index   549

Preface

Kubernetes is an open source container orchestration platform originally developed by Google and made available to the public in 2014. It has made the deployment of container-based, complex, distributed systems simpler for developers. Since its inception, the community has built a large ecosystem around Kubernetes with many open source projects. This book is specially designed to quickly help Kubernetes administrators and **site reliability engineers (SREs)** to find the right tools and get up to speed with Kubernetes. The book covers everything from getting Kubernetes clusters up on most popular cloud and on-premises solutions to recipes that help you automate testing and move your applications out to production environments.

Kubernetes – A Complete DevOps Cookbook gives you clear, step-by-step instructions to install and run your private Kubernetes clusters successfully. It is full of practical and applicable recipes that enable you to use the latest capabilities of Kubernetes, as well as other third-party solutions, and implement them.

Who this book is for

This book targets developers, IT professionals, SREs, and DevOps teams and engineers looking to manage, scale, and orchestrate applications in their organizations using Kubernetes. A basic understanding of Linux, Kubernetes, and containerization is required.

What this book covers

Chapter 1, *Building Production-Ready Kubernetes Clusters*, teaches you how to configure Kubernetes services on different public clouds or on-premises using the popular options available today.

Chapter 2, *Operating Applications on Kubernetes*, teaches you how to deploy DevOps tools and **continuous integration/continuous deployment (CI/CD)** infrastructure on Kubernetes using the most popular life cycle management options.

Chapter 3, *Building CI/CD Pipelines*, teaches you how to build, push, and deploy applications from development to production and also ways to detect bugs, anti-patterns, and license concerns during the process.

Chapter 4, *Automating Tests in DevOps*, teaches you how to automate testing in a DevOps workflow to accelerate time to production, reduce loss-of-delivery risks, and detect service anomalies using known test automation tools in Kubernetes.

Chapter 5, *Preparing for Stateful Workloads*, teaches you how to protect the state of applications from node or application failures, as well as how to share data and reattach volumes.

Chapter 6, *Disaster Recovery and Backup*, teaches you how to handle backup and disaster recovery scenarios to keep applications in production highly available and quickly recover service during cloud-provider or basic Kubernetes node failures.

Chapter 7, *Scaling and Upgrading Applications*, teaches you how to dynamically scale containerized services on running on Kubernetes to handle the changing traffic needs of your service.

Chapter 8, *Observability and Monitoring on Kubernetes*, teaches you how to monitor metrics for performance analysis and also how to monitor and manage the real-time cost of Kubernetes resources.

Chapter 9, *Securing Applications and Clusters*, teaches you how to build DevSecOps into CI/CD pipelines, detect metrics for performance analysis, and securely manage secrets and credentials.

Chapter 10, *Logging on Kubernetes*, teaches you how to set up a cluster to ingest logs, as well as how to view them using both self-managed and hosted solutions.

To get the most out of this book

To use this book, you will need access to computers, servers, or cloud-provider services where you can provision virtual machine instances. To set up the lab environments, you may also need larger cloud instances that will require you to enable billing.

We assume that you are using an Ubuntu host (18.04, codename Bionic Beaver at the time of writing); the book provides steps for Ubuntu environments.

Software/Hardware covered in the book	OS Requirements
GitLab, Jenkins X, OpenShift, Rancher, kops, cURL, Python, Vim or Nano, kubectl, helm	Ubuntu/Windows/macOS

You will need AWS, GCP, and Azure credentials to perform some of the recipes in this book.

If you are using the digital version of this book, we advise you to type the code yourself or access the code via the GitHub repository (link available in the next section). Doing so will help you avoid any potential errors related to copy/pasting of code.

Download the example code files

You can download the example code files for this book from your account at www.packt.com. If you purchased this book elsewhere, you can visit www.packtpub.com/support and register to have the files emailed directly to you.

You can download the code files by following these steps:

1. Log in or register at www.packt.com.
2. Select the **Support** tab.
3. Click on **Code Downloads**.
4. Enter the name of the book in the **Search** box and follow the onscreen instructions.

Once the file is downloaded, please make sure that you unzip or extract the folder using the latest version of:

- WinRAR/7-Zip for Windows
- Zipeg/iZip/UnRarX for Mac
- 7-Zip/PeaZip for Linux

The code bundle for the book is also hosted on GitHub at https://github.com/k8sdevopscookbook/src and https://github.com/PacktPublishing/Kubernetes-A-Complete-DevOps-Cookbook. In case there's an update to the code, it will be updated on the existing GitHub repository.

We also have other code bundles from our rich catalog of books and videos available at https://github.com/PacktPublishing/. Check them out!

Download the color images

We also provide a PDF file that has color images of the screenshots/diagrams used in this book. You can download it here: `http://www.packtpub.com/sites/default/files/downloads/9781838828042_ColorImages.pdf`.

Code in Action

Visit the following link to check out videos of the code being run: `http://bit.ly/2U0Cm8x`

Conventions used

There are a number of text conventions used throughout this book.

`CodeInText`: Indicates code words in text, database table names, folder names, filenames, file extensions, pathnames, dummy URLs, user input, and Twitter handles. Here is an example: "Mount the downloaded `WebStorm-10*.dmg` disk image file as another disk in your system."

A block of code is set as follows:

```
html, body, #map {
  height: 100%;
  margin: 0;
  padding: 0
}
```

When we wish to draw your attention to a particular part of a code block, the relevant lines or items are set in bold:

```
[default]
exten => s,1,Dial(Zap/1|30)
exten => s,2,Voicemail(u100)
exten => s,102,Voicemail(b100)
exten => i,1,Voicemail(s0)
```

Any command-line input or output is written as follows:

```
$ mkdir css
$ cd css
```

Bold: Indicates a new term, an important word, or words that you see onscreen. For example, words in menus or dialog boxes appear in the text like this. Here is an example: "Select **System info** from the **Administration** panel."

Warnings or important notes appear like this.

 Tips and tricks appear like this.

Sections

In this book, you will find several headings that appear frequently (*Getting ready*, *How to do it...*, *How it works...*, *There's more...*, and *See also*).

To give clear instructions on how to complete a recipe, use these sections as follows.

Getting ready

This section tells you what to expect in the recipe and describes how to set up any software or any preliminary settings required for the recipe.

How to do it...

This section contains the steps required to follow the recipe.

How it works...

This section usually consists of a detailed explanation of what happened in the previous section.

There's more...

This section consists of additional information about the recipe in order to make you more knowledgeable about the recipe.

See also

This section provides helpful links to other useful information for the recipe.

Get in touch

Feedback from our readers is always welcome.

General feedback: If you have questions about any aspect of this book, mention the book title in the subject of your message and email us at customercare@packtpub.com.

Errata: Although we have taken every care to ensure the accuracy of our content, mistakes do happen. If you have found a mistake in this book, we would be grateful if you would report this to us. Please visit www.packtpub.com/support/errata, selecting your book, clicking on the Errata Submission Form link, and entering the details.

Piracy: If you come across any illegal copies of our works in any form on the Internet, we would be grateful if you would provide us with the location address or website name. Please contact us at copyright@packt.com with a link to the material.

If you are interested in becoming an author: If there is a topic that you have expertise in and you are interested in either writing or contributing to a book, please visit authors.packtpub.com.

Reviews

Please leave a review. Once you have read and used this book, why not leave a review on the site that you purchased it from? Potential readers can then see and use your unbiased opinion to make purchase decisions, we at Packt can understand what you think about our products, and our authors can see your feedback on their book. Thank you!

For more information about Packt, please visit packt.com.

Building Production-Ready Kubernetes Clusters

This chapter proposes the most common deployment methods that are used on popular cloud services as well as on-premises, although you will certainly find a number of other tutorials on the internet explaining other approaches. This chapter explains the differences between managed/hosted cloud services versus self-managed cloud or on-premises Kubernetes deployments and the advantages of one vendor over another.

In this chapter, we will be covering the following recipes:

- Configuring a Kubernetes cluster on Amazon Web Services
- Configuring a Kubernetes cluster on Google Cloud Platform
- Configuring a Kubernetes cluster on Microsoft Azure
- Configuring a Kubernetes cluster on Alibaba Cloud
- Configuring and managing Kubernetes clusters with Rancher
- Configuring Red Hat OpenShift
- Configuring a Kubernetes cluster using Ansible
- Troubleshooting installation issues

Technical requirements

It is recommended that you have a fundamental knowledge of Linux containers and Kubernetes in general. For preparing your Kubernetes clusters, using a Linux host is recommended. If your workstation is Windows-based, then we recommend that you use **Windows Subsystem for Linux** (**WSL**). WSL gives you a Linux command line on Windows and lets you run ELF64 Linux binaries on Windows.

It's always good practice to develop using the same environment (which means the same distribution and the same version) as the one that will be used in production. This will avoid unexpected surprises such as **It Worked on My Machine** (**IWOMM**). If your workstation is using a different OS, another good approach is to set up a virtual machine on your workstation. VirtualBox (https://www.virtualbox.org/) is a free and open source hypervisor that runs on Windows, Linux, and macOS.

In this chapter, we'll assume that you are using an Ubuntu host (18.04, code name Bionic Beaver at the time of writing). There are no specific hardware requirements since all the recipes in this chapter will be deployed and run on cloud instances. Here is the list of software packages that will be required on your localhost to complete the recipes:

- cURL
- Python
- Vim or Nano (or your favorite text editor)

Configuring a Kubernetes cluster on Amazon Web Services

The recipes in this section will take you through how to get a fully functional Kubernetes cluster with a fully customizable master and worker nodes that you can use for the recipes in the following chapters or in production.

In this section, we will cover both Amazon EC2 and Amazon EKS recipes so that we can run Kubernetes on **Amazon Web Services** (**AWS**).

Getting ready

All the operations mentioned here require an AWS account and an AWS user with a policy that has permission to use the related services. If you don't have one, go to https://aws.amazon.com/account/ and create one.

AWS provides two main options when it comes to running Kubernetes on it. You can consider using the **Amazon Elastic Compute Cloud** (**Amazon EC2**) if you'd like to manage your deployment completely and have specific powerful instance requirements. Otherwise, it's highly recommended to consider using managed services such as **Amazon Elastic Container Service for Kubernetes** (**Amazon EKS**).

How to do it...

Depending on whether you want to use AWS EC2 service or EKS, you can follow the following recipes to get your cluster up and running using either kops or eksctl tools:

- Installing the command-line tools to configure AWS services
- Installing kops to provision a Kubernetes cluster
- Provisioning a Kubernetes cluster on Amazon EC2
- Provisioning a managed Kubernetes cluster on Amazon EKS

Installing the command-line tools to configure AWS services

In this recipe, we will get the AWS **Command-Line Interface (CLI)** awscli and the Amazon EKS CLI eksctl to access and configure AWS services.

Let's perform the following steps:

1. Install awscli on your workstation:

   ```
   $ sudo apt-get update && sudo apt-get install awscli
   ```

2. Configure the AWS CLI so that it uses your access key ID and secret access key:

   ```
   $ aws configure
   ```

3. Download and install the Amazon EKS command-line interface, eksctl:

   ```
   $ curl --silent --location
   "https://github.com/weaveworks/eksctl/releases/download/latest_rele
   ase/eksctl_$(uname -s)_amd64.tar.gz" | tar xz -C /tmp
   $ sudo mv /tmp/eksctl /usr/local/bin
   ```

4. Verify its version and make sure eksctl is installed:

   ```
   $ eksctl version
   ```

   To be able to perform the following recipes, the eksctl version should be 0.13.0 or later.

Installing kops to provision a Kubernetes cluster

In this recipe, we will get the Kubernetes Operations tool, `kops`, and Kubernetes command-line tool, `kubectl`, installed in order to provision and manage Kubernetes clusters.

Let's perform the following steps:

1. Download and install the Kubernetes Operations tool, `kops`:

```
$ curl -LO
https://github.com/kubernetes/kops/releases/download/$(curl -s
https://api.github.com/repos/kubernetes/kops/releases/latest | grep
tag_name | cut -d '"' -f 4)/kops-linux-amd64
$ chmod +x kops-linux-amd64 && sudo mv kops-linux-amd64
/usr/local/bin/kops
```

2. Run the following command to make sure `kops` is installed and confirm that the version is `1.15.0` or later:

```
$ kops version
```

3. Download and install the Kubernetes command-line tool, `kubectl`:

```
$ curl -LO
https://storage.googleapis.com/kubernetes-release/release/$(curl -s
https://storage.googleapis.com/kubernetes-release/release/stable.tx
t)/bin/linux/amd64/kubectl
$ chmod +x ./kubectl && sudo mv ./kubectl /usr/local/bin/kubectl
```

4. Verify its version and make sure `kubectl` is installed:

```
$ kubectl version --short
```

To be able to perform the following recipes, the `kubectl` version should be `v1.15` or later.

Provisioning a Kubernetes cluster on Amazon EC2

This recipe will take you through how to get a fully functional Kubernetes cluster with fully customizable master and worker nodes that you can use for the recipes in the following chapters or in production.

Let's perform the following steps:

1. Create a domain for your cluster.

> It is a cloud management best practice to have subdomains and to divide your clusters with logical and valid DNS names for `kops` to successfully discovery them.

As an example, I will use the `k8s.containerized.me` subdomain as our hosted zone. Also, if your domain is registered with a registrar other than Amazon Route 53, you must update the name servers with your registrar and add Route 53 NS records for the hosted zone to your registrar's DNS records:

```
$ aws route53 create-hosted-zone --name k8s.containerized.me \
--caller-reference k8s-devops-cookbook \
--hosted-zone-config Comment="Hosted Zone for my K8s Cluster"
```

2. Create an S3 bucket to store the Kubernetes configuration and the state of the cluster. In our example, we will use `s3.k8s.containerized.me` as our bucket name:

```
$ aws s3api create-bucket --bucket s3.k8s.containerized.me \
--region us-east-1
```

3. Confirm your S3 bucket by listing the available bucket:

```
$ aws s3 ls
2019-07-21 22:02:58 s3.k8s.containerized.me
```

4. Enable bucket versioning:

```
$ aws s3api put-bucket-versioning --bucket s3.k8s.containerized.me \
--versioning-configuration Status=Enabled
```

5. Set environmental parameters for `kops` so that you can use the locations by default:

```
$ export KOPS_CLUSTER_NAME=useast1.k8s.containerized.me
$ export KOPS_STATE_STORE=s3://s3.k8s.containerized.me
```

6. Create an SSH key if you haven't done so already:

```
$ ssh-keygen -t rsa
```

7. Create the cluster configuration with the list of zones where you want your master nodes to run:

```
$ kops create cluster --node-count=6 --node-size=t3.large \
  --zones=us-east-1a,us-east-1b,us-east-1c \
  --master-size=t3.large \
  --master-zones=us-east-1a,us-east-1b,us-east-1c
```

8. Create the cluster:

```
$ kops update cluster --name ${KOPS_CLUSTER_NAME} --yes
```

9. Wait a couple of minutes for the nodes to launch and validate:

```
$ kops validate cluster
```

10. Now, you can use kubectl to manage your cluster:

```
$ kubectl cluster-info
```

By default, kops creates and exports the Kubernetes configuration under ~/.kube/config. Therefore, no additional steps are required to connect your clusters using kubectl.

Provisioning a managed Kubernetes cluster on Amazon EKS

Perform the following steps to get your managed Kubernetes-as-a-service cluster up and running on Amazon EKS using eksctl:

1. Create a cluster using the default settings:

```
$ eksctl create cluster
...
[√] EKS cluster "great-outfit-123" in "us-west-2" region is ready
```

By default, eksctl deploys a cluster with workers on two m5.large instances using the AWS EKS AMI in the us-west-2 region. eksctl creates and exports the Kubernetes configuration under ~/.kube/config. Therefore, no additional steps are required to connect your clusters using kubectl.

2. Confirm the cluster information and workers:

```
$ kubectl cluster-info && kubectl get nodes
Kubernetes master is running at
https://gr7.us-west-2.eks.amazonaws.com
CoreDNS is running at
https://gr7.us-west-2.eks.amazonaws.com/api/v1/namespaces/kube-syst
em/services/kube-dns:dns/proxy
NAME                                    STATUS ROLES  AGE    VERSION
ip-1-2-3-4.us-west-2.compute.internal Ready  <none> 5m42s v1.13.8-
eks-cd3eb0
ip-1-2-3-4.us-west-2.compute.internal Ready  <none> 5m40s v1.13.8-
eks-cd3eb0
```

Now, you have a two-node Amazon EKS cluster up and running.

How it works...

The first recipe on Amazon EC2 showed you how to provision multiple copies of master nodes that can survive a master node failure as well as single AZ outages. Although it is similar to what you get with the second recipe on Amazon EKS with Multi-AZ support, clusters on EC2 give you higher flexibility. When you run Amazon EKS instead, it runs a single-tenant Kubernetes control plane for each cluster, and the control plane consists of at least two API server nodes and three etcd nodes that run across three AZs within a region.

Let's take a look at the cluster options we used in *step 7* with the kops create cluster command:

- --node-count=3 sets the number of nodes to create. In our example, this is 6. This configuration will deploy two nodes per zone defined with--zones=us-east-1a, us-east-1b, us-east-1c, with a total of three master nodes and six worker nodes.
- --node-size and --master-size set the instance size for the worker and master nodes. In our example, t2.medium is used for worker nodes and t2.large is used for master nodes. For larger clusters, t2.large is recommended for a worker.
- --zones and --master-zones set the zones that the cluster will run in. In our example, we have used three zones called us-east-1a, us-east-1b, and us-east-1c.

For additional zone information, check the AWS Global Infrastructure link in the *See also* section.

 AWS clusters cannot span across multiple regions and all the zones that have been defined for the master and worker nodes should be within the same region.

When deploying multi-master clusters, an odd number of master instances should be created. Also, remember that Kubernetes relies on etcd, a distributed key/value store. etcd quorum requires more than 51% of the nodes to be available at any time. Therefore, with three master nodes, our control plane can only survive a single master node or AZ outages. If you need to handle more than that, you need to consider increasing the number of master instances.

There's more...

It is also useful to have knowledge of the following information:

- Using the AWS Shell
- Using a gossip-based cluster
- Using different regions for an S3 bucket
- Editing cluster configuration
- Deleting your cluster
- Provisioning an EKS cluster using the Amazon EKS dashboard
- Deploying Kubernetes Dashboard

Using the AWS Shell

Another useful tool worth mentioning here is `aws-shell`. It is an integrated shell that works with the AWS CLI. It uses the AWS CLI configuration and improves productivity with an autocomplete feature.

Install `aws-shell` using the following command and run it:

```
$ sudo apt-get install aws-shell && aws-shell
```

You will see the following output:

```
aws> s3api
                abort-multipart-upload
                complete-multipart-upload
                copy-object
                create-bucket
                create-multipart-upload
                delete-bucket
                delete-bucket-analytics-configuration
```

You can use AWS commands with `aws-shell` with less typing. Press the *F10* key to exit the shell.

Using a gossip-based cluster

In this recipe, we created a domain (either purchased from Amazon or another registrar) and a hosted zone, because kops uses DNS for discovery. Although it needs to be a valid DNS name, starting with kops 1.6.2, DNS configuration became optional. Instead of an actual domain or subdomain, a gossip-based cluster can be easily created. By using a registered domain name, we make our clusters easier to share and accessible by others for production use.

If, for any reason, you prefer a gossip-based cluster, you can skip hosted zone creation and use a cluster name that ends with `k8s.local`:

```
$ export KOPS_CLUSTER_NAME=devopscookbook.k8s.local
$ export KOPS_STATE_STORE=s3://devops-cookbook-state-store
```

Setting the environmental parameters for `kops` is optional but highly recommended since it shortens your CLI commands.

Using different regions for an S3 bucket

In order for kops to store cluster configuration, a dedicated S3 bucket is required.

An example for the `eu-west-1` region would look as follows:

```
$ aws s3api create-bucket --bucket s3.k8s.containerized.me \
--region eu-west-1 --create-bucket-configuration \
LocationConstraint=eu-west-1
```

This S3 bucket will become the source of truth for our Kubernetes cluster configuration. For simplicity, it is recommended to use the `us-east-1` region; otherwise, an appropriate `LocationConstraint` needs be specified in order to create the bucket in the desired region.

Editing the cluster configuration

The `kops create cluster` command, which we used to create the cluster configuration, doesn't actually create the cluster itself and launch the EC2 instances; instead, it creates the configuration file in our S3 bucket.

After creating the configuration file, you can make changes to the configuration using the `kops edit cluster` command.

You can separately edit your node instance groups using the following command:

```
$ kops edit ig nodes
$ kops edit ig master-us-east-1a
```

The config file is called from the S3 bucket's state store location. If you prefer a different editor you can, for example, set `$KUBE_EDITOR=nano` to change it.

Deleting your cluster

To delete your cluster, use the following command:

```
$ kops delete cluster --name ${KOPS_CLUSTER_NAME} --yes
```

This process may take a few minutes and, when finished, you will get a confirmation.

Provisioning an EKS cluster using the Amazon EKS Management Console

In the *Provisioning a managed Kubernetes cluster on Amazon EKS* recipe, we used eksctl to deploy a cluster. As an alternative, you can also use the AWS Management Console web user interface to deploy an EKS cluster.

Perform the following steps to get your cluster up and running on Amazon EKS:

1. Open your browser and go to the Amazon EKS console at `https://console.aws.amazon.com/eks/home#/clusters`.
2. Enter a cluster name and click on the **Next Step** button.
3. On the **Create Cluster** page, select **Kubernetes Version**, **Role name**, at least two or more availability zones from the subnets list, and **Security groups**.
4. Click on **Create**.
5. Cluster creation with EKS takes around 20 minutes. Refresh the page in 15-20 minutes and check its status.
6. Use the following command to update your `kubectl` configuration:

   ```
   $ aws eks --region us-east-1 update-kubeconfig \
   --name K8s-DevOps-Cookbook
   ```

7. Now, use `kubectl` to manage your cluster:

   ```
   $ kubectl get nodes
   ```

Now that your cluster has been configured, you can configure `kubectl` to manage it.

Deploying Kubernetes Dashboard

Last but not least, to deploy the Kubernetes Dashboard application on an AWS cluster, you need to follow these steps:

1. At the time I wrote this recipe, Kubernetes Dashboard v.2.0.0 was still in beta. Since v.1.x version will be obsolete soon, I highly recommend that you install the latest version, that is, v.2.0.0. The new version brings a lot of functionality and support for Kubernetes v.1.16 and later versions. Before you deploy Dashboard, make sure to remove the previous version if you have a previous version. Check the latest release by following the link in the following information box and deploy it using the latest release, similar to doing the following:

   ```
   $ kubectl delete ns kubernetes-dashboard
   # Use the latest version link from
   https://github.com/kubernetes/dashboard/releases
   $ kubectl apply -f
   https://raw.githubusercontent.com/kubernetes/dashboard/v2.0.0-beta5
   /aio/deploy/recommended.yaml
   ```

As the Kubernetes version gets upgraded, the dashboard application also gets frequently updated. To use the latest version, find the latest link to the YAML manifest on the release page at `https://github.com/kubernetes/dashboard/releases`. If you experience compatibility issues with the latest version of Dashboard, you can always deploy the previous stable version by using the following command:
```
$ kubectl apply -f
https://raw.githubusercontent.com/kubernetes/dashboard/v1
.10.1/src/depl
oy/recommended/kubernetes-dashboard.yaml
```

2. By default, the `kubernetes-dashboard` service is exposed using the `ClusterIP` type. If you want to access it from outside, edit the service using the following command and replace the `ClusterIP` type with `LoadBalancer`; otherwise, use port forwarding to access it:

   ```
   $ kubectl edit svc kubernetes-dashboard -n kubernetes-dashboard
   ```

3. Get the external IP of your dashboard from the `kubernetes-dashboard` service:

   ```
   $ kubectl get svc kubernetes-dashboard -n kubernetes-dashboard
   NAME                  TYPE          CLUSTER-IP     EXTERNAL-IP
   PORT(S) AGE
   kubernetes-dashboard LoadBalancer 100.66.234.228 myaddress.us-
   east-1.elb.amazonaws.com 443:30221/TCP 5m46s
   ```

4. Open the external IP link in your browser. In our example, it is `https://myaddress.us-east-1.elb.amazonaws.com`.

5. We will use the token option to access Kubernetes Dashboard. Now, let's find the token in our cluster using the following command. In this example, the command returns `kubernetes-dashboard-token-bc2w5` as the token name:

   ```
   $ kubectl get secrets -A | grep dashboard-token
   kubernetes-dashboard kubernetes-dashboard-token-bc2w5
   kubernetes.io/service-account-token 3 17m
   ```

6. Replace the secret name with yours from the output of the previous command. Get the token details from the description of the Secret:

   ```
   $ kubectl describe secrets kubernetes-dashboard-token-bc2w5 -
   nkubernetes-dashboard
   ```

7. Copy the token section from the output of the preceding command and paste it into **Kubernetes Dashboard** to sign in to Dashboard:

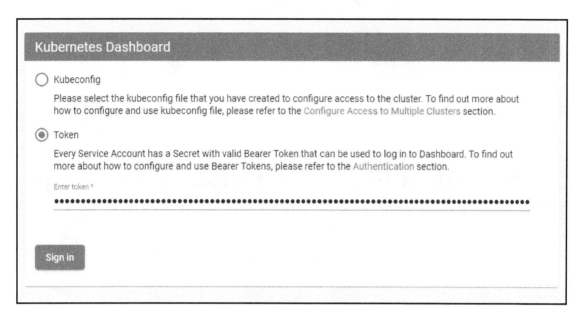

Now, you have access to Kubernetes Dashboard to manage your cluster.

See also

- Kops documentation for the latest version and additional `create cluster` parameters:
    - `https://github.com/kubernetes/kops/blob/master/docs/aws.md`
    - `https://github.com/kubernetes/kops/blob/master/docs/cli/kops_create_cluster.md`
- AWS Command Reference S3 Create Bucket API: `https://docs.aws.amazon.com/cli/latest/reference/s3api/create-bucket.html`
- AWS Global Infrastructure Map: `https://aws.amazon.com/about-aws/global-infrastructure/`
- Amazon EKS FAQ: `https://aws.amazon.com/eks/faqs/`
- The AWS Fargate product, another AWS service, if you would prefer to run containers without managing servers or clusters: `https://aws.amazon.com/fargate/`

- A complete list of CNCF-certified Kubernetes installers: `https://landscape.cncf.io/category=certified-kubernetes-installerformat=card-mode grouping=category`.

- Other recommended tools for getting highly available clusters on AWS:
    - Konvoy: `https://d2iq.com/solutions/ksphere/konvoy`
    - KubeAdm: `https://github.com/kubernetes/kubeadm`
    - KubeOne: `https://github.com/kubermatic/kubeone`
    - KubeSpray: `https://github.com/kubernetes-sigs/kubespray`

Configuring a Kubernetes cluster on Google Cloud Platform

This section will take you through step-by-step instructions to configure Kubernetes clusters on GCP. You will learn how to run a hosted Kubernetes cluster without needing to provision or manage master and etcd instances using GKE.

Getting ready

All the operations mentioned here require a GCP account with billing enabled. If you don't have one already, go to `https://console.cloud.google.com` and create an account.

On **Google Cloud Platform (GCP)**, you have two main options when it comes to running Kubernetes. You can consider using **Google Compute Engine** (GCE) if you'd like to manage your deployment completely and have specific powerful instance requirements. Otherwise, it's highly recommended to use the managed **Google Kubernetes Engine (GKE)**.

How to do it...

This section is further divided into the following subsections to make this process easier to follow:

- Installing the command-line tools to configure GCP services
- Provisioning a managed Kubernetes cluster on GKE
- Connecting to GKE clusters

Installing the command-line tools to configure GCP services

In this recipe, we will get the primary CLI for Google Cloud Platform, gcloud, installed so that we can configure GCP services:

1. Run the following command to download the gcloud CLI:

   ```
   $ curl https://sdk.cloud.google.com | bash
   ```

2. Initialize the SDK and follow the instructions given:

   ```
   $ gcloud init
   ```

3. During the initialization, when asked, select either an existing project that you have permissions for or create a new project.
4. Enable the Compute Engine APIs for the project:

   ```
   $ gcloud services enable compute.googleapis.com
   Operation "operations/acf.07e3e23a-77a0-4fb3-8d30-ef20adb2986a"
   finished successfully.
   ```

5. Set a default zone:

   ```
   $ gcloud config set compute/zone us-central1-a
   ```

6. Make sure you can start up a GCE instance from the command line:

   ```
   $ gcloud compute instances create "devops-cookbook" \
   --zone "us-central1-a" --machine-type "f1-micro"
   ```

7. Delete the test VM:

   ```
   $ gcloud compute instances delete "devops-cookbook"
   ```

If all the commands are successful, you can provision your GKE cluster.

Provisioning a managed Kubernetes cluster on GKE

Let's perform the following steps:

1. Create a cluster:

```
$ gcloud container clusters create k8s-devops-cookbook-1 \
--cluster-version latest --machine-type n1-standard-2 \
--image-type UBUNTU --disk-type pd-standard --disk-size 100 \
--no-enable-basic-auth --metadata disable-legacy-endpoints=true \
--scopes compute-rw,storage-ro,service-management,service-
control,logging-write,monitoring \
--num-nodes "3" --enable-stackdriver-kubernetes \
--no-enable-ip-alias --enable-autoscaling --min-nodes 1 \
--max-nodes 5 --enable-network-policy \
--addons HorizontalPodAutoscaling,HttpLoadBalancing \
--enable-autoupgrade --enable-autorepair --maintenance-window
"10:00"
```

Cluster creation will take 5 minutes or more to complete.

Connecting to Google Kubernetes Engine (GKE) clusters

To get access to your GKE cluster, you need to follow these steps:

1. Configure `kubectl` to access your `k8s-devops-cookbook-1` cluster:

```
$ gcloud container clusters get-credentials k8s-devops-cookbook-1
```

2. Verify your Kubernetes cluster:

```
$ kubectl get nodes
```

Now, you have a three-node GKE cluster up and running.

How it works...

This recipe showed you how to quickly provision a GKE cluster using some default parameters.

In *Step 1*, we created a cluster with some default parameters. While all of the parameters are very important, I want to explain some of them here.

`--cluster-version` sets the Kubernetes version to use for the master and nodes. Only use it if you want to use a version that's different from the default. To get the available version information, you can use the `gcloud container get-server-config` command.

We set the instance type by using the `--machine-type` parameter. If it's not set, the default is `n1-standard-1`. To get the list of predefined types, you can use the `gcloud compute machine-types list` command.

The default image type is COS, but my personal preference is Ubuntu, so I used `--image-type UBUNTU` to set the OS image to `UBUNTU`. If this isn't set, the server picks the default image type, that is, COS. To get the list of available image types, you can use the `gcloud container get-server-config` command.

GKE offers advanced cluster management features and comes with the automatic scaling of node instances, auto-upgrade, and auto-repair to maintain node availability. `--enable-autoupgrade` enables the GKE auto-upgrade feature for cluster nodes and `--enable-autorepair` enables the automatic repair feature, which is started at the time defined with the `--maintenance-window` parameter. The time that's set here is the UTC time zone and must be in `HH:MM` format.

There's more...

The following are some of the alternative methods that can be employed besides the recipe described in the previous section:

- Using Google Cloud Shell
- Deploying with a custom network configuration
- Deleting your cluster
- Viewing the Workloads dashboard

Using Google Cloud Shell

As an alternative to your Linux workstation, you can get a CLI interface on your browser to manage your cloud instances.

Go to `https://cloud.google.com/shell/` to get a Google Cloud Shell.

Deploying with a custom network configuration

The following steps demonstrate how to provision your cluster with a custom network configuration:

1. Create a VPC network:

```
$ gcloud compute networks create k8s-devops-cookbook \
--subnet-mode custom
```

2. Create a subnet in your VPC network. In our example, this is 10.240.0.0/16:

```
$ gcloud compute networks subnets create kubernetes \
--network k8s-devops-cookbook --range 10.240.0.0/16
```

3. Create a firewall rule to allow internal traffic:

```
$ gcloud compute firewall-rules create k8s-devops-cookbook-allow-
int \
--allow tcp,udp,icmp --network k8s-devops-cookbook \
--source-ranges 10.240.0.0/16,10.200.0.0/16
```

4. Create a firewall rule to allow external SSH, ICMP, and HTTPS traffic:

```
$ gcloud compute firewall-rules create k8s-devops-cookbook-allow-
ext \
--allow tcp:22,tcp:6443,icmp --network k8s-devops-cookbook \
--source-ranges 0.0.0.0/0
```

5. Verify the rules:

```
$ gcloud compute firewall-rules list
  NAME                          NETWORK              DIRECTION
PRIORITY ALLOW    DENY     DISABLED
  ...
  k8s-devops-cookbook-allow-ext k8s-devops-cookbook INGRESS    1000
tcp:22,tcp:6443,icmp          False
  k8s-devops-cookbook-allow-int k8s-devops-cookbook INGRESS    1000
tcp,udp,icmp                  False
```

6. Add the --network k8s-devops-cookbook and --subnetwork
kubernetes parameters to your container clusters create command and
run it.

Deleting your cluster

To delete your `k8s-devops-cookbook-1` cluster, use the following command:

```
$ gcloud container clusters delete k8s-devops-cookbook-1
```

This process may take a few minutes and when finished, you will get a confirmation message.

Viewing the Workloads dashboard

On GCP, instead of using the Kubernetes Dashboard application, you can use the built-in Workloads dashboard and deploy containerized applications through Google Marketplace. Follow these steps:

1. To access the Workload dashboard from your GCP dashboard, choose your GKE cluster and click on **Workloads**.
2. Click on **Show system workloads** to see the existing components and containers that have been deployed in the `kube-system` namespace.

See also

- The GCP documentation: `https://cloud.google.com/docs/`
- GKE on-prem installation: `https://cloud.google.com/gke-on-prem/docs/how-to/install-overview-basic`

Configuring a Kubernetes cluster on Microsoft Azure

In this section, we will cover a recipe using Microsoft **Azure Kubernetes Service** (**AKS**) in order to create a Kubernetes cluster on the Microsoft Azure Cloud.

Getting ready

All the operations mentioned here require a Microsoft Azure subscription. If you don't have one already, go to `https://portal.azure.com` and create a free account.

How to do it...

This section will take you through how to configure a Kubernetes cluster on Microsoft Azure. This section is further divided into the following subsections to make this process easier:

- Installing the command-line tools to configure Azure services
- Provisioning a managed Kubernetes cluster on AKS
- Connecting to AKS clusters

Installing the command-line tools to configure Azure services

In this recipe, we will get the Azure CLI tool called `az` and `kubectl` installed.

Let's perform the following steps:

1. Install the necessary dependencies:

   ```
   $ sudo apt-get update && sudo apt-get install -y libssl-dev \
   libffi-dev python-dev build-essential
   ```

2. Download and install the `az` CLI tool:

   ```
   $ curl -L https://aka.ms/InstallAzureCli | bash
   ```

3. Verify the `az` version you're using:

   ```
   $ az --version
   ```

4. Install `kubectl`, if you haven't installed it already:

   ```
   $ az aks install-cli
   ```

   If all commands were successful, you can start provisioning your AKS cluster.

Provisioning a managed Kubernetes cluster on AKS

Let's perform the following steps:

1. Log in to your account:

   ```
   $ az login
   ```

2. Create a resource group named k8sdevopscookbook in your preferred region:

   ```
   $ az group create --name k8sdevopscookbook --location eastus
   ```

3. Create a service principal and take note of your appId and password for the next steps:

   ```
   $ az ad sp create-for-rbac --skip-assignment
   {
     "appId": "12345678-1234-1234-1234-123456789012",
     "displayName": "azure-cli-2019-05-11-20-43-47",
     "name": "http://azure-cli-2019-05-11-20-43-47",
     "password": "12345678-1234-1234-1234-123456789012",
     "tenant": "12345678-1234-1234-1234-123456789012"
   ```

4. Create a cluster. Replace appId and password with the output from the preceding command:

   ```
   $ az aks create --resource-group k8sdevopscookbook \
   --name AKSCluster \
   --kubernetes-version 1.15.4 \
   --node-vm-size Standard_DS2_v2 \
   --node-count 3 \
   --service-principal <appId> \
   --client-secret <password> \
   --generate-ssh-keys
   ```

   Cluster creation will take around 5 minutes. You will see "provisioningState": Succeeded" when it has successfully completed.

Connecting to AKS clusters

Let's perform the following steps:

1. Gather some credentials and configure kubectl so that you can use them:

   ```
   $ az aks get-credentials --resource-group k8sdevopscookbook \
   --name AKSCluster
   ```

2. Verify your Kubernetes cluster:

```
$ kubectl get nodes
```

Now, you have a three-node GKE cluster up and running.

How it works...

This recipe showed you how to quickly provision an AKS cluster using some common options.

In *step 3*, the command starts with `az aks create`, followed by `-g` or `--resource-group`, so that you can select the name of your resource group. You can configure the default group using `az configure --defaults group=k8sdevopscookbook` and skip this parameter next time.

We used the `--name AKSCluster` parameter to set the name of the managed cluster to `AKSCluster`. The rest of the parameters are optional; `--kubernetes-version` or `-k` sets the version of Kubernetes to use for the cluster. You can use the `az aks get-versions --location eastus --output table` command to get the list of available options.

We used `--node-vm-size` to set the instance type for the Kubernetes worker nodes. If this isn't set, the default is `Standard_DS2_v2`.

Next, we used `--node-count` to set the number of Kubernetes worker nodes. If this isn't set, the default is 3. This can be changed using the `az aks scale` command.

Finally, the `--generate-ssh-keys` parameter is used to autogenerate the SSH public and private key files, which are stored in the `~/.ssh` directory.

There's more...

Although Windows-based containers are now supported by Kubernetes, to be able to run Windows Server containers, you need to run Windows Server-based nodes. AKS nodes currently run on Linux OS and Windows Server-based nodes are not available in AKS. However, you can use Virtual Kubelet to schedule Windows containers on container instances and manage them as part of your cluster. In this section, we will take a look at the following:

- Deleting your cluster
- Viewing Kubernetes Dashboard

Deleting your cluster

To delete your cluster, use the following command:

```
$ az aks delete --resource-group k8sdevopscookbook --name AKSCluster
```

This process will take a few minutes and, when finished, you will receive confirmation of this.

Viewing Kubernetes Dashboard

To view Kubernetes Dashboard, you need to follow these steps:

1. To start Kubernetes Dashboard, use the following command:

   ```
   $ az aks browse --resource-group k8sdevopscookbook --name
   AKSCluster
   ```

2. If your cluster is RBAC-enabled, then create `Clusterrolebinding`:

   ```
   $ kubectl create clusterrolebinding kubernetes-dashboard \
   --clusterrole=cluster-admin \
   --serviceaccount=kube-system:kubernetes-dashboard
   ```

3. Open a browser window and go to the address where the proxy is running. In our example, this is `http://127.0.0.1:8001/`.

See also

- Microsoft AKS FAQ: `https://docs.microsoft.com/en-us/azure/aks/faq`
- Repository of the open source core of AKS on GitHub: `https://github.com/Azure/aks-engine`

Configuring a Kubernetes cluster on Alibaba Cloud

Alibaba Cloud (also known as Aliyun) offers multiple templates that you can use to provision a Kubernetes environment. There are four main service categories:

- **Kubernetes**: Self-managed Kubernetes deployed with three masters on ECS instances within a single zone. Worker nodes can be on either ECS or bare-metal.
- **Managed Kubernetes**: Similar to the Kubernetes cluster option, except master nodes are managed by Alibaba Cloud.
- **Multi-AZ Kubernetes**: Similar to the Kubernetes cluster option, except the self-managed master and worker instances can be deployed in separate availability zones.
- **Serverless Kubernetes**: A Kubernetes service offering where you deploy container applications without having to manage and maintain clusters instances:

In this section, we will cover how to provision a highly available Multi-AZ Kubernetes cluster without needing to provision or manage master and etcd instances.

Getting ready

All the operations mentioned here require an Alibaba Cloud account (also known as Aliyun) with an AccessKey. If you don't have one already, go to `https://account.alibabacloud.com` and create an account.

How to do it...

This section will take you through how to configure a Kubernetes cluster on Alibaba Cloud. This section is further divided into the following subsections to make this process easier:

- Installing the command-line tools to configure Alibaba Cloud services
- Provisioning a highly available Kubernetes cluster on Alibaba Cloud
- Connecting to Alibaba Container Service clusters

Installing the command-line tools to configure Alibaba Cloud services

For this recipe, we will use the Alibaba Cloud console and generate the API request parameters from the dashboard that will be used with the CLI. You will also need the Alibaba Cloud CLI, `aliyun`, and `kubectl` installed.

1. Run the following command to download the `aliyun` tool:

```
$ curl -O
https://aliyuncli.alicdn.com/aliyun-cli-linux-3.0.15-amd64.tgz
```

 You can find the link to the latest version here: `https://github.com/aliyun/aliyun-cli`.

2. Extract the files and install them:

```
$ tar -zxvf aliyun-cli*.tgz && sudo mv aliyun /usr/local/bin/.
```

3. Verify the `aliyun` CLI version you're using:

```
$ aliyun --version
```

4. If you haven't created an AccessKey, go to **Security Management** in your account and create one (`https://usercenter.console.aliyun.com/#/manage/ak`).

5. Complete the CLI configuration by entering your AccessKey ID, AccessKey Secret, and region ID:

```
$ aliyun configure
Configuring profile '' in '' authenticate mode...
Access Key Id []: <Your AccessKey ID>
Access Key Secret []: <Your AccessKey Secret>
Default Region Id []: us-west-1
Default Output Format [json]: json (Only support json))
Default Language [zh|en] en: en
Saving profile[] ...Done.
```

6. Enable `bash/zsh` autocompletion:

```
$ aliyun auto-completion
```

7. Go to the Container Service console (`https://cs.console.aliyun.com`) to give permissions to the container service to access cloud resources. Here, select `AliyunCSDefaultRole`, `AliyunCSServerlessKuberentesRole`, `AliyunCSClusterRole`, and `AliyunCSManagedKubernetesRole` and click on **Confirm Authorization Policy.**

Make sure you have the **Resource Orchestration Service (ROS)** and Autoscaling services enabled since they are required to get Kubernetes clusters deployed. ROS is used to automatically provision and configure resources for auto-deployment, operation, and maintenance based on your template, while Autoscaling is used to adjust compute resources based on demand.

Provisioning a highly available Kubernetes cluster on Alibaba Cloud

Let's perform the following steps:

1. Open a browser window and go to the Alibaba Cloud Virtual Private Cloud console at `https://vpc.console.aliyun.com`.
2. Make sure you select a region with at least three zones (most of the regions in mainland China have more than three zones) and click on **Create VPC**.
3. Give a unique name to your VPC and select an **IPv4 CIDR** block. In our example, this is `10.0.0.0/8`.

4. Enter a name for your first VSwitch (`k8s-1`), and select a zone (`Beijing Zone A`).

5. Set an **IPv4 CIDR** block. In our example, we used `10.10.0.0./16`.

6. Click on the **Add** button and repeat *steps 4* and *5* to get different zones. Use the following CIDR block information:

	VSwitch 2	VSwitch 3
Name:	k8s-2	k8s-3
Zone:	Beijing Zone B	Beijing Zone E
IPv4 CIDR Block:	10.20.0.0/16	10.30.0.0/16

7. Click **OK** to create your VPC and VSwitches.

8. Open the Aliyun Web console on your web browser (`https://cs.console.aliyun.com.`).

9. Click on **Create Kubernetes Cluster**.

10. Select **Standard Managed Cluster**.

11. Click on the **Multi-AZ Kubernetes** tab, give your cluster a name, and select the same region that you used to create your VPCs and VSwitches.

12. If you have selected the same region, the **VPC** dropdown will be populated with `k8s-devops-cookbook-vpc`. Now, select all three **VSwitches** that we've created:

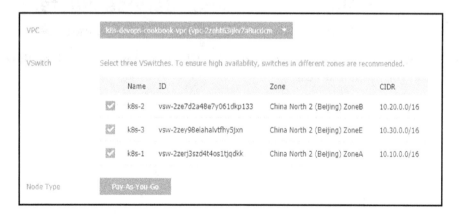

13. Set the instance types for the **Master** node configuration in each zone.

14. Set the instance type for the **Worker** node configuration in each zone and the number of nodes in every zone to 3. Otherwise, use the defaults.

15. Select the Kubernetes version (`1.12.6-aliyun.1`, at the time of writing).

16. Select **Key Pair Name** from the drop-down menu, or create one by clicking **Create a new key pair**:

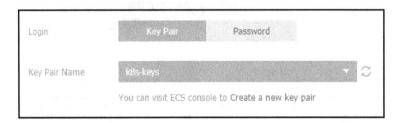

17. Alibaba offers two CNI options: Flannel and Terway. The difference is explained in the *There's more...* section of this recipe. Leave the default network options using `Flannel`. The default parameters support up to 512 servers in the cluster.

18. Monitoring and logging will be explained in `Chapter 8`, *Observability and Monitoring on Kubernetes*, and `Chapter 10`, *Logging on Kubernetes*. Therefore, this step is optional. Check the `Install cloud monitoring plug-in on your ECS` and `Using Log Service` options to enable monitoring and logging.

19. Now, click on **Create** to provision your Multi-AZ Kubernetes cluster. This step may take 15-20 minutes to complete.

Connecting to Alibaba Container Service clusters

To get access to your cluster on Alibaba Cloud, you need to follow these steps:

1. To get the cluster's credentials, go to the **Clusters** menu and click on the cluster name you want to access:

2. Copy the content displayed in the **KubeConfig** tab to your local machine's $HOME/.kube/config file:

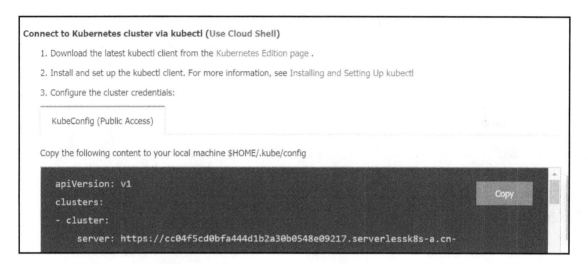

3. Verify your Kubernetes cluster:

```
$ kubectl get nodes
```

As an alternative, see the *Viewing the Kubernetes Dashboard* instructions under the *There's more...* section to manage your cluster.

How it works...

This recipe showed you how to provision a managed Kubernetes cluster on Alibaba Cloud using a cluster template.

Under the **Container Service** menu, Alibaba Cloud provides a few Kubernetes cluster, where you are offered seven cluster templates. We used the **Standard** Managed Cluster here. This option lets you manage the worker nodes only and saves you the cost of resources and management for the master nodes:

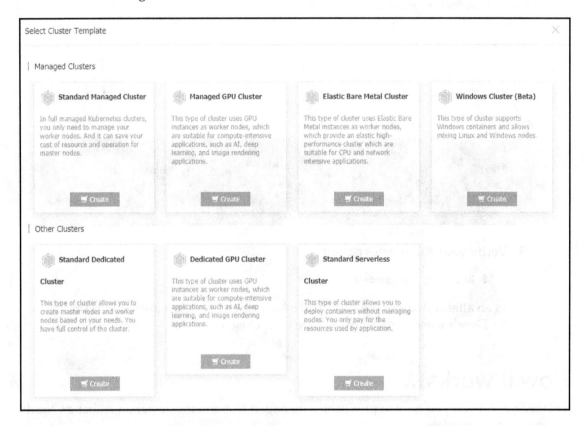

By default, accounts support up to 20 clusters and 40 nodes in each cluster. You can request a quota increase by submitting a support ticket.

There's more...

As an alternative way of using the Alibaba Cloud console, you can use REST API calls through `aliyuncli` to create the ECS instances and your cluster. Follow these steps to do so:

1. After you've configured your cluster options on your Alibaba Cloud console, click on **Generate API request Parameters** right under the **Create** button to generate POST request body content to be used with the `aliyun` CLI.
2. Save the content in a file. In our case, this file is called `cscreate.json`.
3. For an explanation of the additional parameters listed in this section, please refer to the *Create a Kubernetes* section at `https://www.alibabacloud.com/help/doc-detail/87525.htm`.
4. Use the following command to create your cluster:

   ```
   $ aliyun cs POST /clusters --header "Content-Type=application/json" \
   --body "$(cat cscreate.json)"
   ```

   The Alibaba Cloud Container Service provides two network plugin options for their Kubernetes clusters: Terway and Flannel.

   Flannel is based on the community Flannel CNI plugin. Flannel is a very common and stable networking plugin that provides basic networking functionality. It is the recommended option for most use cases, except it does not support the Kubernetes NetworkPolicy. Terway is a network plugin developed by Alibaba Cloud CS. It is fully compatible with Flannel. Terway can define access policies between containers based on the Kubernetes NetworkPolicy. Terway also supports bandwidth limiting for containers.

Configuring and managing Kubernetes clusters with Rancher

Rancher is a container management platform with the flexibility to create Kubernetes clusters with **Rancher Kubernetes Engine (RKE)** or cloud-based Kubernetes services, such as GKE, AKS, and EKS, which we discussed in the previous recipes.

In this section, we will cover recipes for configuring Rancher so that we can deploy and manage Kubernetes services.

Getting ready

Rancher can be installed on Ubuntu, RHEL/CentOS, RancherOS, or even on Windows Server. You can bring up Rancher Server in a high availability configuration or a single node. Refer to the *See also...* section for links to the alternative installation instructions. In this recipe, we will run Rancher on a single node.

How to do it...

This section will take you through how to configure and manage Kubernetes clusters with Rancher. To that end, this section is further divided into the following subsections to make this process easier:

- Installing Rancher Server
- Deploying a Kubernetes cluster
- Importing an existing cluster
- Enabling cluster and node providers

Installing Rancher Server

Follow these steps to install Rancher Server:

1. Install a supported version of Docker. You can skip this step if you have Docker installed already:

    ```
    $ sudo apt-get -y install apt-transport-https ca-certificates curl \
    software-properties-common
    $ curl -fsSL https://download.docker.com/linux/ubuntu/gpg | sudo apt-key add -
    $ sudo add-apt-repository "deb [arch=amd64]
    https://download.docker.com/linux/ubuntu $(lsb_release -cs) stable"
    $ sudo apt-get -y install docker-ce && docker --version
    ```

2. Add a user to a Docker group:

    ```
    $ sudo usermod -a -G docker $USER
    ```

3. To install Rancher Server, run the following command:

    ```
    docker run -d --restart=unless-stopped \
    -p 80:80 -p 443:443 rancher/rancher:latest
    ```

4. Open a browser window and go to `https://localhost`.
   Replace `localhost` with your host's IP if necessary.
5. Set a new password and click on **Continue**.
6. Set the public IP address of Rancher server and click on **Save URL**. This IP needs to be externally accessible from your clusters.

Deploying a Kubernetes cluster

To deploy a new cluster, you need to follow these steps:

1. Click on **Add Cluster.**
2. Choose a provider. In our example, we will use GKE. Some settings for other providers might be slightly different:

3. Enter a cluster name.

   If you have your GCP service account JSON file that we saved previously, skip to *step 10*.

4. From the GCP navigation menu, go to **IAM** and click on the **Service accounts** link.
5. Click on **Create Service Account**.
6. Enter a service account name and click **Create**.
7. Add the required minimum permissions; that is, **Compute Viewer**, **Viewer**, **Kubernetes Engine Admin**, and **Service Account User**, and click **Continue**.

8. Click on **Create Key**. Use **JSON** as the key type in order to save your service account.

9. On the Rancher UI, click on **Read from a file** and load the service account JSON file you saved previously.

10. Customize the **Cluster Options** as needed; otherwise, use the default settings and click on **Create** to deploy your Kubernetes cluster:

Your cluster will be listed and ready to be managed immediately on your Rancher dashboard.

Importing an existing cluster

To import an existing cluster, you need to follow these steps:

1. Click on **Add Cluster**

2. Click on **Import**:

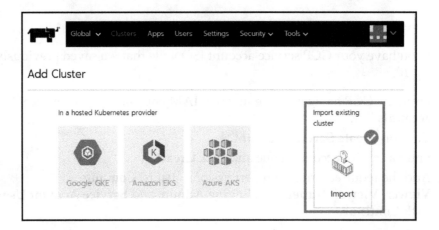

3. Enter a cluster name and click on **Create**.

4. Follow the instructions shown and copy and run the `kubectl` command displayed on the screen to an existing Kubernetes cluster. This command will look similar to the following if you are running with an untrusted/self-signed SSL certificate:

```
curl --insecure -sfL
https://54.184.9.87/v3/import/5nvrfch6x66xgqfj5nh5ghwtllvhf9v6gwwbnj7qb69jtpl9v8c2bn.yaml
| kubectl apply -f -
```

5. By clicking on **Done**, your cluster will be listed and ready to manage immediately on your Rancher dashboard:

The last step may take a minute to complete. Eventually, the state of your cluster will turn from **Pending** to **Active** when it is ready.

Enabling cluster and node providers

To be able to support multiple providers, Rancher uses cluster and node drivers. If you don't see your provider on the list, then it is most likely not enabled.

To enable additional providers, follow these steps:

1. From **Tools**, click on **Drivers**.
2. Find your provider on the list and click **Activate**:

From the same page, you can also deactivate the providers you don't intend to use.

How it works...

This recipe showed you how to quickly run Rancher Server to manage your Kubernetes clusters.

In *step 1*, we used a single node installation using a default self-signed certificate method. For security purposes, SSL is required to interact with the clusters. Therefore, a certificate is required.

If you prefer to use your own certificate signed by a recognized CA instead, you can use the following command and provide the path to your certificates to mount them in your container by replacing the FULLCHAIN.pem and PRIVATEKEY.pem files with your signed certificates:

```
$ docker run -d --restart=unless-stopped \
 -p 80:80 -p 443:443 \
 -v /<CERTDIRECTORY>/<FULLCHAIN.pem>:/etc/rancher/ssl/cert.pem \
 -v /<CERTDIRECTORY>/<PRIVATEKEY.pem>:/etc/rancher/ssl/key.pem \
 rancher/rancher:latest --no-cacerts
```

Using a recognized certificate will eliminate the security warning on the login page.

There's more...

It is also useful to have knowledge of the following information:

- Bind mounting a host volume to keep data
- Keeping user volumes persistent
- Keeping data persistent on a host volume
- Running Rancher on the same Kubernetes nodes

Bind mounting a host volume to keep data

When using the single node installation?, the persistent data is kept on the /var/lib/rancher path in the container.

To keep data on the host, you can bind mount a host volume to a location using the following command:

```
$ docker run -d --restart=unless-stopped \
  -p 80:80 -p 443:443 \
  -v /opt/rancher:/var/lib/rancher \
  -v /var/log/rancher/auditlog:/var/log/auditlog \
  rancher/rancher:latest
```

Bind mounts have limited functionality compared to volumes. When Rancher is started using the bind mount, a directory on the host machine will be mounted to the specified directory in the container.

Keeping user volumes persistent

When using RancherOS, only specific directories keep the data defined by the user-volumes parameter persistent.

To add additional persistent user-volumes, for example, add the /var/openebs directory:

```
$ ros config set rancher.services.user-volumes.volumes
\[/home:/home,/opt:/opt,/var/lib/kubelet:/var/lib/kubelet,/etc/kubernet
es:/etc/kubernetes,/var/openebs]
$ system-docker rm all-volumes
$ reboot
```

After rebooting, data in the specified directories will be persistent.

Running Rancher on the same Kubernetes nodes

To add the node where you run Rancher Server on a cluster, replace the default ports -p 80:80 -p 443:443 as follows and use the following command to start Rancher:

```
$ docker run -d --restart=unless-stopped \
  -p 8080:80 -p 8443:443 rancher/rancher:latest
```

In this case, Rancher Server will be accessible through https://localhost:8443 instead of the standard 443 port.

See also

- The Rancher 2.x Documentation: `https://rancher.com/docs/rancher/v2.x/en/`
- K3s, a lightweight Kubernetes from Rancher Labs: `https://k3s.io/`
- Rio, an application deployment engine for Kubernetes from Rancher Labs: `https://rio.io/`

Configuring Red Hat OpenShift

In this recipe, we will learn how to deploy Red Hat OpenShift on AWS, bare-metal, or VMware vSphere VMs.

The steps in the *Provisioning an OpenShift cluster recipe* can be applied to deploy OpenShift on either VMs running on a virtualized environment or bare-metal servers.

Getting ready

All the operations mentioned here require a Red Hat account with active Red Hat Enterprise Linux and OpenShift Container Platform subscriptions. If you don't have one already, go to `https://access.redhat.com` and create an account.

> When you deploy on VMs, make sure to plan that the zones you create on Kubernetes nodes are actually physically located on separate hypervisor nodes.

For this recipe, we need to have a minimum of six nodes with Red Hat Enterprise CoreOS installed on them. These nodes can be either bare-metal, VMs, or a mix of bare-metal and VMs.

How to do it...

This section will take you through how to configure Red Hat OpenShift. To that end, this section is further divided into the following subsections to make this process easier:

- Downloading OpenShift binaries
- Provisioning an OpenShift cluster
- Connecting to OpenShift clusters

Downloading OpenShift binaries

Make sure you are on the Terminal of your first master and that you have an account with root access, or you are running as a superuser. Follow these steps:

1. Go to `https://cloud.redhat.com/openshift/install` and download the latest `OpenShift Installer`:

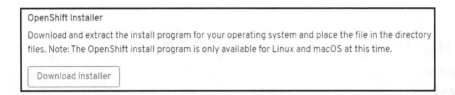

2. Extract the installer files on your workstation:

```
$ tar -xzf openshift-install-linux-*.tar.gz
```

The preceding command will create a file called `openshift-install` in the same folder.

Provisioning an OpenShift cluster

In this recipe, we will use the AWS platform to deploy OpenShift:

1. To get your OpenShift cluster up, use the following command:

```
$ ./openshift-install create cluster
```

2. Choose `aws` as your platform and enter your `AWS Access Key ID` and `Secret Access Key`.
3. Choose your region. In our example, this is `us-east-1`.
4. Select a base domain. In our example, this is `k8s.containerized.me`.
5. Enter a cluster name.
6. Copy **Pull Secret** from the Red Hat site and paste it onto the command line:

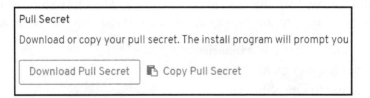

7. After the installation is complete, you will see the console URL and credentials for accessing your new cluster, similar to the following:

```
INFO Install complete!
INFO To access the cluster as the system:admin user when using
'oc', run 'export KUBECONFIG=/home/ubuntu/auth/kubeconfig'
INFO Access the OpenShift web-console here:
https://console-openshift-console.apps.os.k8s.containerized.me
INFO Login to the console with user: kubeadmin, password: ABCDE-
ABCDE-ABCDE-ABCDE
```

8. Switch to the Red Hat site and click on the Download Command-Line Tools link to download openshift-client.

9. Extract the openshift-client files in your workstation:

```
$ tar -xzf openshift-client-linux-*.tar.gz && sudo mv oc
/usr/local/bin
```

The preceding command will create the kubectl and oc files on the same folder and move the oc binary to PATH.

Connecting to OpenShift clusters

To connect to OpenShift clusters, follow these steps:

1. To get access to your OpenShift cluster, use the following command:

```
$ export KUBECONFIG=~/auth/kubeconfig
```

2. Log in to your OpenShift cluster after replacing password and cluster address:

```
$ oc login -u kubeadmin -p ABCDE-ABCDE-ABCDE-ABCDE \
https://api.openshift.k8s.containerized.me:6443 \
--insecure-skip-tls-verify=true
```

If you prefer to use the web console instead, open the web console URL address from the *Provisioning an OpenShift cluster* recipe, in *step 7*.

How it works...

This recipe showed you how to quickly deploy an OpenShift cluster on AWS.

In *step 1*, we created a cluster using the default configuration of the installer-provisioned infrastructure.

The installer asked a series of questions regarding user information and used mostly default values for other configuration options. These defaults can be edited and customized if needed using the install-config.yaml file.

To see the defaults that were used for the deployment, let's create an install-config.yaml file and view it:

```
$ ./openshift-install create install-config && cat install-config.yaml
```

As you can see from the following output, the file's default configuration creates a cluster consisting of three master and three worker nodes:

```
apiVersion: v1
baseDomain: k8s.containerized.me
compute:
- hyperthreading: Enabled
  name: worker
  platform: {}
  replicas: 3
controlPlane:
  hyperthreading: Enabled
  name: master
  platform: {}
  replicas: 3
...
```

Edit install-config.yaml as needed. Next time you create the cluster, new parameters will be used instead.

There's more...

It is also useful to have knowledge of the following information:

- Deleting your cluster

Deleting your cluster

To delete your cluster, use the following command:

```
$ ./openshift-install destroy cluster
```

This process will take a few minutes and, when finished, you will get a confirmation message.

See also

- The OpenShift Container Platform 4.3 Documentation: https://docs.openshift.com/container-platform/4.3/welcome/index.html

Configuring a Kubernetes cluster using Ansible

Powerful IT automation engines such as Ansible can be used to automate pretty much any day-to-day IT task, including the deployment of Kubernetes clusters on bare-metal clusters. In this section, we will learn how to deploy a simple Kubernetes cluster using Ansible playbooks.

Getting ready

In this recipe, we will use an Ansible playbook. The examples that will be used in these recipes are accessible through the k8sdevopscookbook GitHub repository.

Before you start executing the commands in this section's recipes, clone the Ansible playbook examples using the following command:

```
$ git clone https://github.com/k8sdevopscookbook/src.git
```

You will find the examples stored under the k8sdevopscookbook/src directory.

How to do it...

This section will take you through how to configure a Kubernetes cluster using Ansible. To that end, this section is further divided into the following subsections to make this process easier:

- Installing Ansible
- Provisioning a Kubernetes cluster using an Ansible playbook
- Connecting to the Kubernetes cluster

Installing Ansible

In order to provision a Kubernetes cluster using an Ansible playbook, follow these steps:

1. To install Ansible on your Linux workstation, first, we need to add the necessary repositories:

```
$ sudo apt-get install software-properties-common
$ sudo apt-add-repository --yes --update ppa:ansible/ansible
```

2. Install Ansible using the following command:

```
$ sudo apt-get update && sudo apt-get install ansible -y
```

3. Verify its version and make sure Ansible is installed:

```
$ ansible --version
```

At the time this recipe was written, the latest Ansible version was 2.9.4.

Provisioning a Kubernetes cluster using an Ansible playbook

In order to provision a Kubernetes cluster using an Ansible playbook, follow these steps:

1. Edit the hosts.ini file and replace the master and node IP addresses with your node IPs where you want Kubernetes to be configured:

```
$ cd src/chapter1/ansible/ && vim hosts.ini
```

2. The `hosts.ini` file should look as follows:

```
[master]
192.168.1.10
[node]
192.168.1.[11:13]
[kube-cluster:children]
master
node
```

3. Edit the `groups_vars/all.yml` file to customize your configuration. The following is an example of how to do this:

```
kube_version: v1.14.0
token: b0f7b8.8d1767876297d85c
init_opts: ""
kubeadm_opts: ""
service_cidr: "10.96.0.0/12"
pod_network_cidr: "10.244.0.0/16"
calico_etcd_service: "10.96.232.136"
network: calico
network_interface: ""
enable_dashboard: yes
insecure_registries: []
systemd_dir: /lib/systemd/system
system_env_dir: /etc/sysconfig
network_dir: /etc/kubernetes/network
kubeadmin_config: /etc/kubernetes/admin.conf
kube_addon_dir: /etc/kubernetes/addon
```

4. Run the `site.yaml` playbook to create your cluster:

```
$ ansible-playbook site.yaml
```

Your cluster will be deployed based on your configuration.

Connecting to the Kubernetes cluster

To get access to your Kubernetes cluster, you need to follow these steps:

1. Copy the configuration file from the `master1` node:

```
$ scp root@master:/etc/kubernetes/admin.conf ~/.kube/config
```

2. Now, use `kubectl` to manage your cluster.

See also

- The Ansible module for working with Kubernetes: `https://docs.ansible.com/ansible/latest/modules/k8s_module.html`
- Kubernetes Operators examples using Ansible and the Operator SDK: `https://github.com/operator-framework/operator-sdk/blob/master/doc/ansible/user-guide.md`

Troubleshooting installation issues

Kubernetes consists of many loosely coupled components and APIs. Based on environmental differences, you may run into problems where a little bit more attention is required to get everything up and running. Fortunately, Kubernetes provides many ways to point out problems.

In this section, we will learn how to get cluster information in order to troubleshoot potential issues.

How to do it...

Follow these steps to gather cluster information in order to troubleshoot potential issues:

1. Create a file dump of the cluster state called `cluster-state`:

```
$ kubectl cluster-info dump --all-namespaces \
  --output-directory=$PWD/cluster-state
```

2. Display the master and service addresses:

```
$ kubectl cluster-info
Kubernetes master is running at https://172.23.1.110:6443
Heapster is running at
https://172.23.1.110:6443/api/v1/namespaces/kube-system/services/he
apster/proxy
KubeDNS is running at
https://172.23.1.110:6443/api/v1/namespaces/kube-system/services/ku
be-dns:dns/proxy
```

3. Show the resource usage of the `us-west-2.compute.internal` node:

```
$ kubectl top node us-west-2.compute.internal
NAME CPU(cores) CPU% MEMORY(bytes) MEMORY%
us-west-2.compute.internal 42m 2% 1690Mi 43%
```

4. Mark the `us-west-2.compute.internal` node as unschedulable:

```
$ kubectl cordon us-west-2.compute.internal
```

5. Safely evict all the pods from the `us-west-2.compute.internal` node for maintenance:

```
$ kubectl drain us-west-2.compute.internal
```

6. Mark the `us-west-2.compute.internal` node as schedulable after maintenance:

```
$ kubectl uncordon us-west-2.compute.internal
```

How it works...

This recipe showed you how to quickly troubleshoot common Kubernetes cluster issues.

In step 1, when the `kubectl cluster-info` command was executed with the `--output-directory` parameter, Kubernetes dumped the content of the cluster state under a specified folder. You can see the full list using the following command:

```
$ tree ./cluster-state
./cluster-state
├── default
│   ├── daemonsets.json
│   ├── deployments.json
│   ├── events.json
│   ├── pods.json
│ ....
```

In step 4, we marked the node as unavailable using the `kubectl cordon` command. Kubernetes has a concept of scheduling applications, meaning that it assigns pods to nodes that are available. If you know in advance that an instance on your cluster will be terminated or updated, you don't want new pods to be scheduled on that specific node. Cordoning means patching the node with `node.Spec.Unschedulable=true`. When a node is set as unavailable, no new pods will be scheduled on that node.

In step 5, we use, the `kubectl drain` command to evict the existing pods, because cordoning alone will not have an impact on the currently scheduled pods. Evict APIs take disruption budgets into account. If set by the owner, disruption budgets limit the number of pods of a replicated application that are down simultaneously from voluntary disruptions. If this isn't supported or set, Evict APIs will simply delete the pods on the node after the grace period.

There's more...

It is also useful to have knowledge of the following information:

- Setting log levels

Setting log levels

When using the `kubectl` command, you can set the output verbosity with the `--v` flag, followed by an integer for the log level, which is a number between 0 and 9. The general Kubernetes logging conventions and the associated log levels are described in the Kubernetes documentation at `https://kubernetes.io/docs/reference/kubectl/cheatsheet/#kubectl-output-verbosity-and-debugging`.

It is useful to get the output details in a specific format by adding one of the following parameters to your command:

- `-o=wide` is used to get additional information on a resource. An example is as follows:

```
$ kubectl get nodes -owide
NAME STATUS ROLES AGE VERSION INTERNAL-IP EXTERNAL-IP OS-IMAGE
KERNEL-VERSION CONTAINER-RUNTIME
ip-192-168-41-120.us-west-2.compute.internal Ready <none> 84m
v1.13.8-eks-cd3eb0 192.168.41.120 34.210.108.135 Amazon Linux 2
4.14.133-113.112.amzn2.x86_64 docker://18.6.1
ip-192-168-6-128.us-west-2.compute.internal Ready <none> 84m
v1.13.8-eks-cd3eb0 192.168.6.128 18.236.119.52 Amazon Linux 2
4.14.133-113.112.amzn2.x86_64 docker://18.6.1
```

- `-o=yaml` is used to return the output in YAML format. An example is as follows:

```
$ kubectl get pod nginx-deployment-5c689d88bb-qtvsx -oyaml
apiVersion: v1
kind: Pod
metadata:
```

```
    annotations:
      kubernetes.io/limit-ranger: 'LimitRanger plugin set: cpu
  request for container
        nginx'
    creationTimestamp: 2019-09-25T04:54:20Z
    generateName: nginx-deployment-5c689d88bb-
    labels:
      app: nginx
      pod-template-hash: 5c689d88bb
    name: nginx-deployment-5c689d88bb-qtvsx
    namespace: default
  ...
```

As you can see, the output of the -o=yaml parameter can be used to create a manifest file out of an existing resource as well.

See also

- An overview and detailed uses of the kubectl command: https://kubernetes. io/docs/reference/kubectl/overview/
- kubectl cheat sheet: https://kubernetes.io/docs/reference/kubectl/ cheatsheet/
- A visual guide on troubleshooting Kubernetes deployments: https://learnk8s. io/a/troubleshooting-kubernetes.pdf
- K9s – the Kubernetes CLI to manage your clusters in style: https://github.com/ derailed/k9s

2
Operating Applications on Kubernetes

In this chapter, we will discuss the provisioning tools available to deploy cloud-native applications on Kubernetes. You will learn how to deploy DevOps tools and **CI/CD** (short for **continuous integration/continuous delivery** or **continuous deployment**) infrastructure on Kubernetes using the most popular life cycle management options. You will gain the skills to perform Day 1 and some Day 2 operations, such as installing, upgrading, and version controlling Deployments, ruling out a new application, and removing Deployments when they are no longer needed.

In this chapter, we will be covering the following topics:

- Deploying workloads using YAML files
- Deploying workloads using Customize
- Deploying workloads using Helm charts
- Deploying and operating applications using Kubernetes operators
- Deploying and managing the life cycle of Jenkins X
- Deploying and managing the life cycle of GitLab

Technical requirements

Recipes in this section assume that you have a functional Kubernetes cluster deployed following one of the recommended methods described in `Chapter 1`, *Building Production-Ready Kubernetes Clusters*.

The Kubernetes Operations tool kubectl will be used for the rest of the recipes in this section since it's the main command-line interface for running commands against Kubernetes clusters. If you are using a Red Hat OpenShift cluster, you can replace `kubectl` with `oc` and all commands are expected to function similarly.

Deploying workloads using YAML files

In this section, we will create the resource configurations required to deploy your applications in Kubernetes. You will learn how to create a Kubernetes manifest, deploy a workload, and roll out a new version using **Yet Another Markup Language** (**YAML**) files.

Getting ready

Before you start, clone the repository of the examples used in this chapter:

```
$ git clone https://github.com/k8sdevopscookbook/src.git
```

Make sure you have a Kubernetes cluster ready and kubectl configured to manage the cluster resources.

How to do it...

This section is further divided into the following subsections to ease the process:

- Creating a Deployment
- Verifying a Deployment
- Editing a Deployment
- Rolling back a Deployment
- Deleting a Deployment

Creating a Deployment

This recipe will take you through instructions to create a Deployment using a manifest file that keeps a set of pods running. Deployments are used to declare how many replicas of a pod should be running. A Deployment can be scaled up and down; we will see more on that topic later in Chapter 7, *Scaling and Upgrading Applications*.

Let's perform the following steps:

1. Change directory to src/chapter2/yaml/, where the example files for this recipe are located:

```
$ cd src/chapter2/yaml/
```

2. Review the Deployment manifest:

```
$ cat deployment-nginx.yaml
apiVersion: apps/v1
kind: deployment
metadata:
  name: nginx-deployment
  labels:
    app: nginx
spec:
  replicas: 2
  selector:
    matchLabels:
      app: nginx
# actual file is longer, shortened to show structure of the file
only
```

YAML is white space sensitive. Review the example file to understand the structure of the file. You will see that YAML files do not use tabs instead of a space character.
If in doubt, use a linter for your YAML files.

3. Create a Deployment by applying the YAML manifest:

```
$ kubectl apply -f deployment-nginx.yaml
```

After you run the preceding command, the container image mentioned in the YAML manifest will be pulled from the container registry and the application will be scheduled in your Kubernetes cluster as defined in the Deployment manifest. Now you should be able to verify the Deployment by following the next recipe.

Verifying a Deployment

This recipe will take you through the instructions to verify the status of the Deployment and troubleshoot it if needed.

Let's perform the following steps:

1. Confirm that the Deployment status shows a successfully rolled out message by watching the rollout status:

```
$ kubectl rollout status deployment nginx-deployment
deployment "nginx-deployment" successfully rolled out
```

2. Verify that the number of DESIRED and CURRENT values is equal, in our case 2:

```
$ kubectl get deployments
NAME               DESIRED CURRENT UP-TO-DATE AVAILABLE AGE
nginx-deployment 2        2       2          2         2m40s
```

3. Finally, also check the ReplicaSets (rs) and pods deployed as part of the Deployment:

```
$ kubectl get rs,pods
NAME                                 DESIRED CURRENT READY AGE
nginx-deployment-5c689d88bb          2       2       2     28m
NAME                                 READY STATUS   RESTARTS AGE
nginx-deployment-5c689d88bb-r2pp9 1/1   Running 0        28m
nginx-deployment-5c689d88bb-xsc5f 1/1   Running 0        28m
```

Now you have verified that the new Deployment is successfully deployed and running. In a production environment, you will also need to edit, update, and scale an existing application. In the next recipe, you will learn how to perform these modify operations on an existing Deployment.

Editing a Deployment

This recipe will take you through the instructions to edit an existing Kubernetes object, and you will learn how to change a Deployment object's parameters when needed.

Let's perform the following steps:

1. Edit the Deployment object and change the container image from image nginx 1.7.9 to image nginx 1.16.0:

```
$ kubectl edit deployment nginx-deployment
```

2. You can see that the Deployment first goes into pending termination and later the rollout status shows a successfully rolled out message after you run the following command:

```
$ kubectl rollout status deployment nginx-deployment
Waiting for deployment "nginx-deployment" rollout to finish: 1 old
replicas are pending termination...
deployment "nginx-deployment"
```

3. Confirm that your Deployment spins up the new pods by creating a new ReplicaSet and scaling down the old one from 2 to 0:

```
$ kubectl get rs
NAME                           DESIRED CURRENT READY AGE
nginx-deployment-5c689d88bb 0      0       0     36m
nginx-deployment-f98cbd66f  2      2       2     46s
```

4. We will create a change cause annotation. The following command will add the description defined in the `kubernetes.io/change-cause` parameter to your current Deployment:

```
$ kubectl annotate deployment nginx-deployment
kubernetes.io/change-cause="image updated to 1.16.0"
```

5. Now, as an alternative way to edit a Deployment, edit the `deployment-nginx.yaml` file and change the replicas from `replicas: 2` to `replicas: 3` and `nginx:1.7.9` to `image: nginx:1.17.0`:

```
$ nano deployment-nginx.yaml
```

6. Update the Deployment by applying the updated YAML manifest with your changes. This step will apply the change of image tag used for the Deployment and the number of replicas we increased in *step 5*:

```
$ kubectl apply -f deployment-nginx.yaml
```

7. Confirm that your Deployment spins up the new pods by creating a new ReplicaSet and scaling down the old pods:

```
$ kubectl get rs
NAME                           DESIRED CURRENT READY AGE
nginx-deployment-5c689d88bb 0      0       0     56m
nginx-deployment-5d599789c6 3      3       3     15s
nginx-deployment-f98cbd66f  0      0       0     20m
```

8. Create another change cause annotation by defining the changes we made using the `kubernetes.io/change-cause` parameter:

```
$ kubectl annotate deployment nginx-deployment
kubernetes.io/change-cause="image updated to 1.17.0 and scaled up
to 3 replicas"
```

Now you have learned how to edit, scale up, and also roll out a new version of the application using a ReplicaSet.

Rolling back a deployment

This recipe will take you through the instructions for reviewing changes made by comparing the annotations and rolling back the Deployment to an older revision when needed.

Let's perform the following steps:

1. Check the details and events for the Deployment and note recent `ScalingReplicaSet` events:

   ```
   $ kubectl describe deployments
   ```

2. Now, display the rollout history for the Deployment. The output will show the revisions along with the annotations we have created:

   ```
   $ kubectl rollout history deployment nginx-deployment
   deployment.extensions/nginx-deployment
   REVISION CHANGE-CAUSE
   1        <none>
   2        image updated to 1.16.0
   3        image updated to 1.17.0 and scaled up to 3 replicas
   ```

3. Roll back the last rollout. This command will take your Deployment to the previous revision, in this recipe, revision 2:

   ```
   $ kubectl rollout undo deployment nginx-deployment
   deployment.apps/nginx-deployment rolled back
   ```

4. Confirm that the Deployment has rolled back to the previous version:

   ```
   $ kubectl get rs
   NAME                          DESIRED CURRENT READY AGE
   nginx-deployment-5c689d88bb   0       0       0     69m
   nginx-deployment-5d599789c6   0       0       0     12m
   nginx-deployment-f98cbd66f    3       3       3     33m
   ```

 Notice that the rollback command only takes the Deployments back to different image version rollouts, and does not undo the other spec changes, such as the number of replicas.

5. Now, roll back to a specific revision. This command will take your Deployment to a specific revision defined using the `--to-revision` parameter:

   ```
   $ kubectl rollout undo deployment nginx-deployment --to-revision=1
   ```

Now you have learned how to review the rollout history and roll back a change when required.

Deleting a Deployment

Kubernetes schedules resources on the worker nodes based on the availability of resources. If you are using a small cluster with limited CPU and memory resources, you may easily run out of resources, which would cause new Deployments to fail to get scheduled on worker nodes. Therefore, unless it is mentioned in the requirement of the recipe, always clean up the old Deployments before you move onto the next recipe.

Let's perform the following step to remove `nginx-deployment`:

1. Delete the Deployment before moving onto the next recipes:

   ```
   $ kubectl delete deployment nginx-deployment
   ```

   The preceding command will immediately terminate the Deployment and remove the application from your cluster.

How it works...

The *Creating a Deployment* recipe showed you how to apply the desired state of your pods and ReplicaSets to the Deployment controller using YAML manifest files.

In step 2, we used the `kubectl apply` command, which is a part of the declarative management approach and makes incremental changes rather than overwriting them. The first time you create a resource intent, you could instead use the `kubectl create` command, which is considered an imperative management method.

I prefer to use the `apply` command, where declarative patterns are allowed, instead of `create` since it is better for creating the CI script and does not raise an error if the resource already exists.

Now you have learned the fundamental steps to get a single Deployment running in Kubernetes, we can move on to more complex Deployment use cases to compose a collection of objects using Kustomize, Helm, and Operator frameworks.

See also

- A linter for YAML files: `https://github.com/adrienverge/yamllint`
- Online Kubernetes YAML validator: `https://kubeyaml.com/`
- Read more on the declarative management of Kubernetes objects using configuration files: `https://kubernetes.io/docs/tasks/manage-kubernetes-objects/declarative-config/`
- Authoring Kubernetes manifests guide: `https://github.com/bitnami/charts/blob/master/_docs/authoring-kubernetes-manifests.md`

Deploying workloads using Kustomize

In this section, we will show you how to generate resources from files and compose and customize collections of resources in Kubernetes. You will learn about the declarative management of Kubernetes objects using Kustomize.

Getting ready

Make sure you have a Kubernetes cluster ready and `kubectl` configured to manage the cluster resources.

The source files created in this section can be found on my GitHub repository located at `https://github.com/k8sdevopscookbook/src/tree/master/chapter2/kustomize`. It is recommended that you follow the instructions to create and edit them and only use the files in the repository to compare with your files if you run into an issue.

How to do it...

This section is further divided into the following subsections to ease the process:

- Validating the Kubernetes cluster version
- Generating Kubernetes resources from files
- Creating a base for a development and production Deployment

Validating the Kubernetes cluster version

For Kustomize to function, Kubernetes cluster version 1.14.0 or later is required, since Kustomize support is only included with kubectl v.1.14.0 and later.

1. List the nodes to confirm your Kubernetes cluster version and make sure that it is 1.14.0 or later:

   ```
   $ kubectl get nodes
   NAME STATUS ROLES AGE VERSION
   ip-172-20-112-25.ec2.internal Ready master 7h19m v1.15.0
   ip-172-20-126-108.ec2.internal Ready node 7h18m v1.15.0
   ip-172-20-51-209.ec2.internal Ready node 7h18m v1.15.0
   ip-172-20-92-89.ec2.internal Ready node 7h19m v1.15.0
   ```

   In the preceding example, the version shows v1.15.0.

Generating Kubernetes resources from files

Let's learn how to customize the nginx rollout we did in the previous recipe using Kustomize this time:

1. Create a directory named nginx:

   ```
   $ mkdir nginx
   ```

2. Copy the deployment-nginx.yaml file you created in the *Deploying workload using YAML files* recipe under the nginx directory. This file still uses image: nginx:1.7.9 as the container image:

   ```
   $ cp deployment-nginx.yaml ./nginx/
   ```

3. Create a kustomization.yaml file by specifying a new image version:

   ```
   $ cat <<EOF >./nginx/kustomization.yaml
   apiVersion: kustomize.config.k8s.io/v1beta1
   kind: Kustomization
   resources:
   - deployment-nginx.yaml
   images:
     - name: nginx
       newName: nginx
       newTag: 1.16.0
   commonAnnotations:
     kubernetes.io/change-cause: "Initial deployment with 1.16.0"
   EOF
   ```

4. Check that the new version is injected into your Deployment by running the following command. In the output, you will see `image: nginx:1.16.0` instead of the original image version `nginx:1.7.9` that we have previously used in the `deployment-nginx.yaml` file:

```
$ kubectl kustomize ./nginx/
```

5. Apply the Deployment with customizations using the `-k` parameter:

```
$ kubectl apply -k nginx
```

6. Create a new `kustomization.yaml` file by specifying a newer image version:

```
$ cat <<EOF > nginx/kustomization.yaml
apiVersion: kustomize.config.k8s.io/v1beta1
kind: Kustomization
resources:
  - deployment-nginx.yaml
images:
  - name: nginx
    newName: nginx
    newTag: 1.17.0
commonAnnotations:
  kubernetes.io/change-cause: "image updated to 1.17.0"
EOF
```

7. Apply the customized Deployment using the `-k` parameter:

```
$ kubectl apply -k nginx
```

8. Now, display the rollout history for the Deployment:

```
$ kubectl rollout history deployment nginx-deployment
deployment.extensions/nginx-deployment
REVISION CHANGE-CAUSE
1          Initial deployment with 1.16.0
2          image updated to 1.17.0
```

Now you have learned how to edit, scale up, and also roll out a new version of the application using Kustomize.

Creating a base for a development and production Deployment

Let's perform the following steps to create a base for a local Docker image registry Deployment that we will use later in this chapter:

1. Create a directory named `registry` and another one underneath called `base`:

   ```
   $ mkdir registry && mkdir registry/base
   ```

2. Under `registry/base`, download the Deployment file named `deployment-registry.yaml` from the example repository:

   ```
   $ cd registry/base/
   $ wget
   https://raw.githubusercontent.com/k8sdevopscookbook/src/master/chapter2/kustomize/registry/base/deployment-registry.yaml
   ```

3. Review the file to understand its structure. You will see that it is a `Deployment` manifest consisting of two containers named `registry` and `registryui`. You will see that the registry container has a `volumeMount` named `registry-storage` and this volume is provided by a persistent volume claim named `registry-pvc`:

   ```
   $ cat deployment-registry.yaml
   apiVersion: extensions/v1beta1
   kind: Deployment
   # actual file is longer, shortened to highlight important structure
   of the file only
         - image: registry:2
   #....#
         - name: registry-storage
           mountPath: /var/lib/registry
   #....#
         - name: registryui
           image: hyper/docker-registry-web:latest
   #....#
         - name: registry-storage
           persistentVolumeClaim:
             claimName: registry-pvc
   ```

4. Under the same `registry/base`, download the service manifest file named `service-registry.yaml` from the example repository:

```
$ wget
https://raw.githubusercontent.com/k8sdevopscookbook/src/master/chap
ter2/kustomize/registry/base/service-registry.yaml
```

5. Review the file to understand its structure. You will see that it is a service manifest that exposes the service on each Node's IP at a static port; in this recipe, port 5000 for the `registry` service and port 80 for the `registry-ui`:

```
$ cat <<EOF > registry/base/service-registry.yaml
kind: Service
# actual file is longer, shortened to highlight important structure
of the file only
  type: NodePort
  ports:
    - name: registry
      port: 5000
      protocol: TCP
      nodePort: 30120
    - name: registry-ui
      port: 80
      protocol: TCP
      nodePort: 30220
#....#
```

6. Create a `PersistentVolumeClaim` manifest file named `pvc-registry.yaml` with the following content:

```
$ cat <<EOF > registry/base/pvc-registry.yaml
apiVersion: v1
kind: PersistentVolumeClaim
metadata:
  name: registry-pvc
  labels:
    app: kube-registry-pv-claim
spec:
  accessModes:
    - ReadWriteOnce
  resources:
    requests:
      storage: 10G
EOF
```

At this point, you can deploy the workload using all the resource files under the `registry` directory, by using `kubectl apply -f registry/base`. But every time you need to change a parameter in resources, such as `app` or `label`, you need to edit the files. The whole point of using Kustomize is to take advantage of reusing the files without modifying the source of the files.

7. And finally, create the `kustomization.yaml` file. The following command will create the Kustomize resource content with the three separate manifest files we created previously:

```
$ cat <<EOF >./registry/base/kustomization.yaml
apiVersion: kustomize.config.k8s.io/v1beta1
kind: Kustomization
resources:
  - deployment-registry.yaml
  - service-registry.yaml
  - pvc-registry.yaml
EOF
```

8. Now, create two overlays to be used for development and production Deployments. The first one is for development:

```
$ mkdir registry/overlays && mkdir registry/overlays/dev
$ cat <<EOF >./registry/overlays/dev/kustomization.yaml
apiVersion: kustomize.config.k8s.io/v1beta1
kind: Kustomization
bases:
  - ../../base
namePrefix: dev-
commonAnnotations:
  note: Hello, I am development!
EOF
```

9. And the second manifest will create the overlay for production:

```
$ mkdir registry/overlays/prod
$ cat <<EOF >./registry/overlays/prod/kustomization.yaml
apiVersion: kustomize.config.k8s.io/v1beta1
kind: Kustomization
bases:
  - ../../base
namePrefix: prod-
commonAnnotations:
  note: Hello, I am production!
EOF
```

10. Check that `dev` and `prod` prefixes are injected into your Deployment. When you point to the `prod` folder, the annotation note will display `"Hello, I am production!"`:

```
$ kubectl kustomize ./registry/overlays/prod/
# result shortened to highlight the annotation
metadata:
  annotations:
    note: Hello, I am production!
  labels:
    app: kube-registry-pv-claim
  name: prod-registry-pvc
#...#
```

11. When you point to the `dev` folder, the annotation note will display `"Hello, I am development!"`:

```
$ kubectl kustomize ./dev/
... # removed
metadata:
  annotations:
    note: Hello, I am development!
  labels:
    app: kube-registry-pv-claim
  name: dev-registry-pvc
... # removed
```

12. Now, deploy the `dev` version of your application:

```
$ kubectl apply -k ./registry/overlays/dev
```

Similarly, you can inject labels, patch image versions, change the number of replicas, and deploy resources into a different namespace.

How it works...

This recipe showed you how to manage and implement basic version control of your configuration files using Git.

In the *Creating a base for a development and production Deployment* recipe, the resources we created between step 2 and step 6 under the `base` directory represents an upstream repository of the application/workload, and the customizations we created between step 8 and step 10 under the `overlay` directory are the changes you control and store in your repository.

Later, if you need to see the difference of a variant, you can use the `diff` parameter as follows:

```
$ kubectl diff -k registry/overlays/prod/
```

By separating the changes from the base, we were able to customize template-free YAML files for multiple purposes, leaving the original YAML files unchanged, making the version controlling of source and changes possible.

See also

- Kustomize concepts overview slides: `https://speakerdeck.com/spesnova/introduction-to-kustomize`
- Declarative application management in Kubernetes background whitepaper – a highly recommended read: `https://goo.gl/T66ZcD`
- Common terms in Kustomize: `https://github.com/kubernetes-sigs/kustomize/blob/master/docs/glossary.md`
- Additional Kustomize examples: `https://github.com/kubernetes-sigs/kustomize/tree/master/examples`

Deploying workloads using Helm charts

In this section, we will show you how to use Helm charts in Kubernetes. Helm is the package manager for Kubernetes, which helps developers and SREs to easily package, configure, and deploy applications.

You will learn how to install Helm on your cluster and use Helm to manage the life cycle of third-party applications.

Getting ready

Make sure you have a Kubernetes cluster ready and `kubectl` configured to manage the cluster resources.

How to do it...

This section is further divided into the following subsections to ease the process:

- Installing Helm 2.x
- Installing an application using Helm charts
- Searching for an application in Helm repositories
- Updating an application using Helm
- Rolling back an application using Helm
- Adding new Helm repositories
- Deleting an application using Helm
- Building a Helm chart

Installing Helm 2.x

Let's perform the following steps to configure the prerequisites and install Helm:

1. Create a `ServiceAccount` by using the following command:

```
$ cat <<EOF | kubectl apply -f -
apiVersion: v1
kind: ServiceAccount
metadata:
  name: tiller
  namespace: kube-system
EOF
```

2. Create a `ClusterRoleBinding` by using the following command:

```
$ cat <<EOF | kubectl apply -f -
apiVersion: rbac.authorization.k8s.io/v1
kind: ClusterRoleBinding
metadata:
  name: tiller
roleRef:
  apiGroup: rbac.authorization.k8s.io
  kind: ClusterRole
  name: cluster-admin
subjects:
  - kind: ServiceAccount
    name: tiller
    namespace: kube-system
EOF
```

3. Download the Helm installation script. This `install-helm.sh` script will detect the architecture of your system and get the latest correct binaries to install Helm:

```
$ curl
https://raw.githubusercontent.com/kubernetes/helm/master/scripts/ge
t > install-helm.sh
```

4. Run the script to install Helm. The following command will install the two important binaries, Helm and Tiller, required to run Helm:

```
$ chmod u+x install-helm.sh && ./install-helm.sh
```

5. Run the `init` parameter to configure Helm with the service account we created in step 1. The `--history-max` parameter is used to purge and limit the Helm history, since without this setting the history can grow indefinitely and cause problems:

```
$ helm init --service-account tiller --history-max 200
```

This process with install the Helm server-side component Tiller in your cluster.

If you get a message complaining that `Tiller is already installed in the cluster.`, you can run the same command by adding the `--upgrade` parameter to the end of the command and force-upgrading the existing version.

6. Confirm the Helm version by running the following command:

```
$ helm version --short
```

At the time of writing this recipe, the latest stable version of Helm was v2.15.1 and the next version, Helm 3, was still in beta. In the following chapters and recipes, we will base our instruction on the Helm 2.x version.

Installing an application using Helm charts

Let's perform the following steps to install a Helm chart from the official Helm repository location:

1. Before you install a chart, always sync the repository to pull the latest content. Otherwise, you may end up with the old version of the Helm charts:

```
$ helm repo update
```

2. Install an example chart, in this case, `stable/mysql`:

```
$ helm install --name my-mysqlrelease stable/mysql
```

Similarly, you can install other applications from the Helm charts stable repository or add your own repositories for custom charts.

Every time you install a chart, a new release with a random name is created unless specified with the `--name` parameter. Now, list the releases:

```
$ helm ls
NAME                    REVISION UPDATED                      STATUS    CHART
APP VERSION NAMESPACE
my-mysqlrelease 1               Thu Aug 8 02:30:27 2019 DEPLOYED
mysql-1.3.0 5.7.14          default
```

3. Check the status in the release, in our example, `my-mysqlrelease`:

```
$ helm status my-mysqlrelease
```

You will get the Deployment status and information on all resources.

Searching for an application in Helm repositories

Let's perform the following steps to search for an application you would like to deploy on Kubernetes from the Helm chart repositories:

1. Search for a chart in the repository. The following command will look for your search words in the Helm repositories that you have access to:

```
$ helm search redis
NAME CHART VER APP VER DESCRIPTION
stable/prometheus-redis-exporter 3.0.0 1.0.3 Prometheus export
stable/redis 9.0.1 5.0.5 Open source, adva
stable/redis-ha 3.6.2 5.0.5 Highly available
stable/sensu 0.2.3 0.28 Sensu monitoring
```

You can find the complete list of workloads in helm/stable and the source of the repository at the following GitHub link: `https://github.com/helm/charts/tree/master/stable`

2. Your `search` keyword doesn't have to be the exact name of the project. You can also search for keywords such as `Storage`, `MQ`, or `Database`:

```
$ helm search storage
NAME                 CHART VERSION APP VERSION DESCRIPTION ...
stable/minio         2.5.4 RELEASE.2019-07-17T22-54-12Z MinIO is a
hi
stable/nfs-server-pr 0.3.0 2.2.1-k8s1.12 nfs-server-provisioner is
an
stable/openebs       1.0.0 1.0.0 Containerized Storage for
Containers
```

By default, your repository list is limited to the `helm/stable` location but later, in the *Adding new Helm repositories* recipe, you will also learn how to add new repositories to extend your search coverage to other repositories.

Upgrading an application using Helm

There are a couple of ways to use an upgrade. Let's perform the following steps:

1. Upgrade the release, in our case, `my-mysqlrelease`, with a newer chart version when available:

   ```
   $ helm upgrade my-mysqlrelease stable/mysql
   ```

2. In the future, you may find a specific version of the application that is more stable in your environment or keep the installations identical in multiple clusters. In that case, you can update the chart version with your preferred chart version using the following command:

   ```
   $ helm upgrade my-mysqlrelease stable/mysql --version 1.2.0
   ```

3. Confirm the chart version change using the following command. After upgrading the version in step 2, you should expect to see `mysql --version 1.2.0`:

   ```
   $ helm ls
   NAME                 REVISION UPDATED                      STATUS    CHART
   APP VERSION NAMESPACE
   my-mysqlrelease 3         Tue Jul 30 22:44:07 2019 DEPLOYED
   mysql-1.2.0 5.7.14       default
   ```

4. See the history of revisions using the following command. Since we recently updated the chart version, you should see at least two revisions in the history:

```
$ helm history my-mysqlrelease stable/mysql
REV UPDATED              STATUS      CHART        DESCRIPTION
1    Oct 1 22:47:37 2019 SUPERSEDED mysql-1.3.3 Install complete
2    Oct 1 22:57:32 2019 SUPERSEDED mysql-1.3.3 Upgrade complete
3    Oct 1 23:00:44 2019 DEPLOYED    mysql-1.2.0 Upgrade complete
```

5. Use the `helm upgrade` function to update a parameter on an existing release by specifying a parameter using the `--set key=value[,key=value]` argument. The following command will set two MySQL password using the `--set mysqlRootPassword` parameter:

```
$ helm upgrade my-mysqlrelease stable/mysql --version 1.2.0 --set
mysqlRootPassword="MyNevvPa55w0rd"
```

6. Confirm that the password is actually updated. You should expect to get the same password you set in step 4:

```
$ kubectl get secret --namespace default my-mysqlrelease -o
jsonpath="{.data.mysql-root-password}" | base64 --decode; echo
MyNevvPa55w0rd
```

Now you have learned how to upgrade a Helm release with new parameters.

Rolling back an application using Helm

Let's perform the following steps to recall an upgrade and bring your application status to a previous revision:

1. List the revision history for your release, in our example, `coy-jellyfish`:

```
$ helm history my-mysqlrelease
REV UPDATED                  STATUS      CHART        DESCRIPTION
1    Tue Oct 1 22:47:37 2019 SUPERSEDED mysql-1.3.3 Install complete
2    Tue Oct 1 22:57:32 2019 SUPERSEDED mysql-1.3.3 Upgrade complete
3    Tue Oct 1 23:00:44 2019 SUPERSEDED mysql-1.2.0 Upgrade complete
4    Tue Oct 1 23:07:23 2019 SUPERSEDED mysql-1.3.3 Upgrade complete
5    Tue Oct 1 23:10:39 2019 DEPLOYED    mysql-1.2.0 Upgrade complete
```

2. Let's say you need to roll back from the last upgrade to revision 4. Roll back to a specific revision:

```
$ helm rollback my-mysqlrelease 4
Rollback was a success.
```

3. The revision history will be updated to reflect your rollback:

```
$ helm history my-mysqlrelease
REV UPDATED                       STATUS      CHART       DESCRIPTION
...
5   Tue Jul 30 22:44:07 2019 SUPERSEDED mysql-1.2.0 Upgrade
complete
6   Tue Jul 30 23:11:52 2019 DEPLOYED   mysql-1.3.0 Rollback to 4
```

Now you have learned how to review the release history and roll back a Helm release when needed.

Deleting an application using Helm

Let's perform the following steps to remove an application deployed with Helm from your Kubernetes cluster:

1. Use the `helm ls` command with the `--all` parameter to list all the releases, including deleted revisions:

```
helm ls --all
NAME REVISION UPDATED STATUS CHART APP VERSION NAMESPACE
my-mysqlrelease 6 Thu Aug 8 02:34:13 2019 DEPLOYED mysql-1.3.0
5.7.14 default
```

2. Delete a release using the `--purge` parameter. The following command will completely remove the application from your cluster:

```
helm delete --purge my-mysqlrelease
```

The preceding command will immediately terminate the Deployment and remove the Helm release from your cluster.

Adding new Helm repositories

By default, Helm only uses the official Helm/stable repository for lookups and often in the following chapters, we will need to add additional repositories from third-party vendors using the method explained in this recipe.

Let's perform the following steps to add additional Helm repositories to your source list:

1. Check the list of existing repositories. You should only see `stable` and `local` on the list:

   ```
   $ helm repo list
   NAME    URL
   stable https://kubernetes-charts.storage.googleapis.com
   local  http://127.0.0.1:8879/charts
   ```

2. We need a persistent volume and authentication configured for our repository server. Create a file called `customhelmrepo.yaml` using the following content:

   ```
   cat <<EOF >customhelmrepo.yaml
   env:
    open:
     STORAGE: local
   persistence:
     enabled: true
     accessMode: ReadWriteOnce
     size: 10Gi
     secret:
        BASIC_AUTH_USER: helmcurator
        BASIC_AUTH_PASS: myhelmpassword
   EOF
   ```

3. Create a repository server using a persistent volume:

   ```
   $ helm install --name my-chartmuseum -f customhelmrepo.yaml
   stable/chartmuseum
   ```

4. Get the service IP for `chartmuseum`. The following command will return an IP address, in our example, `10.3.0.37`:

   ```
   $ kubectl get svc --namespace default -l "app=chartmuseum" -l \
   "release=my-chartmuseum" -o jsonpath="{.items[0].spec.clusterIP}";
   echo
   10.3.0.37
   ```

5. Add the new Helm repository to your list of repositories; in our case, the IP is `10.3.0.37`:

   ```
   $ helm repo add chartmuseum http://10.3.0.37:8080
   ```

6. Check the list of existing repositories:

```
$ helm repo list
NAME           URL
stable         https://kubernetes-charts.storage.googleapis.com
local          http://127.0.0.1:8879/charts
chartmuseum    http://10.3.0.37:8080
```

There are many options available to host your chart repository. You can deploy a local repository using an open source Helm repository server called **ChartMuseum**, on an S3 bucket, GitHub pages, or a classic web server. For simplicity, we used Helm itself to deploy a server. You can find alternative hosting methods for Helm charts under the *See also* section.

Building a Helm chart

Let's perform the following steps to build a custom Helm chart to be published in your local chartmuseum repository:

1. Create a chart called mychart:

```
$ helm create mychart
```

2. Edit your chart structure as you like and test the templates for possible errors:

```
$ helm lint ./mychart
==> Linting ./mychart
[INFO] Chart.yaml: icon is recommended
1 chart(s) linted, no failures
```

3. Test your application using --dry-run:

```
$ helm install ./mychart --debug --dry-run
```

4. Build the Helm chart. By running the following command, you will generate a tarball package of your Helm repository from the mychart location:

```
$ helm package .
```

5. Replace the Helm repository server address with your Helm server and upload this Helm chart package using a URL:

```
$ cd mychart && curl --data-binary "@mychart-0.1.0.tgz"
http://10.3.0.37:8080/api/charts
```

Now you have learned how to create, lint, test, package, and upload your new chart to your local ChartMuseum-based Helm repository.

How it works...

This recipe showed you how to install the Helm package manager and build your first Helm chart.

When we built the Helm chart in the *Building a Helm chart* recipe, in step 1, the `helm create` command created a couple of files as a template under the `chart` folder. You can start by editing these files or create them from scratch when you become more comfortable with the structure.

The `helm create` command creates the templates that construct our Helm chart. The contents and their functionality are explained here:

```
mychart
├─── Chart.yaml          --> Description of the chart
├─── charts              --> Directory for chart dependencies
├─── mychart-0.1.0.tgz   --> Packaged chart following the SemVer 2
standard
├─── templates           --> Directory for chart templates
│    ├─── NOTES.txt       --> Help text displayed to users
│    ├─── _helpers.tpl    --> Helpers that you can re-use
│    ├─── deployment.yaml --> Application - example deployment
│    ├─── service.yaml    --> Application - example service endpoint
└─── values.yaml         --> Default values for a chart
```

In the *Building a Helm chart* recipe, in step 3, `helm install`, when used along with the `--dry-run` parameter, sends the chart to the server and returns the rendered template only instead of installing it. This is usually used for testing Helm charts.

In the same recipe, in step 4, the `helm package` command packages your complete chart into a chart archive, basically a tarball.

In step 5, we used the `curl` command to send the packaged tarball binary to our ChartMuseum server, an HTTP server, so it can serve our Helm chart archives when it receives GET requests from the `helm` command.

Now you have learned how to install Helm charts and create your Helm charts in your local repositories, you will be able to install the third-party charts required in the next chapters, as well as building your own artifacts in your CI/CD pipelines.

See also

- The Helm documentation: `https://docs.helm.sh`
- Alternative hosting methods for Helm charts: https://v2.helm.sh/docs/chart_repository/
- Getting started with a chart template: `https://helm.sh/docs/chart_template_guide/`
- Fields required to build the `Chart.yaml` file: `https://v2.helm.sh/docs/chart_template_guide/`

- J-Frog Container Registry, a powerful Hybrid Docker and Helm registry: `https://jfrog.com/container-registry/`

Deploying and operating applications using Kubernetes operators

Kubernetes operators are another method of bundling, deploying, and managing application for Kubernetes. Operators are a bit more complex than a package manager like Helm. An operator helps to remove manual steps, application-specific preparation, and post-deployment steps, and even automates second-day operations such as scaling or upgrading them for the user.

As an example, an application's requirements might be validated differently based on the platform on which it is installed or may require changes to its configuration and interaction with external systems.

In this section, we will deploy two operators for popular stateful applications based on two different operator frameworks and learn what functionalities they offer.

Getting ready

Make sure you have a Kubernetes cluster ready and kubectl configured to manage the cluster resources.

How to do it...

This section is further divided into the following subsections to ease the process:

- Installing **KUDO** (short for **Kubernetes Universal Declarative Operator**) and the KUDO kubectl plugin
- Installing the Apache Kafka operator using KUDO
- Installing Operator Lifecycle Manager
- Installing the Zalando PostgreSQL operator

Installing KUDO and the KUDO kubectl plugin

Before you can install applications using KUDO operators, you need to install KUDO. We will install KUDO using `brew`, a package manager used in Linux for the simple installation of binaries on Linux; therefore, you will also need brew installed if you haven't done it already:

1. Follow the Helm instructions in the *Deploying workloads using Helm charts* recipe to get Helm running.
2. Install `brew` by using the following commands:

   ```
   $ sh -c "$(curl -fsSL
   https://raw.githubusercontent.com/Linuxbrew/install/master/install.
   sh)"
   $ PATH=/home/linuxbrew/.linuxbrew/bin/:$PATH
   ```

3. Install KUDO and the `kudo kubectl` plugin using `brew install` by running the following command:

   ```
   $ brew tap kudobuilder/tap && brew install kudo-cli
   ```

4. Install KUDO as follows:

   ```
   $ kubectl kudo init
   ```

    It is worth mentioning that Kubernetes operators are a developing concept in the Kubernetes community. There are multiple operator frameworks, such as the Red Hat Operator Framework, D2iQ's KUDO, and many others out there. Also, for each workload, you will find a number of operators developed by the community. I recommend testing a few flavors before you decide to use an operator to find the operator that fits your use case.

Now you have the KUDO controller installed to test some stateful running applications using Kubernetes Operators.

Installing the Apache Kafka Operator using KUDO

There are multiple Kafka operators listed in the *See also* section, such as Strimzi, Banzai Cloud, Confluent, krallistic, and others. Although I don't have any preference in this recipe, as an example, we will deploy the Apache Kafka Operator based on the KUDO Operator.

Let's perform the following steps:

1. Kafka requires ZooKeeper. Let's create a ZooKeeper cluster:

   ```
   $ kubectl kudo install zookeeper --instance=zk
   ```

2. Create a Kafka cluster using the KUDO Kafka Operator:

   ```
   $ kubectl kudo install kafka --instance=kafka
   ```

3. List KUDO Operators by querying the Operators CRD APIs as follows. After deploying Kafka, which also has a ZooKeeper dependency, you should see both kafka and zookeeper operators:

   ```
   $ kubectl get Operators
   NAME        AGE
   kafka       9s
   zookeeper   17s
   ```

4. List KUDO instances:

   ```
   $ kubectl get instances
   NAME    AGE
   kafka   25s
   zk      33s
   ```

Now you have learned how to deploy both ZooKeeper and Kafka using the KUDO Operator.

Installing Operator Lifecycle Manager

Before you can install applications using Red Hat Operator Framework Operators, you need to install **Operator Lifecycle Manager (OLM)**. Note that OLM is installed by default in OpenShift 4.0 and precedent.

1. Install OLM. It is required for our next recipe, *Installing the Zalando PostgreSQL Operator*:

   ```
   $ kubectl create -f
   https://raw.githubusercontent.com/Operator-framework/Operator-lifec
   ycle-manager/master/deploy/upstream/quickstart/crds.yaml
   $ kubectl create -f
   https://raw.githubusercontent.com/Operator-framework/Operator-lifec
   ycle-manager/master/deploy/upstream/quickstart/olm.yaml
   ```

Now you have OLM installed to test some stateful running applications using an Operator Framework.

Installing the Zalando PostgreSQL Operator

There are multiple PostgreSQL Operators listed in the *See also* section, such as CrunchyDB and Zalando. In this recipe, as an example, we will deploy the Zalando PostgreSQL Operator to manage the life cycle of PostgreSQL Deployments in your Kubernetes cluster.

Let's perform the following steps to get the Zalando PostgreSQL Operator deployed using the Operator Hub:

1. Install the `postgres-Operator` from the Operator Hub:

   ```
   $ kubectl create -f
   https://Operatorhub.io/install/postgres-Operator.yaml
   ```

2. Verify that `postgres-Operator` is running:

   ```
   $ kubectl get pods -n Operators
   NAME                                 READY STATUS    RESTARTS AGE
   postgres-Operator-5cd9d99494-5nl5r 1/1   Running 0          3m56s
   ```

3. Now that the PostgreSQL Operator is up and running, let's deploy the Postgres Operator UI:

   ```
   $ kubectl apply -f
   https://raw.githubusercontent.com/k8sdevopscookbook/src/master/chap
   ter2/postgres-Operator/ui/postgres-ui.yaml
   ```

4. Deploy PostgreSQL. The following command will create a small two-instance PostgreSQL cluster:

```
$ kubectl create -f
https://raw.githubusercontent.com/zalando/postgres-Operator/master/
manifests/minimal-postgres-manifest.yaml
```

6. List PostgreSQL instances that are managed by the Zalando Operator. It will show a cluster named `acid-minimal-cluster`:

```
$ kubectl get postgresql
NAME                     TEAM VERSION PODS VOLUME CPU-REQUEST MEMORY-
REQUEST AGE STATUS
acid-minimal-cluster acid 11       2      1Gi
7s
```

7. First get your cluster credentials and connect to your PostgreSQL using the `psql` interactive PostgreSQL terminal as follows:

```
$ export PGPASSWORD=$(kubectl get secret postgres.acid-minimal-
cluster.credentials -o 'jsonpath={.data.password}' | base64 -d)
$ export PGSSLMODE=require
$ psql -U postgres
```

8. Delete your PostgreSQL cluster:

```
$ kubectl delete postgresql acid-minimal-cluster
```

Now you have learned how to simply use popular Kubernetes Operators to deploy and manage workloads on Kubernetes. You can apply this knowledge later to simplify the life cycle management of stateful workloads you use in the development and production environment.

See also

- Deep dive on the Kubernetes Operators at KubeCon 2018: `https://developers.redhat.com/blog/2018/12/18/kubernetes-Operators-in-depth/`
- List of Kubernetes Operators by community: `https://github.com/Operator-framework/awesome-Operators`
- List of Kubernetes Operators build using the Red Hat Operator SDK: `https://Operatorhub.io/`
- The **Kubernetes Universal Declarative Operator** (**KUDO**): `https://kudo.dev/`

- Repository for KUDO-based Operators: `https://github.com/kudobuilder/Operators`
- A Python framework to write Kubernetes Operators in just a few lines of code: `https://github.com/zalando-incubator/kopf`
- A list of alternative Kafka Operators:
    - Apache Kafka Operator running on OpenShift: `http://strimzi.io/`
    - KUDO Kafka Operator: `https://github.com/kudobuilder/Operators/tree/master/repository/kafka`
    - Yet another Kafka Operator for Kubernetes: `https://github.com/banzaicloud/kafka-Operator`
- Istio Operator: `https://github.com/banzaicloud/istio-Operator`
- A list of alternative PostgreSQL Operators:
    - Crunchy Data PostgreSQL Operator: `https://github.com/CrunchyData/postgres-Operator`
    - Zalando PostgreSQL Operator: `https://github.com/zalando/postgres-Operator`

Deploying and managing the life cycle of Jenkins X

Jenkins X is an open source solution that offers software developers pipeline automation, built-in GitOps, CI, automated testing, and CD, known as CI/CD, in Kubernetes. Jenkins X is highly focused on accelerating software delivery at a large scale using the Kubernetes ecosystem.

In this section, we will focus on Jenkins X recipes and create a Kubernetes cluster with CI/CD capabilities on your cloud provider.

Getting ready

In the following recipes, you will learn how to create a static Jenkins Server to deploy Kubernetes clusters with pipeline automation and automated CI/CD with GitOps promotion and preview environments.

This recipe requires kubectl and Helm. For this recipe, we will use **GKE** (short for **Google Kubernetes Engine**), therefore the gcloud CLI tool needs to be installed as well. You also need to have a proper GitHub organization and GitHub account created.

How to do it...

This section is further divided into the following subsections to ease the process:

- Installing the Jenkins X CLI
- Creating a Jenkins X Kubernetes cluster
- Verifying Jenkins X components
- Switching Kubernetes clusters
- Validating cluster conformance

Installing the Jenkins X CLI

The Jenkins X CLI jx is used along with your preferred cloud provider CLI to orchestrate the Deployment of the Kubernetes cluster. Jenkins X supports Azure, AWS, **GCP** (short for **Google Cloud Platform**), IBM Cloud, Oracle Cloud, Minikube, Minishift, and OpenShift as the provider for the Deployment. For this recipe, we will use GKE. See the Jenkins X documentation for other vendor instructions.

Let's perform the following steps to install Jenkins X CLI tool:

1. Visit the JX release site (https://github.com/jenkins-x/jx/releases) and note the latest release version. At the time of writing, the latest release was v2.0.905.
2. Update the release version in the following command. Download and install the latest version of the Jenkins X CLI:

```
$ curl -L
https://github.com/jenkins-x/jx/releases/download/v2.0.905/jx-linux
-amd64.tar.gz | tar xzv
$ sudo mv jx /usr/local/bin
```

Now you have the Jenkins X CLI installed, you can move on to the next recipe.

Creating a Jenkins X Kubernetes cluster

You may prefer other cloud vendors or on-premises deployment. For this recipe, we will use GKE. See the Jenkins X documentation for other vendor instructions.

Let's perform the following steps to create your first Jenkins X Kubernetes cluster using `jx`:

1. Create a Kubernetes cluster with GKE using the `jx` command with the `gke` parameter as follows:

   ```
   $ jx create cluster gke --skip-login
   ```

2. Select your Google Cloud project; in our example, `devopscookbook`.
3. Select `us-central1-a` when asked to pick a Google Cloud zone.
4. Select **Static Jenkins Server** and **Jenkinsfiles** as the installation type.
5. Enter your GitHub username:

   ```
   Creating a local Git user for GitHub server
   ? GitHub username:
   ```

6. Enter your GitHub API token. Go to the GitHub Token page at `https://github.com/settings/tokens/new?scopes=`
   `repo,read:user,read:org,user:email,write:repo_hook,delete_repo` to get your API token:

   ```
   Please click this URL and generate a token
   https://github.com/settings/tokens/new?scopes=repo,read:user,read:o
   rg,user:email,write:repo_hook,delete_repo
   Then COPY the token and enter it following:
   ? API Token:
   ```

7. By default, Jenkins X will set the ingress rules to use the magic DNS `nip.io` domain:

   ```
   ? Domain [? for help] (your_IP.nip.io)
   ```

8. Enter `Yes` to the following question:

   ```
   ? Do you wish to use GitHub as the pipelines Git server: (Y/n)
   ```

9. Select the GitHub organization where you want to create the environment repository; in our case, `k8devopscookbook`.

10. You will see a message similar to the following when your Deployment is successful:

```
Jenkins X installation completed successfully
        ******************************************************
              NOTE: Your admin password is: your_password
        ******************************************************
...
Context "gke_devopscookbook_us-central1-a_slayersunset" modified.
NAME               HOSTS                               ADDRESS PORTS AGE
chartmuseum        chartmuseum.jx.your_IP.nip.io       your_IP 80
7m43s
docker-registry docker-registry.jx.your_IP.nip.io your_IP 80
7m43s
jenkins            jenkins.jx.your_IP.nip.io           your_IP 80
7m43s
nexus              nexus.jx.your_IP.nip.io             your_IP 80
7m43s
```

You can also find your admin password in the preceding output.

Verifying Jenkins X components

Let's perform the following steps to verify that all Jenkins X components are running as expected:

1. Confirm that all pods are running. All pods in the `jx` namespace should be in a running state:

```
$ kubectl get pods -n jx
NAME                                             READY STATUS
RESTARTS AGE
jenkins-956c58866-pz5vl                          1/1   Running 0
11m
jenkins-x-chartmuseum-75d45b6d7f-5bckh           1/1   Running 0
11m
jenkins-x-controllerrole-bd4d7b5c6-sdkbg         1/1   Running 0
11m
jenkins-x-controllerteam-7bdd76dfb6-hh6c8        1/1   Running 0
11m
jenkins-x-controllerworkflow-7545997d4b-hlvhm 1/1   Running 0
11m
jenkins-x-docker-registry-6d555974c7-sngm7       1/1   Running 0
11m
jenkins-x-heapster-7777b7d7d8-4xgb2              2/2   Running 0
11m
```

```
jenkins-x-nexus-6ccd45c57c-btzjr          1/1    Running 0
11m
maven-brcfq                               2/2    Running 0
63s
maven-qz0lc                               2/2    Running 0
3m
maven-vqw91                               2/2    Running 0
32s
```

2. Get the list of Jenkins X service URLs that we will need to connect. You will have a list of `jenkins`, `chartmuseum`, `docker-registry`, and `nexus` URLs similar to the following:

```
$ jx get urls
NAME                         URL
jenkins                      http://jenkins.jx.your_IP.nip.io
jenkins-x-chartmuseum        http://chartmuseum.your_IP.nip.io
jenkins-x-docker-registry    http://docker-registry.jx.your_IP.nip.io
nexus                        http://nexus.jx.your_IP.nip.io
```

Now you can connect to the Jenkins UI by visiting the first URL from the preceding output of the `jx get urls` command.

Switching Kubernetes clusters

Let's perform the following steps to switch between the Kubernetes clusters that you have access to using Jenkins X:

1. Get the existing Kubernetes clusters by listing the contexts:

```
$ jx context
```

2. Select the cluster you would like to use. In our case, we switch to the `gke_devopscookbook` cluster that we created using Jenkins X:

```
Change Kubernetes context: [Use arrows to move, space to select,
type to filter]
> gke_devopscookbook_us-central1-a_slayersunset
eks_devopscookbook_us-west
openshift_cluster
```

Now you know how to switch context using the Jenkins X CLI.

Validating cluster conformance

If you switch between the existing Kubernetes clusters, it is suggested that you validate the cluster configuration before you run your pipelines. Let's perform the following steps:

1. Validate that your cluster is compliant. These tests will typically take an hour:

   ```
   jx compliance run
   ```

2. Check the status. This command will return a `Compliance tests completed` message only after tests are completed:

   ```
   $ jx compliance status
   Compliance tests completed.
   ```

3. Review the results. If your cluster is compliant all executed test results should be displayed as `PASSED`:

   ```
   $ jx compliance results
   ```

   Now you know how to check cluster conformance results.

How it works...

The *Creating a Jenkins X Kubernetes cluster* recipe showed you how to provision the Kubernetes cluster for pipeline automation and automated CI/CD.

In the *Creating a Jenkins X Kubernetes cluster* recipe, in step 1, we created the cluster using the Jenkins X CLI. By default, Jenkins X uses `n1-standard-2` as the machine type on GKE and creates a cluster with a minimum of three and a maximum of five nodes settings. Remember that you could also use an existing Kubernetes cluster instead of creating a new one. Most of the settings will be saved and remembered next time you run the `create cluster` command.

Jenkins X deploys a couple of services, including Jenkins, a private Docker registry, a private Helm repository ChartMuseum, Monocular to manage Helm charts, and a Maven and npm repository called **Nexus**.

As you will find in your repository after the installation, Jenkins X creates two Git repositories, one for your staging environment and one for production. Jenkins X uses the GitOps approach to promote code from one repo to another through Git **pull requests** (**PRs**). Therefore each repo contains a Jenkins pipeline to handle promotions.

In the *Creating a Jenkins X Kubernetes cluster* recipe, in step 7, Jenkins X uses the magic DNS service and converts the IP address of your GKE cluster into a DNS discoverable hostname using a service via `nip.io`. If you have your own domain and the DNS is configured to point to your cluster, you can update the settings later using the `jx upgrade ingress --cluster` command.

Later, in step 10, you will get the default password assigned to your admin user. You will be asked to change this password when you first connect to the Jenkins UI via the URL provided in this step.

There's more...

It is also useful to have knowledge of the following information:

- Importing an application
- Upgrading Jenkins X
- Deleting a Jenkins X Kubernetes cluster

Importing an application

Let's perform the following steps to import an existing application into the Jenkins X environment:

1. Clone or use an existing application. As an example, we will create a clone of the `hello-world` example:

```
$ mkdir import && cd import
$ git clone https://github.com/k8sdevopscookbook/hello-world.git
```

2. Remove the Git files from the `cloned` directory. This will remove the Git history from the directory:

```
$ cd hello-world & sudo rm -r .git/
```

3. Run the following command in the folder to import the source code into Jenkins X:

```
$ jx import
```

Upgrading a Jenkins X application

Let's perform the following steps to upgrade a Jenkins X application and its components:

1. First, upgrade the `jx` CLI. This command will upgrade the application if there is a new version available in the remote repository:

   ```
   $ jx upgrade cli
   ```

2. Once you are on the latest CLI, upgrade the platform using the following command. The new `jx` CLI command will upgrade the platform components if a new version exists:

   ```
   $ jx upgrade platform
   ```

Deleting a Jenkins X Kubernetes cluster

Removing managed Kubernetes clusters may be tricky, especially if you are not the one who created them. Since we used GKE to create them, it is faster to use the gcloud CLI tool to delete them. Let's perform the following steps to delete the Kubernetes cluster we created with Jenkins X:

1. Use your cloud provider's instructions to delete the Kubernetes cluster. In our case, we used GKE for the recipe. First, list the clusters:

   ```
   $ gcloud container clusters list
   NAME LOCATION MASTER_VERSION MASTER_IP MACHINE_TYPE NODE_VERSION
   NUM_NODES STATUS
   clustername us-central1-a 1.12.8-gke.10 your_IP n1-standard-2
   1.12.8-gke.10 3 RUNNING
   ```

2. Delete the cluster using the `clustername` from the output of step 1:

   ```
   $ gcloud container clusters delete <clustername>
   ```

   Now you have learned how to use Jenkins X to create your cluster. This knowledge has prepared you for `Chapter 3`, *Building CI/CD Pipelines*, where you will continue to use the environment and learn to import an application as a pipeline in Jenkins X.

See also

- Introduction to Jenkins: `https://jenkins.io/blog/2018/03/19/introducing-jenkins-x/`
- Jenkins X repository and binaries: `https://github.com/jenkins-x/jx`
- Jenkins X tutorials: `https://jenkins-x.io/tutorials/`
- Jenkins X getting started instructions: `https://jenkins-x.io/getting-started/install-on-cluster/`
- Jenkins X CLI commands and an explanation of how to use them: `https://jenkins-x.io/commands/jx/`

Deploying and managing the life cycle of GitLab

GitLab is a complete DevOps tool chain, delivered in a single application platform. GitLab provides all the necessary tooling you need to manage, plan, create, verify, package, release, configure, monitor, and secure your applications.

In this section, we will cover the deployment and life cycle management of GitLab using Helm charts.

Getting ready

In the following recipe, you will learn how to install GitLab on an existing Kubernetes cluster where you can manage the entire DevOps life cycle.

This recipe requires kubectl and Helm, as well as an existing Kubernetes cluster. For this recipe, we will use the cluster we deployed on AWS in Chapter 1, *Building Production-Ready Kubernetes Clusters*. You should be able to run the same recipe on any Kubernetes cluster version 1.11 or higher with a minimum of 6vCPU and 16 GB of RAM.

How to do it...

This section is further divided into the following subsections to ease the process:

- Installing GitLab using Helm
- Connecting to the GitLab dashboard

- Creating the first GitLab user
- Upgrading GitLab
- Deleting GitLab

Installing GitLab using Helm

For this recipe, we will use the Kubernetes cluster on Amazon EC2, which we deployed in Chapter 1, *Building Production-Ready Kubernetes Clusters* under the *Configuring a Kubernetes cluster on Amazon Web Services* section:

1. Add GitLab Helm chart repos to your local repository:

```
$ helm repo add gitlab https://charts.gitlab.io/
$ helm repo update
```

2. Replace the following externalUrl with your domain name and deploy GitLab using Helm in the gitlab namespace:

```
$ helm upgrade --install gitlab gitlab/gitlab --namespace gitlab \
--timeout 600 \
--set global.edition=ce \
--set certmanager-issuer.email=youremail@domain.com \
--set global.hosts.domain=yourdomain.com
```

 For simplicity, I would recommend using your own certificates following the *Using auto-generated self-signed certificates* sections. Then you can map your DNS name to the created ELB using a CNAME record.

3. The deployment may take around 10-15 minutes. Confirm the service status and note the external IP of the gitlab-gitlab-ce service:

```
$ kubectl get svc -n gitlab
```

Connecting to the GitLab dashboard

Let's perform the following steps to get the GitLab service address to connect using your web browser:

1. Get the external address of your GitLab service:

```
$ echo http://$(kubectl get svc --namespace gitlab \
gitlab-nginx-ingress-controller \
-o jsonpath='{.status.loadBalancer.ingress[0].hostname}')
```

2. Open the address returned to the preceding command in a browser.
3. Get the default root password created by GitLab by running the following command:

```
$ kubectl get secret gitlab-gitlab-initial-root-password \
-ojsonpath='{.data.password}' | base64 --decode ; echo
```

4. Set a new password and sign in using the `root` user and your new password.
5. To use a custom URL, create a `CNAME` record on your DNS with an alias to the external URL used in step 1.

Creating the first GitLab user

By default, we use the root account to manage the GitLab Deployment. All new users need to log in to GitLab using their own credentials.

Let's perform the following steps to create new users:

1. Log in as the `root` user.
2. After you log in to the GitLab dashboard, you will see a welcome screen similar to the following. Click **Add people** on the **Welcome to GitLab** screen:

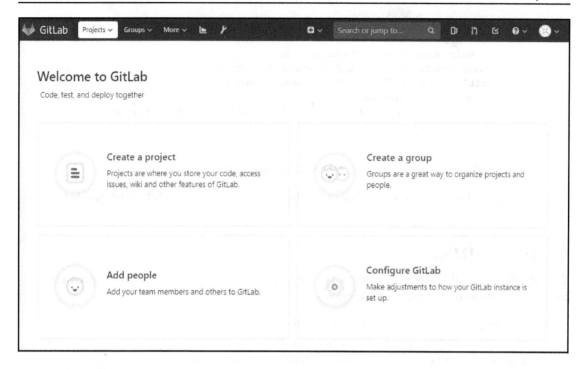

3. Under the **New User** menu, enter at least the name, username, and email fields, and then click on **Create User** to save the changes.

Upgrading GitLab

GitLab frequently releases new versions with additional functionality. Once in a while, you may also need to upgrade to get bug fixes. Upgrading can be done easily using the Helm upgrade. Let's perform the following steps to upgrade GitLab to a new version:

1. First, export the currently used arguments into a YAML file using the `helm get values` command as follows:

```
$ helm get values gitlab > gitlab.yaml
```

2. Upgrade the chart repositories to get new versions available from the remote repository:

```
$ helm repo update
```

3. List the available chart versions:

```
$ helm search -1 gitlab/gitlab
NAME CHART VERSION APP VERSION DESCRIPTION
gitlab/gitlab 2.1.7 12.1.6 Web-based Git-repository manager with
wiki and issue-trac...
gitlab/gitlab 2.1.6 12.1.4 Web-based Git-repository manager with
wiki and issue-trac...
...
```

4. Use the same arguments with the new version to upgrade:

```
$ helm upgrade gitlab gitlab/gitlab --version 2.1.7 -f gitlab.yaml
```

How it works...

The *Installing GitLab using Helm* recipe showed you how to provision GitLab with all built-in components and external dependencies.

In the *Installing GitLab using Helm* recipe, in step 1, we made sure that official up-to-date GitLab Helm chart repos were added into the local repository list. Otherwise, older versions of the GitLab charts from the stable/gitlab repo would be used.

In the same recipe, in step 2, we deployed GitLab using Helm charts in the `gitlab` namespace using the `--namespace gitlab` parameter. This command not only deployed GitLab components but also Redis, PostgreSQL, Minio object storage for data persistence, Cert Manager, a local container registry, and the nginx ingress controller.

 To use existing Deployments of PostgreSQL, Redis, Gitaly, S3 Storage, and the ingress controller, follow the advanced configuration instruction a described here: `https://docs.gitlab.com/charts/advanced/`.

By default, GitLab Helm charts deploy the enterprise version of GitLab. By using the `--set global.edition=ce` parameter, we switched the Deployment to the free Community Edition.

After we executed the command in the *Installing GitLab using Helm* recipe, in step 2, the Helm chart assumes that we have an existing default storage class and it uses the default one to create the PVCs and PVs for the stateful application.

There's more...

It is also useful to have knowledge of the following information:

- Using your own wildcard certificate
- Using autogenerated self-signed certificates
- Enabling a GitLab Operator
- Deleting GitLab

Using your own wildcard certificate

Helm chart installation of GitLab supports TLS termination using the nginx controller. When you install GitLab, you have options. For improved security, you can use Cert Manager and Let's Encrypt or choose to use your own wildcard certificate. In this recipe, we will explain using your own wildcard certificates option, as follows:

1. Add your certificate and key to the cluster as a secret:

   ```
   $ kubectl create secret tls mytls --cert=cert.crt --key=key.key
   ```

2. Deploy GitLab from the Helm chart using the following additional parameters:

   ```
   $ helm upgrade --install gitlab gitlab/gitlab --namespace gitlab \
   --timeout 600 \
   --set global.edition=ce \
   --version 2.1.6 \
   --set certmanager.install=false \
   --set global.ingress.configureCertmanager=false \
   --set global.ingress.tls.secretName=mytls
   ```

Using autogenerated self-signed certificates

If you can't effo using your own wildcard certificate and still want to get GitLab quickly up for testing or smaller use cases, you can also use autogenerated self-signed certificates. In this recipe, we will explain using self-signed certificates, which can be useful in environments where Let's Encrypt is not an option, but SSL security is still needed:

1. In cases where your domain is not reachable from the Let's Encrypt servers, you can provide an autogenerated self-signed wildcard certificate:

   ```
   $ helm upgrade --install gitlab gitlab/gitlab --namespace gitlab \
   --timeout 600 \
   --set global.edition=ce \
   ```

```
--version 2.1.6 \
--set certmanager.install=false \
--set global.ingress.configureCertmanager=false \
--set gitlab-runner.install=false
```

2. Retrieve the certificate, which can be imported into a web browser or system store later:

```
$ kubectl get secret gitlab-wildcard-tls-ca -n gitlab \
-ojsonpath='{.data.cfssl_ca}' | base64 --decode >
gitlab.mydomain.com.ca.pem
```

Enabling the GitLab Operator

GitLab provides an experimental Operator. This Operator controls the upgrade process and helps to perform rolling upgrades without downtime. Let's perform the following steps to get the GitLab Operator running:

1. First, make sure CRD is in place by enabling the global Operator using the Helm parameters as follows:

```
$ helm upgrade --install gitlab . --set
global.Operator.enabled=true \
--set global.Operator.bootstrap=true
```

2. Deploy the GitLab Operator using the Helm charts:

```
$ helm upgrade gitlab . --set global.Operator.enabled=true \
--set global.Operator.bootstrap=false
```

Deleting GitLab

Let's perform the following steps to completely remove the GitLab Deployment we created in this section:

1. Delete the existing release of GitLab using Helm:

```
$ helm delete --purge gitlab
```

2. You may also want to remove the namespace to make sure there is nothing left behind:

```
$ kubectl delete ns gitlab
```

Now you have learned how to get GitLab up and running on Kubernetes. This knowledge will be required in `Chapter 3`, *Building CI/CD Pipelines*, in the *GitLab* section, where you will learn how to import an application and create a pipeline in GitLab.

See also

- GitLab cloud-native Helm chart documentation: `https://docs.gitlab.com/charts/`
- Advanced configuration options: `https://docs.gitlab.com/charts/advanced/`
- GitLab Operator: `https://docs.gitlab.com/charts/installation/Operator.html`
- Alternative ways to install GitLab Community Edition: `https://about.gitlab.com/install/?version=ce/`

3
Building CI/CD Pipelines

In this chapter, we will discuss the configuration of end-to-end **Continuous Integration/Continuous Delivery (CI/CD)** pipelines using the most popular CI/CD tools on both self-managed public clouds and SaaS solutions using Kubernetes. After following the recipes in this chapter, you will have gained the skills needed to build, deploy, and promote applications from development to a production environment. You will be able to use the tools that we will implement in these recipes to detect bugs, anti-patterns, and license concerns during the continuous integration process.

In this chapter, we will cover the following recipes:

- Creating a CI/CD pipeline in Jenkins X
- Creating a CI/CD pipeline in GitLab
- Creating a CI/CD pipeline using CircleCI
- Setting up a CI/CD pipeline using GitHub Actions
- Setting up a CI/CD pipeline on Amazon Web Services
- Setting up a CI/CD pipeline with Spinnaker on Google Cloud Build
- Setting up a CI/CD pipeline on Azure DevOps

Technical requirements

The recipes in this section assume that you have a functional Kubernetes cluster deployed after following one of the recommended methods described in Chapter 1, *Building Production-Ready Kubernetes Clusters*.

Kubernetes' command-line interface, kubectl, will be used for the rest of the recipes in this section since it's the main command-line interface for running commands against Kubernetes clusters. If you are using a Red Hat OpenShift cluster, you can replace kubectl with oc. All the commands are expected to function similarly.

The recipes in this section require a Git repository with a containerized project.

Creating a CI/CD pipeline in Jenkins X

Jenkins X is a fairly new open source solution that extends the Jenkins ecosystem and solves the problem of automating CI/CD in the cloud using Kubernetes.

In this section, we will learn how to get your application as a pipeline into Jenkins X, which you will have deployed by following the *Deploying and managing the life cycle of Jenkins X* recipe instructions in Chapter 2, *Operating Applications on Kubernetes*. With that, you will learn how to create a CI/CD pipeline with automated GitOps and promote an application from staging to production, all by using simple commands.

Getting ready

Make sure you have followed the instructions in Chapter 2, *Operating Applications on Kubernetes*, in the *Deploying and managing the life cycle of Jenkins X* recipe and have a functional Kubernetes cluster with a Jenkins X deployment ready. You can find the instructions to install helm in that chapter as well.

In the following recipe, you will learn how to create a pipeline with GitOps promotion.

This recipe requires kubectl, helm, the Jenkins X CLI, jx, and your preferred cloud provider CLI where you installed your Kubernetes cluster using Jenkins X.

Jenkins X supports Azure, AWS, GCP, IBM Cloud, Oracle Cloud, minikube, minishift, and OpenShift as providers for the deployment process. You also need to have a GitHub organization and GitHub account.

How to do it...

This section is further divided into the following subsections to make this process easier:

- Connecting to the Jenkins pipeline console
- Importing an application as a pipeline
- Checking application status
- Promoting an application to production
- Creating a pipeline using a quick-start application

Connecting to Jenkins Pipeline Console

Let's perform the following steps to access the Jenkins Pipeline Console web interface:

1. Switch to the `jx` namespace where Jenkins X is deployed:

```
$ jx ns
? Change namespace: [Use arrows to move, space to select, type to
filter]
  default
> jx
  jx-production
  jx-staging
  kube-public
  kube-system
```

2. Using the following command to get the Jenkins (Blue Ocean) console address and open the link in your browser. In this recipe, the console address is the output to the following `jx console` command, that is, `http://jenkins.jx.your_ip.nip.io/blue`:

```
$ jx console
Jenkins Console: http://jenkins.jx.your_ip.nip.io/blue
```

3. After you've opened the Jenkins Console link from the output of *step 2*, click on one of the pipelines from the list. As an example, you can see two pipelines in our following demo environment:

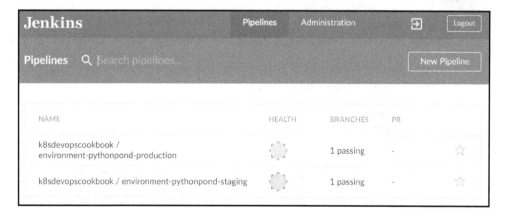

4. Select the last run and make sure both pipelines are healthy, meaning that your environment works. Similar to the following screenshot, you should see green check marks at the **Validate Environment** and **Update Environment** stages:

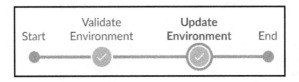

Now that we've validated that the environment is functional, we can start adding a new pipeline for our own application.

Importing an application as a pipeline

Most of the time, you will be required to import a local project or Git repository into Jenkins. Let's perform the following steps to create a local clone of an existing repository and import it as a pipeline:

1. First, fork your copy of the example code to your account. Go to `https://github.com/k8sdevopscookbook/python-flask-docker` in your browser and click on the **Fork** button in the upper-right corner.

2. Clone the repository to your local machine. Make sure that you replace `your_github_username` with your GitHub username where you forked the example:

   ```
   $ git clone
   https://github.com/your_github_username/python-flask-docker.git
   ```

3. Now, you should have a local copy of the `python-flask-docker` application. Use the following commands to import the project:

   ```
   $ cd python-flask-docker
   $ jx import
   ```

4. Now, you can watch the pipeline activity either from the Jenkins Blue Ocean view or the CLI. The following screenshot shows the pipeline activity on the Jenkins Blue Ocean dashboard:

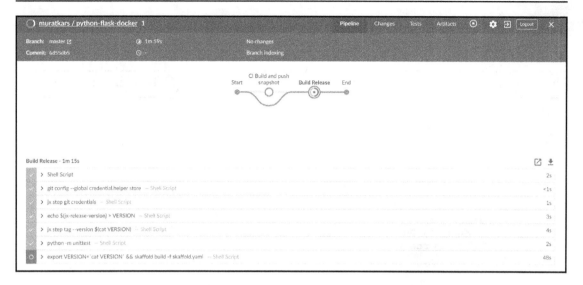

5. As an alternative, you can watch the activity on the CLI using the `jx get activity` command:

```
$ jx get activity -f python-flask-docker -w
STEP STARTED AGO DURATION STATUS
muratkars/python-flask-docker/master #1 1m3s Running
  Checkout Source 22s 5s Succeeded
  CI Build and push snapshot 17s NotExecuted
  Build Release 17s Pending
...
    Promoted 2m5s 2m0s Succeeded Application is at:
http://python-flask-docker.jx-staging.35.188.140.152.nip.io
    Clean up 1s 0s Succeeded
```

Checking application status

After you've created the pipeline, you need to confirm its status. Let's perform the following steps make sure the application has been deployed in staging before we move it into production:

1. If the pipeline has been built successfully, you should have version 0.0.1 in your staging environment. List the applications when the pipeline is complete:

```
$ jx get applications
APPLICATION STAGING PODS URL
python-flask-docker 0.0.1 1/1
http://python-flask-docker.jx-staging.35.188.140.152.nip.io
```

2. Here, you can see that the application has been deployed. Visit the URL to see the application:

The hostname of the container is **jx-python-flask-docker-8564f5b4cb-ff97f** and its IP is **10.48.0.12**.

3. Our pod is currently running in the jx-staging namespace. Confirm the pods in the jx-staging and jx-production namespaces. The second namespace shouldn't return anything until we promote our application to production:

```
$ kubectl get pods -n jx-staging
NAME READY STATUS RESTARTS AGE
jx-python-flask-docker-8564f5b4cb-ff97f 1/1 Running 0 21m
$ kubectl get pods -n jx-production
No resources found.
```

Promoting an application to production

Once an application has been deployed in staging, the next step is to promote it into the production environment. Let's perform the following steps to promote an application from staging to production:

1. After you've confirmed that an application is stable, the next step is to promote it into production. Let's use the following command to push the current version from staging to production:

```
$ jx promote python-flask-docker --version 0.0.1 --env production
```

2. For various reasons, mostly environmental limitations, the successful deployment of an application into staging doesn't guarantee successful deployment into production. After promoting the application, use the following command to check the progress of the production deployment. You need to see a Succeeded message after you run this command:

```
$ jx get activity -f python-flask-docker -w
```

3. Our pod has been promoted to the jx-production namespace. Confirm that the pods are now running in the jx-production namespace as well:

```
$ kubectl get pods -n jx-production
NAME                                      READY STATUS  RESTARTS AGE
jx-python-flask-docker-8564f5b4cb-fhcpm 1/1   Running 0        104m
```

4. List the applications. You will get both staging and production links for the same application:

```
$ jx get applications
APPLICATION              STAGING PODS URL
PRODUCTION PODS URL
python-flask-docker 0.0.1    1/1
http://python-flask-docker.jx-staging.35.188.140.152.nip.io 0.0.1
1/1  http://python-flask-docker.jx-production.35.188.140.152.nip.io
```

Creating a pipeline using a QuickStart application

If you don't have a project to import, then you can create a new app from QuickStart and import the newly generated code into Git and Jenkins for CI/CD by performing the following steps:

1. Create a build from a standardized template. This command will show you application templates that you can use to create a new application:

   ```
   $ jx create quickstart
   ```

2. Select your GitHub username and organization:

   ```
   ? Git user name?
   ? Which organisation do you want to use?
   ```

3. Enter a new repository name. In this recipe, this is chapter2-jx-tutorial:

   ```
   Enter the new repository name: chapter2-jx-tutorial
   ```

4. Select the QuickStart example you wish to create. In our recipe, this is golang-http.

5. Specify Yes to the following question:

   ```
   Would you like to initialise git now? (Y/n) y
   ```

6. The pipelines will take some time to complete. List the available pipelines with the following command:

   ```
   $ jx get pipelines
   ```

How it works...

The second recipe of this section, *Importing an application as a pipeline*, showed you how to create a Jenkins pipeline using an existing project.

In *step 3*, the following happens when you import the application using the `jx import` command:

1. First, the project source is checked out from the repository and a new semantic version number is applied. Then, with the help of Skaffold, a command-line tool that facilitates continuous development for Kubernetes applications, Git tag v0.0.1 is created and unit tests are executed (in our example, there were no unit tests).

2. After the unit tests have been executed, a Docker image is created and pushed to the local Container Registry. You can see this process on the following code:

   ```
   Starting build...
   Building [devopscookbook/python-flask-docker]...
   Sending build context to Docker daemon    127kB
   Step 1/8 : FR
   OM python:3.6
   3.6: Pulling from library/python
   4ae16bd47783: Pulling fs layer
   bbab4ec87ac4: Pulling fs layer
   ...
   ```

3. After the container image has been pushed to the registry, you can find it in your Docker Registry:

4. During the Promote to Environments stage, a Helm build will be executed. After the charts have been pushed to the local `chartmuseum` repository, you can find the Helm chart in the repository:

   ```
   $ helm search python-flask-docker
   NAME CHART VERSION APP VERSION DESCRIPTION
   jenkins-x-chartmuseum/python-flask-docker 0.0.1 0.0.1 A Helm chart
   for Kubernetes
   ```

5. Finally, the staging pipeline runs from the master branch and deploys our pod from the Helm repository into the `jx-staging` namespace. Both the staging and application pipelines will be completed after this step.

Creating a CI/CD pipeline in GitLab

GitLab is a complete DevOps toolchain that's delivered in a single application platform. GitLab provides all the necessary tooling you need to manage, plan, create, verify, package, release, configure, monitor, and secure your applications.

In this section, we will focus on the CI/CD pipeline features of GitLab that can be consumed as SaaS or self-hosted service. We will import an application and create a pipeline in GitLab. You will learn how to create a CI/CD pipeline with Auto DevOps and promote an application from staging into production.

Getting ready

In the following recipe, you will learn how to create a pipeline with Auto DevOps. This recipe requires GitLab (self-managed or SaaS) and an account with your preferred cloud vendor where you installed your Kubernetes cluster using GitLab.

The Community Edition of GitLab includes the Auto Build, Auto Test, Auto Review Apps, Auto Deploy, and Auto Monitoring features. In addition to these features, the subscription-based SaaS version of GitLab also provides Auto Code Quality, Auto **Static Application Security Testing** (**SAST**), Auto Dependency Scanning, Auto License Compliance, Auto Container Scanning, Auto **Dynamic Application Security Testing** (**DAST**), and Auto Browser Performance Testing functionalities, depending on your subscription plan.

Make sure you have followed the instructions in `Chapter 2`, *Operating Applications on Kubernetes*, in the *Deploying and managing the life cycle of GitLab* recipe and deployed a self-hosted GitLab.

If you prefer, you can also use the SaaS offering hosted by GitLab. In that case, visit the GitLab website at `https://about.gitlab.com/free-trial/` and sign in to your account.

GitLab Auto DevOps supports GKE for creating new Kubernetes clusters, as well as existing clusters, on any public or private clouds.

How to do it...

This section is further divided into the following subsections to make this process easier:

- Creating a project using templates
- Importing an existing project from GitHub
- Enabling Auto DevOps
- Enabling Kubernetes cluster integration
- Creating a pipeline using Auto DevOps
- Incrementally rolling out applications to production

Creating a project using templates

Most of the actions on GitLab are done on projects. When you start a project for the first time, you have a couple of options. You can create a project using one of the project templates, import an existing project, or start a blank project. In this recipe, you will learn how to create a project using the project templates by performing the following steps:

1. Log in to GitLab with a non-root user account.
2. Click the **Create a project** button on the **Welcome to GitLab** screen:

3. Select the **Create from template** tab and choose one of the code templates listed by clicking on the **Use template** button. For this example, we will use the following **Pages/GitBook** template:

4. GitLab projects can be either **Private, Internal,** or **Public.** This project access level is determined by the visibility field in the project. Give your new project a name and set the **Visibility Level** to **Public:**

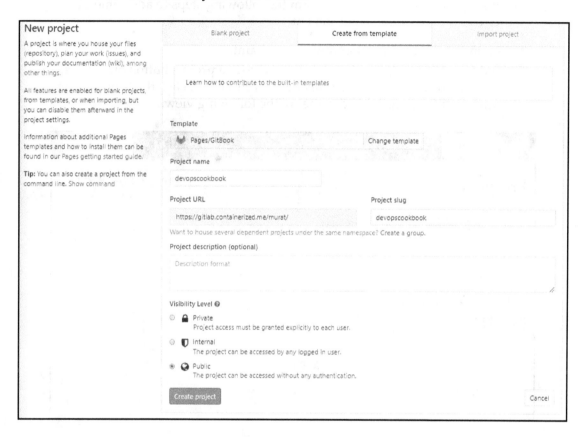

5. Click on the **Create project** button.

Now, you will see that the template project has been successfully imported.

Importing an existing project from GitHub

It is not always possible to start with clean project templates. Often, you will need to create a pipeline for an existing project. Let's perform the following steps to add some existing project source code into a GitLab environment:

1. Log in to GitLab with a non-root user account.
2. If you don't have a project yet, click the **Create a project** button on the **Welcome to GitLab** screen. If you have created projects before, click the **New project** button in the top right-hand corner of the following view:

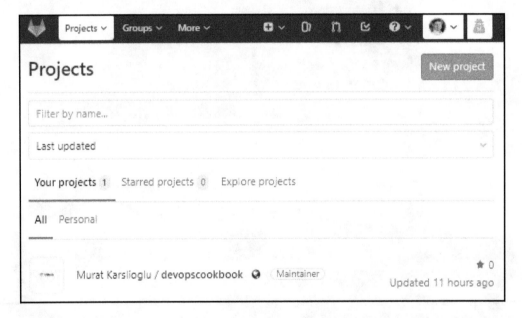

3. GitLab can import projects from various Git repositories, including GitHub, Bitbucket, Google Code, Fogbugz, Gitea, and GitLab itself. Here, select the **Import project** tab and choose **GitHub**:

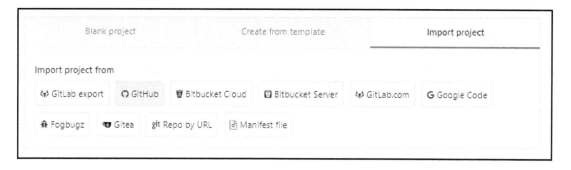

4. Open `https://github.com/settings/tokens` in a new window and go to your GitHub account.

5. Click on **Generate new Token** on your GitHub account.

6. For GitLab to be able to access your GitHub account, an access token needs to be created. On the **New personal access token** page, select the **repo** scope and click on the **Generate Token** button. This page shows the permissions that you can assign with the token:

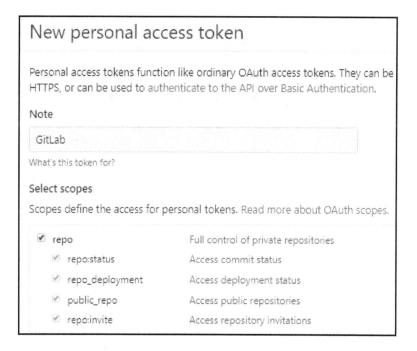

7. Copy the new personal access token created on GitHub, paste it into GitLab, and click on the **List your GitHub repositories** button:

8. GitLab will access and discover projects in your GitHub repository location. Import the repository that you want to use with this recipe. In this example, we will use the project from the `https://github.com/k8sdevopscookbook/auto-devops-example` repository. This is where all the examples in this book are located:

When importing is complete, the status will show **Done**. Finally, click on the **Go to project** button to see your project in GitLab.

Enabling Auto DevOps

GitLab's Auto DevOps functionality provides predefined CI/CD configuration that automatically detects, builds, tests, deploys, and monitors your applications. Let's perform the following steps to enable the Auto DevOps option for your existing project:

1. Log in with your project user account.
2. On the **Welcome to GitLab** screen, you will see links that will help you get started. Here, click the **Configure GitLab** button to access the configuration options:

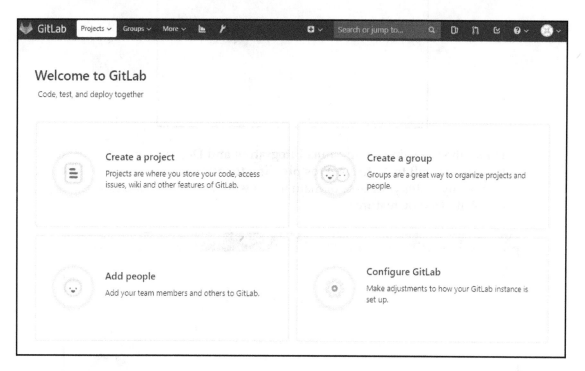

3. Only the project users with Maintainers and Admin permissions have access to the project settings. From the **Admin Area** menu on the left-hand side of the screen, select the **Settings | CI/CD** menu to access the CI/CD options. The following screenshot shows where the CI/CD settings are located:

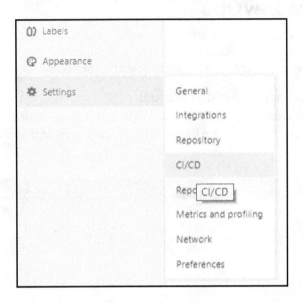

4. Under the following **Continuous Integration and Deployment** page, make sure that the **Default to Auto DevOps pipeline for all projects** checkbox is checked. Optionally, enter your base domain if you want to use the Auto Review Apps and Auto Deploy features:

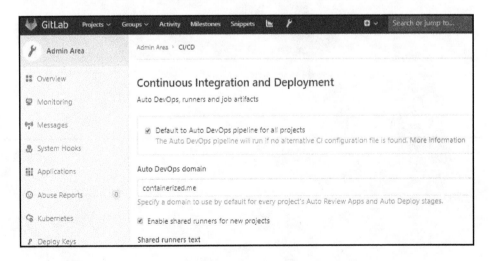

5. Click on the **Save changes** button.

Enabling Kubernetes cluster integration

GitLab works with or within Kubernetes in multiple ways. Let's perform the following steps and add Kubernetes automation so that we can share the cluster across multiple projects:

1. Log in as root user.
2. Select a project under the **Your Projects** page.
3. From the project's **Details** page, click on the **Add Kubernetes cluster** button:

4. You can either **Create a new cluster on GKE** or **Add an existing cluster**. Assuming that you have created a cluster by following the recipes in Chapter 1, *Building Production-Ready Kubernetes Clusters*, we will add an existing cluster. On the view shown in the following screenshot, select the **Add existing cluster** tab:

5. Enter a Kubernetes cluster name. In our example, this is AWSCluster.

6. From the command line where your kubectl instance has been configured so that you can access your existing Kubernetes cluster, use the following command to get the API URL:

```
$ kubectl cluster-info | grep 'Kubernetes master' | awk '/http/
{print $NF}'
```

7. For GitLab to be able to access your cluster using APIs, an authentication token is required. Kubernetes stores the `default-token` as a secret. To find that token, list the secrets on your cluster using the following command:

```
$ kubectl get secrets | grep default-token
default-token-75958 kubernetes.io/service-account-token 3 4d12h
```

8. Use the token name that was returned by the preceding command and get the CA certificate:

```
$ kubectl get secret <secret name> -o
jsonpath="{['data']['ca\.crt']}" | base64 --decode
-----BEGIN CERTIFICATE-----
MID...h5x
-----END CERTIFICATE-----
```

9. Create a GitLab admin called `ServiceAccount` on your cluster:

```
cat <<EOF | kubectl apply -f -
apiVersion: v1
kind: ServiceAccount
metadata:
  name: gitlab-admin
  namespace: kube-system
EOF
```

10. Create a GitLab admin called `ClusterRoleBinding` on your cluster:

```
cat <<EOF | kubectl apply -f -
apiVersion: rbac.authorization.k8s.io/v1beta1
kind: ClusterRoleBinding
metadata:
  name: gitlab-admin
roleRef:
  apiGroup: rbac.authorization.k8s.io
  kind: ClusterRole
  name: cluster-admin
subjects:
- kind: ServiceAccount
  name: gitlab-admin
  namespace: kube-system
EOF
```

11. Get the service account token. The following command will return your token in the **Token** section:

```
$ kubectl -n kube-system describe secret $(kubectl -n kube-system
get secret | grep gitlab-admin | awk '{print $1}')
```

```
Name: gitlab-admin-token-xkvss
...
Data
====
ca.crt: 1119 bytes
namespace: 11 bytes
token:
<your_token_here>
```

12. Once you've copied the token information from the output of *step 11*, click on the
    Add Kubernetes cluster button on the same window. You should see something
    similar to the following view, which is where we add our cluster into GitLab:

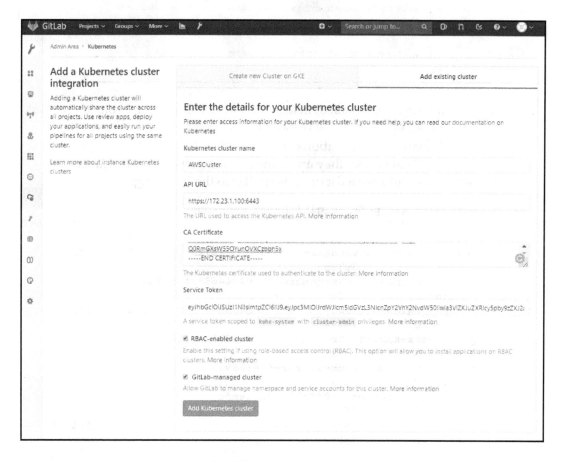

13. Next, enter your Base domain name. In our example, we use the
    `k8s.containerized.me` subdomain as our hosted zone, which we created in
    `Chapter 1`, *Building Production-Ready Kubernetes Clusters*, in the *Provisioning a
    Kubernetes cluster on Amazon EC2* recipe.

14. Click on the **Install** button next to Helm Tiller. This option will deploy the Helm
    server into your cluster:

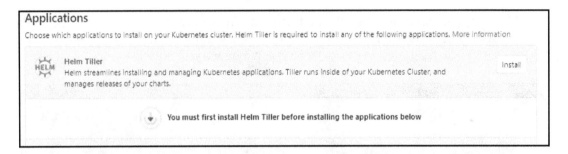

15. Once Helm has been installed, install Ingress, Cert-Manager, Prometheus, and
    GitLab Runner by clicking the **Install** buttons next to those options.

16. All GitLab managed applications are installed under the `gitlab-managed-apps`
    namespace. Validate that they are in the `Running` state on your Kubernetes
    cluster. You should see a list of pods similar to the following:

```
$ kubectl get pods -n gitlab-managed-apps
NAME                                                       READY STATUS
RESTARTS AGE
certmanager-cert-manager-574b6d6cdd-s87kn                  1/1
Running 0        3m39s
ingress-nginx-ingress-controller-7d44688bf-8x7ld           1/1
Running 0        4m39s
ingress-nginx-ingress-default-backend-66645696bf-sz545 1/1
Running 0        4m39s
prometheus-kube-state-metrics-744949b679-2rwnh             1/1
Running 0        2m8s
prometheus-prometheus-server-646888949c-j4wn7              2/2
Running 0        2m8s
runner-gitlab-runner-84fc959dcf-4wxfc                      1/1
Running 0        56s
tiller-deploy-5d76d4796c-fdtxz                             1/1
Running 0        7m13s
```

Creating a pipeline using Auto DevOps

Once it's enabled, Auto DevOps simplifies the setup and execution of the software development life cycle. Let's perform the following steps to take advantage of Auto DevOps and create our first automated pipeline:

1. If you have more than one project, you need to select the target project where you would like to run your pipeline. First, select your project in the **Your Projects** page.

2. Click on **Pipelines** under the **CI/CD** menu. This option will take you to the page where existing pipelines can be viewed. On this page, click on the **Run Pipeline** button. This option will help us manually run the pipeline:

3. Here, you have the option to run the pipeline on different branches. For this example, select the master branch to run the pipeline on. In the following screenshot, you see the pipeline stages being completed:

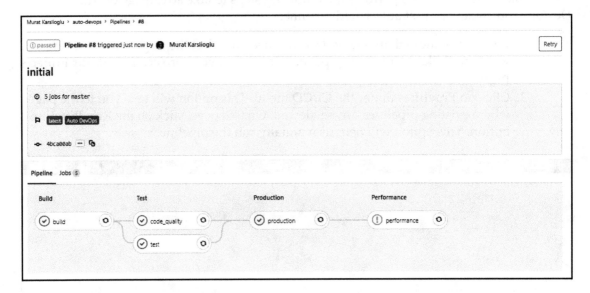

When the pipeline is complete, you will see the results for every job that was executed and your application should be accessible at `http://application_name.your_domain.com`. In our case, this address is `http://murat-auto-devops.k8s.containerized.me`.

Incrementally rolling out applications to production

By default, Auto DevOps uses a Continuous Deployment to production strategy. If you would like to change that setting to perform incremental rollouts, perform the following steps:

1. Select your project in the **Your Projects** page.
2. Click on **CI/CD** in the **Settings** menu.
3. Expand the **Auto DevOps** section by clicking on the **Expand** button.

4. Change the **Deployment strategy** to **Automatic deployment to staging, manual deployment to production** and click on the **Save changes** button. You will see the other Auto DevOps options as well:

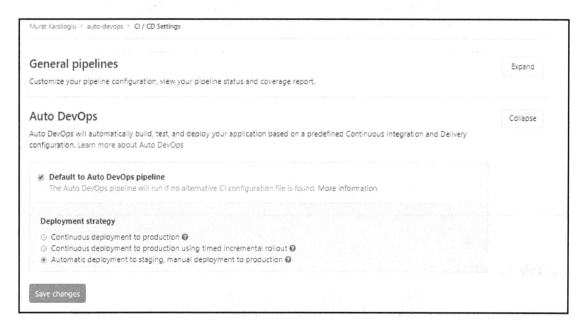

5. Click on **Pipelines** under the **CI/CD** menu. Click on the **Run Pipeline** button to manually run the pipeline.

6. When the staging job is complete, the pipeline will be paused. You will see the results for every job that has been executed and your application should be accessible at `http://application-name-staging.your_domain.com`. In our case, this address is `http://murat-auto-devops-staging.k8s.containerized.me`

7. Now, click on **Environments** in the **Operations** menu.

8. Once your application is in the staging environment, you can gradually move it into production. To be able to do that while in the staging environment, click on the **Deploy to** button (the one that looks like a play button) and choose a percentage to roll out to, as shown in the following view. In the dropdown menu, you will see options for 10%, 25%, 50%, and 100%:

How it works...

The preceding recipe, *Creating a pipeline using Auto DevOps*, showed you how to take advantage of the functionality of Auto DevOps to simplify the creation of pipelines.

In *step 2*, after you run the pipeline, GitLab Auto DevOps saves you time and effort from creating the stages and jobs manually when no `.gitlab-ci.yml` files are found in the project. This file is created by GitLab and provides CI/CD configuration for all the projects that don't have one.

If you like to use the `.gitlab-ci.yaml` file instead, disable Auto DevOps and use the **Set up CI/CD** button on your project to create your GitLab CI/CD YAML file from a template. Follow the link regarding the *Creating a simple .gitlab-ci.yaml file* instructions in the *See also* section to learn more about creating the YAML file.

During *step 3*, Auto DevOps uses Herokuish Buildpacks, a tool for emulating Heroku build and runtime tasks in containers. By using Herokuish, GitLab detects the language your project is written in and automatically creates the pipeline.

There's more...

You will also benefit from learning about the following:

- GitLab Web IDE
- Monitoring environments

GitLab Web IDE

GitLab is not just a CI/CD solution, it has many other functionalities and provides you with a private code repository similar to GitHub. You can use GitLab Web IDE to edit and commit your changes and push them to production. To edit your code without cloning to your own machine, perform the following steps:

1. Select your project on the **Your Projects** page.
2. Click on the **Web IDE** button.
3. Select a file from the repository to edit.
4. Edit the file and once done, click on the **Commit...** button, as shown in the following screenshot:

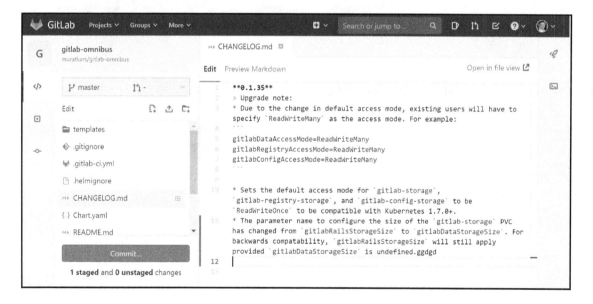

5. Create a commit message and click on the **Stage & Commit** button, as shown in the following screenshot:

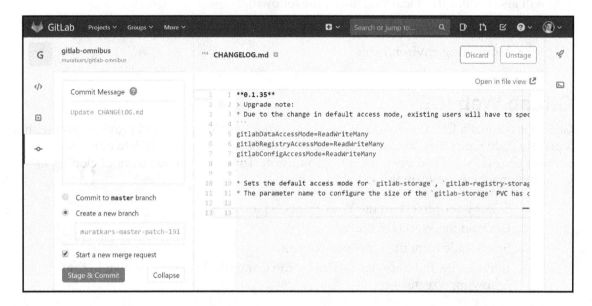

Your commit will trigger a new pipeline. As a result, GitLab will build, test, and stage your changes.

Monitoring environments

Using GitLab, you can monitor Kubernetes cluster resource usage and application response metrics. If you haven't enabled Prometheus on your Kubernetes cluster, follow the instructions in the *Enabling Kubernetes cluster integration* recipe and then perform the following steps:

1. Select your project on the **Your Projects** page.
2. Click on **Metrics** in the **Operations** menu.

3. Select the **Production** environment from the drop-down menu. On the dropdown menu, you will have **production** and **staging** environments:

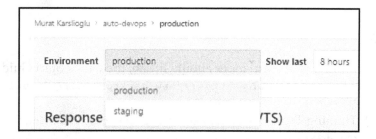

4. GitLab will show a page similar to the following with the last 8 hours of your application performance data and Kubernetes resource utilization metrics. In this view, you will be able to see the historical average and total CPU and memory utilization of the applications:

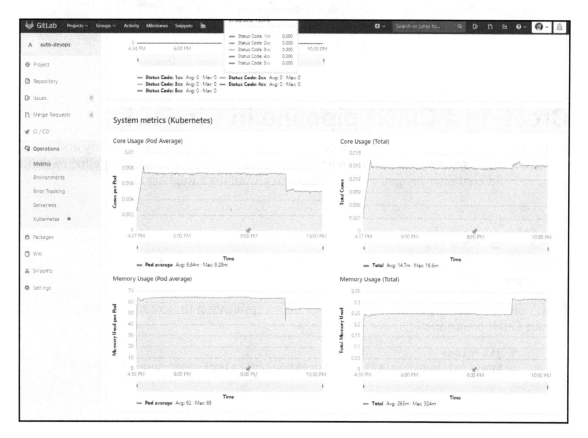

Now, you know how to create projects on GitLab and use Auto DevOps functionality to automate the creation of CI/CD pipelines.

See also

- If you would like to learn more about GitLab, the Quick Start Guide by Adam O'Grady is a great resource: `https://www.packtpub.com/virtualization-and-cloud/gitlab-quick-start-guide`
- GitLab Training Tracks: `https://about.gitlab.com/training/`
- GitLab Git cheat sheet: `https://about.gitlab.com/images/press/git-cheat-sheet.pdf`
- Learning GitLab: `https://www.packtpub.com/application-development/learning-gitlab-video`
- Hands-On Auto DevOps with the GitLab CI: `https://github.com/PacktPublishing/Hands-On-Auto-DevOps-with-GitLab-CI`
- Creating a simple `.gitlab-ci.yaml` file: `https://docs.gitlab.com/ee/ci/quick_start/#creating-a-simple-gitlab-ciyml-file`

Creating a CI/CD pipeline in CircleCI

In this section, we will cover the initial configuration and requirements to deploy and manage Kubernetes services using CircleCI. You will learn how to create a pipeline so that you can build container images and store them in a Container Registry.

Getting ready

This recipe requires an active GitHub account with a project to build. We will use AWS EKS to demonstrate CI with CircleCI.

First, visit the following GitHub page of our demo application project and fork your copy to your GitHub account:

```
$ git clone
https://github.com/k8sdevopscookbook/circleci-demo-aws-eks.git
```

Clone the `k8sdevopscookbook/circleci-demo-aws-eks` repository to your workstation in order to use the `circleci-demo-aws-eks` example at `https://github.com/k8sdevopscookbook/circleci-demo-aws-eks`.

How to do it...

This section is further divided into the following subsections to make this process easier:

- Getting started with CircleCI
- Deploying changes to a Kubernetes cluster on Amazon EKS

Getting started with CircleCI

Circle CI is a continuous integration platform that automatically runs your build in a clean container or virtual machine, allowing the code stored on your repository to be directly tested for every commit. CircleCI can be used in the cloud as a SaaS solution or installed as a self-hosted solution on your environment. Let's perform the following steps to get started using the cloud version of CircleCI:

1. Sign up for CircleCI using your GitHub account by going to `https://circleci.com/signup/`.

2. After you've signed up, click on the **ADD PROJECTS** button on the left-hand side of the Dashboard view:

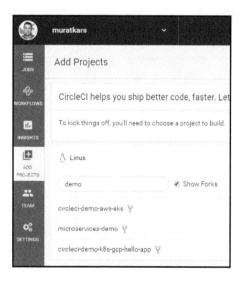

3. From the upper-left drop-down menu, select the GitHub account where you want to build your projects.

Deploying changes to a Kubernetes cluster on EKS

In this recipe, we will use Amazon EKS. Let's perform the following steps to get started:

1. Create a new AWS IAM user specifically for CircleCI and take note of your new user's access key ID and secret access key.

2. Create a repository named `eks_orb_demo_app` on the AWS Elastic Container Registry ECR. Take note of your ECR URL. It should look similar to `1234567890.dkr.ecr.us-east-2.amazonaws.com`.

3. Make sure you are signed in to Circle CI. Click on the **Add Projects** button, search for the `demo-aws` keyword, and click on the **Set Up Project** button next to it:

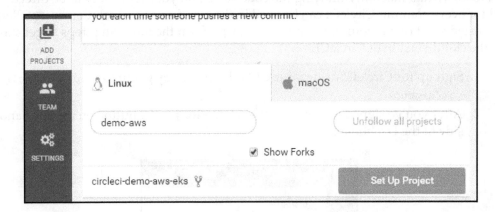

4. Click on **build**. The build will fail since it is missing the environment variables to access your AWS account.

5. Click on **Project Settings**. Go to the **Environmental Variables** page under **Build Settings**. Create the following four variables by clicking the **Add Variable** button:

```
AWS_DEFAULT_REGION = us-east-2
AWS_ACCESS_KEY_ID = [Enter your Access key ID here]
AWS_SECRET_ACCESS_KEY = [Enter your Secret Access Key here]
AWS_ECR_URL = [Enter your ECR URL here]
```

The output of this can be seen in the following screenshot:

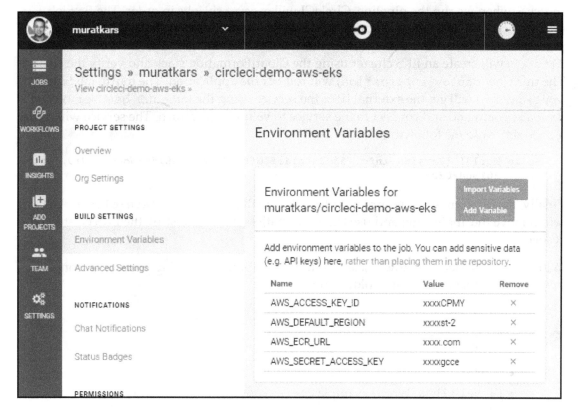

6. Setting environmental variables will allow your pipeline to access AWS resources. After the cloud variables have been defined, click on the **Build** button to start the build.

7. The build may fail if your AWS user does not have the required permissions; otherwise, this should be completed successfully in 35-40 mins.

How it works...

This recipe showed you how to quickly create a CI/CD pipeline using a demo application running on a Kubernetes cluster.

In *step 2* of the *Deploying changes to a Kubernetes cluster on EKS* recipe, we created a repository on AWS ECR to push our container images that were built by CircleCI. After a successful build, the images will be saved and accessible through the private registry location.

In *step 6*, when we run the pipeline, CircleCI will execute six jobs in order. The first job (`build-and-push-image`) will bring up a VM, check out our code, install any prerequisites, and build the image from the code. The second job (`aws-eks/create-cluster`) will create an EKS cluster using the CloudFormation stack and verify the cluster. The third job (`deploy-application`) will roll out the application. The fourth job (`test-application`) will get the external IP of the service using the `kubectl get service demoapp` command and connect to the service to validate the return. The service will return a page similar to the following:

```
Hello World! (Version info: 63d25fd14ef8dfb1c718cf81a815b36d80138d19, build
date: 20190820224253)
```

Finally, the fifth (`undeploy-application`) and sixth (`aws-eks/delete-cluster`) jobs will remove the application and use CloudFormation again to destroy the EKS cluster, respectively.

With that, you've learned how to easily build your application using predefined container environments that have been deployed on CircleCI.

See also

- Circle CI documentation: `https://circleci.com/docs/`
- Circle CI Hello World examples: `https://circleci.com/docs/2.0/hello-world/`
- Circle CI AWS EKS demo application: `https://github.com/k8sdevopscookbook/circleci-demo-aws-eks`
- Circle CI GCP demo application: `https://github.com/k8sdevopscookbook/circleci-demo-k8s-gcp-hello-app`

Setting up a CI/CD pipeline using GitHub Actions

GitHub Actions enable you to create custom software development workflows directly in your GitHub repository. If you are already using GitHub as your code repository, built-in CI/CD capabilities make this option very compelling.

In this section, we will cover the GitHub Actions workflow configuration and built-in CI/CD capabilities. You will learn how to manage workflows and create new GitHub Actions.

Getting ready

In the following recipe, you will learn how to create a basic action example in a repository you own by adding a Dockerfile. This recipe requires an active GitHub account with a project to build. We will use AWS EKS to demonstrate CI with GitHub.

How to do it...

This section is further divided into the following subsections to make this process easier:

- Creating a workflow file
- Creating a basic Docker build workflow
- Building and publishing images to Docker Registry
- Adding a workflow status badge

Creating a workflow file

GitHub flow is a lightweight branch that was recently introduced by GitHub. Let's perform the following steps to create our first workflow:

1. Sign in to your GitHub account at `https://github.com/`.
2. Select a repository where you have maintainer access. In our example, we are using the fork of the `k8sdevopscookbook/python-flask-docker` project.

3. Create a `ci.yml` file in the `.github/workflows` directory with the following content:

```yaml
name: My Application
on:
  pull_request:
    branches:
    - master
jobs:
  build:
    runs-on: ubuntu-16.04
    steps:
    - uses: actions/checkout@v1
    - name: Set up Python 3.7
      uses: actions/setup-python@v1
      with:
        python-version: 3.7
```

4. Add the following lines to install any dependencies:

```yaml
- name: Install dependencies
  run: |
    python -m pip install --upgrade pip
    pip install -r requirements.txt
```

5. When using computer programming languages, lint tools are used to perform static analysis of source code to check for semantic discrepancies. In our example, we will use `flake8` to lint our Python code using the following command:

```yaml
- name: Lint with flake8
  run: |
    pip install flake8
    # stop the build if there are Python syntax errors or undefined names
    flake8 . --count --select=E9,F63,F7,F82 --show-source --statistics
    # exit-zero treats all errors as warnings. The GitHub editor is 127 chars wide
    flake8 . --count --exit-zero --max-complexity=10 --max-line-length=127 --statistics
```

6. If you have unit tests, add the following lines to test your application with `pytest`, a framework that's used in Python programming to write small tests:

```yaml
- name: Test with pytest
  run: |
    pip install pytest
    pytest
```

7. After the configuration is complete, send a pull request to your repository to trigger the pipeline:

After the pipeline is complete, you will be able to see a green checkmark on your **Pull Request (PR)**. In the preceding screenshot, you can see that all the checks have passed and that the pull request was successful.

Creating a basic Docker build workflow

Let's perform the following steps to automate the Docker image build directly from our GitHub repository:

1. Sign in to your GitHub account.
2. Select a repository where you have maintainer access. In our example, we are using the fork of the `k8sdevopscookbook/python-flask-docker` project.
3. Click the **Actions**tab.
4. From here, click on **Add a new workflow**.
5. Create a `dockerimage.yml` file under the `.github/workflows` directory with the following content:

```
name: Docker Image CI
on: [push]
jobs:
  build:
    runs-on: ubuntu-latest
    steps:
    - uses: actions/checkout@v1
    - name: Build the Docker image
      run: docker build . --file Dockerfile --tag my-image-
name:$(date +%s)
```

The workflow will create a new Docker image every time new code is pushed to the repository.

Building and publishing images to Docker Registry

Instead of creating multiple actions to build, tag, login, and push to Docker Repository, you can use one action to achieve all at once. Let's perform the following steps:

1. Sign in to your GitHub account.
2. Select a repository where you have maintainer access. In our example, we are using the fork of the `k8sdevopscookbook/python-flask-docker` project.
3. Click the **Actions**tab.
4. From here, click on **Add a new workflow**.
5. Create a `dockerpush.yml` file under the `.github/workflows` directory with the following content. Make sure to change `MyDockerRepo/repository` so that it uses the name of the image you would like to push:

```yaml
name: Build and Push to DockerHub
on: [push]
jobs:
  build:
    runs-on: ubuntu-latest
    steps:
    - uses: actions/checkout@master
    - name: Publish to Registry
      uses: elgohr/Publish-Docker-Github-Action@master
      with:
        name: MyDockerRepo/repository
        username: ${{ secrets.DOCKER_USERNAME }}
        password: ${{ secrets.DOCKER_PASSWORD }}
```

6. Click on the **Settings** tab and go to the **Secrets** menu.
7. Create a `DOCKER_USERNAME` secret with the value equals to the username you used to log in to your Docker Registry.
8. Create `DOCKER_PASSWORD` secrets with a value equals to the password you used to log in to your Docker Registry. After both secrets have been created, you should be able to see them in the **Secrets** menu, as shown in the following screenshot:

Environmental variables stored as secrets will be encrypted and are only available for selected actions.

Adding a workflow status badge

Many good source code repositories on GitHub use badges on their main page to display the status of various tests that have been completed on the repositories. Similarly, in this recipe, we will add an action status summary to our repository to inform our visitors and users about the current workflow status:

1. Sign in to your GitHub account and select a repository where you have maintainer access. In our example, we are using the fork of the k8sdevopscookbook/python-flask-docker project.
2. Edit the README.md file in the top directory of your repository.
3. Add the link to the badge by following the format https://github.com/{owner}/{repo}/workflows/{workflow_name}/badge.svg, as shown in the following example:

```
[![Actions
Status](https://github.com/muratkars/python-flask-docker/workflows/
.github/workflows/dockerpush.yml/badge.svg)
```

See also

- GitHub Actions for interacting with Docker: `https://github.com/docker-actions`
- GitHub Actions for AWS: `https://github.com/aws-actions`
- GitHub Actions for Azure: `https://github.com/Azure/k8s-actions`
- GitHub Actions for GCP: `https://github.com/GoogleCloudPlatform/github-actions`

Setting up a CI/CD pipeline on Amazon Web Services

In this section, we will cover the CI/CD pipeline construction workflow on AWS and built-in CI/CD capabilities. You will learn how to manage pipelines, how to run build commands during the pipeline steps, and how to store build result images on the Amazon **Elastic Container Registry (ECR)**.

Getting ready

In the following recipe, you will learn how to build, test, and deploy an example service based on AWS services. All the operations mentioned here require an AWS account and an AWS user with a policy that has permission to use the related services, have HTTPS Git credentials for CodeCommit assigned, and a Kubernetes cluster deployed using AWS EKS. If you don't have one, go to `https://aws.amazon.com/account/` and create one.

How to do it...

This section is further divided into the following subsections to make this process easier:

- Creating an AWS CodeCommit code repository
- Building projects with AWS CodeBuild
- Creating an AWS CodeDeploy deployment
- Creating a pipeline with AWS CodePipeline

Creating an AWS CodeCommit code repository

The AWS CodeCommit service is a managed source control service that hosts secure Git-based repositories on the AWS platform. In this recipe, we will learn how to create our first repository on CodeCommit:

1. Sign in to your AWS account and open AWS Developer Tools at `https://us-west-2.console.aws.amazon.com/codesuite`.

2. From the **Developer Tools** menu, expand the **Source** menu and click on **Repositories**. You can see the complete menu content in the following screenshot:

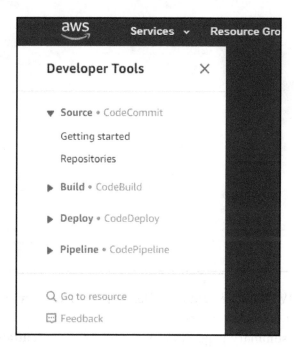

3. On the **Repositories** page, click on the **Create repository** button to start your code repository on CodeCommit.

4. Enter a **Repository name** and click on the **Create** button. In this example, the repository name is `k8sdevopscookbook`:

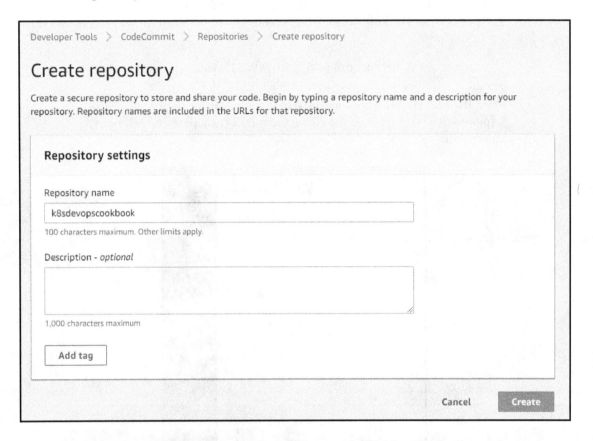

5. From the AWS Management Console, go to the IAM service.
6. From the list of existing users, select an IAM user that you would like to use.
7. On the user summary page, click on the **Security credentials** tab. The following screenshot shows the location of the tab:

8. Under **HTTPS Git credentials for AWS CodeCommit**, click on the **Generate** button. This will create a username and password that we will use for authentication later:

9. On the **Git credentials generated** window, click on the **Download credentials** button to record your CodeCommit credentials. The following screenshot shows the username and password that was created for me. This is the only chance you will get to view or copy your credentials:

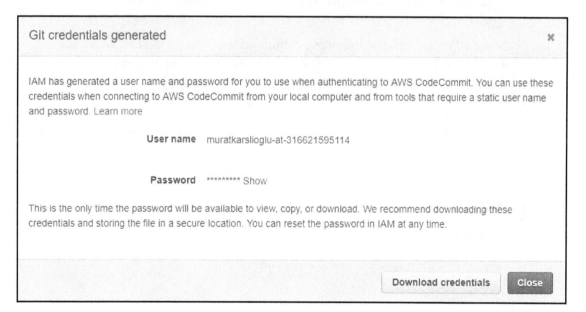

8. From the AWS Management Console, go to the CodeCommit service.

9. Under the **Clone URL** column, select **HTTPS**. In this recipe, our example repository is located at `https://git-codecommit.us-west-2.amazonaws.com/v1/` `repos/k8sdevopscookbook`.

10. On your Linux workstation, clone the empty repository:

```
$ git clone <your_new_repo>
```

11. Clone the repository using your CodeCommit credentials.

12. Download our example application and extract it:

```
$ wget
https://github.com/k8sdevopscookbook/python-flask-docker/archive/ma
ster.zip && unzip master.zip
```

13. Now, copy the example application to your clone of the repository:

```
$ cp -r python-flask-docker-master/. k8sdevopscookbook/.
$ cd k8sdevopscookbook
```

14. Stage all your files. The following command will find all the new and updated files on the project directory and add them to the staging area before it is pushed to the target repository:

```
$ git add -A
```

15. Commit the files with a message. The following command, when used with the -m parameter, adds the commit:

```
$ git commit -m "Add example application files"
```

16. Push the files from your local repository folder to your CodeCommit repository:

```
$ git push
```

Now, you will be able to view files in your CodeCommit repository.

Building projects with AWS CodeBuild

Let's perform the following steps to build a project from the CodeCommit repository that we created in the previous recipe:

1. Sign in to your AWS account and open AWS Developer Tools at `https://us-west-2.console.aws.amazon.com/codesuite`.

2. From the **Developer Tools** menu, expand the **Build** menu and click on **Build Projects**. The following screenshot shows the menu's location:

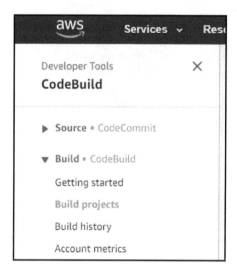

3. On the **Build projects** page, click on the **Create build project** button. The following screenshot shows the other available menu options and the location of the **Create build project** button:

4. Enter a project name.

5. Now, we will set the primary source of the project. In the **Source** box, select **AWS CodeCommit** as a source provider. Select the repository you created in the *Creating an AWS CodeCommit code repository* recipe. Select the **master** branch. In our example, the repository's name is `k8sdevopscookbook`:

6. In the **Environment** box, select **Managed image** and **Ubuntu** as your OS.

7. Select **New service role**:

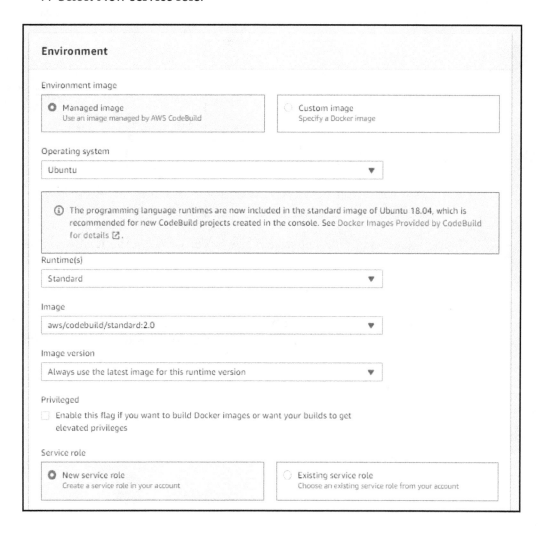

8. Expand the additional configuration settings. Add the AWS_DEFAULT_REGION, AWS_ACCOUNT_ID, IMAGE_TAG, and IMAGE_REPO_NAME environment variables, as shown in the following screenshot:

 Never store environmental variables in a repository location. Always use environmental parameters to provide the values during the build process.

9. In the **Buildspec** box, select **Use a buildspec file**. Make sure the buildspec.yaml file exists in the root of your code repository. This file should look something like this:

```
version: 0.2
phases:
 install:
 runtime-versions:
 docker: 18
 pre_build:
 commands:
 - echo Logging in to Amazon ECR...
 - $(aws ecr get-login --no-include-email --region
$AWS_DEFAULT_REGION)
 build:
 commands:
 - echo Build started on `date`
 - echo Building the Docker image...
 - docker build -t $IMAGE_REPO_NAME:$IMAGE_TAG .
 ...
```

10. Finally, click on **Create build project**.

11. Find the Service Role you created in *step 7* in **Identity and Access Management (IAM)** and add this statement to the policy attached to the CodeBuild service role:

```
{
  "Version": "2012-10-17"
  "Statement": [       ### BEGIN ADDING STATEMENT HERE ###      {
  "Action": [
        "ecr:BatchCheckLayerAvailability",
        "ecr:CompleteLayerUpload",
        "ecr:GetAuthorizationToken",
        "ecr:InitiateLayerUpload",
        "ecr:PutImage",
        "ecr:UploadLayerPart"            ],
      "Resource": "*",
      "Effect": "Allow"
  },       ### END ADDING STATEMENT HERE ###      ...    ],
}
```

12. Now that the project is ready, click on the **Start build** button on the upper right-hand corner of the page. In the following screenshot, you can view its status under the **Build history** tab, after it's been started. In our example, it shows that the build **Succeeded**:

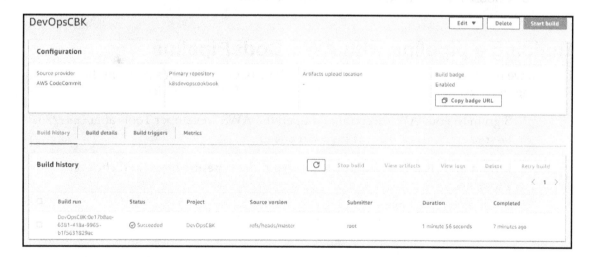

If your builds fail, make sure that the `AmazonEC2ContainerRegistryPowerUser` policy is assigned to your IAM role.

Creating an AWS CodeDeploy deployment

Let's perform the following steps to create a deployment from the CodeBuild builds:

1. Sign in to your AWS account and open the AWS Developer Tools at `https://us-west-2.console.aws.amazon.com/codesuite`.
2. From the **Developer Tools** menu, expand the **Deploy** menu and click on **Applications**.
3. Click on the **Create application** button:

4. Enter an application name.
5. Choose **AWS Lambda** as a compute platform.

Building a pipeline with AWS CodePipeline

Finally, we have reached the last stage of AWS Developer Tools. Let's perform the following steps to build a pipeline using the AWS CodePipeline service:

1. Sign in to your AWS account and open the AWS Developer Tools at `https://us-west-2.console.aws.amazon.com/codesuite`.

2. From the **Developer Tools** menu, expand the **Pipeline** menu and click on **Pipelines**.
3. Enter a pipeline name.
4. Select **New service role** and click on **Next**.

5. Now, we will set the primary source of the pipeline. Select **AWS CodeCommit** as a source provider. Select the repository you created in the *Creating an AWS CodeCommit code repository* recipe. Click on the **Next** button to confirm these changes. The following screenshot shows that, in our example, the source is k8sdevopscookbook:

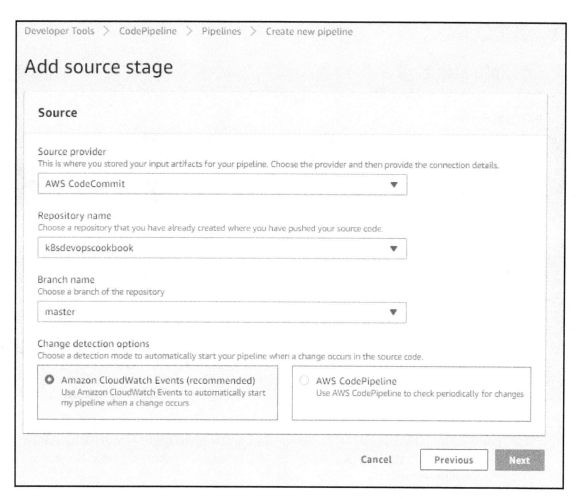

6. Select **AWS CodeBuild** as the **Build provider**. Select the project name you created in the *Building projects with AWS CodeBuild* recipe (or create a new project). Click on **Next** to confirm these changes. The following screenshot shows that, in our example, the region is US West and that the project name is **DevOpsCookbookExample**:

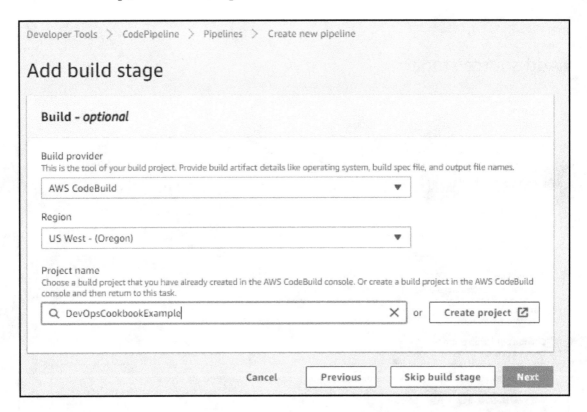

7. Click on **Skip deploy stage**. As a deployment alternative, you can invoke a Lambda function to call the CloudFormation template and deploy a Kubernetes cluster. You can find the AWS CodeSuite example that shows how to do this in the *See also* section.

8. Click on **Create Pipeline**.

9. When the pipeline has been executed, you will see a build similar to the following:

With that, you have successfully built a pipeline using the AWS CodePipeline service.

How it works...

This recipe showed you how to quickly create a pipeline using AWS Developer Tools.

In the *Building a pipeline with AWS CodePipeline* recipe, after you create the pipeline, AWS CodePipeline watches for changes in AWS CodeCommit. When a new PR is merged into the master branch stored in your CodeCommit repository, CodePipeline automatically detects the changes to the branch and triggers the pipeline.

During the build job, CodeBuild packages the code and any dependencies described in the Docker file into a Docker image. This Docker image is pushed to the Amazon ECR container registry you specified during the recipe.

This pipeline is also fully extensible. In fact, you have the option to also invoke a serverless function through AWS Lambda to either create a Kubernetes cluster or deploy the code on an existing Kubernetes cluster so that you can test it. You can find additional examples at the AWS Blog link provided in the *See also* section.

See also

- AWS CodeCommit documentation: `https://docs.aws.amazon.com/codecommit/latest/userguide/welcome.html`
- AWS CodeBuild documentation: `https://docs.aws.amazon.com/codebuild/latest/userguide/welcome.html`
- AWS CodeDeploy documentation: `https://docs.aws.amazon.com/codedeploy/latest/userguide/welcome.html`
- AWS CodePipeline documentation: `https://docs.aws.amazon.com/codepipeline/latest/userguide/welcome.html`
- AWS Blog on Continuous Deployment to Kubernetes using AWS Developer Tools: `https://aws.amazon.com/blogs/devops/continuous-deployment-to-kubernetes-using-aws-codepipeline-aws-codecommit-aws-codebuild-amazon-ecr-and-aws-lambda/`
- CodeSuite – Continuous Deployment Reference Architecture for Kubernetes: `https://github.com/aws-samples/aws-kube-codesuite`
- A similar example of a Lambda function for EKS deployment: `https://github.com/muratkars/lambda-eks`

Setting up a CI/CD pipeline with Spinnaker on Google Cloud Build

Google Cloud Build is a managed CI/CD and deployment platform that lets you build, test, and deploy in the cloud. In this section, we will cover the CI/CD pipeline with Google Cloud Build configuration using Spinnaker capabilities, an open source, multi-cloud continuous delivery platform.

Getting ready

Clone the `k8sdevopscookbook/src` repository to your workstation to use the manifest files under the `chapter3` directory:

```
$ git clone https://github.com/k8sdevopscookbook/src.git
$ cd /src/chapter3
```

Make sure you have the necessary credentials to use GCP services and have access to the current project. If you don't have one already, go to `https://console.cloud.google.com` and create an account.

How to do it...

This section is further divided into the following subsections to make this process easier:

- Installing and configuring the Spin CLI
- Configuring a service account for the CI/CD
- Configuring events to trigger the pipeline
- Installing Spinnaker using Helm
- Creating a Google Cloud Source code repository
- Building projects with Google Cloud Build
- Configuring a Spinnaker pipeline
- Rolling out an application to production

Installing and configuring the Spin CLI

The operations mentioned in the following recipes require the spin CLI, gcloud, and a GCP account with a project that has billing enabled. We will enable related APIs using the gcloud CLI:

1. Run the following command to download the gcloud CLI. If you have the gcloud CLI installed and a project already, skip to *step 4*:

   ```
   $ curl https://sdk.cloud.google.com | bash
   ```

2. Initialize the SDK and follow the instructions given:

   ```
   $ gcloud init
   ```

3. Select a project that you have permissions for or create a new one.
4. Enable the Kubernetes Engine API, the Cloud Build API, and the Cloud Source Repositories API for the project:

   ```
   $ gcloud services enable compute.googleapis.com
   cloudapis.googleapis.com sourcerepo.googleapis.com
   Operation "operations/acf.d1f2c714-9258-4784-a8a9-6648ab4c59fe"
   finished successfully.
   ```

5. Download and install the `spin` CLI:

```
$ curl -LO \
https://storage.googleapis.com/spinnaker-artifacts/spin/$(curl -s \
https://storage.googleapis.com/spinnaker-artifacts/spin/latest)/lin
ux/amd64/spin
$ chmod +x spin
$ sudo mv spin /usr/local/bin/spin
```

Now you have GCP services enabled and the `spin` CLI installed.

Configuring a service account for the CI/CD

To use CI/CD services on Google Cloud, your user needs to have the right permissions assigned to them. Let's perform the following steps to configure a service account for the CI/CD:

1. Follow the instructions in the *Provisioning a managed Kubernetes cluster on the GKE* recipe of Chapter 1, *Building Production-Ready Kubernetes Clusters*, to deploy a GKE cluster. If you already have one, skip to *step 2* to create a service account that will be used by the pipeline later:

```
$ gcloud iam service-accounts create cicd-account \
--display-name "My CICD Service Account"
```

2. Replace the following `devopscookbook` in both places with your project name and add storage admin role binding to your service account:

```
$ gcloud projects \
    add-iam-policy-binding \
    devopscookbook --role \
    roles/storage.admin --member \
    serviceAccount:cicd-
account@devopscookbook.iam.gserviceaccount.com
```

3. Store your `cicd-account` key:

```
$ gcloud iam service-accounts keys \
    create cicd-key.json \
    --iam-account cicd-
account@devopscookbook.iam.gserviceaccount.com
```

With that, you have assigned the permissions to your service account.

Configuring events to trigger a pipeline

Google Pub/Sub is a cloud service best described as a managed version of Kafka or Rabbit MQ. We will use Google Pub/Sub to deliver notifications when a change is detected in our container registry. Let's perform the following steps:

1. Use the following `gcloud` command to create a Cloud Pub/Sub topic:

    ```
    $ gcloud pubsub topics create
    projects/devopscookbook/topics/gcrgcloud pubsub topics create
    projects/devopscookbook/topics/gcr
    Created topic [projects/devopscookbook/topics/gcrgcloud].
    Created topic [projects/devopscookbook/topics/pubsub].
    Created topic [projects/devopscookbook/topics/topics].
    Created topic [projects/devopscookbook/topics/create].
    Created topic [projects/devopscookbook/topics/gcr].
    ```

2. Create a `pubsub` subscription. The following command should return a `Created subscription` message, similar to the following:

    ```
    $ gcloud pubsub subscriptions create gcr-triggers --topic
    projects/devopscookbook/topics/gcr
    Created subscription [projects/devopscookbook/subscriptions/gcr-
    triggers].
    ```

3. Replace the following `devopscookbook` in both places with your project name and add permission to your CI/CD service account, that is, `cicd-account`:

    ```
    $ gcloud pubsub subscriptions add-iam-policy-binding \
        gcr-triggers --role roles/pubsub.subscriber \
        --member serviceAccount:cicd-
    account@devopscookbook.iam.gserviceaccount.com
    ```

With that, you've learned how to configure events to trigger a pipeline.

Deploying Spinnaker using Helm

Let's perform the following steps to deploy the Spinnaker tool using Helm charts:

1. Verify that `helm` is installed and initialized on your GKE cluster. If not, follow the instructions in Chapter 2, *Operating Applications on Kubernetes*, in the *Deploying workloads using Helm charts* recipe to install Helm. The following command will return the client and server of Helm if it's installed on your cluster:

```
$ helm version --short
Client: v2.14.3+g0e7f3b6
Server: v2.14.3+g0e7f3b6
```

2. Create `clusterrolebinding` for the `ci-admin` service account:

```
$ kubectl create clusterrolebinding \
    --clusterrole=cluster-admin \
    --serviceaccount=default:default \
    ci-admin
```

3. Create a pipeline configuration bucket using the following command. Make sure to replace the `devopscookbook-ci-config` bucket name with a unique name. This will create an object storage bucket on Google Cloud Storage:

```
$ gsutil mb -c regional -l us-central1 gs://devopscookbook-ci-
config
```

4. Create a variable with the content of the `cicd-account` key:

```
$ export CICDKEY_JSON=$(cat cicd-key.json)
```

5. Edit the `spinnaker-config.yaml` file in the `cd /src/chapter3/gcp` directory and replace the following bucket name with the bucket name you used in *step 3*:

```
gcs:
  enabled: true
  bucket: devopscookbook-ci-config
  project: devopscookbok
  jsonKey: '$CICDKEY_JSON'
...
```

6. Deploy Spinnaker on your Kubernetes cluster using the custom `spinnaker-config.yaml` file from *step 5*:

```
$ helm install -n cd stable/spinnaker -f \
    spinnaker-config.yaml --timeout 600 --wait
```

7. Create port forwarding tunnels to access the Spinnaker UI:

```
$ export DECK_POD=$(kubectl get pods --namespace default -l
"cluster=spin-deck" -o jsonpath="{.items[0].metadata.name}")
$ kubectl port-forward --namespace default $DECK_POD 8080:9000 >>
/dev/null &
$ export GATE_POD=$(kubectl get pods --namespace default -l
"cluster=spin-gate" -o jsonpath="{.items[0].metadata.name}")
$ kubectl port-forward --namespace default $GATE_POD 8084
```

To be able to access the Spinnaker UI, we created port forwarding tunnels for our workstation. We could also create a cloud LoadBalancer to open ports to the internet, but port forwarding is safer.

Creating a Google Cloud Source code repository

Let's perform the following steps to create a code repository on the Google Cloud Source Code service:

1. Download our example application and extract it:

```
$ wget
https://github.com/k8sdevopscookbook/src/raw/master/chapter3/gcp/sa
mple-app-v2.tgz && tar xzfv sample-app-v2.tgz
```

2. After the example code has been extracted, change directories to our source code directory:

```
$ cd sample-app
```

3. Make the initial commit to your repository using the following commands:

```
$ git init && git add . && git commit -m "Initial commit"
```

4. Create a Google Cloud Code repository named `sample-app`:

```
$ gcloud source repos create sample-app
```

5. Set `credential.helper` for the Google Cloud repository:

```
$ git config credential.helper gcloud.sh
```

6. Replace `devopscookbook` with your project name. Add your new repository as `remote` and push your code:

```
$ git remote add origin
https://source.developers.google.com/p/devopscookbook/r/sample-app
$ git push origin master
```

7. Now, you will be able to view the files in your Google Cloud Source Code repository in the `sample-app` repository, as shown in the following screenshot:

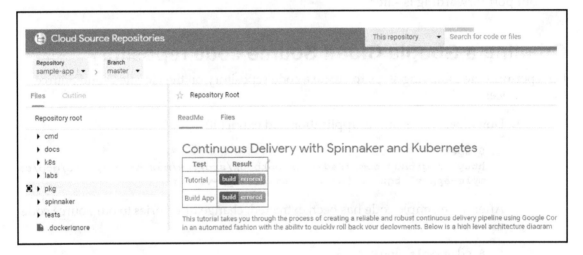

With that, you've learned how to create a code repository on Google Cloud Source. In the next recipe, we will use the Cloud Source repository location to build our project.

Building projects with Google Cloud Build

Let's perform the following steps to build the project from the Cloud Source repository that we created in the previous recipe:

1. Here, we are going to use the Cloud Build product to build our project. First, log in to your GCP account. From the main **Products** menu, click on **Cloud Build**. As shown in the following screenshot, it is located under **TOOLS**:

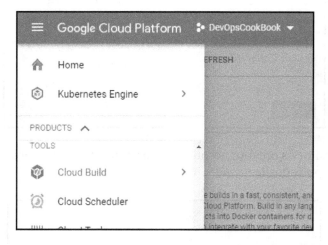

2. In the **Cloud Build** menu, choose **Triggers** and click on the **Create trigger** button, as shown in the following screenshot:

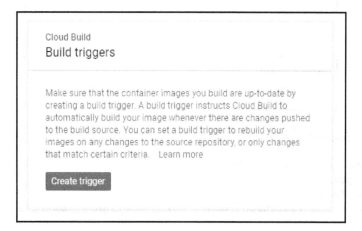

3. Our code is in a Cloud Source repository, so select **Cloud Source Repository** and click on the **Continue** button. As you can see, the other options are **Bitbucket** and **GitHub**:

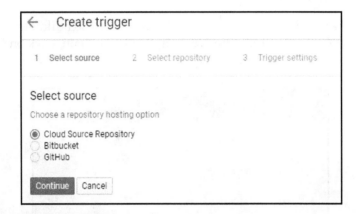

4. The repositories on your account will be detected automatically. Select the **sample-app** repository and click on the **Continue** button:

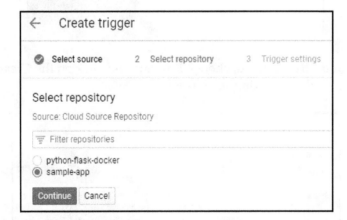

5. Set the following settings and leave the others unchanged:

```
Name: devopscookbook-trigger-1
Trigger type: Tag
Tag (regex): v.*
Build configuration: Cloud Build configuration file (yaml or json)
```

6. Click on the **Create trigger** button.

7. Switch back to the command line where `kubectl` has been configured to access your Kubernetes cluster and create a bucket. Replace the `devopscookbook-kubernetes-manifests` bucket name with a unique bucket name before you create it:

```
$ gsutil mb -l us-central1 gs://devopscookbook-kubernetes-manifests
```

8. Enable bucket versioning on the bucket you created in *step 6*. This following command will enable versioning on Cloud Storage and let the bucket keep old versions of objects:

```
$ gsutil versioning set on gs://devopscookbook-kubernetes-manifests
```

9. If you are not already in the source code folder, change directories to our source code:

```
$ cd sample-app
```

10. Change the project ID in our Kubernetes deployment manifest files to your project:

```
$ sed -i s/PROJECT/devopscookbook/g k8s/deployments/*
```

11. Commit the changes with a meaningful commit message similar to the following:

```
$ git commit -a -m "Change placeholder project ID to
devopscookbook"
```

12. Create a Git tag for the release and push the tag:

```
$ git tag v1.0.0 && git push --tags
```

13. Switch back to the browser and click on **History** from the **Cloud Code** menu and confirm that the build has been triggered and successful:

With that, you've learned how to build a project using Google Cloud Build.

Configuring a Spinnaker pipeline

Let's perform the following steps to upload your configuration to Spinnaker:

1. Replace the following email in the `owner-email` section with yours and create the provided application in Spinnaker using the following command:

    ```
    $ spin application save \
    --application-name sample \
    --owner-email \
    youremail@domain.com \
    --cloud-providers kubernetes \
    --gate-endpoint \
    http://localhost:8080/gate
    ```

2. Upload the example pipeline to Spinnaker:

    ```
    $ sed s/PROJECT/devopscookbook/g spinnaker/pipeline-deploy.json >
    pipeline.json
    $ spin pipeline save --gate-endpoint http://localhost:8080/gate -f
    pipeline.json
    ```

The preceding command will export the configuration into a file called `pipeline.json` and upload it to Spinnaker.

Rolling out an application to production

Once an application has been deployed to staging, the next step is to promote it into the production environment. Let's perform the following steps to promote an application from staging to production on Spinnaker:

1. On the Spinnaker UI, select the `sample` application that we created in the *Configuring a Spinnaker pipeline* recipe:

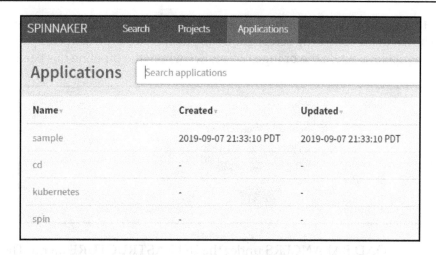

2. Click on the **PIPELINES** tab shown in the following screenshot:

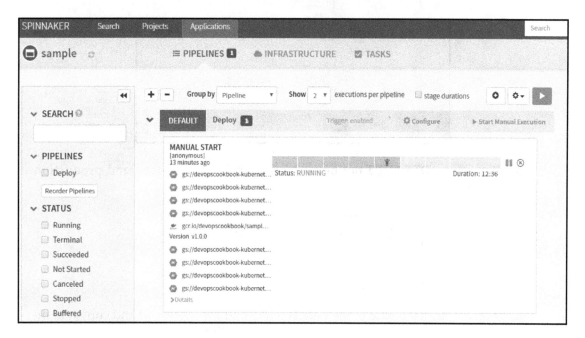

3. Hover your mouse over the orange box and click on the **Continue** button. As shown in the following screenshot, the green boxes represent completed parts of the pipeline, while the orange box shows where the pipeline has been paused:

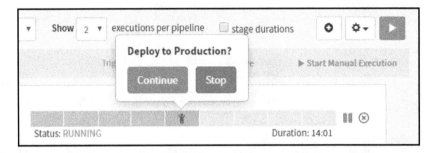

4. Select **LOAD BALANCERS** under the **INFRASTRUCTURE** menu. The following screenshot shows the **INFRASTRUCTURE** menu:

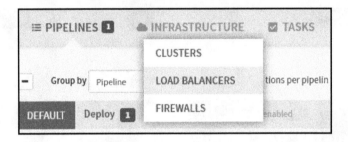

5. Click on the **DEFAULT** button under the **service sample-frontend-production** load balancer:

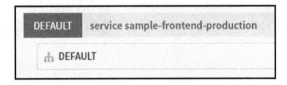

6. On the right-hand side of the details pane, find the Ingress IP and copy it to the clipboard by clicking the copy icon next to the IP address:

7. Open the IP address in your browser to confirm that the production application is accessible. You will see a screen similar to the following view showing the **Pod Name**, **Node Name**, and its **Version**:

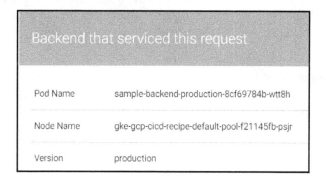

With that, you know how to use Google Cloud Platform services and Spinnaker to create your CI/CD pipeline on GKE.

See also

- CI/CD on Google Cloud Quickstarts: `https://cloud.google.com/docs/ci-cd/`
- Cloud Source Repositories documentation: `https://cloud.google.com/source-repositories/docs/`

Setting up a CI/CD pipeline on Azure DevOps

Azure DevOps provides version control, reporting, automated builds, and project/lab/testing and release management capabilities. Azure DevOps is available as a SaaS or on-premises server product. In this section, we will cover the Azure DevOps workflow configuration and built-in CI/CD capabilities using the SaaS product. You will learn how to manage workflows and create Azure pipelines.

Getting ready

In the following recipe, you will learn how to create a pipeline example in a repository you own by adding a YAML file. This recipe requires an active GitHub account with a project ready to be built. We will use AKS to demonstrate continuous delivery with Azure Pipelines.

All the operations mentioned here require an Azure DevOps account. If you don't have one, go to `https://azure.microsoft.com/services/devops/` and create one. Deploying the application on Azure Kubernetes Service also requires an active Azure Cloud subscription.

How to do it...

This section is further divided into the following subsections to make this process easier:

- Getting started with Azure DevOps
- Configuring Azure Pipelines
- Deploying changes to an AKS cluster

Getting started with Azure DevOps

Azure DevOps is a set of DevOps tools provided by Microsoft that includes CI/CD and project management services such as Azure Pipelines, Azure Boards, Azure Artifacts, Azure Repos, and Azure Test Plans.

Let's perform the following steps to create our first project before we use Azure Pipelines:

1. Sign in to Azure DevOps at `https://azure.microsoft.com/en-us/services/devops/`.
2. Create a project name.
3. Choose **Visibility**. In our example, this is set to **Public:**

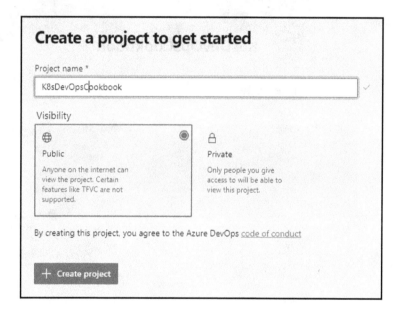

4. Click on the **Create project** button.

Configuring Azure Pipelines

Azure Pipelines lets you build, test, and deploy with the CI/CD with any language, platform, and cloud provider. Let's perform the following steps to configure Azure Pipelines for the first time:

1. After you log in to your Azure DevOps account, you will see the links to the main functionality on the left-hand **Overview** menu. From the **Overview** menu, click on the **Pipelines** menu. The following screenshot shows the **Welcome to the project!** page:

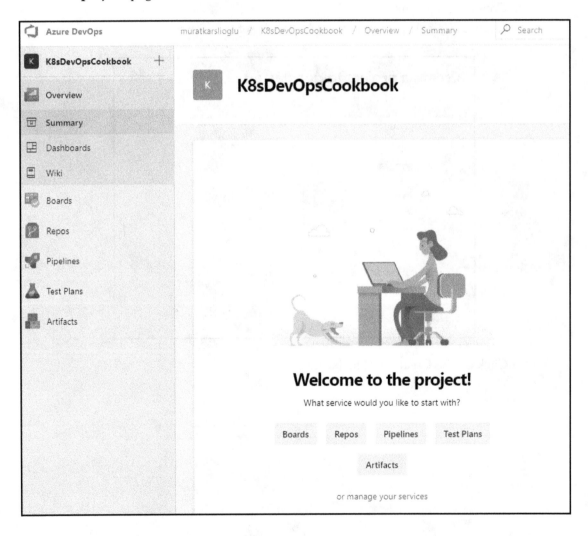

2. Click on the **Create Pipeline** button.

3. As part of the pipeline creation process, you need to set your code repository location. You can import a project from any Git repository. In our example, we will use **GitHub** as our repository. The following screenshot shows all the other available options:

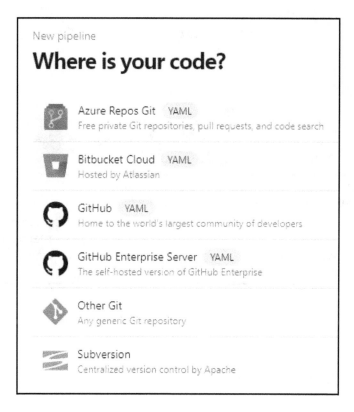

4. Click on **Authorize AzurePipelines**:

5. Select a repository and click on **Approve & Install**:

6. Now, select the repository you would like to configure a pipeline.
7. Choose **Docker** to build and push an image to Azure Container Registry. This option will upload the container artifact to the Azure Container Registry service. The following screenshot shows the **Docker** option that we will be using:

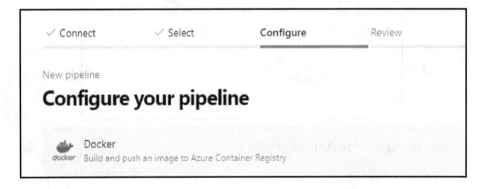

8. Review your pipeline YAML and click **Save and run** to approve it.
9. You will see the pipeline. Click on the **Build** job to view its details:

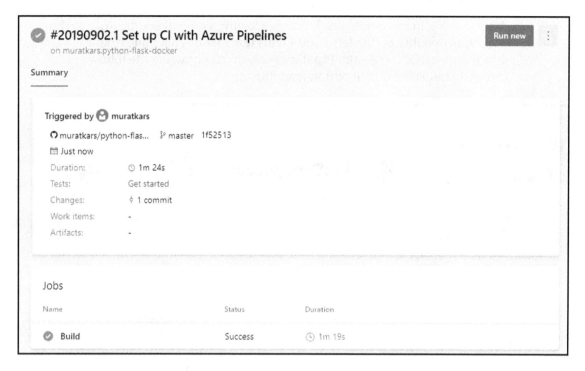

With that, you've learned how to configure an Azure Pipeline.

Deploying changes to an AKS cluster

Let's perform the following steps:

1. After you log in to your Azure DevOps account, you will see the links to the main functionality on the left-hand **Overview** menu. This time, from the **Overview** menu, choose the **Pipelines** option. As shown in the following screenshot, it is the fourth option from the top:

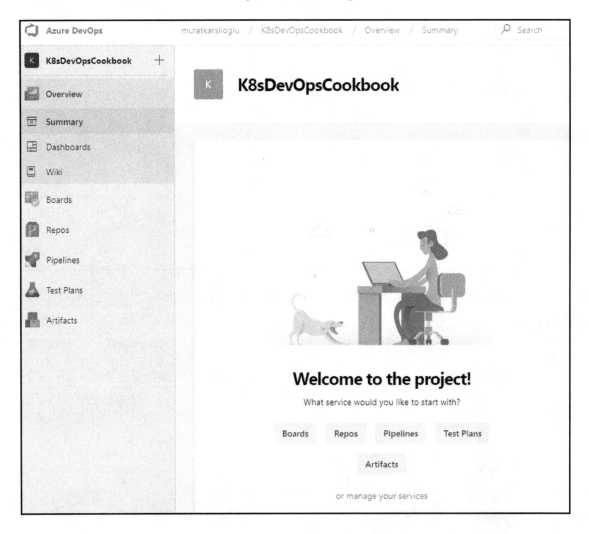

2. Next, you need to create a pipeline. The following screenshot shows the
   Pipelines menu. Click on the **New pipeline** button located in the upper-right
   corner of the page:

3. Choose **GitHub** as your repository. Again, all the other repository options are
   visible in the following screenshot:

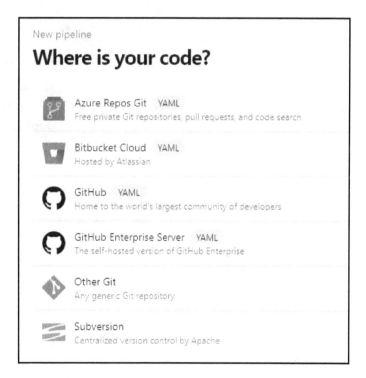

4. Select a repository and click on **Approve & Install**. The following screenshot shows that my own repository is selected. In your case, the repository name will be different:

5. Now, select the repository you would like to configure a pipeline.

6. As shown in the following screenshot, you will be offered predefined alternatives for configuring your pipelines. For this example, choose **Deploy to Azure Kubernetes Service** to build and push an image to Azure Container Registry and to deploy to AKS:

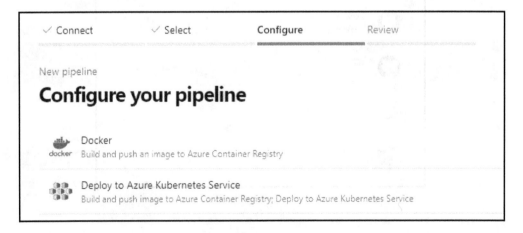

7. Select your Azure Cloud subscription.
8. Select an existing AKS cluster.
9. Choose **Existing** and select **default** in the **Namespace** field.
10. Enter the name of your Container Registry. In the following screenshot, you can see the options that I have selected. In your case, **Container registry** and **Image Name** will be different:

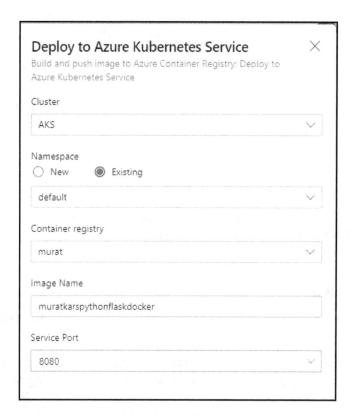

11. Click on the **Validate and configure** button.
12. Review your pipeline YAML and click **Save and run** to approve it.

13. You will see the pipeline. Click on the **Build** job to view its details:

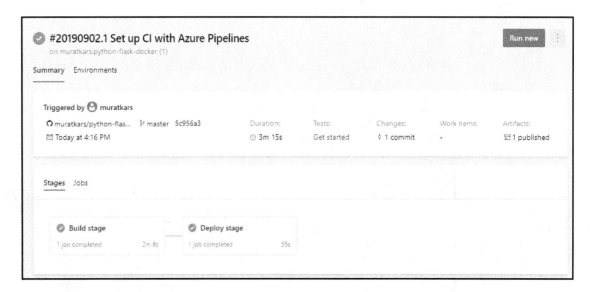

As shown in the preceding screenshot, our simple pipeline only includes only two stages. These will be explained in the *How it works...* section.

How it works...

This recipe showed you how to quickly create an Azure DevOps CI/CD pipeline using a demo application running on an AKS cluster.

In the *Deploying changes to an AKS cluster* recipe, after *step 9*, while we build the job, Azure Pipelines will create your pipeline. It will create the following two stages:

1. In stage 1, which is the Build Stage, it creates a Docker image and pushes images into your Azure Container Registry. When it is successful, you can find the new image stored in your existing registry in Azure portal. As an example, the following screenshot shows the image that was created as a result of my pipeline under the Azure Container Registry and its details:

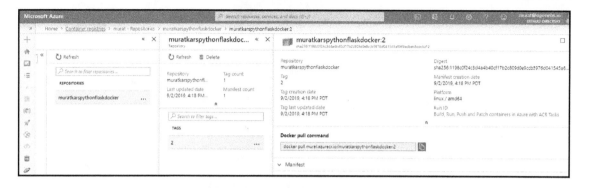

2. In stage 2, which is the Deploy stage, it creates the image pull secrets to access your registry and rolls out your application as a deployment.

The application will be deployed into the namespace you specified during the pipeline creation.

Later, you can create multiple environments that can be used for the different stages (preview, staging, and production) of your application and change where your application needs to be deployed in the pipelines.

See also

- Azure DevOps documentation: `https://docs.microsoft.com/en-us/azure/devops/?view=azure-devops`
- Azure Pipelines documentation: `https://docs.microsoft.com/en-us/azure/devops/pipelines/index?view=azure-devops`
- Canary deployment strategy for Kubernetes deployments: `https://docs.microsoft.com/en-us/azure/devops/pipelines/ecosystems/kubernetes/canary-demo?view=azure-devops`

4
Automating Tests in DevOps

In this chapter, we will discuss automating tests in DevOps workflow to accelerate time to production, reduce the loss of delivery risks, and detect service anomalies using known test automation tools on Kubernetes. After following the recipes in this chapter, you will have gained the skills to prevent known defects as well as quickly find new defects to reduce service downtime.

In this chapter, we will cover the following recipes:

- Building event-driven automation with StackStorm
- Automating tests with the Litmus framework
- Automating Chaos Engineering with Gremlin
- Automating your code review with Codacy
- Detecting bugs and anti-patterns with static code analysis with SonarQube
- Detecting license compliance issues with Fossa

Technical requirements

The recipes in this section assume that you have a functional Kubernetes cluster deployed by following one of the recommended methods described in Chapter 1, *Building Production-Ready Kubernetes Clusters*.

The Kubernetes command-line tool, `kubectl`, will be used for the rest of the recipes in this chapter, since it's the main command-line interface for running commands against Kubernetes clusters. We will also use `helm`, where Helm charts are available to deploy solutions.

Building event-driven automation with StackStorm

StackStorm is an open source, event-driven automation platform. Using the GitOps approach, it helps run workflows based on events. In this section, we will perform arbitrary automation or remediation tasks using StackStorm on Kubernetes. You will learn how to deploy StackStorm in a highly available configuration on Kubernetes using Helm charts and get started by deploying examples of rules, custom sensors, actions, and workflows.

Getting ready

Make sure you have a Kubernetes cluster ready, as well as `kubectl` and `helm` configured so that you can manage the cluster resources.

How to do it...

This section is further divided into the following subsections to make this process easier:

- Installing StackStorm
- Accessing the StackStorm UI
- Using the st2 CLI
- Defining a rule
- Deploying a rule

Installing StackStorm

Although StackStorm can be distributed as a **Red Hat Package Manager/Debian (RPM/Deb)** for Linux systems and as a Docker images, if you plan to run business-critical automation tasks, it is recommended to deploy StackStorm **High Availability (HA)** cluster on Kubernetes.

In this recipe, we will learn how to deploy StackStorm on Kubernetes by following these steps:

1. Add the Helm repository to your list of local charts:

    ```
    $ helm repo add stackstorm https://helm.stackstorm.com/
    ```

2. Install the StackStorm HA cluster using the Helm chart. The following command will deploy StackStorm and its dependencies, such as MongoDB and RabbitMQ:

    ```
    $ helm install stackstorm/stackstorm-ha --name=st2 --
    namespace=stackstorm
    ```

3. The installation process may take 2 to 3 minutes. Confirm that the release has been deployed and running:

    ```
    $ helm ls st2
    NAME REVISION  UPDATED                      STATUS    CHART
    APP VERSION NAMESPACE
    st2  1          Wed Oct 30 23:06:34 2019 DEPLOYED stackstorm-
    ha-0.22.0 3.2dev        stackstorm
    ```

    Now, you have StackStorm running in our cluster. Next, we will access the UI or use the CLI to interact with StackStorm.

Accessing the StackStorm UI

The StackStorm Helm installation assumes you are running in a single-node Minikube cluster and the instructions provided alongside it serve smaller deployments. We are running StackStorm on a large cluster with multiple nodes. We will expose the web server externally to access the StackStorm UI.

Let's perform the following steps to create a cloud load balancer so that we can access the StackStorm web interface:

1. Create a load balancer. The following command will create a load balancer through your cloud provider and expose the web service on port 80:

    ```
    $ cat <<EOF | kubectl apply -f -
    apiVersion: v1
    kind: Service
    metadata:
      name: st2-service
      namespace: stackstorm
    spec:
    ```

```
        type: LoadBalancer
        ports:
          - port: 80
            targetPort: 80
            protocol: TCP
        selector:
          app: st2web
    EOF
```

2. Find the external service IP. In the following example, we have used a Kubernetes cluster deployed on AWS. Although the output might be different, the following command should result in the same on other platforms:

```
$ kubectl get svc st2-service -nstackstorm
NAME          TYPE          CLUSTER-IP      EXTERNAL-IP PORT(S) AGE
st2-service LoadBalancer 100.68.68.243
a022d6921df2411e9bd5e0a92289be87-2114318237.us-
east-1.elb.amazonaws.com 80:31874/TCP 6m38s
```

3. Open the external IP address from *step 2* in a browser:

4. Log in with the necessary credentials, that is, username as st2admin and password as Ch@ngeMe :

Now, you have access to the StackStorm interface. Now, we will click on the menu items and explore the actions before we create our first rule in the *Defining a rule* recipe.

Using the st2 CLI

The StackStorm web interface is useful if we want to get familiar with the product, but, if you are going to use StackStorm in production, you need to learn the CLI commands. Now, perform the following steps to access the st2 CLI from the pod:

1. Find the st2 client's pod name:

```
$ export ST2CLIENT=$(kubectl get --namespace stackstorm pod -l
app=st2client -o jsonpath="{.items[0].metadata.name}")
```

2. Execute the following commands via the st2 CLI. This command will execute the st2 --version command from the pod:

```
$ kubectl exec -it ${ST2CLIENT} -n stackstorm -- st2 --version
st2 3.2dev (a643ba7), on Python 2.7.12
```

3. Authenticate to StackStorm using the following CLI command and save the password using the $-w$ parameter. If you don't want to save the password, then you can remove the $-w$ parameter at the end:

```
$ kubectl exec -it ${ST2CLIENT} -n stackstorm -- st2 login st2admin
-p 'Ch@ngeMe' -w
Logged in as st2admin
```

4. List the available actions from the core pack:

```
$ kubectl exec -it ${ST2CLIENT} -n stackstorm -- st2 action list --
pack=core
```

5. List the actions from the core pack. You can also try the other pack options for Linux, ChatOps, and packs:

```
$ kubectl exec -it ${ST2CLIENT} -n stackstorm -- st2 action list --
pack=core
```

All StackStorm CLI operations are available via REST API, Python, and JavaScript bindings. You can find more information at the *StackStorm CLI and Python Client* reference link in the *See also* section.

Defining a rule

StackStorm uses rules to run available actions when events occur. StackStorm comes with default actions and the catalog of actions can be increased by adding new actions from the community. Follow these steps to create your first rule:

1. Rules are created in a familiar YAML format and consist of three sections: trigger, criteria, and action. Before we create the rule file, we will get familiar with the available triggers we can use in our rule. Use the following command to list the available triggers:

```
$ kubectl exec -it ${ST2CLIENT} -n stackstorm -- st2 trigger list
```

2. Check the details of the webhook trigger. The following command will return the description, parameters, and payload schema for the trigger.
Review `parameters_schema` since we will use this in our example rule later:

```
$ kubectl exec -it ${ST2CLIENT} -n stackstorm -- st2 trigger get
core.st2.webhook
...
| parameters_schema | {                                              |
|                   |              "additionalProperties": false,  |
```

```
|              |              | "type": "object",            |
|              |              | "properties": {              |
|              |              |     "url": {                 |
|              |              |         "required": true,    |
|              |              |         "type": "string"     |
...
```

3. Use the following command to list the available actions:

```
$ kubectl exec -it ${ST2CLIENT} -n stackstorm -- st2 action list
```

4. Check the details of the `core.local` action. This action executes an arbitrary Linux command on the localhost. The following command returns the parameters it can take, as follows:

```
$ kubectl exec -it ${ST2CLIENT} -n stackstorm -- st2 action get
core.local
...
| parameters    | {                                                    |
|               | "cmd": {                                             |
|               |     "required": true,                                |
|               |     "type": "string",                                |
|               |     "description": "Arbitrary Linux command to       |
|               | be executed on the local host."                      |
|               |     },                                               |
|               |     "sudo": {                                        |
|               |         "immutable": true                            |
|               |     }                                                |
|               | }                                                    |
| metadata_file | actions/local.yaml                                   |
...
```

5. Let's use the preceding trigger and action in a rule, and set up a webhook to listen to the URL at `https://{host}/api/v1/webhooks/sample` using the following rule and create a `first_rule.yaml` file. Once you've done this, copy the file into the container. The action will be triggered when a POST request is made to this URL:

```
$ cat > first_rule.yaml <<EOF
name: "sample_rule_with_webhook"
pack: "examples"
description: "Sample rule dumping webhook payload to a file."
enabled: true
trigger:
type: "core.st2.webhook"
parameters:
url: "sample"
```

```
criteria:
trigger.body.name:
pattern: "st2"
type: "equals"
action:
ref: "core.local"
parameters:
cmd: "echo \"{{trigger.body}}\" >> ~/st2.webhook_sample.out ;
sync"
EOF
```

With that, you've learned how to find and use available actions and triggers to construct a rule. Next, we will learn how to run it in StackStorm.

Deploying a rule

StackStorm rules can be deployed through its UI, a CLI, or APIs. In this recipe, we will use the rule we defined previously and deploy it using the following steps:

1. Create the rule using the YAML file we created in the *Defining a rule* recipe:

   ```
   $ kubectl exec -it ${ST2CLIENT} -n stackstorm -- st2 rule create
   first_rule.yaml
   ```

2. List the rules and confirm that the new rule has been created. You should see the examples.sample_rule_with_webhook rule on the list, as follows:

   ```
   $ kubectl exec -it ${ST2CLIENT} -n stackstorm -- st2 rule list
   +-------------------+----------+---------------------------+----------+
   | ref | pack | description | enabled |
   +-------------------+----------+---------------------------+----------+
   | chatops.notify | chatops | Notification rule to | True |
   | | | send results of action | |
   | | | executions to stream | |
   | | | for chatops | |
   | examples.sample | examples | Sample rule dumping | True |
   | rule_with_webhook| | webhook payload to a | |
   | | | file. | |
   +-------------------+----------+---------------------------+----------+
   ```

With the new rule we created here, the webhook has started to listen on
`https://{host}/api/v1/webhooks/sample`.

See also

- StackStorm documentation: `https://docs.stackstorm.com/install/k8s_ha.html`
- StackStorm CLI and Python client: `https://docs.stackstorm.com/reference/cli.html`
- StackStorm examples: `https://github.com/StackStorm/st2/tree/master/contrib/examples`

Automating tests with the Litmus framework

Litmus is an open source toolset that's used to run chaos experiments in Kubernetes. Litmus provides the Chaos **Central Registration Depository (CRD)** for cloud-native developers and SREs to inject, orchestrate, and monitor chaos to find potential weaknesses in Kubernetes deployments in real time in production. In this section, we will run some of these chaos experiments to validate the resiliency of the systems. You will learn how to build pipelines for CI and end-to-end testing in order to validate and certify the new Kubernetes version.

Getting ready

Clone the `k8sdevopscookbook/src` repository to your workstation to be able to use the manifest files under the `chapter4` directory:

```
$ git clone https://github.com/k8sdevopscookbook/src.git
$ cd src/chapter4
```

Make sure you have a Kubernetes cluster ready and `kubectl` and `helm` configured so that you can manage the cluster resources.

How to do it...

This section is further divided into the following subsections to make this process easier:

- Installing the Litmus Operator
- Using Chaos Charts for Kubernetes
- Creating a container kill chaos experiment
- Reviewing chaos experiment results
- Viewing chaos experiment logs

Installing the Litmus Operator

The Litmus Chaos Engineering tool can be installed using the Helm chart. Books are defined as Kubernetes jobs.

Let's perform the following steps to install Litmus in our cluster:

1. Install the Litmus Chaos Operator:

   ```
   $ kubectl apply -f
   https://litmuschaos.github.io/pages/litmus-operator-latest.yaml
   ```

2. Verify that the Litmus Chaos Operator pod is running:

   ```
   $ kubectl get pods -n litmus
   NAME                                      READY  STATUS    RESTARTS  AGE
   chaos-operator-ce-554d6c8f9f-46kf6 1/1     Running 0               50s
   ```

3. Verify that the cluster role and cluster role bindings have been applied:

   ```
   $ kubectl get clusterroles,clusterrolebinding,crds | grep
   "litmus\|chaos"
   ```

   Now, we have the Litmus Chaos Operator running in our cluster. Next, we need to deploy chaos experiments to test the resiliency of our cluster resources.

Using Chaos Charts for Kubernetes

Similar to workload Helm charts, Litmus Chaos Charts are used to install chaos experiment bundles. Chaos experiments contain the actual chaos details. In this recipe, we will learn how to list chaos experiment bundles and download the Kubernetes chaos experiment bundle. Let's perform the following steps to install Chaos Charts for the Litmus Operator:

1. Open the Chaos Charts for Kubernetes website at `https://hub.litmuschaos.io` on your browser and search for `generic` in the search field:

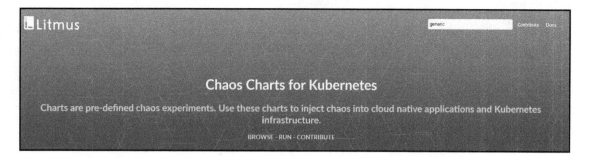

2. Click on the **Generic Chaos** chart:

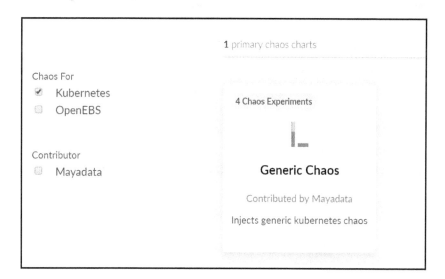

3. Click on the **Install All Experiments** button:

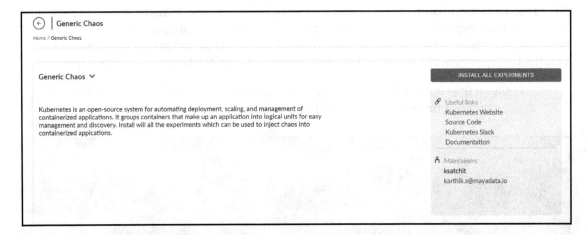

4. Copy the chaos experiment manifest link:

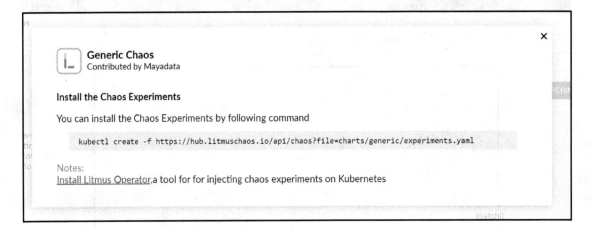

5. Install the chaos experiment:

```
$ kubectl create -f
https://hub.litmuschaos.io/api/chaos?file=charts/generic/experiment
s.yaml
```

6. Get the list of chaos experiments that have been created:

```
$ kubectl get chaosexperiments
NAME                   AGE
container-kill         19s
pod-delete             19s
pod-network-latency    19s
pod-network-loss       19s
```

Chaos experiment scenarios such as pod delete, network latency, network loss, and container kill are available under generic Chaos Chart. You can also install or build your own application-specific Chaos Charts to run application-specific Chaos.

Creating a pod deletion chaos experiment

Chaos experiments bundle the reproducible chaos situations in order to run them as a Kubernetes job. In this recipe, we will deploy an example application and use a Kubernetes chaos experiment on the application. Let's perform the following steps to test the impact of pod deletion in our cluster:

1. Deploy a sample application:

```
$ kubectl apply -f litmus/nginx/nginx.yaml
```

2. List the pods and confirm they are running:

```
$ kubectl get pods |grep nginx
nginx-deployment-5c689d88bb-24n4m 1/1 Running 0 4m31s
nginx-deployment-5c689d88bb-qtvsx 1/1 Running 0 4m31s
```

3. Annotate the deployment for chaos using `litmuschaos.io/chaos="true"`:

```
$ kubectl annotate deploy nginx-deployment
litmuschaos.io/chaos="true"
deployment.extensions/nginx-deployment annotated
```

4. Create a `ServiceAccount` for the chaos executor:

```
$ cat <<EOF | kubectl apply -f -
apiVersion: v1
kind: ServiceAccount
metadata:
  name: nginx
  labels:
    app: nginx
EOF
```

5. Create a cluster role:

```
$ cat <<EOF | kubectl apply -f -
kind: ClusterRole
apiVersion: rbac.authorization.k8s.io/v1
metadata:
  name: nginx
rules:
- apiGroups: ["", "extensions", "apps", "batch", "litmuschaos.io"]
  resources: ["daemonsets", "deployments", "replicasets", "jobs",
"pods", "pods/exec", "events", "chaosengines", "chaosexperiments",
"chaosresults"]
  verbs: ["*"]
EOF
```

6. Create a `ClusterRoleBinding`:

```
$ cat <<EOF | kubectl apply -f -
kind: ClusterRoleBinding
apiVersion: rbac.authorization.k8s.io/v1
metadata:
  name: nginx
subjects:
- kind: ServiceAccount
  name: nginx
  namespace: default
roleRef:
  kind: ClusterRole
  name: nginx
  apiGroup: rbac.authorization.k8s.io
EOF
```

7. Review the experiment CRs to view the chaos parameters. In this case, let's review the `pod-delete` and `container-kill` experiments:

```
$ kubectl get chaosexperiment pod-delete -o yaml
$ kubectl get chaosexperiment container-kill -o yaml
```

8. Create a Chaos Engine using the preceding two experiments you've reviewed:

```
cat <<EOF | kubectl apply -f -
apiVersion: litmuschaos.io/v1alpha1
kind: ChaosEngine
metadata:
  name: engine-nginx
spec:
  appinfo:
    appns: default
    applabel: "app=nginx"
    appkind: deployment
  chaosServiceAccount: nginx
  experiments:
    - name: pod-delete
      spec:
        rank: 1
    - name: container-kill
      spec:
        components:
EOF
```

With that, you've learned how to create chaos experiments based on predefined Chaos Charts.

Reviewing chaos experiment results

Chaos experiments are executed as Kubernetes jobs and affected pods will be taken down by the chaos executor based on the experiment definition.

Let's perform the following steps to review the results of our chaos experiments:

1. Watch the experiment in progress:

```
$ watch kubectl get pods
Every 2.0s: kubectl get pods ip-172-20-50-43: Wed Sep 25 05:17:55
2019
NAME                             READY STATUS      RESTARTS AGE
container-kill-klfr5-rgddd       0/1   Completed   0        2m39s
engine-nginx-runner              1/2   Running     0        4m53s
```

```
nginx-deployment-5c689d88bb-qtvsx 1/1   Terminating  1        23m
nginx-deployment-5c689d88bb-rwtk9 1/1   Running      0        3m12s
pod-delete-wzj6w-x6k5t            0/1   Completed    0        4m8s
```

2. Get the list of results:

```
$ kubectl get chaosresults
NAME                           AGE
engine-nginx-container-kill    9m
engine-nginx-pod-delete        10m
```

3. View the engine-nginx-container-kill experiment results:

```
$ kubectl describe chaosresults engine-nginx-container-kill
...
Spec:
  Experimentstatus:
    Phase: <nil>
    Verdict: pass
Events: <none>
```

4. View the engine-nginx-pod-delete experiment results:

```
$ kubectl describe chaosresults engine-nginx-pod-delete
...
Spec:
  Experimentstatus:
    Phase: <nil>
    Verdict: pass
Events: <none>
```

In this recipe, we have tested and reviewed a simple scenario. You can combine existing Chaos Charts to create your experiments and write your application chaos experiments using the Litmus framework.

Viewing chaos experiment logs

Logs are always collected and stored by the standard Kubernetes logging frameworks that are used on your cluster. In cases where you need to review them quickly, you can use access to the kubelet logs.

Let's perform the following steps to take a deeper look at the tasks that are executed during the chaos experiments:

1. Get the list of pods that were created by the completed jobs:

```
$ kubectl get pods |grep Completed
container-kill-klfr5-rgddd 0/1 Completed 0 35m
pod-delete-wzj6w-x6k5t     0/1 Completed 0 37m
```

2. View the logs using the `kubectl logs` command:

```
$ kubectl logs container-kill-klfr5-rgddd
...

TASK [Force kill the application pod using pumba]
*****************************

...

TASK [Verify restartCount]
*****************************************

...

PLAY RECAP
*****************************************************************
127.0.0.1 : ok=29 changed=18 unreachable=0 failed=0
2019-09-25T05:15:56.151497 (delta: 1.254396) elapsed: 35.944704
*******
```

Inside the logs, you will be able to see the individual tasks that have been executed and the summary of passed or failed tasks.

How it works...

This recipe showed you how to quickly run a predefined chaos experiment on your applications running on Kubernetes.

Litmus experiments can be easily created from scratch and integrated into an application developer's CI pipeline, post the build and unit/integration test phases, to test chaos behavior on Kubernetes clusters.

In the *Running a Litmus chaos experiment* recipe, in *step 8*, we created a Chaos Engine to test a pod delete experiment, followed by a container kill experiment. These two experiments use Chaoskube, a tool that periodically kills random pods in your Kubernetes cluster, and Pumba, a chaos testing and network emulation tool, as the end injectors of chaos.

See also

- Litmus documentation: `https://docs.litmuschaos.io/`
- Chaos Charts for Kubernetes: `https://hub.litmuschaos.io/`
- Chaoskube project: `https://github.com/linki/chaoskube`
- Pumba project: `https://github.com/alexei-led/pumba`

Automating Chaos Engineering with Gremlin

Gremlin is a Chaos Engineering service that prevents outages and builds more reliable systems. In this section, we will run chaos attacks in production to validate the resiliency of the systems using Gremlin. You will learn how to create CPU and node shutdown attacks to test the resiliency of your infrastructure.

Getting ready

For this recipe, we need to have the Kubernetes command-line tool, `kubectl`, and `helm` installed.

All the operations mentioned here require a Gremlin account. If you don't have one, go to `https://app.gremlin.com/signup` and create one.

How to do it...

This section is further divided into the following subsections to make this process easier:

- Setting up Gremlin credentials
- Installing Gremlin on Kubernetes
- Creating a CPU attack against a Kubernetes worker
- Creating a node shutdown attack against a Kubernetes worker
- Running predefined scenario-based attacks
- Deleting Gremlin from your cluster

Setting up Gremlin credentials

To connect to Gremlin services from our Kubernetes cluster, we will need to store our Gremlin credentials as a Kubernetes Secret.

Let's perform the following steps to configure our Gremlin credentials:

1. Log in to the Gremlin service at `https://app.gremlin.com/`.
2. From the account menu, click on **Company Settings**:

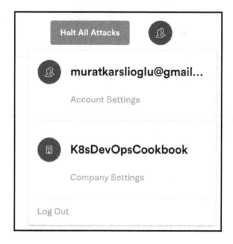

3. Click on the **Teams** tab and select your team:

4. Click on the **Configuration** tab and download your certificates:

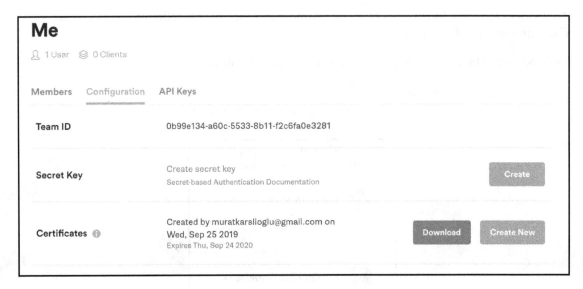

5. Copy the `certificates.zip` file to your host where kubectl has been configured.

6. Extract the files:

```
$ unzip certificate.zip
```

7. Rename the certificate files accordingly:

```
$ mv Me-client.pub_cert.pem gremlin.cert && mv Me-client.priv_key.pem gremlin.key
```

8. Create a Secret resource in your cluster:

```
$ kubectl create secret generic gremlin-team-cert --from-file=./gremlin.cert --from-file=./gremlin.key
```

With that, we have converted our credentials into secret resources in Kubernetes. This secret will be used later to connect Gremlin to our cluster.

Installing Gremlin on Kubernetes

The easiest way to install Gremlin on Kubernetes is by using Helm charts. Make sure you have created a gremlin team cert secret, as described in the *Setting up Gremlin credentials* recipe, before you proceed.

Let's perform the following steps to install Gremlin using Helm charts:

1. Add the Gremlin Helm repository:

   ```
   $ helm repo add gremlin https://helm.gremlin.com
   ```

2. Update the repositories:

   ```
   $ helm repo update
   ```

3. Install the Gremlin client using your Team ID:

   ```
   $ helm install --name gremlin --set gremlin.teamID=abc1234-
   a12b-1234-1234-abcdefgh gremlin/gremlin
   ```

4. Gremlin will create a DaemonSet that will run on every node in your cluster. Validate that the DESIRED and AVAILABLE pods are equal:

   ```
   $ kubectl get daemonsets
   NAME     DESIRED CURRENT READY UP-TO-DATE AVAILABLE NODE SELECTOR
   AGE
   gremlin 3       3       3     3          3         <none>
   11m
   ```

   Gremlin is running in your cluster. Next, we need to trigger some chaos through our Gremlin account.

Creating a CPU attack against a Kubernetes worker

Gremlin can generate various infrastructure attacks that impact cores, workers, and memory.

Let's perform the following steps to attack the CPU:

1. Deploy a sample application:

   ```
   $ kubectl apply -f ./src/chapter4/gremlin/nginx.yaml
   ```

2. List the pods and confirm they are running:

```
$ kubectl get pods |grep nginx
nginx-deployment-5c689d88bb-24n4m 1/1 Running 0 4m31s
nginx-deployment-5c689d88bb-rwtk9 1/1 Running 0 4m31s
```

3. Get the node name for one of the pods:

```
$ kubectl get pod nginx-deployment-5c689d88bb-rwtk9 -o
jsonpath="{.spec.nodeName}"
ip-172-20-50-43.ec2.internal
```

4. Watch the `pods` status:

```
$ watch kubectl get pods
```

5. Log in to your Gremlin account at `https://app.gremlin.com/`.
6. From the **Attacks** menu, click on **Infrastructure.**
7. Click on the **New Attack** button:

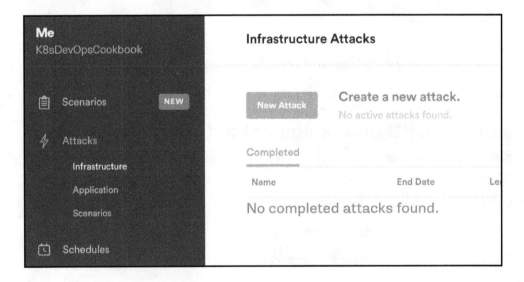

8. Under the **Choose Hosts to target** tab, pick the node's local hostname from *step 3*:

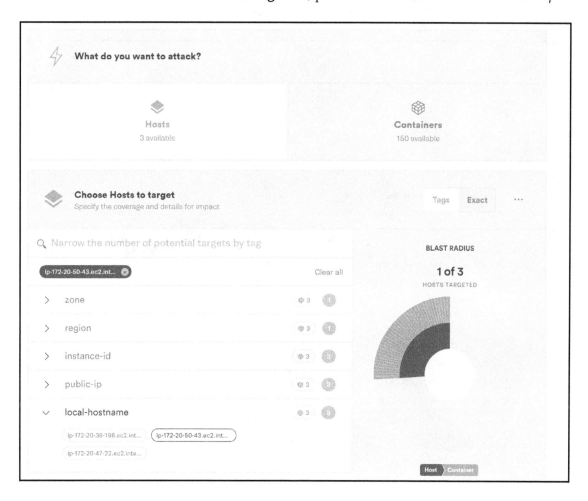

9. Under the **Choose a Gremlin** tab, click on **Resource**, select **CPU** attack, set **CPU Capacity** to 90, and consume all CPU cores:

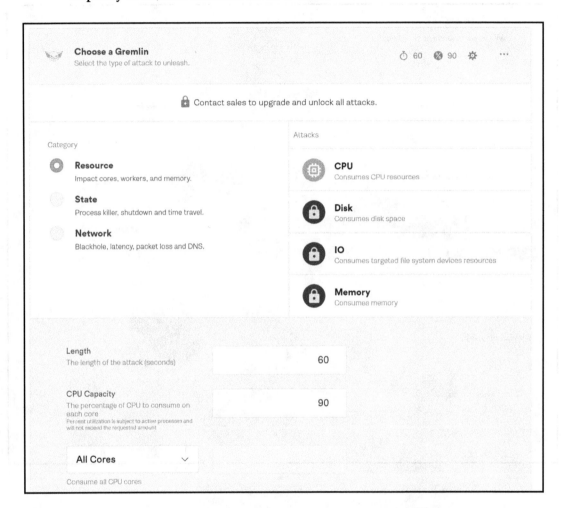

10. Click on **Unleash Gremlin** to run the attack:

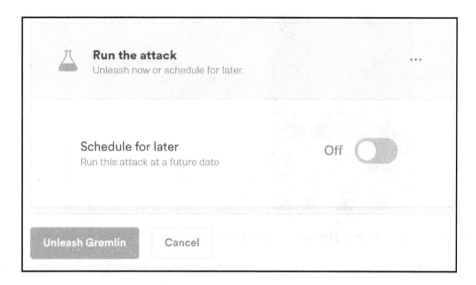

Now, the actions you triggered on your Gremlin account will be executed on your cluster through the agent.

Creating a node shutdown attack against a Kubernetes worker

Gremlin can generate various infrastructure attacks that impact cores, workers, and memory.

Let's perform the following steps to attack the CPU:

1. Log in to your Gremlin account at `https://app.gremlin.com/`.
2. From the **Attacks** menu, click on **Infrastructure**.

3. Click on the **New Attack** button:

4. Under the **Choose Hosts to target** tab, pick the node's local hostname:

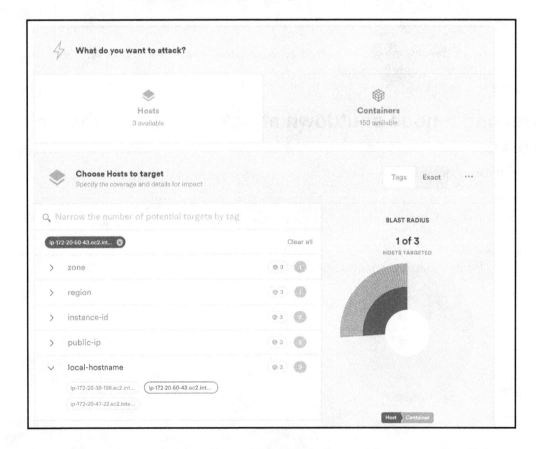

5. Under the **Choose a Gremlin** tab, click on **State** and select **Shutdown**:

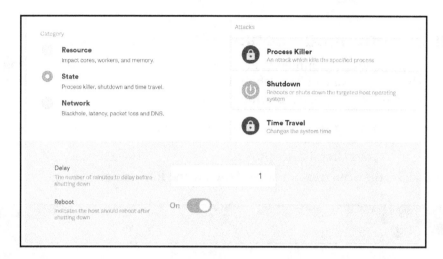

6. Click on **Unleash Gremlin** to run the attack:

7. Get the pods on the node we executed a Shutdown attack on:

```
$ kubectl get pod -owide |grep ip-172-20-50-43.ec2.internal
NAME                    READY STATUS  RESTARTS AGE IP          NODE
NOMINATED NODE
engine-nginx-runner 1/2    Running 1        24h 100.96.0.65
ip-172-20-50-43.ec2.internal <none>
gremlin-rpp22        1/1    Running 1        88m 100.96.0.60
ip-172-20-50-43.ec2.internal <none>
nginx-deployment-5c689d88bb-rwtk9 1/1 Running 1 24h 100.96.0.63
ip-172-20-50-43.ec2.internal <none>
```

You will notice that the pods are restarted.

Running predefined scenario-based attacks

Gremlin chaos scenarios help bundle attacks together to generate real-world outage scenarios. In this recipe, we will learn about the predefined scenarios that we can use to validate how our system responds to common failures.

Let's perform the following steps to validate autoscaling:

1. Log in to your Gremlin account at `https://app.gremlin.com/`.
2. Click on the **Scenarios** menu and review the **Recommended** scenarios:

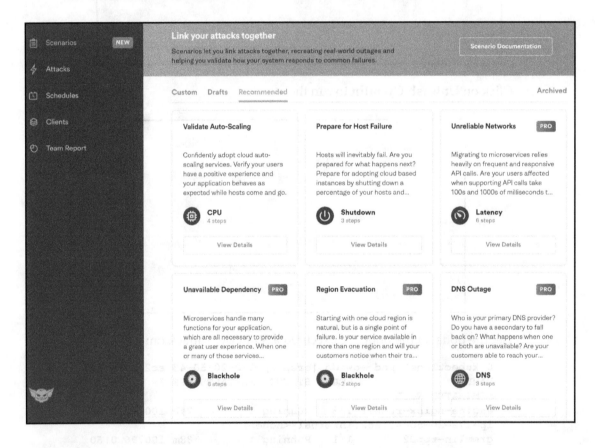

3. Make sure autoscaling is enabled on your Kubernetes cluster and select the **Validate Auto-Scaling** scenario.

4. Click on the **Add targets and run** button:

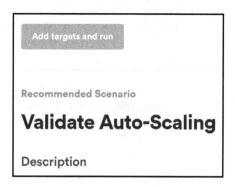

5. Click on **Run Scenario** to execute the attack.

   As a result, Gremlin will execute a CPU attack on the existing nodes to put pressure on the cluster, which should ideally trigger the autoscaling feature of the cluster to reduce CPU pressure.

Deleting Gremlin from your cluster

Let's perform the following steps to remove the components of Gremlin from your Kubernetes cluster:

1. List the Gremlin Helm releases:

   ```
   $ helm ls |grep gremlin
   gremlin 1 Thu Sep 26 04:37:05 2019 DEPLOYED gremlin-0.1.3 2.11.8
   ```

2. Remove the Helm release using the release name:

   ```
   $ helm delete gremlin --purge
   ```

   Helm will remove the release from your cluster.

How it works...

This recipe showed you how to quickly run a predefined chaos attack on your worker nodes where applications are scheduled to run by Kubernetes.

Keep in mind that, although we were looking for the impact on specific pods in the *Creating a CPU attack* and *Creating a node shutdown attack* recipes, the whole node was under attack, so the other pods on the node were also impacted.

Especially in small clusters, it is suggested to limit your blast radius and start targeting a single container of a pod. This can be done using network latency attacks and by specifying the ports that are relevant to the containers you wish to see the attack work on.

See also

- Gremlin documentation: `https://www.gremlin.com/docs/`

Automating your code review with Codacy

In this section, we will use Codacy to automate code reviews without having to make any additional code changes to our repositories and generate notifications on code quality and security issues. You will learn how to automate one of the most underestimated tasks when it comes to the development of code reviews and checks.

Getting ready

All the operations mentioned here require a Codacy account. If you don't have one, go to `https://www.codacy.com/pricing` and create one.

How to do it...

This section is further divided into the following subsections to make this process easier:

- Accessing the Project Dashboard
- Reviewing commits and PRs

- Viewing issues by category
- Adding a Codacy badge to your repository

Accessing the Project Dashboard

Let's perform the following steps to access the Codacy Project Dashboard:

1. Log in to Codacy at `https://app.codacy.com`, which will bring you to your Organization Dashboard.
2. Click on **Projects** on the left menu:

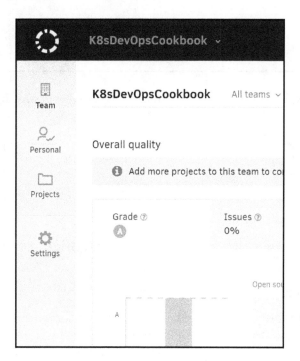

3. Click on a specific project to get to the project view:

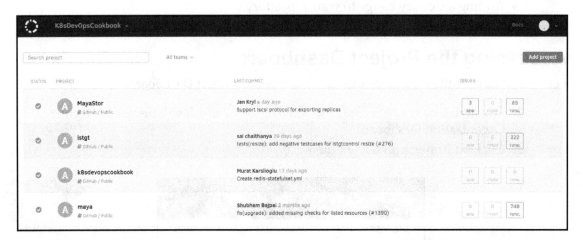

4. Find the **Project grading** option on the Project Dashboard. In our example, the following project has been graded **A**:

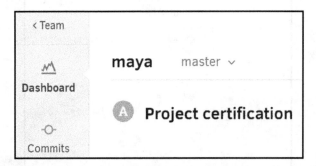

5. Find the **Quality evolution** graph and view the comparison of the number of issues versus industry average. If your average is higher than the industry standard, you need to review the commit and reduce the number of issues:

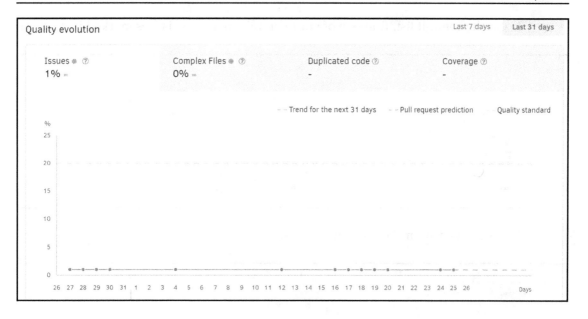

Reviewing commits and PRs

Let's perform the following steps to review code commits on the Codacy Dashboard:

1. On the Project Dashboard, click on the **Commits** menu.
2. Select the **master** branch from the drop-down menu:

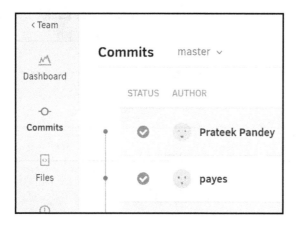

3. On the commit list, find one of your commits with new issues marked in red:

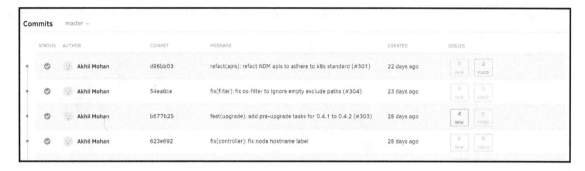

4. Click on a **Commit** to view its details:

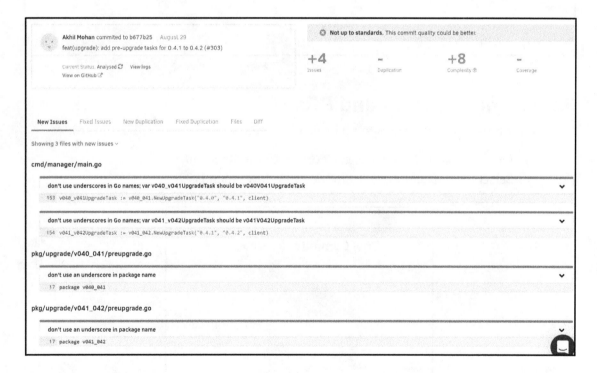

5. Implement the suggested fixes to clear the issues or open a GitHub issue for the developer team to fix.

6. Now, click on the **Open Pull Requests** menu:

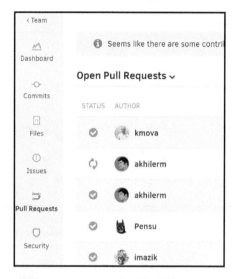

7. Repeat *steps 3* to *5* to review the issues and recommended solutions to clear them before the code is merged. This will improve code quality.

Viewing issues by category

Not all issues are the same and require the same amount of work to be fixed. Most of the time, security issues should be the top concern and code styles should be an ongoing engineering effort so that they're fixed with improving internal review processes.

Let's perform the following steps to see the issue breakdown:

1. Log in to `https://app.codacy.com`, which will bring you to your Organization Dashboard.

2. Click on **Projects** on the left menu.

3. Select a project to analyze.

4. Scroll down the Dashboard until you see the **Issues breakdown** chart:

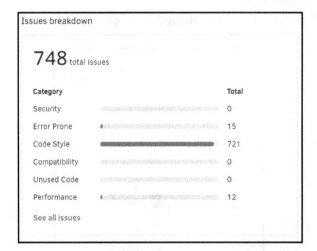

5. Click on a category with issues and use the provided information on issues in code reviews:

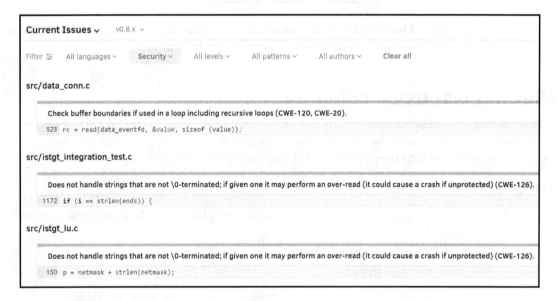

6. If you are peer-reviewing or checking your own code, you can filter issues from an author by clicking on the **All authors** filter and changing it to a name.

Adding a Codacy badge to your repository

Badges are used to represent the high-level project status and its stability to the users coming to your repository or website. Since Codacy can show the quality of your code, it is definitely something you may want to display on your repository in the README.MD file.

Let's perform the following steps to add a Codacy badge to your GitHub repository:

1. Log in to `https://app.codacy.com`, which will bring you to your Organization Dashboard.
2. Click on **Projects** on the left menu.
3. Select a project to analyze.
4. Click on the **Badge** icon next to your project name:

5. Click on **Add badge to repository** to create a **Pull Request (PR)** to your repository:

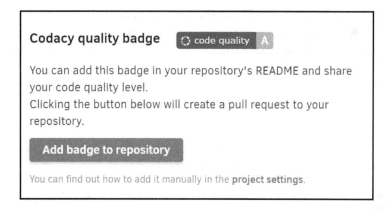

6. Review the content of the PR and merge it. Once it's been merged, you will see the code quality score on your repository **Overview** page, similar to what's shown in the following screenshot:

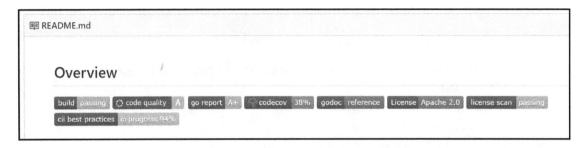

Badges are used to highlight important tests and information for your repository visitors.

See also

- Codacy documentation: `https://support.codacy.com/hc/en-us`

Detecting bugs and anti-patterns with SonarQube

SonarQube is a popular development tool that is used in software development to catch bugs and vulnerabilities in your applications. In this section, we will learn how to automate static code analysis to detect bugs and anti-patterns that you can use in your CI/CD pipelines.

Getting ready

Clone the `k8sdevopscookbook/src` repository to your workstation in order to use the manifest files under the `chapter4` directory:

```
$ git clone https://github.com/k8sdevopscookbook/src.git
$ cd src/chapter4
```

Make sure you have a Kubernetes cluster ready and `kubectl` and `helm` configured so that you can manage the cluster resources.

How to do it...

This section is further divided into the following subsections to make this process easier:

- Installing SonarQube using Helm
- Accessing the SonarQube Dashboard
- Creating a new user and tokens
- Enabling Quality Profiles
- Adding a project
- Analyzing a project
- Viewing issues by category
- Adding a SonarQube badge to your repository
- Adding marketplace plugins
- Deleting SonarQube from your cluster

Installing SonarQube using Helm

SonarQube is a leading open source solution for code quality and security analysis for adopting code quality in your CI/CD. It can be installed as a standalone solution from binaries. In this recipe, we will install it on a Kubernetes cluster using Helm charts.

Let's perform the following steps to get SonarQube up and running:

1. Update your repositories:

   ```
   $ helm repo update
   ```

2. Install SonarQube:

   ```
   $ helm install stable/sonarqube --name sonar --namespace sonarqube
   ```

3. Validate that the PostgreSQL and SonarQube pods are ready:

   ```
   $ kubectl get pods -n sonarqube
   NAME                                READY  STATUS   RESTARTS  AGE
   sonar-postgresql-68b88ddc77-146wc 1/1    Running  0         16m
   sonar-sonarqube-995b9cc79-9vzjn    1/1    Running  1         16m
   ```

With that, you've learned how to get SonarQube deployed on the Kubernetes cluster.

Accessing the SonarQube Dashboard

When installed using Helm charts, SonarQube creates a load balancer and exposes an external IP to connect. We will discover the IP first and connect to the SonarQube Dashboard using the service IP.

Let's perform the following steps to expose SonarQube through a cloud load balancer:

1. Get the SonarQube load balancer's external IP:

    ```
    $ export SONAR_SVC=$(kubectl get svc --namespace sonarqube sonar-
    sonarqube -o jsonpath='{.status.loadBalancer.ingress[0].hostname}')
    $ echo http://$SONAR_SVC:9000
    ```

2. Open the address in your browser:

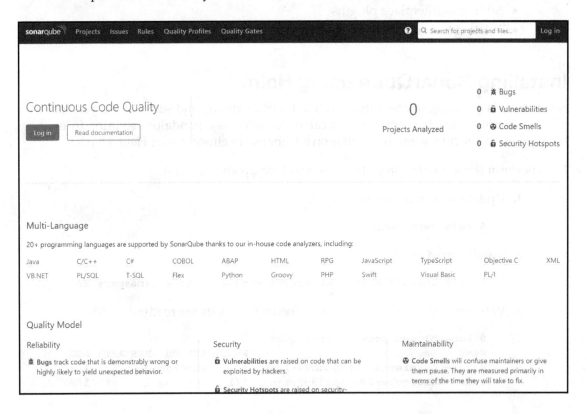

3. Click on **Log in** and use `admin` as both your username and password to log in to the Dashboard:

4. Click on the account profile logo on the top right of the screen and select **My Account**:

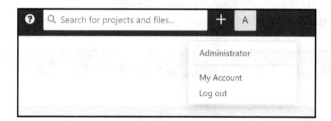

5. Select the **Security** tab:

6. Change the default admin password and save it by clicking the **Change password** button:

Since the service port is accessible externally, it is important to change the default credentials of SonarQube.

Creating a new user and tokens

Team members need to have their own user accounts to access the Dashboard. It is recommended that you generate tokens in order to manage accounts. You can use them to run analyses or invoke web services without needing to access the user's actual credentials. This way, your analysis of the user's password does not go through the network.

Let's perform the following steps to create new users that can access SonarQube:

1. From the top menu, click on **Administration**.
2. Click on the **Security** tab and select **Users**:

3. Click on the **Create User** button:

4. Enter the **Name**, **Email**, and **Password** of the user and click on **Create**:

5. On the **Users** table, click the **Update Tokens** button under the **Tokens** column:

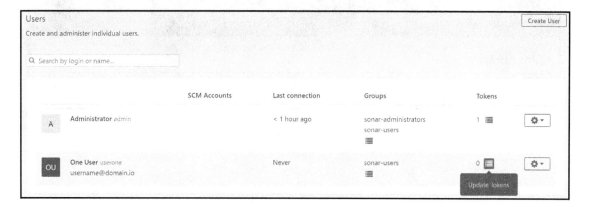

6. Set a token name and click on the **Generate** button.

7. Make sure that you copy the token and take note of it for the upcoming recipes.

Enabling quality profiles

To be able to analyze a project, first, you need to install specific programming language plugins. Let's perform the following steps to install Java plugins that we'll use in the next recipe, *Adding a project:*

1. Click on **Quality Profiles**. If you see a message saying **There are no languages available**, then you need to install the language plugins:

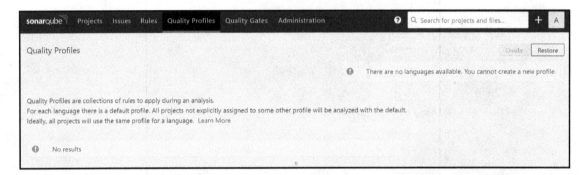

2. Click on the **Administration** menu and switch to the **Marketplace** tab:

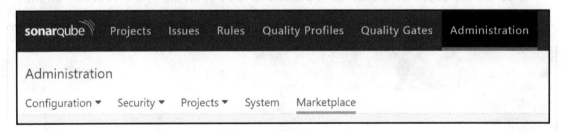

3. On the **Marketplace** search field, search for the language you would like to enable. For this recipe, this is `java`:

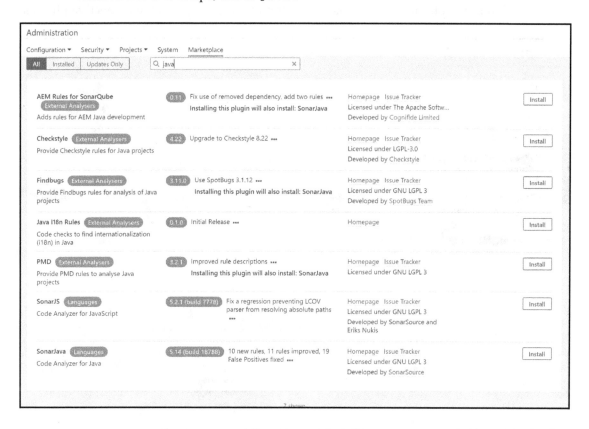

4. Add **Adobe Experience Manager** (**AEM**) rules for SonarQube, Checkstyle, Findbugs, Java i18n rules, **Programming Mistake Detector** (**PMD**), and SonarJava plugins by clicking on the **Install** button next to the respective plugins:

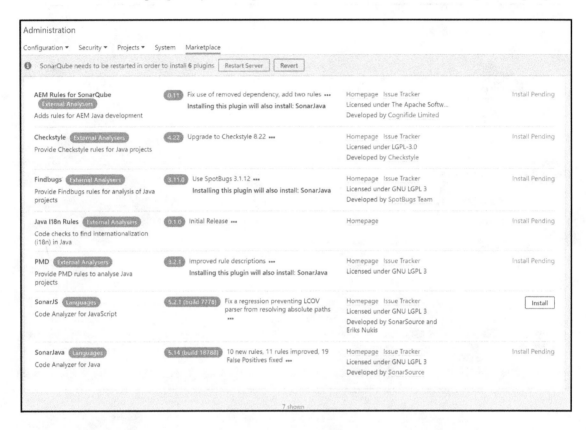

5. This action requires a restart. Click on **Restart Server** and log in to the Dashboard after it's restarted:

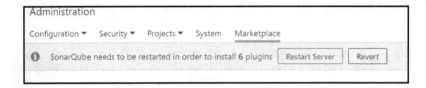

6. Once you've logged back into the Dashboard, click on **Quality Profiles**. This time, you should see Java profiles:

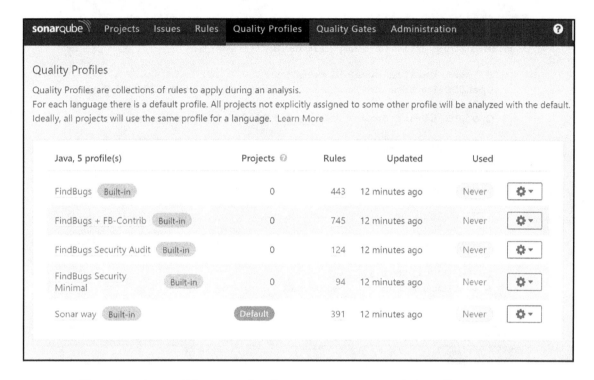

Repeat *steps 1* to *5* for any other languages you want to install.

Adding a project

A project is created in SonarQube automatically on its first analysis. Before we can scan a project, we need to choose an analysis method. In this recipe, we will launch a Gradle analysis. The other available methods are listed in the *See also* section.

Let's perform the following steps to add a new project to SonarQube:

1. Clone an example repository to scan:

```
$ git clone https://github.com/javajon/code-analysis.git
$ cd code-analysis/microservice/
```

2. For this example, we also need Java 1.8 installed on our node. If you already have it, skip to *step 4*:

```
$ sudo apt install openjdk-8-jre-headless default-jdk
```

3. Confirm the version of Java you're using:

```
$ java -version openjdk version "1.8.0_222"
OpenJDK Runtime Environment (build 1.8.0_222-8u222-b10-1~deb9u1-
b10)
OpenJDK 64-Bit Server VM (build 25.222-b10, mixed mode)
```

4. Get the SonarQube service's external IP:

```
$ export SONAR_SVC=$(kubectl get svc --namespace sonarqube sonar-
sonarqube -o jsonpath='{.status.loadBalancer.ingress[0].hostname}')
```

5. Run the analysis. The analysis will complete in a couple of minutes:

```
$ ./gradlew -Dsonar.host.url=http://$SONAR_SVC:9000 sonarqube
....
BUILD SUCCESSFUL in 13s
6 actionable tasks: 1 executed, 5 up-to-date
```

6. Switch back to the SonarQube portal to see the new project:

Now, you will be able to see your new project on the SonarQube portal.

Reviewing a project's quality

SonarQube's analysis varies, depending on the language that's scanned, but, in most cases, it generates good-quality measures, issues reports, and finds where coding rules were broken. In this recipe, you will learn where to find types of issues and look into issues by severity.

Make sure that you added the sample project to SonarQube by following the *Adding a project* recipe. Now, perform the following steps:

1. Click on the **Issues** menu:

2. Known vulnerabilities are considered blockers and need to be addressed immediately. Under **Filters**, expand **Severity** and select **Blocker:**

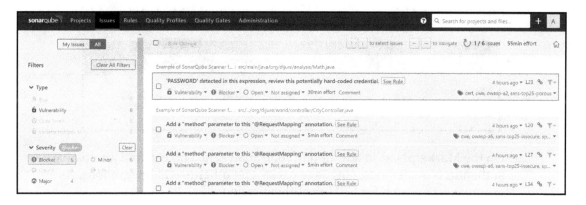

3. A hardcoded credential has been detected in the example code, which is a serious vulnerability. To assign this issue to a team member, click on the **Not assigned** dropdown and type in the person's name to assign it to them:

4. Eventually, all the issues need to be either confirmed and assigned or resolved as fixed, false positive, or won't be fixed. The status can be set by clicking on the **Open** dropdown and changing it to a new status value.

Adding marketplace plugins

Let's perform the following steps to add new plugins to SonarQube from the marketplace:

1. Click on the **Administration** menu and switch to the **Marketplace** tab:

2. On the **Marketplace**, in addition to code analyzers, you can find alternative authentication methods, language packs, and other useful integrations. As an example, let's search for GitHub authentication:

3. Click on the **Install** button next to the plugin.
4. Now, click on **Restart Server** and log in to the Dashboard after it's been restarted.
5. With SonarQube, go to **Administration** | **Configuration** | **General Settings** | **GitHub**.
6. Set **Enabled** to true:

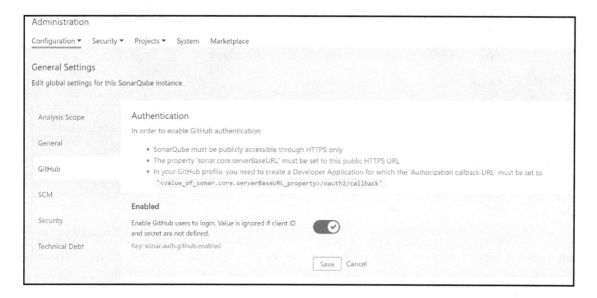

7. Set the `client ID` and `client secret` to the values provided by the GitHub developer application. Register a new OAuth application with GitHub by going to `https://github.com/settings/applications/new`.
8. Save the settings and log out from SonarQube:

New, users will be asked to log in with a GitHub user.

Deleting SonarQube from your cluster

Let's perform the following steps to remove SonarQube from your Kubernetes cluster:

1. List the SonarQube Helm releases:

   ```
   $ helm ls |grep sonarqube
   sonar 1 Thu Sep 26 22:01:24 2019 DEPLOYED sonarqube-2.3.0 7.9
   sonarqube
   ```

2. Remove the Helm release using the release name:

   ```
   $ helm delete sonar --purge
   ```

   Helm will remove the SonarQube release and its components from your cluster.

How it works...

This recipe showed you how to quickly detect security vulnerabilities and bugs in your project.

In the *Adding a project* recipe, in *step 5*, when we start analyzing our example, the files that are provided to the analysis are analyzed on the server-side, and the result of the analysis is sent back to the server as a report. This report is analyzed in an asynchronous way on the server-side.

Reports are added to a queue and processed by the server in order. If multiple reports are sent back to the server, the results may take some time to be displayed on the SonarQube Dashboard.

By default, only the files that can be detected by the installed code analyzer are loaded into the project. This means that if you only have SonarJava code written in C or Go and YAML files that are very common in the Kubernetes world, they will be ignored.

See also

- SonarQube Documentation: https://docs.sonarqube.org/latest/setup/overview/
- Static code analysis example using SonarScanner for Gradle: https://github.com/javajon/code-analysis
- SonarScanner for Jenkins: https://docs.sonarqube.org/latest/analysis/scan/sonarscanner-for-jenkins/

- SonarQube extension for Azure DevOps: `https://docs.sonarqube.org/latest/analysis/scan/sonarscanner-for-azure-devops/`
- SonarQube Scanner for MSBuild: `https://docs.sonarqube.org/display/SCAN/Analyzing+with+SonarQube+Scanner+for+MSBuild`
- SonarQube Scanner for Maven: `https://docs.sonarqube.org/display/SCAN/Analyzing+with+SonarQube+Scanner+for+Maven`
- SonarQube Scanner for Ant: `https://docs.sonarqube.org/display/SCAN/Analyzing+with+SonarQube+Scanner+for+Ant`
- SonarQube Scanner to launch analysis from the CLI: `https://docs.sonarqube.org/display/SCAN/Analyzing+with+SonarQube+Scanner`
- Plugin Library: `https://docs.sonarqube.org/display/PLUG/Plugin+Library`
- SonarQube Community: `https://community.sonarsource.com/`

Detecting license compliance issues with FOSSA

FOSSA is an open source software license compliance tool that allows modern teams to be successful with open source software development. In this section, we will scan software licenses with the FOSSA framework. You will learn how to automate license compliance and vulnerability checks.

Getting ready

All the operations mentioned here require a FOSSA account. If you don't have one, go to `https://app.fossa.com/account/register` and create one.

How to do it...

This section is further divided into the following subsections to make this process easier:

- Adding projects to FOSSA
- Triaging licensing issues
- Adding a FOSSA badge to your project

Adding projects to FOSSA

Let's perform the following steps to add projects to FOSSA:

1. Log in to FOSSA at `https://app.fossa.com/projects`.
2. Click on the **ADD PROJECTS** button:

3. Select **QUICK IMPORT** and then **Continue**:

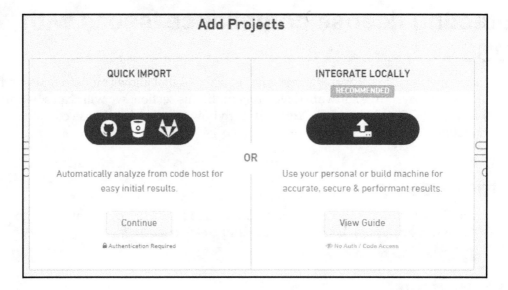

4. Select your repository location. In this recipe, we will use **Gitlab**:

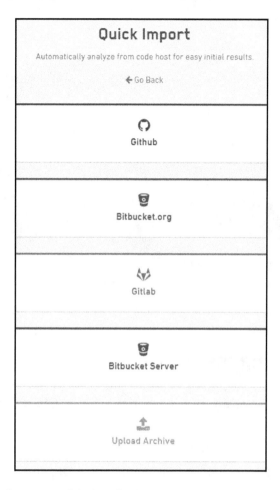

5. Click on the **Connect with Service** button.

6. Select the repositories you would like to scan and click on the **IMPORT** button:

FOSSA will import and automatically scan for license compliance issues.

Triaging licensing issues

FOSSA does not require any additional steps or code to scan your projects. It runs the license scans as soon as you add your repositories to your FOSSA account. Let's take a look:

1. Log in to https://app.fossa.com/projects.
2. Select **Projects**.
3. The **SUMMARY** tab will display any **Flagged Dependencies** that have been detected:

4. Click on the **ISSUES** tab:

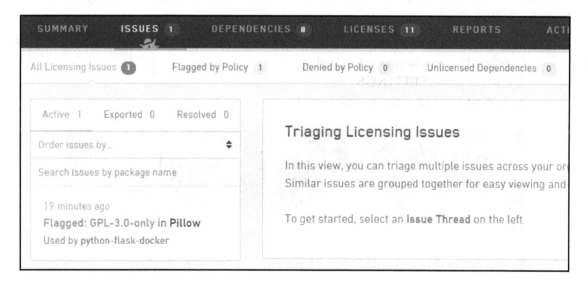

5. Select an **Issue Thread** from the left menu.

6. Review the issue and the recommended resolution:

Based on the action that needs to be taken for the issue, you can either decide to create a ticket, leave a comment for discussion with a team member, or resolve it with an explanation.

Adding a FOSSA badge to your project

Let's perform the following steps to add a FOSSA license check badge to our GitHub repository page:

1. Log in to FOSSA at `https://app.fossa.com/projects`.
2. Select **Projects** to generate a badge.
3. Switch to the **SETTINGS** tab.
4. Select **SHEILD** as the badge format:

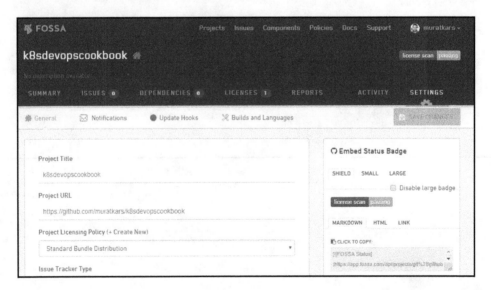

5. Copy the **MARKDOWN** content to the clipboard.
6. Edit the README.md file on the GitHub repository you scanned. Paste the **MARKDOWN** badge code you copied in *step 5* to the beginning of the file:

7. Once you've saved the file, the results of the FOSSA scan will be displayed in the badge on your repository.

5
Preparing for Stateful Workloads

In this chapter, we will discuss using popular open source storage solutions on Kubernetes and how to protect the state of applications from node or application failures and share the same data, or how to handle reattaching volumes when the pod is rescheduled on a different node. After following the recipes in this chapter, you will have acquired the skills to use both block and file storage options in self-managed infrastructure or private clouds.

In this chapter, we will be covering the following recipes:

- Managing Amazon EBS volumes in Kubernetes
- Managing GCE PD volumes in Kubernetes
- Managing Azure Disk volumes in Kubernetes
- Configuring and managing persistent storage using Rook
- Configuring and managing persistent storage using OpenEBS
- Setting up NFS for shared storage on Kubernetes
- Troubleshooting storage issues

Technical requirements

Recipes in this section assume that you have a functional Kubernetes cluster deployed according to one of the recommended methods described in Chapter 1, *Building Production-Ready Kubernetes Clusters*.

Kubernetes' command-line tool, kubectl, will be used for the remainder of the recipes in this section since it is the main command-line interface for running commands against Kubernetes clusters. We will also use helm where helm charts are available to deploy solutions.

Managing Amazon EBS volumes in Kubernetes

Amazon Elastic Block Store (Amazon EBS) provides persistent block-level storage volumes for Amazon EC2 instances used in both `kops`-created Kubernetes clusters and Amazon EKS clusters in AWS. In this section, we will create storage classes for your applications in Kubernetes running in AWS. You will learn how to create a StorageClass resource in Kubernetes, you will learn about the parameters available with the variation in performance of EBS volume types and also use the new **Container Storage Interface** (CSI) to consume EBS volumes.

Getting ready

Clone the `k8sdevopscookbook/src` repository to your workstation in order to be able to use manifest files under the `chapter5` directory:

```
$ git clone https://github.com/k8sdevopscookbook/src.git
$ cd chapter5
```

Make sure that you have a Kubernetes cluster ready and `kubectl` configured to manage the cluster resources.

How to do it...

This section is sub-divided further into the following subsections to facilitate the process:

- Creating an EBS storage class
- Changing the default storage class
- Using EBS volumes for persistent storage
- Using EBS storage classes to dynamically create persistent volumes
- Deleting EBS persistent volumes
- Installing the EBS CSI driver to manage EBS volumes

Creating an EBS storage class

Let's perform the following steps to learn the storage class parameters required to construct an EBS storage class that we can use to dynamically request new persistent volumes from AWS Cloud:

1. Create a basic storage class with the provisioner, `kubernetes.io/aws-ebs`, and `gp2` type specified:

   ```
   $ cat <<EOF | kubectl apply -f -
   apiVersion: storage.k8s.io/v1
   kind: StorageClass
   metadata:
    name: aws-gp2
   provisioner: kubernetes.io/aws-ebs
   parameters:
    type: gp2
    fsType: ext4
   reclaimPolicy: Retain
   allowVolumeExpansion: true
   mountOptions:
    - debug
   volumeBindingMode: Immediate
   EOF
   ```

   Other type values accepted here include `io1`, `sc1`, and `st1`. You can find the definition and use cases for different volume types on the AWS EBS volume types link in the *See also* section.

   On Amazon EKS clusters, the default EBS volume type is `gp2`. For database workloads, such as MongoDB, Cassandra, and PostgreSQL, `io1-type`, high-performance SSDs are recommended.

2. List the storage classes. Confirm that you have new `aws-gp2` on the list. Depending on the cloud provider or Kubernetes deployment tool, you may see other storage classes on the list similar to the following:

   ```
   $ kubectl get sc
   NAME                    PROVISIONER                     AGE
   aws-gp2                 kubernetes.io/aws-ebs           8s
   default                 kubernetes.io/aws-ebs           25h
   gp2 (default)           kubernetes.io/aws-ebs           25h
   openebs-hostpath        openebs.io/local                175m
   openebs-jiva-default    openebs.io/provisioner-iscsi    175m
   ```

Storage classes are the foundation of dynamic provisioning. As you can see in our example, you may have more than one storage class in your cluster. Ideally, storage classes should be created with an application's requirements in mind, since certain applications require faster volumes, while others may take advantage of multi-availability zone replication provided by solutions such as Rook and OpenEBS, which we will deploy later in this chapter.

Changing the default storage class

Dynamic storage provisioning is a key part of scaling applications. When a storage class is not specified by a **Persistent Volume Claim** (**PVC**), Kubernetes uses the default option. Let's perform the following steps to set our preferred storage class as the default:

1. Create a new storage class and define it as the default at the same time by setting the is-default-class value to true. Our example here uses the io1 volume type and limits iopsPerGB to 10. It also sets reclaimPolicy to Retain, meaning that, if the user deletes the related PVC, the volume will be retained (the other two retain policy options are Recycle and Delete):

```
$ cat <<EOF | kubectl apply -f -
apiVersion: storage.k8s.io/v1
kind: StorageClass
metadata:
 name: aws-io1-slow
 annotations:
  storageclass.kubernetes.io/is-default-class: "true"
provisioner: kubernetes.io/aws-ebs
parameters:
 type: io1
 iopsPerGB: "10"
 fsType: ext4
reclaimPolicy: Retain
allowVolumeExpansion: true
EOF
```

2. To change the status of an existing storage class after it has been created, first pick a storage class:

```
$ kubectl get sc
NAME                   PROVISIONER              AGE
aws-gp2                kubernetes.io/aws-ebs  6m28s
aws-io1-slow (default) kubernetes.io/aws-ebs  4m29s
```

3. Let's set the existing storage class, `aws-io1-slow`, as the non-default option:

```
$ kubectl patch storageclass aws-io1-slow -p '{"metadata":
{"annotations":{"storageclass.kubernetes.io/is-default-
class":"false"}}}'
```

4. Now, define `aws-gp2` as the default storage class again:

```
$ kubectl patch storageclass aws-gp2 -p '{"metadata":
{"annotations":{"storageclass.kubernetes.io/is-default-
class":"true"}}}'
```

5. Confirm the new default storage class:

```
$ kubectl get sc
NAME                  PROVISIONER            AGE
aws-gp2 (default)    kubernetes.io/aws-ebs 10m
aws-io1-slow         kubernetes.io/aws-ebs 8m
```

Make sure that there is always one default storage class at a time, otherwise PVCs without a storage class defined that are expecting a default storage class will fail.

Using EBS volumes for persistent storage

As an alternative to creating PVCs and dynamically creating volumes, you can also manually create a volume and attach it to your application directly as a persistent volume by carrying out the following steps:

1. Create an EBS volume in the same zone as your worker nodes by using the following `aws` CLI:

```
$ aws ec2 create-volume --availability-zone=us-west-2a --size=10 --
volume-type=gp2
```

2. Deploy a test application using the EBS `volumeID` you created in *Step 1:*

```
$ cat <<EOF | kubectl apply -f -
apiVersion: v1
kind: Pod
metadata:
  name: test-server
spec:
  containers:
  - image: gcr.io/google_containers/test-webserver
    name: test-container
    volumeMounts:
```

```
      - mountPath: /test-ebs
        name: test-volume
  volumes:
  - name: test-volume
    awsElasticBlockStore:
      volumeID: vol-02f4bc9b938604f72
      fsType: ext4
EOF
```

3. Verify that your pod is in the `Running` state:

```
$ kubectl get pods
NAME            READY STATUS   RESTARTS AGE
test-server 1/1    Running 0          4m32s
```

The main advantage of manually created persistent volumes (PVs) is that PVs are not attached to a single cluster or namespace. They exist as a resource on your AWS cloud account and they can even be shared across clusters where dynamically created PVCs only exist in the namespace created and can only be used by a pod within that same namespace.

Using EBS storage classes to dynamically create persistent volumes

As part of a StatefulSet, `volumeClaimTemplates` can provide persistent storage using `PersistentVolumes` provisioned by a `PersistentVolume` provisioner of your choice. In this recipe, we will use StorageClass to dynamically create PVs for your application. Let's begin with the following steps:

1. Add the `aws-gp2` storage class line under the `volumeClaimTemplates` section of your application deployment manifest, similar to the following example:

```
...
  volumeClaimTemplates:
  - metadata:
      name: datadir
      annotations:
        volume.beta.kubernetes.io/storage-class: aws-gp2
    spec:
      accessModes: [ "ReadWriteOnce" ]
      resources:
        requests:
          storage: 1G
...
```

2. In this recipe, we will deploy the Redis StatefulSet using the `aws-gp2` storage class. Review the YAML manifest under the `src/chapter5/aws` directory in the example repository before we execute it:

```
$ cat aws/redis-statefulset.yml
```

3. Create the Redis StatefulSet using the following example:

```
$ kubectl apply -f aws/redis-statefulset.yml
```

4. Verify that pods have been created. In this recipe, our example has StatefulSet with three replicas. As a result, you should see three replicas running, similar to the following output:

```
$ kubectl get pods
NAME READY STATUS   RESTARTS AGE
rd-0 1/1   Running 0        9m9s
rd-1 1/1   Running 0        7m56s
rd-2 1/1   Running 0        6m47s
```

5. List the PVC and PVs created. You should expect to see three PVCs and three PVs created similar to our example output here:

```
$ kubectl get pvc,pv
NAME STATUS VOLUME CAPACITY ACCESS MODES STORAGECLASS AGE
datadir-rd-0 Bound pvc-8a538aa3-7382-4147-adde-1ea3dbaaafb4 1Gi RWO
aws-gp2 10m
datadir-rd-1 Bound pvc-171fbee3-39bf-4450-961f-6c1417ff3897 1Gi RWO
aws-gp2 9m1s
datadir-rd-2 Bound pvc-b40df89b-5349-4f02-8510-917012579746 1Gi RWO
aws-gp2 7m52s$
NAME CAPACITY ACCESS MODES RECLAIM POLICY STATUS CLAIM STORAGECLASS
REASON AGE
pvc-171fbee3-39bf-4450-961f-6c1417ff3897 1Gi RWO Retain Bound
default/datadir-rd-1 aws-gp2 9m18s
pvc-8a538aa3-7382-4147-adde-1ea3dbaaafb4 1Gi RWO Retain Bound
default/datadir-rd-0 aws-gp2 10m
pvc-b40df89b-5349-4f02-8510-917012579746 1Gi RWO Retain Bound
default/datadir-rd-2 aws-gp2 8m10s
```

Now, you know how to dynamically create persistent volumes as part of your deployment.

Deleting EBS persistent volumes

When the reclaim policy is set to retain the volumes, they need to be removed separately by observing the following steps:

1. Remember that deleting your workload will not remove the PVCs and PVs, unless the PVC manifest was included in the manifest:

```
$ kubectl delete -f redis-statefulset.yml
```

2. List the remaining PVs:

```
$ kubectl get pv
NAME CAPACITY ACCESS MODES RECLAIM POLICY STATUS CLAIM STORAGECLASS
REASON AGE
pvc-171fbee3-39bf-4450-961f-6c1417ff3897 1Gi RWO Retain Bound
default/datadir-rd-1 aws-gp2 13m
pvc-8a538aa3-7382-4147-adde-1ea3dbaaafb4 1Gi RWO Retain Bound
default/datadir-rd-0 aws-gp2 15m
pvc-b40df89b-5349-4f02-8510-917012579746 1Gi RWO Retain Bound
default/datadir-rd-2 aws-gp2 12m
```

3. Delete the PVCs. You can delete multiple PVCs at once by adding their names in a single command, similar to the following:

```
$ kubectl delete pvc datadir-rd-0 datadir-rd-1 datadir-rd-2
```

4. Delete the PVs. You can delete multiple PVs at once by adding their names in a single command, similar to the following:

```
$ kubectl delete pv <pv-name-1> <pv-name-2> <pv-name-3>
```

Although we removed PVCs and PVs, our EBS volumes are still retained. Let's now remove these as well:

5. Open your AWS Management Console and click on **EC2** under the **Compute** options:

6. Under the **Resources** section, click on **Volumes**:

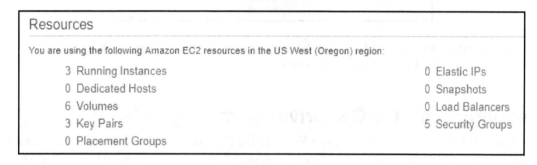

7. Select the available and unused volumes. From the *Using EBS storage classes to create dynamic persistent volumes* recipe, we have three unused volumes:

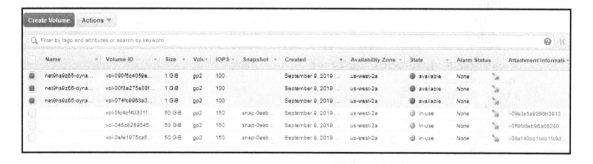

8. From the **Actions** drop-down menu, select **Delete Volumes**:

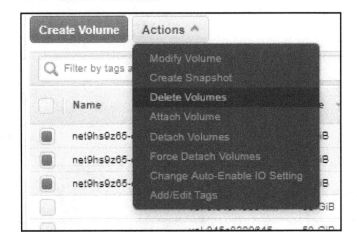

We have successfully removed all storage resources related to the application that was created as part of the Redis StatefulSet resource.

Installing the EBS CSI driver to manage EBS volumes

The Amazon EBS CSI driver provides a Kubernetes CSI interface that allows Amazon EKS clusters to simply manage the life cycle of Amazon EBS volumes for persistent volumes. In this recipe, we will learn how to install the EBS CSI driver by observing the following steps:

1. EBS CSI communicates with your AWS volume to create volumes on demand. Therefore, it requires access credentials. Replace the `key_id` and `access_key` values here with your AWS credentials and configure CSI driver permission using a secret resource:

```
$ cat <<EOF | kubectl apply -f -
apiVersion: v1
kind: Secret
metadata:
 name: aws-secret
 namespace: kube-system
stringData:
 key_id: "YOUR_KEY_ID_HERE"
 access_key: "YOUR_ACCESS_KEY_HERE"
EOF
```

2. Deploy the AWS EBS CSI driver from its repository location. The following command will create ClusterRoleBindings, CSI controller deployment, and an `ebs-csi-node` DaemonSet that will run every worker node you have:

```
$ kubectl apply -k "github.com/kubernetes-sigs/aws-ebs-csi-
driver/deploy/kubernetes/overlays/stable/?ref=master"
```

3. Verify that the driver is running:

```
$ kubectl get pods -n kube-system | grep ebs-csi
ebs-csi-controller-8579f977f4-ljfhm 4/4 Running 0 2m37s
ebs-csi-controller-8579f977f4-qw6ld 4/4 Running 0 2m37s
ebs-csi-node-5x8nh 3/3 Running 0 2m37s
ebs-csi-node-cfghj 3/3 Running 0 2m37s
ebs-csi-node-xp569 3/3 Running 0 2m37s
ebs-csi-node-z45hn 3/3 Running 0 2m37s
```

4. Now, create a new storage class that will use `ebs.csi.aws.com` as the provisioner:

```
$ cat <<EOF | kubectl apply -f -
kind: StorageClass
apiVersion: storage.k8s.io/v1
metadata:
  name: aws-csi-ebs
provisioner: ebs.csi.aws.com
volumeBindingMode: WaitForFirstConsumer
EOF
```

5. Create a PVC:

```
$ cat <<EOF | kubectl apply -f -
apiVersion: v1
kind: PersistentVolumeClaim
metadata:
  name: csi-ebs-pvc
spec:
  accessModes:
    - ReadWriteOnce
  storageClassName: aws-csi-ebs
  resources:
    requests:
      storage: 4Gi
EOF
```

6. Create a pod that will use the PVC and that writes to the /data/out.txt file:

```
$ cat <<EOF | kubectl apply -f -
apiVersion: v1
kind: Pod
metadata:
  name: app
spec:
  containers:
  - name: app
    image: centos
    command: ["/bin/sh"]
    args: ["-c", "while true; do echo $(date -u) >> /data/out.txt;
sleep 5; done"]
    volumeMounts:
    - name: persistent-storage
      mountPath: /data
  volumes:
  - name: persistent-storage
    persistentVolumeClaim:
      claimName: csi-ebs-pvc
EOF
```

7. Verify that our mytestapp pod writes data to the volume:

```
$ kubectl exec -it mytestapp cat /data/out.txt
Mon Sep 9 17:40:25 UTC 2019
```

8. Remove resources by deleting the pod and the PVC by using the following command:

```
$ kubectl delete pod mytestapp && kubectl delete pvc csi-ebs-pvc
```

Now you know how to use CSI drivers to provision EBS volumes. A CSI driver provides a unified interface to answer storage requests on Kubernetes. As long as the driver is installed and has the functionality implemented by the driver, it can be consumed by the user regardless of the underlying storage system.

See also

- AWS EBS volume types: https://docs.aws.amazon.com/AWSEC2/latest/UserGuide/EBSVolumeTypes.html

- AWS EBS CSI driver repository: `https://github.com/kubernetes-sigs/aws-ebs-csi-driver`
- AWS EBS CSI driver documentation: `https://docs.aws.amazon.com/eks/latest/userguide/ebs-csi.html`

Managing GCE PD volumes in Kubernetes

Google Cloud Platform (**GCP**) provides persistent block-level storage volumes for use with **Google Kubernetes Engine** (**GKE**) instances. In this section, we will create storage classes for your applications in Kubernetes running in the GKE. You will learn to create a StorageClass resource in Kubernetes, you will learn about the parameters available with the variation in performance of GCP PD volume types, and also use the new CSI.

Getting ready

Clone the `k8sdevopscookbook/src` repository to your workstation:

```
$ git clone https://github.com/k8sdevopscookbook/src.git
$ cd src/chapter5
```

Make sure that you have a regional GKE cluster ready and `kubectl` configured to manage the cluster resources.

How to do it...

This section is sub-divided further into the following subsections to facilitate the process:

- Creating a GCE persistent disk storage class
- Changing the default storage class
- Using GCE PD volumes for persistent storage
- Using GCE PD storage classes to create dynamic persistent volumes
- Deleting GCE PD persistent volumes
- Installing the GCP Compute PD CSI driver to manage PD volumes

Creating a GCE persistent disk storage class

Let's perform the following steps to learn the storage class parameters to construct a GCE PD storage class that we can use to dynamically request new persistent volumes:

1. GKE-based Kubernetes clusters are created with a default storage class. List the storage classes as follows:

```
$ kubectl get sc
NAME                   PROVISIONER           AGE
standard (default) kubernetes.io/gce-pd 81s
```

2. Describe the `standard` storage class:

```
$ kubectl describe sc standard
Name: standard
IsDefaultClass: Yes
Annotations: storageclass.beta.kubernetes.io/is-default-class=true
Provisioner: kubernetes.io/gce-pd
Parameters: type=pd-standard
AllowVolumeExpansion: <unset>
MountOptions: <none>
ReclaimPolicy: Delete
VolumeBindingMode: Immediate
Events: <none>
```

3. Create a basic storage class with the provisioner, `kubernetes.io/gce-pd`, and the `pd-standard` type specified:

```
$ cat <<EOF | kubectl apply -f -
kind: StorageClass
apiVersion: storage.k8s.io/v1
metadata:
 name: gce-pd
provisioner: kubernetes.io/gce-pd
parameters:
 type: pd-standard
volumeBindingMode: WaitForFirstConsumer
allowedTopologies:
- matchLabelExpressions:
  - key: failure-domain.beta.kubernetes.io/zone
    values:
    - us-central1-a
    - us-central1-b
EOF
```

You can find the definition and use cases for different volume types on the *GCE PD volume types* link in the *See also* section.

On GKE clusters, the default PD volume type is `pd-standard`. For database workloads, such as MongoDB, Cassandra, and PostgreSQL, `pd-ssd-type`, high-performance SSDs are recommended.

4. List the storage classes:

```
$ kubectl get sc
NAME                      PROVISIONER                 AGE
gce-pd                    kubernetes.io/gce-pd        3s
standard (default)        kubernetes.io/gce-pd        17m
```

GKE comes with a default storage class called `standard`. You may have more than one storage class in your cluster. Ideally, storage classes should be created with an application's requirements in mind, since certain applications require faster volumes, while others may take advantage of multi-availability zone replication provided by other solutions.

Changing the default storage class

Dynamic storage provisioning is a key part of scaling applications. When a storage class is not specified by a PVC, Kubernetes uses the default option. Let's perform the following steps to set our preferred storage class as the default:

1. Let's create a new storage class and define it as the default option at the same time by setting `is-default-class` to `true`:

```
$ cat <<EOF | kubectl apply -f -
kind: StorageClass
apiVersion: storage.k8s.io/v1
metadata:
  name: gce-pd-ssd
  annotations:
    storageclass.kubernetes.io/is-default-class: "true"
provisioner: kubernetes.io/gce-pd
parameters:
  type: pd-ssd
reclaimPolicy: Retain
allowVolumeExpansion: true
volumeBindingMode: WaitForFirstConsumer
allowedTopologies:
- matchLabelExpressions:
  - key: failure-domain.beta.kubernetes.io/zone
```

```
        values:
        - us-central1-a
        - us-central1-b
    EOF
```

2. Having more than one default storage class will cause a problem. You need to remove one. To change the status of an existing storage class after it has been created, first pick a storage class:

```
$ kubectl get sc
NAME                     PROVISIONER AGE
gce-pd                   kubernetes.io/gce-pd 3m52s
gce-pd-ssd (default)     kubernetes.io/gce-pd 4s
standard (default)       kubernetes.io/gce-pd 21m
```

3. Let's set the standard and gce-pd-ssd storage classes as non-default:

```
$ kubectl patch storageclass standard -p '{"metadata":
{"annotations":{"storageclass.beta.kubernetes.io/is-default-
class":"false"}}}'
$ kubectl patch storageclass gce-pd-ssd -p '{"metadata":
{"annotations":{"storageclass.kubernetes.io/is-default-
class":"false"}}}'
```

4. Let's now define gce-pd as the default storage class again:

```
$ kubectl patch storageclass gce-pd -p '{"metadata":
{"annotations":{"storageclass.kubernetes.io/is-default-
class":"true"}}}'
```

5. Confirm the new default storage class:

```
$ kubectl get sc
NAME                    PROVISIONER            AGE
gce-pd (default)        kubernetes.io/gce-pd 8m25s
gce-pd-ssd              kubernetes.io/gce-pd 4m37s
standard                kubernetes.io/gce-pd 25m
```

Now you have learned how to replace the default storage class with a new storage class. Make sure that there is always one default storage class at a time; otherwise PVCs without a storage class defined that are expecting a default storage class will fail.

Using GCE PD volumes for persistent storage

As an alternative to creating PVCs and dynamically creating volumes, you can also create a volume manually and attach it to your application directly as a persistent volume by observing the following steps:

1. Create a GCE PD volume in the same zone as your worker nodes:

```
$ gcloud beta compute disks create gce-disk-1 --region us-central1 --
replica-zones us-central1-b,us-central1-c
Created
[https://www.googleapis.com/compute/beta/projects/devopscookbook/region
s/us-central1/disks/gce-disk-1].
NAME         ZONE SIZE_GB TYPE         STATUS
gce-disk-1        500     pd-standard READY
```

2. Create a PV using the existing volume name, gce-disk-1:

```
$ cat <<EOF | kubectl apply -f -
apiVersion: v1
kind: PersistentVolume
metadata:
  name: gce-disk-1
spec:
  storageClassName: ""
  capacity:
    storage: 500G
  accessModes:
    - ReadWriteOnce
  gcePersistentDisk:
    pdName: gce-disk-1
    fsType: ext4
EOF
```

3. Create a PVC using the PV name, gce-disk-1:

```
$ cat <<EOF | kubectl apply -f -
apiVersion: v1
kind: PersistentVolumeClaim
metadata:
  name: pvc-gcedisk1
spec:
```

```
        storageClassName: ""
        volumeName: gce-disk-1
        accessModes:
          - ReadWriteOnce
        resources:
          requests:
            storage: 500G
    EOF
```

4. Deploy a test application using the `volumeMounts` name, `gce-disk-1`, that you have created in *Step 1:*

```
$ cat <<EOF | kubectl apply -f -
apiVersion: v1
kind: Pod
metadata:
  name: test-server
spec:
  containers:
  - image: gcr.io/google_containers/test-webserver
    name: test-container
    volumeMounts:
    - mountPath: /test-ebs
      name: test-volume
  volumes:
  - name: test-volume
    persistentVolumeClaim:
      claimName: pvc-gcedisk1
EOF
```

5. Verify that your pod is in the `Running` state:

```
$ kubectl get pods
NAME            READY STATUS  RESTARTS AGE
test-server 1/1    Running 0         4m32s
```

The main advantage of manually created PVs is that PVs are not attached to a single cluster or namespace. They exist as a resource on your GCP account and they can even be shared across clusters. On the other hand, dynamically created PVCs only exist in the namespace created and can only be used by a pod within that same namespace.

Using GCE PD storage classes to create dynamic persistent volumes

As part of a StatefulSet, `volumeClaimTemplates` can provide persistent storage using `PersistentVolumes` provisioned by a `PersistentVolume` provisioner of your choice. In this recipe, we will use StorageClass to dynamically create PVs for your application:

1. Add the `gce-pd` storage class line under the `volumeClaimTemplates` section of your application deployment manifest, similar to the following example:

   ```
   ...
   volumeClaimTemplates:
   - metadata:
   name: datadir
   annotations:
   volume.beta.kubernetes.io/storage-class: gce-pd
   spec:
   accessModes: [ "ReadWriteOnce" ]
   resources:
   requests:
   storage: 1G
   ...
   ```

2. In this recipe, we will deploy the Redis Statefulset using the `gce-pd` storage class. Review the YAML manifest under the `src/chapter5/gcp` directory in the example repository before we execute it:

   ```
   $ cat gcp/redis-statefulset.yml
   ```

3. Create the Redis StatefulSet:

   ```
   $ kubectl apply -f redis-statefulset.yml
   ```

4. Verify that pods have been created:

   ```
   $ kubectl get pods
   NAME READY STATUS    RESTARTS AGE
   rd-0 1/1   Running 0         2m27s
   rd-1 1/1   Running 0         81s
   rd-2 0/1   Running 0         19s
   ```

5. List the PVCs and PVs created:

   ```
   $ kubectl get pvc, pv
   NAME STATUS VOLUME CAPACITY ACCESS MODES STORAGECLASS AGE
   datadir-rd-0 Bound pvc-3481b73c-d347-11e9-b514-42010a80005e 1Gi RWO
   ```

```
gce-pd 3m1s
datadir-rd-1 Bound pvc-5b8cc2d6-d347-11e9-b514-42010a80005e 1Gi RWO
gce-pd 115s
datadir-rd-2 Bound pvc-80d826b9-d347-11e9-b514-42010a80005e 1Gi RWO
gce-pd 53s
NAME CAPACITY ACCESS MODES RECLAIM POLICY STATUS CLAIM STORAGECLASS
REASON AGE
pvc-3481b73c-d347-11e9-b514-42010a80005e 1Gi RWO Delete Bound
default/datadir-rd-0 gce-pd 3m16s
pvc-5b8cc2d6-d347-11e9-b514-42010a80005e 1Gi RWO Delete Bound
default/datadir-rd-1 gce-pd 2m11s
pvc-80d826b9-d347-11e9-b514-42010a80005e 1Gi RWO Delete Bound
default/datadir-rd-2 gce-pd 68s
```

Now you know how to dynamically create GCE PD persistent volumes as part of your application deployment.

Deleting GCE PD persistent volumes

When the reclaim policy is set to retain the volumes, they need to be removed separately by observing the following steps:

1. Remember that deleting your workload will not remove the PVCs and PVs, unless a PVC manifest was included in the manifest:

```
$ kubectl delete -f redis-statefulset.yml
statefulset.apps "rd" deleted
service "redis" deleted
```

2. List the remaining PVs:

```
$ kubectl get pv
NAME CAPACITY ACCESS MODES RECLAIM POLICY STATUS CLAIM STORAGECLASS
REASON AGE
pvc-171fbee3-39bf-4450-961f-6c1417ff3897 1Gi RWO Retain Bound
default/datadir-rd-1 aws-gp2 13m
pvc-8a538aa3-7382-4147-adde-1ea3dbaaafb4 1Gi RWO Retain Bound
default/datadir-rd-0 aws-gp2 15m
pvc-b40df89b-5349-4f02-8510-917012579746 1Gi RWO Retain Bound
default/datadir-rd-2 aws-gp2 12m
```

3. Delete the PVCs. You can delete multiple PVCs at once by adding their names in a single command, similar to the following:

```
$ kubectl delete pvc datadir-rd-0 datadir-rd-1 datadir-rd-2
```

We have successfully removed all storage resources related to the application that was created as part of the Redis StatefulSet resource.

Installing the GCP Compute PD CSI driver to manage PD volumes

The GCP Compute PD CSI driver provides a Kubernetes CSI interface that allows GKE clusters to simply manage the life cycle of GKE volumes for persistent volumes. In this recipe, we will learn the steps required to install the GCP Compute PD CSI driver by observing the following steps:

1. Clone the GCP CSI driver project:

```
$ git clone
https://github.com/kubernetes-sigs/gcp-compute-persistent-disk-csi-driv
er.git
$ cd gcp-compute-persistent-disk-csi-driver/
```

2. Replace the PROJECT name with your GCP project name, GCE_PD_SA_DIR, in the location where your service account private key file is stored and set the GCP service account variables:

```
$ EXPORT PROJECT="DevOpsCookBook"
$ GCE_PD_SA_NAME=my-gce-pd-csi-sa
$ GCE_PD_SA_DIR=/my/safe/credentials/directory
$ ./deploy/setup-project.sh
```

3. Deploy the GCP Compute PD CSI driver:

```
$ GCE_PD_SA_DIR=/my/safe/credentials/directory
$ GCE_PD_DRIVER_VERSION=stable
$ ./deploy/kubernetes/deploy-driver.sh
```

4. Verify that the driver is running:

```
$ kubectl get pods -n kube-system | grep ebs-csi
csi-gce-pd-controller    4/4 Running 0 31s
csi-gce-pd-node-f8w8w    3/3 Running 0 31s
csi-gce-pd-node-g8qn5    3/3 Running 0 31s
csi-gce-pd-node-n2fhp    3/3 Running 0 31s
```

5. Now, create a new regional storage class using the `pd.csi.storage.gke.io` provisioner:

```
$ cat <<EOF | kubectl apply -f -
apiVersion: storage.k8s.io/v1
kind: StorageClass
metadata:
  name: gcp-csi-pd
provisioner: pd.csi.storage.gke.io
parameters:
  type: pd-standard
  replication-type: regional-pd
volumeBindingMode: WaitForFirstConsumer
EOF
```

6. Create a PVC:

```
$ cat <<EOF | kubectl apply -f -
apiVersion: v1
kind: PersistentVolumeClaim
metadata:
  name: csi-gcp-pd-pvc
spec:
  accessModes:
    - ReadWriteOnce
  storageClassName: gcp-csi-pd
  resources:
    requests:
      storage: 4Gi
EOF
```

7. Create a pod that will use the PVC and that writes to the `/data/out.txt` file:

```
$ cat <<EOF | kubectl apply -f -
apiVersion: v1
kind: Pod
metadata:
 name: mytestapp
spec:
 containers:
 - name: app
 image: centos
 command: ["/bin/sh"]
 args: ["-c", "while true; do echo $(date -u) >> /data/out.txt; sleep
5; done"]
 volumeMounts:
 - name: persistent-storage
 mountPath: /data
```

```
  volumes:
  - name: persistent-storage
  persistentVolumeClaim:
  claimName: csi-gcp-pd-pvc
EOF
```

8. Verify that our `mytestapp` pod writes data to the volume:

```
$ kubectl exec -it mytestapp cat /data/out.txt
Mon Sep 9 18:20:38 UTC 2019
```

9. Remove the resources:

```
$ kubectl delete pod mytestapp && kubectl delete pvc csi-gcp-pd-pvc
```

Now you know how to utilize a CSI driver to deploy GCE PD volumes on GKE clusters.

How it works...

This recipe showed you how to quickly provision a dynamic persistent volume using Kubernetes storage classes, and PVC and PV concepts.

In the *Creating a GCP persistent disk storage class* recipe, in *Step 3*, you created `gce-pd` storage classes by using the `allowedTopologies` parameter and set two GKE zones, `us-central1-a` and `us-central1-b`, under the values.

When `allowedTopologies` is defined in a storage class, GCP creates a regional persistent disk and replicates the data between two zones in the same region for higher availability.

Volumes that are created with this option also get labeled in a similar manner to the label here: `failure-domain.beta.kubernetes.io/region : us-central1` and `failure-domain.beta.kubernetes.io/region : us-central1-a`

Regional PDs help to survive a zonal outage. In that case, your Kubernetes cluster will failover workloads using the volume to the other zone.

This option is recommended when building highly available stateful workloads on GKE clusters.

See also

- GCE PD types: `https://cloud.google.com/persistent-disk/`
- GCE PD CSI driver repository: `https://github.com/kubernetes-sigs/gcp-compute-persistent-disk-csi-driver`

Managing Azure Disk volumes in Kubernetes

Azure Cloud provides persistent block-level storage volumes for use with **Azure Kubernetes Engine** (**AKS**). In this section, we will create storage classes for your applications in Kubernetes running in the AKS. You will learn how to create a StorageClass resource in Kubernetes, you will learn about the parameters available with the variation in performance of Azure Disk volume types, and you will also learn how to use the new CSI.

Getting ready

Clone the `k8sdevopscookbook/src` repository to your workstation in order to use manifest files under the `chapter5` directory:

```
$ git clone https://github.com/k8sdevopscookbook/src.git
$ cd src/chapter5
```

Make sure you have a regional GKE cluster ready and `kubectl` configured to manage the cluster resources.

How to do it...

This section is sub-divided further into the following subsections to facilitate the process:

- Creating an Azure Disk storage class
- Changing the default storage class to ZRS
- Using Azure Disk storage classes to create dynamic PVs
- Deleting Azure Disk persistent volumes
- Installing the Azure Disk CSI driver

Creating an Azure Disk storage class

Let's perform the following steps to learn the storage class parameters required to construct an Azure Disk storage class that we can use to dynamically request new persistent volumes from AKS:

1. AKS-based Kubernetes clusters are created with two locally redundant (LRS) storage classes by default. Let's list the storage classes on your AKS cluster:

```
$ kubectl get sc
NAME PROVISIONER AGE
default (default) kubernetes.io/azure-disk 13m
managed-premium kubernetes.io/azure-disk 13m
```

2. Describe the `default` storage class:

```
$ kubectl describe sc default
Name: default
IsDefaultClass: Yes
...
Provisioner: kubernetes.io/azure-disk
Parameters:
cachingmode=ReadOnly,kind=Managed,storageaccounttype=Standard_LRS
AllowVolumeExpansion: <unset>
MountOptions: <none>
ReclaimPolicy: Delete
VolumeBindingMode: Immediate
Events: <none>
```

3. Create a zone-redundant storage class with the provisioner, `kubernetes.io/azure-disk`, and the `Standard_ZRS` skuName specified:

```
$ cat <<EOF | kubectl apply -f -
kind: StorageClass
apiVersion: storage.k8s.io/v1
metadata:
  name: azure-zrs
provisioner: kubernetes.io/azure-disk
parameters:
  storageaccounttype: Standard_ZRS
  kind: Shared
reclaimPolicy: Retain
allowVolumeExpansion: true
volumeBindingMode: Immediate
EOF
```

You can find the definition and use cases for different volume types on the *Azure Disk volume types* link in the *See also* section.

 On Azure Cloud clusters, the default Azure Disk volume type is `Standard_LRS`. For database workloads, such as MongoDB, Cassandra, and PostgreSQL, `Premium_LRS`-type, high-performance SSDs are recommended.

4. List the storage classes:

```
$ kubectl get sc
NAME                     PROVISIONER                 AGE
azure-zrs                kubernetes.io/azure-disk 4s
default (default)        kubernetes.io/azure-disk 18m
managed-premium          kubernetes.io/azure-disk 18m
```

As you can see in our example, AKS clusters come with two predefined storage classes.

Changing the default storage class to ZRS

Dynamic storage provisioning is a key part of scaling applications. When a storage class is not specified by a PVC, Kubernetes uses the default option. Let's perform the following steps to set our preferred storage class as the default:

1. Let's set the existing `default` storage class as the non-default option:

```
$ kubectl patch storageclass default -p '{"metadata":
{"annotations":{"storageclass.beta.kubernetes.io/is-default-
class":"false"}}}'
```

2. Now, define `azure-zrs` as the default storage class again:

```
$ kubectl patch storageclass azure-zrs -p '{"metadata":
{"annotations":{"storageclass.kubernetes.io/is-default-
class":"true"}}}'
```

3. Confirm the new default storage class. You should see new `azure-zrs` as the default, similar to the following output:

```
$ kubectl get sc
NAME                     PROVISIONER AGE
azure-zrs (default)      kubernetes.io/azure-disk 4m38s
default                  kubernetes.io/azure-disk 23m
managed-premium          kubernetes.io/azure-disk 23m
```

Now you know how to set your preferred storage class as the default on your AKS cluster.

Using Azure Disk storage classes to create dynamic PVs

As part of a StatefulSet, `volumeClaimTemplates` can provide persistent storage using `PersistentVolumes` provisioned by a `PersistentVolume` provisioner of your choice. In this recipe, we will use the Azure storage class to dynamically create PVs for your application:

1. Add the `azure-zrs` storage class line under the `volumeClaimTemplates` section of your application deployment manifest, similar to the following example:

```
...
volumeClaimTemplates:
- metadata:
    name: datadir
    annotations:
      volume.beta.kubernetes.io/storage-class: azure-zrs
  spec:
    accessModes: [ "ReadWriteOnce" ]
    resources:
      requests:
        storage: 1G
...
```

2. In this recipe, we will deploy Redis Statefulset using the `azure-zrs` storage class. Review the YAML manifest under the `src/chapter5/azure` directory in the example repository before we execute it:

```
$ cat azure/redis-statefulset.yml
```

3. Create the Redis StatefulSet:

```
$ kubectl apply -f redis-statefulset.yml
```

4. Verify that pods have been created. In this recipe, our example has StatefulSet with three replicas. As a result, you should see three replicas running, similar to the following output:

```
$ kubectl get pods
NAME READY STATUS    RESTARTS AGE
rd-0 1/1   Running 0          6m24s
```

```
rd-1 1/1   Running 0      4m14s
rd-2 1/1   Running 0      2m13s
```

5. List the PVCs and PVs created. You should expect to see three PVCs and three PVs created, similar to our example output here:

```
$ kubectl get pvc, pv
NAME STATUS VOLUME CAPACITY ACCESS MODES STORAGECLASS AGE
datadir-rd-0 Bound pvc-afaafb97-d376-11e9-88a2-a2c82783dcda 1Gi RWO
azure-zrs 4m31s
datadir-rd-1 Bound pvc-fc9f3a35-d376-11e9-88a2-a2c82783dcda 1Gi RWO
azure-zrs 2m22s
datadir-rd-2 Bound pvc-453d185d-d377-11e9-88a2-a2c82783dcda 1Gi RWO
azure-zrs 20s
NAME CAPACITY ACCESS MODES RECLAIM POLICY STATUS CLAIM STORAGECLASS
REASON AGE
pvc-453d185d-d377-11e9-88a2-a2c82783dcda 1Gi RWO Delete Bound
default/datadir-rd-2 azure-zrs 22s
pvc-afaafb97-d376-11e9-88a2-a2c82783dcda 1Gi RWO Delete Bound
default/datadir-rd-0 azure-zrs 4m42s
pvc-fc9f3a35-d376-11e9-88a2-a2c82783dcda 1Gi RWO Delete Bound
default/datadir-rd-1 azure-zrs 2m38s
```

Now you know how to dynamically create persistent volumes as part of your application deployment on AKS clusters.

Deleting Azure Disk persistent volumes

When the reclaim policy is set to retain the volumes, they need to be removed separately by observing the following steps:

1. Remember that deleting your workload will not remove the PVCs and PVs unless the PVC manifest was included in the manifest:

```
$ kubectl delete -f redis-statefulset.yml
statefulset.apps "rd" deleted
service "redis" deleted
```

2. List the remaining PVs:

```
$ kubectl get pv
NAME CAPACITY ACCESS MODES RECLAIM POLICY STATUS CLAIM STORAGECLASS
REASON AGE
pvc-171fbee3-39bf-4450-961f-6c1417ff3897 1Gi RWO Retain Bound
default/datadir-rd-1 aws-gp2 13m
pvc-8a538aa3-7382-4147-adde-1ea3dbaaafb4 1Gi RWO Retain Bound
```

```
default/datadir-rd-0 aws-gp2 15m
pvc-b40df89b-5349-4f02-8510-917012579746 1Gi RWO Retain Bound
default/datadir-rd-2 aws-gp2 12m
```

3. Delete the PVCs. You can delete multiple PVCs at once by adding their names in a single command, similar to the following:

```
$ kubectl delete pvc datadir-rd-0 datadir-rd-1 datadir-rd-2
```

We have now successfully removed all storage resources related to the application that was created as part of the Redis StatefulSet resource.

Installing the Azure Disk CSI driver

The Azure Disk CSI driver provides a Kubernetes CSI that allows AKS clusters to simply manage the life cycle of Azure Disk volumes for persistent volumes. In this recipe, we will learn the steps required to install the Azure Disk CSI driver by observing the following steps:

1. Deploy the Azure Disk CSI driver:

```
$ kubectl apply -f
https://raw.githubusercontent.com/kubernetes-sigs/azuredisk-csi-driver/
master/deploy/crd-csi-driver-registry.yaml
$ kubectl apply -f
https://raw.githubusercontent.com/kubernetes-sigs/azuredisk-csi-driver/
master/deploy/crd-csi-node-info.yaml
$ kubectl apply -f
https://raw.githubusercontent.com/kubernetes-sigs/azuredisk-csi-driver/
master/deploy/rbac-csi-azuredisk-controller.yaml
$ kubectl apply -f
https://raw.githubusercontent.com/kubernetes-sigs/azuredisk-csi-driver/
master/deploy/csi-azuredisk-controller.yaml
$ kubectl apply -f
https://raw.githubusercontent.com/kubernetes-sigs/azuredisk-csi-driver/
master/deploy/csi-azuredisk-node.yaml
```

2. Verify that the driver is running that controller and that the `azuredisk-node` DaemonSet is running:

```
$ kubectl get po -o wide -n kube-system | grep csi-azuredisk
csi-azuredisk-controller-9bc7f4d77-cbgxs 6/6 Running 0 5m31s 10.244.2.4
aks-agentpool-40109510-2 <none> <none>
csi-azuredisk-node-7kqzm 3/3 Running 0 5m27s 10.240.0.5 aks-
agentpool-40109510-1 <none> <none>
csi-azuredisk-node-gm6dr 3/3 Running 0 5m27s 10.240.0.4 aks-
```

```
agentpool-40109510-2 <none> <none>
csi-azuredisk-node-wqsls 3/3 Running 0 5m27s 10.240.0.6 aks-
agentpool-40109510-0 <none> <none>
```

3. Now, create a new storage class:

```
$ cat <<EOF | kubectl apply -f -
apiVersion: storage.k8s.io/v1
kind: StorageClass
metadata:
  name: disk.csi.azure.com
provisioner: disk.csi.azure.com
parameters:
  skuname: Standard_LRS
  kind: managed
  cachingMode: ReadOnly
reclaimPolicy: Delete
volumeBindingMode: Immediate
EOF
```

4. Create a PVC using the storage class name, `disk.csi.azure.com`:

```
cat <<EOF | kubectl apply -f -
apiVersion: v1
kind: PersistentVolumeClaim
metadata:
  name: csi-azure-pvc
spec:
  accessModes:
    - ReadWriteOnce
  storageClassName: disk.csi.azure.com
  resources:
    requests:
      storage: 4Gi
EOF
```

5. Create a pod that will use the `csi-azure-pvc` PVC and that writes to the `/data/out.txt` file:

```
$ cat <<EOF | kubectl apply -f -
apiVersion: v1
kind: Pod
metadata:
 name: mytestapp
spec:
 containers:
 - name: app
  image: centos
```

```
command: ["/bin/sh"]
args: ["-c", "while true; do echo $(date -u) >> /data/out.txt; sleep
5; done"]
volumeMounts:
- name: persistent-storage
mountPath: /data
volumes:
- name: persistent-storage
persistentVolumeClaim:
claimName: csi-azure-pvc
EOF
```

6. Verify that our `mytestapp` pod writes data to the volume:

```
$ kubectl exec -it mytestapp cat /data/out.txt
Mon Sep 9 19:23:29 UTC 2019
```

Now you know how to use the Azure Disk CSI driver to provision persistent volumes on your AKS clusters.

See also

- Azure Disk volume types: `https://azure.microsoft.com/en-us/pricing/details/managed-disks/`
- AWS EBS CSI driver repository: `https://github.com/kubernetes-sigs/azuredisk-csi-driver`

Configuring and managing persistent storage using Rook

Rook is a cloud-native, open source storage orchestrator for Kubernetes. Rook provides self-managing, self-scaling, and self-healing distributed storage systems in Kubernetes. In this section, we will create multiple storage providers using the Rook storage orchestrator for your applications in Kubernetes. You will learn to create a Ceph provider for your stateful applications that require persistent storage.

Getting ready

Make sure that you have a Kubernetes cluster ready and `kubectl` configured to manage the cluster resources.

How to do it...

This section is sub-divided further into the following subsections to facilitate the process:

- Installing a Ceph provider using Rook
- Creating a Ceph cluster
- Verifying a Ceph cluster's health
- Create a Ceph block storage class
- Using a Ceph block storage class to create dynamic PVs

Installing a Ceph provider using Rook

Let's perform the following steps to get a Ceph scale-out storage solution up and running using the Rook project:

1. Clone the Rook repository:

```
$ git clone https://github.com/rook/rook.git
$ cd rook/cluster/examples/kubernetes/ceph/
```

2. Deploy the Rook Operator:

```
$ kubectl create -f common.yaml
$ kubectl create -f operator.yaml
```

3. Verify the Rook Operator:

```
$ kubectl get pod -n rook-ceph
NAME                                    READY STATUS   RESTARTS AGE
rook-ceph-operator-6b66859964-vnrfx 1/1     Running 0        2m12s
rook-discover-8snpm                     1/1   Running 0        97s
rook-discover-mcx9q                     1/1   Running 0        97s
rook-discover-mdg2s                     1/1   Running 0        97s
```

Now you have learned how to deploy the Rook orchestration components for the Ceph provider running on Kubernetes.

Creating a Ceph cluster

Let's perform the following steps to deploy a Ceph cluster using the Rook Operator:

1. Create a Ceph cluster:

```
$ cat <<EOF | kubectl apply -f -
apiVersion: ceph.rook.io/v1
kind: CephCluster
metadata:
  name: rook-ceph
  namespace: rook-ceph
spec:
  cephVersion:
    image: ceph/ceph:v14.2.3-20190904
  dataDirHostPath: /var/lib/rook
  mon:
    count: 3
  dashboard:
    enabled: true
  storage:
    useAllNodes: true
    useAllDevices: false
    directories:
    - path: /var/lib/rook
EOF
```

2. Verify that all pods are running:

```
$ kubectl get pod -n rook-ceph
```

Within a minute, a fully functional Ceph cluster will be deployed and ready to be used. You can read more about Ceph in the *Rook Ceph Storage Documentation* link in the *See also* section.

Verifying a Ceph cluster's health

The Rook toolbox is a container with common tools used for rook debugging and testing. Let's perform the following steps to deploy the Rook toolbox to verify cluster health:

1. Deploy the Rook toolbox:

```
$ kubectl apply -f toolbox.yaml
```

2. Verify that the toolbox is running:

```
$ kubectl -n rook-ceph get pod -l "app=rook-ceph-tools"
NAME                                READY STATUS    RESTARTS AGE
rook-ceph-tools-6fdfc54b6d-4kdtm 1/1    Running 0          109s
```

3. Connect to the toolbox:

```
$ kubectl -n rook-ceph exec -it $(kubectl -n rook-ceph get pod -l
"app=rook-ceph-tools" -o jsonpath='{.items[0].metadata.name}') bash
```

4. Verify that the cluster is in a healthy state (HEALTH_OK):

```
# ceph status
  cluster:
    id: 6b6e4bfb-bfef-46b7-94bd-9979e5e8bf04
    health: HEALTH_OK
  services:
    mon: 3 daemons, quorum a,b,c (age 12m)
    mgr: a(active, since 12m)
    osd: 3 osds: 3 up (since 11m), 3 in (since 11m)
  data:
    pools: 0 pools, 0 pgs
    objects: 0 objects, 0 B
    usage: 49 GiB used, 241 GiB / 291 GiB avail
    pgs:
```

5. When you are finished troubleshooting, remove the deployment using the following command:

```
$ kubectl -n rook-ceph delete deployment rook-ceph-tools
```

Now you know how to deploy the Rook toolbox with its common tools that are used to debug and test Rook.

Create a Ceph block storage class

Let's perform the following steps to create a storage class for Ceph storage.:

1. Create CephBlockPool:

```
$ cat <<EOF | kubectl apply -f -
apiVersion: ceph.rook.io/v1
kind: CephBlockPool
metadata:
```

```
    name: replicapool
    namespace: rook-ceph
  spec:
    failureDomain: host
    replicated:
      size: 3
  EOF
```

2. Create a Rook Ceph block storage class:

```
$ cat <<EOF | kubectl apply -f -
apiVersion: storage.k8s.io/v1
kind: StorageClass
metadata:
    name: rook-ceph-block
provisioner: rook-ceph.rbd.csi.ceph.com
parameters:
    clusterID: rook-ceph
    pool: replicapool
    imageFormat: "2"
    imageFeatures: layering
    csi.storage.k8s.io/provisioner-secret-name: rook-ceph-csi
    csi.storage.k8s.io/provisioner-secret-namespace: rook-ceph
    csi.storage.k8s.io/node-stage-secret-name: rook-ceph-csi
    csi.storage.k8s.io/node-stage-secret-namespace: rook-ceph
    csi.storage.k8s.io/fstype: xfs
reclaimPolicy: Delete
EOF
```

3. Confirm that the storage class has been created:

```
$ kubectl get sc
NAME                PROVISIONER                 AGE
default (default) kubernetes.io/azure-disk    6h27m
rook-ceph-block    rook-ceph.rbd.csi.ceph.com 3s
```

As you can see from the preceding provisioner name, `rook-ceph.rbd.csi.ceph.com`,
Rook also uses CSI to interact with Kubernetes APIs. This driver is optimized for RWO pod
access where only one pod may access the storage.

Using a Ceph block storage class to create dynamic PVs

In this recipe, we will deploy Wordpress using dynamic persistent volumes created by the Rook Ceph block storage provider. Let's perform the following steps:

1. Clone the examples repository:

```
$ git clone https://github.com/k8sdevopscookbook/src.git
$ cd src/chapter5/rook/
```

2. Review both `mysql.yaml` and `wordpress.yaml`. Note that PVCs are using the `rook-ceph-block` storage class:

```
$ cat mysql.yaml && cat wordpress.yaml
```

3. Deploy MySQL and WordPress:

```
$ kubectl apply -f mysql.yaml
$ kubectl apply -f wordpress.yaml
```

4. Confirm the persistent volumes created:

```
$ kubectl get pv
NAME CAPACITY ACCESS MODES RECLAIM POLICY STATUS CLAIM STORAGECLASS
REASON AGE
pvc-eb2d23b8-d38a-11e9-88a2-a2c82783dcda 20Gi RWO Delete Bound
default/mysql-pv-claim rook-ceph-block 38s
pvc-eeab1ebc-d38a-11e9-88a2-a2c82783dcda 20Gi RWO Delete Bound
default/wp-pv-claim rook-ceph-block 38s
```

5. Get the external IP of the WordPress service:

```
$ kubectl get service
NAME                 TYPE          CLUSTER-IP    EXTERNAL-IP   PORT(S)       AGE
kubernetes           ClusterIP     10.0.0.1      <none>        443/TCP
6h34m
wordpress            LoadBalancer  10.0.102.14   13.64.96.240  80:30596/TCP
3m36s
wordpress-mysql      ClusterIP     None          <none>        3306/TCP
3m42s
```

6. Open the external IP of the WordPress service in your browser to access your Wordpress deployment:

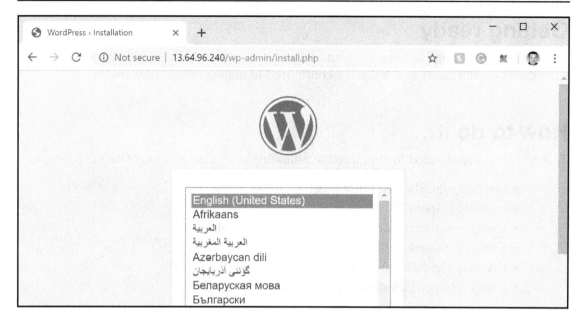

Now you know how to get the popular WordPress service, with persistent storage stored on Rook-based Ceph storage, up and running.

See also

- Rook documentation: `https://rook.io/docs/rook/master/`
- Rook Ceph storage documentation: `https://rook.io/docs/rook/master/ceph-storage.html`
- Rook community slack channel: `https://slack.rook.io/`

Configuring and managing persistent storage using OpenEBS

OpenEBS is a popular open source, cloud-native storage (CNS) project with a large community. In this section, we will install an OpenEBS persistent storage provider. You will learn how to create volumes using different types of storage engine options for stateful workloads on Kubernetes.

Getting ready

For this recipe, we need to have `helm` and `kubectl` installed. Make sure you have a Kubernetes cluster ready and `kubectl` configured to manage the cluster resources.

How to do it...

This section is sub-divided further into the following subsections to facilitate the process:

- Installing iSCSI client prerequisites
- Installing OpenEBS
- Using ephemeral storage to create persistent volumes
- Creating storage pools
- Creating OpenEBS storage classes
- Using an OpenEBS storage class to create dynamic PVs

Installing iSCSI client prerequisites

The OpenEBS storage provider requires that the iSCSI client runs on all worker nodes:

1. On all your worker nodes, follow the steps to install and enable `open-iscsi`:

```
$ sudo apt-get update && sudo apt-get install open-iscsi && sudo
service open-iscsi restart
```

2. Validate that the iSCSI service is running:

```
$ systemctl status iscsid
● iscsid.service – iSCSI initiator daemon (iscsid)
   Loaded: loaded (/lib/systemd/system/iscsid.service; enabled; vendor
preset: enabled)
   Active: active (running) since Sun 2019-09-08 07:40:43 UTC; 7s ago
     Docs: man:iscsid(8)
```

3. If the service status is showing as inactive, then enable and start the iscsid service:

```
$ sudo systemctl enable iscsid && sudo systemctl start iscsid
```

After installing the iSCSI service, you are ready to install OpenEBS on your cluster.

Installing OpenEBS

Let's perform the following steps to quickly get the OpenEBS control plane installed:

1. Install OpenEBS services by using the operator:

    ```
    $ kubectl apply -f
    https://openebs.github.io/charts/openebs-operator.yaml
    ```

2. Confirm that all OpenEBS pods are running:

    ```
    $ kubectl get pods --namespace openebs
    NAME                                          READY STATUS   RESTARTS AGE
    maya-apiserver-dcbc87f7f-k99fz                0/1   Running  0        88s
    openebs-admission-server-585c6588d-j29ng      1/1   Running  0        88s
    openebs-localpv-provisioner-cfbd49877-jzjxl   1/1   Running  0        87s
    openebs-ndm-fcss7                             1/1   Running  0        88s
    openebs-ndm-m4qm5                             1/1   Running  0        88s
    openebs-ndm-operator-bc76c6ddc-4kvxp          1/1   Running  0        88s
    openebs-ndm-vt76c                             1/1   Running  0        88s
    openebs-provisioner-57bbbd888d-jb94v          1/1   Running  0        88s
    openebs-snapshot-operator-7dd598c655-2ck74    2/2   Running  0        88s
    ```

OpenEBS consists of the core components listed here. Node Disk Manager (NDM) is one of the important pieces of OpenEBS that is responsible for detecting disk changes and runs as DaemonSet on your worker nodes.

Using ephemeral storage to create persistent volumes

OpenEBS currently provides three storage engine options (Jiva, cStor, and LocalPV). The first storage engine option, `Jiva`, can create replicated storage on top of the ephemeral storage. Let's perform the following steps to get storage using ephemeral storage configured:

1. List the default storage classes:

    ```
    $ kubectl get sc
    NAME                    PROVISIONER
    AGE
    openebs-device          openebs.io/local
    25m
    openebs-hostpath        openebs.io/local
    25m
    openebs-jiva-default    openebs.io/provisioner-iscsi
    25m
    ```

```
openebs-snapshot-promoter volumesnapshot.external-
storage.k8s.io/snapshot-promoter 25m
```

2. Describe the `openebs-jiva-default` storage class:

```
$ kubectl describe sc openebs-jiva-default
Name: openebs-jiva-default
IsDefaultClass: No
Annotations: cas.openebs.io/config=- name: ReplicaCount
  value: "3"
- name: StoragePool
  value: default
```

3. Create a persistent volume claim using `openebs-jiva-default`:

```
$ cat <<EOF | kubectl apply -f -
kind: PersistentVolumeClaim
apiVersion: v1
metadata:
  name: demo-vol1-claim
spec:
  storageClassName: openebs-jiva-default
  accessModes:
    - ReadWriteOnce
  resources:
    requests:
      storage: 5G
EOF
```

4. Confirm that the PVC status is BOUND:

```
$ kubectl get pvc
NAME STATUS VOLUME CAPACITY ACCESS MODES STORAGECLASS AGE
demo-vol1-claim Bound pvc-cb7485bc-6d45-4814-adb1-e483c0ebbeb5 5G RWO
openebs-jiva-default 4s
```

5. Now, use the PVC to dynamically provision a persistent volume:

```
$ kubectl apply -f
https://raw.githubusercontent.com/openebs/openebs/master/k8s/demo/perco
na/percona-openebs-deployment.yaml
```

6. Now list the pods and make sure that your workload, OpenEBS controller, and replicas are all in the running state:

```
$ kubectl get pods
NAME                                                         READY
STATUS   RESTARTS AGE
```

```
percona-767db88d9d-2s8np                                            1/1
Running 0              75s
pvc-cb7485bc-6d45-4814-adb1-e483c0ebbeb5-ctrl-54d7fd794-s8svt 2/2
Running 0              2m23s
pvc-cb7485bc-6d45-4814-adb1-e483c0ebbeb5-rep-647458f56f-2b9q4 1/1
Running 1              2m18s
pvc-cb7485bc-6d45-4814-adb1-e483c0ebbeb5-rep-647458f56f-nkbfq 1/1
Running 0              2m18s
pvc-cb7485bc-6d45-4814-adb1-e483c0ebbeb5-rep-647458f56f-x7s9b 1/1
Running 0              2m18s
```

Now you know how to get highly available, cloud-native storage configured for your stateful applications on Kubernetes.

Creating storage pools

In this recipe, we will use raw block devices attached to your nodes to create a storage pool. These devices can be AWS EBS volumes, GCP PDs, Azure Disk, virtual disks, or vSAN volumes. Devices can be attached to your worker node VMs, or basically physical disks if you are using a bare-metal Kubernetes cluster. Let's perform the following steps to create a storage pool out of raw block devices:

1. List unused and unclaimed block devices on your nodes:

```
$ kubectl get blockdevices -n openebs
NAME NODENAME SIZE CLAIMSTATE STATUS AGE
blockdevice-24d9b7652893384a36d0cc34a804c60c ip-172-23-1-176.us-
west-2.compute.internal 107374182400 Unclaimed Active 52s
blockdevice-8ef1fd7e30cf0667476dba97975d5ac9 ip-172-23-1-25.us-
west-2.compute.internal 107374182400 Unclaimed Active 51s
blockdevice-94e7c768ef098a74f3e2c7fed6d82a5f ip-172-23-1-253.us-
west-2.compute.internal 107374182400 Unclaimed Active 52s
```

In our example, we have a three-node Kubernetes cluster on AWS EC2 with one additional EBS volume attached to each node.

2. Create a storage pool using the unclaimed devices from *Step 1*:

```
$ cat <<EOF | kubectl apply -f -
apiVersion: openebs.io/v1alpha1
kind: StoragePoolClaim
metadata:
  name: cstor-disk-pool
  annotations:
    cas.openebs.io/config: |
      - name: PoolResourceRequests
```

```
        value: |-
            memory: 2Gi
      - name: PoolResourceLimits
        value: |-
            memory: 4Gi
  spec:
    name: cstor-disk-pool
    type: disk
    poolSpec:
      poolType: striped
    blockDevices:
      blockDeviceList:
      - blockdevice-24d9b7652893384a36d0cc34a804c60c
      - blockdevice-8ef1fd7e30cf0667476dba97975d5ac9
      - blockdevice-94e7c768ef098a74f3e2c7fed6d82a5f
  EOF
```

3. List the storage pool claims:

```
$ kubectl get spc
NAME AGE
cstor-disk-pool 29s
```

4. Verify that a cStor pool has been created and that its status is `Healthy`:

```
$ kubectl get csp
NAME                    ALLOCATED  FREE   CAPACITY  STATUS   TYPE     AGE
cstor-disk-pool-8fnp 270K         99.5G  99.5G     Healthy  striped  3m9s
cstor-disk-pool-nsy6 270K         99.5G  99.5G     Healthy  striped  3m9s
cstor-disk-pool-v6ue 270K         99.5G  99.5G     Healthy  striped  3m10s
```

5. Now we can use the storage pool in storage classes to provision dynamic volumes.

Creating OpenEBS storage classes

Let's perform the following steps to create a new storage class to consume StoragePool, which we created previously in the *Creating storage pools* recipe:

1. Create an OpenEBS cStor storage class using the cStor `StoragePoolClaim` name, `cstor-disk-pool`, with three replicas:

```
$ cat <<EOF | kubectl apply -f -
apiVersion: storage.k8s.io/v1
kind: StorageClass
metadata:
```

```
    name: openebs-cstor-default
    annotations:
      openebs.io/cas-type: cstor
      cas.openebs.io/config: |
        - name: StoragePoolClaim
          value: "cstor-disk-pool"
        - name: ReplicaCount
          value: "3"
  provisioner: openebs.io/provisioner-iscsi
  EOF
```

2. List the storage classes:

```
$ kubectl get sc
NAME                    PROVISIONER                 AGE
default                 kubernetes.io/aws-ebs       25m
gp2 (default)           kubernetes.io/aws-ebs       25m
openebs-cstor-default openebs.io/provisioner-iscsi 6s
openebs-device          openebs.io/local            20m
openebs-hostpath        openebs.io/local            20m
openebs-jiva-default    openebs.io/provisioner-iscsi 20m
openebs-snapshot-promoter volumesnapshot.external-
storage.k8s.io/snapshot-promoter 20m
ubun
```

3. Set the gp2 AWS EBS storage class as the non-default option:

```
$ kubectl patch storageclass gp2 -p '{"metadata":
{"annotations":{"storageclass.beta.kubernetes.io/is-default-
class":"false"}}}'
```

4. Define openebs-cstor-default as the default storage class:

```
$ kubectl patch storageclass openebs-cstor-default -p '{"metadata":
{"annotations":{"storageclass.kubernetes.io/is-default-
class":"true"}}}'
```

Make sure that the previous storage class is no longer set as the default and that you only have one default storage class.

Using an OpenEBS storage class to create dynamic PVs

Let's perform the following steps to deploy dynamically created persistent volumes using the OpenEBS storage provider:

1. Clone the examples repository:

```
$ git clone https://github.com/k8sdevopscookbook/src.git
$ cd src/chapter5/openebs/
```

2. Review `minio.yaml` and note that PVCs are using the `openebs-stor-default` storage class.

3. Deploy Minio:

```
$ kubectl apply -f minio.yaml
deployment.apps/minio-deployment created
persistentvolumeclaim/minio-pv-claim created
service/minio-service created
```

4. Get the Minio service load balancer's external IP:

```
$ kubectl get service
NAME TYPE CLUSTER-IP EXTERNAL-IP PORT(S) AGE
kubernetes ClusterIP 10.3.0.1 <none> 443/TCP 54m
minio-service LoadBalancer 10.3.0.29
adb3bdaa893984515b9527ca8f2f8ca6-1957771474.us-west-2.elb.
amazonaws.com 9000:32701/TCP 3s
```

5. Add port `9000` to the end of the address and open the external IP of the Minio service in your browser:

6. Use the username `minio`, and the password `minio123` to log in to the Minio deployment backed by persistent OpenEBS volumes:

You have now successfully deployed a stateful application that is deployed on the OpenEBS cStor storage engine.

How it works...

This recipe showed you how to quickly provision a persistent storage provider using OpenEBS.

In the *Using ephemeral storage to create persistent volumes* recipe, in *Step 6*, when we deployed a workload using the `openebs-jiva-default` storage class, OpenEBS launched OpenEBS volumes with three replicas.

To set one replica, as is the case with a single-node Kubernetes cluster, you can create a new storage class (similar to the one we created in the *Creating OpenEBS storage class* recipe) and set the `ReplicaCount` variable value to 1:

```
apiVersion: openebs.io/v1alpha1
kind: StoragePool
metadata:
  name: my-pool
  type: hostdir
spec:
  path: "/my/openebs/folder"
```

When ephemeral storage is used, the OpenEBS Jiva storage engine uses the `/var/openebs` directory on every available node to create replica sparse files. If you would like to change the default or create a new StoragePool resource, you can create a new storage pool and set a custom path.

See also

- OpenEBS documentation: `https://docs.openebs.io/`
- Beyond the basics: OpenEBS workshop: `https://github.com/openebs/community/tree/master/workshop`
- OpenEBS Community Slack channel: `https://openebs.io/join-our-slack-community`
- OpenEBS enterprise platform: `https://mayadata.io/product`
- OpenEBS director for managing stateful workloads: `https://account.mayadata.io/login`

Setting up NFS for shared storage on Kubernetes

Although it's not the best-performing solution, NFS is still used with cloud-native applications where multi-node write access is required. In this section, we will create an NFS-based persistent storage for this type of application. You will learn how to use OpenEBS and Rook to **ReadWriteMany** (**RWX**) accessible persistent volumes for stateful workloads that require shared storage on Kubernetes.

Getting ready

For this recipe, we need to have either `rook` or `openebs` installed as an orchestrator. Make sure that you have a Kubernetes cluster ready and `kubectl` configured to manage the cluster resources.

How to do it...

There are two popular alternatives when it comes to providing an NFS service. This section is sub-divided further into the following subsections to explain the process using Rook and OpenEBS:

- Installing NFS prerequisites
- Installing an NFS provider using a Rook NFS operator
- Using a Rook NFS operator storage class to create dynamic NFS PVs

- Installing an NFS provider using OpenEBS
- Using the OpenEBS operator storage class to create dynamic NFS PVs

Installing NFS prerequisites

To be able to mount NFS volumes, NFS client packages need to be preinstalled on all worker nodes where you plan to have NFS-mounted pods:

1. If you are using Ubuntu, install nfs-common on all worker nodes:

```
$ sudo apt install -y nfs-common
```

2. If using CentOS, install nfs-common on all worker nodes:

```
$ yum install nfs-utils
```

Now we have nfs-utils installed on our worker nodes and are ready to get the NFS server to deploy.

Installing an NFS provider using a Rook NFS operator

Let's perform the following steps to get an NFS provider functional using the Rook NFS provider option:

1. Clone the Rook repository:

```
$ git clone https://github.com/rook/rook.git
$ cd rook/cluster/examples/kubernetes/nfs/
```

2. Deploy the Rook NFS operator:

```
$ kubectl create -f operator.yaml
```

3. Confirm that the operator is running:

```
$ kubectl get pods -n rook-nfs-system
NAME READY STATUS RESTARTS AGE
rook-nfs-operator-54cf68686c-f66f5 1/1 Running 0 51s
rook-nfs-provisioner-79fbdc79bb-hf9rn 1/1 Running 0 51s
```

4. Create a namespace, rook-nfs:

```
$ cat <<EOF | kubectl apply -f -
apiVersion: v1
kind: Namespace
```

```
    metadata:
      name: rook-nfs
    EOF
```

5. Make sure that you have defined your preferred storage provider as the default storage class. In this recipe, we are using `openebs-cstor-default`, defined in persistent storage using the OpenEBS recipe.

6. Create a PVC:

```
$ cat <<EOF | kubectl apply -f -
apiVersion: v1
kind: PersistentVolumeClaim
metadata:
  name: nfs-default-claim
  namespace: rook-nfs
spec:
  accessModes:
  - ReadWriteMany
  resources:
    requests:
      storage: 1Gi
EOF
```

7. Create the NFS instance:

```
$ cat <<EOF | kubectl apply -f -
apiVersion: nfs.rook.io/v1alpha1
kind: NFSServer
metadata:
  name: rook-nfs
  namespace: rook-nfs
spec:
  serviceAccountName: rook-nfs
  replicas: 1
  exports:
  - name: share1
    server:
      accessMode: ReadWrite
      squash: "none"
    persistentVolumeClaim:
      claimName: nfs-default-claim
  annotations:
  # key: value
EOF
```

8. Verify that the NFS pod is in the `Running` state:

```
$ kubectl get pod -l app=rook-nfs -n rook-nfs
NAME           READY   STATUS   RESTARTS  AGE
rook-nfs-0 1/1         Running 0          2m
```

By observing the preceding command, an NFS server instance type will be created.

Using a Rook NFS operator storage class to create dynamic NFS PVs

NFS is used in the Kubernetes environment on account of its `ReadWriteMany` capabilities for the application that requires access to the same data at the same time. In this recipe, we will perform the following steps to dynamically create an NFS-based persistent volume:

1. Create Rook NFS storage classes using `exportName`, `nfsServerName`, and `nfsServerNamespace` from the *Installing an NFS provider using a Rook NFS operator* recipe:

```
$ cat <<EOF | kubectl apply -f -
apiVersion: storage.k8s.io/v1
kind: StorageClass
metadata:
  labels:
    app: rook-nfs
  name: rook-nfs-share1
parameters:
  exportName: share1
  nfsServerName: rook-nfs
  nfsServerNamespace: rook-nfs
provisioner: rook.io/nfs-provisioner
reclaimPolicy: Delete
volumeBindingMode: Immediate
EOF
```

2. Now, you can use the `rook-nfs-share1` storage class to create PVCs for applications that require `ReadWriteMany` access:

```
$ cat <<EOF | kubectl apply -f -
apiVersion: v1
kind: PersistentVolumeClaim
metadata:
  name: rook-nfs-pv-claim
spec:
  storageClassName: "rook-nfs-share1"
```

```
        accessModes:
          - ReadWriteMany
        resources:
          requests:
            storage: 1Mi
    EOF
```

By observing the preceding command, an NFS PV will be created.

Installing an NFS provisioner using OpenEBS

OpenEBS provides an NFS provisioner that is protected by the underlying storage engine options of OpenEBS. Let's perform the following steps to get an NFS service with OpenEBS up and running:

1. Clone the examples repository:

    ```
    $ git clone https://github.com/k8sdevopscookbook/src.git
    $ cd src/chapter5/openebs
    ```

2. In this recipe, we are using the `openebs-jiva-default` storage class. Review the directory content and apply the `YAML` file under the NFS directory:

    ```
    $ kubectl apply -f nfs
    ```

3. List the PVCs and confirm that a PVC named `openebspvc` has been created:

    ```
    $ kubectl get pvc
    NAME          STATUS VOLUME                                    CAPACITY
    ACCESS MODES STORAGECLASS        AGE
    openebspvc Bound   pvc-9f70c0b4-efe9-4534-8748-95dba05a7327 110G    RWO
    openebs-jiva-default 13m
    ```

Using the OpenEBS NFS provisioner storage class to create dynamic NFS PVs

Let's perform the following steps to dynamically deploy an NFS PV protected by the OpenEBS storage provider:

1. List the storage classes, and confirm that `openebs-nfs` exists:

    ```
    $ kubectl get sc
    NAME                             PROVISIONER                 AGE
    openebs-cstor-default (default) openebs.io/provisioner-iscsi 14h
    ```

```
openebs-device              openebs.io/local              15h
openebs-hostpath            openebs.io/local              15h
openebs-jiva-default        openebs.io/provisioner-iscsi 15h
openebs-nfs                 openebs.io/nfs                5s
openebs-snapshot-promoter   volumesnapshot.external-
storage.k8s.io/snapshot-promoter 15h
```

2. Now, you can use the `openebs-nfs` storage class to create PVCs for applications that require `ReadWriteMany` access:

```
$ cat <<EOF | kubectl apply -f -
apiVersion: v1
kind: PersistentVolumeClaim
metadata:
  name: openebs-nfs-pv-claim
spec:
  storageClassName: "openebs-nfs"
  accessModes:
    - ReadWriteMany
  resources:
    requests:
      storage: 1Mi
EOF
```

See also

- Rook NFS operator documentation: `https://github.com/rook/rook/blob/master/Documentation/nfs.md`
- OpenEBS provisioning read-write-many PVCs: `https://docs.openebs.io/docs/next/rwm.html`

Troubleshooting storage issues

In this section, you will learn how to solve the most common storage issues associated with Kubernetes. After following the recipes in this chapter, you will gain the basic skills required to troubleshoot persistent volumes stuck in pending or termination states.

Getting ready

Make sure that you have a Kubernetes cluster ready and `kubectl` configured to manage the cluster resources.

How to do it...

This section is sub-divided further into the following subsections to facilitate the process:

- Persistent volumes in the pending state
- A PV is stuck once a PVC has been deleted

Persistent volumes in the pending state

You have deployed an application, but both pods and persistent volume claims are stuck in the pending state, similar to the following:

```
$ kubectl get pvc
NAME STATUS VOLUME CAPACITY ACCESS MODES STORAGECLASS AGE
mysql-pv-claim Pending rook-ceph-block 28s
```

Let's perform the following steps to start troubleshooting:

1. First, describe the PVC to understand the root cause:

```
$ kubectl describe pvc mysql-pv-claim
...
Events:
 Type Reason Age From Message
 ---- ------ ---- ---- -------
 Warning ProvisioningFailed 3s (x16 over 3m42s) persistentvolume-
controller storageclass.storage.k8s.io "rook-ceph-block" not found
```

2. A PVC is stuck due to an incorrect or non-existing storage class. We need to change the storage class with a valid resource. List the storage classes as follows:

```
$ kubectl get sc
NAME                             PROVISIONER
AGE
default                          kubernetes.io/aws-ebs
102m
gp2                              kubernetes.io/aws-ebs
102m
openebs-cstor-default (default)  openebs.io/provisioner-iscsi
77m
openebs-device                   openebs.io/local
97m
openebs-hostpath                 openebs.io/local
97m
openebs-jiva-default             openebs.io/provisioner-iscsi
97m
```

```
openebs-snapshot-promoter          volumesnapshot.external-
storage.k8s.io/snapshot-promoter 97m
```

3. Delete the deployment using `kubectl delete -f <deployment.yaml>`.

4. Edit the deployment and replace the `storageClassName` field with a valid storage class from the output of the previous step, in our case, `openebs-cstor-default`.

5. Redeploy the application using `kubectl apply -f <deployment.yaml>`.

6. Confirm that the PVC status is `Bound`:

```
$ kubectl get pvc
NAME STATUS VOLUME CAPACITY ACCESS MODES STORAGECLASS AGE
mysql-pv-claim Bound pvc-bbf2b01e-2a69-4c4c-b9c2-48921959c363 20Gi RWO
openebs-cstor-default 5s
```

Now you have successfully troubleshooted PVC issues caused by a missing StorageClass resource.

A PV is stuck once a PVC has been deleted

You have deleted a PVC. However, either the PVC or PV deletion is stuck in the terminating state, similar to the following:

```
$ kubectl get pv
NAME CAPACITY ACCESS MODES RECLAIM POLICY STATUS CLAIM STORAGECLASS
REASON AGE
pvc-bbf2b01e-2a69-4c4c-b9c2-48921959c363 20Gi RWO Delete Terminating
default/mysql-pv-claim gp2 7m45s
```

Edit the stuck PVs or PVCs in the terminating state:

```
$ kubectl edit pv <PV_Name>
```

Remove finalizers similar to – `kubernetes.io/pv-protection`, and save the changes.

Disaster Recovery and Backup

6

In this chapter, we will focus on the backup and disaster recovery scenarios that keep applications in production highly available and allow them to quickly recover services during cloud provider or basic Kubernetes node failures. After following the recipes in this chapter, you will have gained the skills to operate the tools that are used for **disaster recovery (DR)** and be able to live-migrate applications across clusters and clouds.

In this chapter, we will cover the following recipes:

- Configuring and managing S3 object storage using MinIO
- Managing Kubernetes Volume Snapshots and restore
- Application backup and recovery using Velero
- Application backup and recovery using Kasten
- Cross-cloud application migration

Technical requirements

The recipes in this chapter assume that you have a functional Kubernetes cluster deployed by following one of the recommended methods described in `Chapter 1`, *Building Production-Ready Kubernetes Clusters*.

The Kubernetes Operations tool `kubectl` will be used for the rest of the recipes in this chapter since it's the main command-line interface for running commands against Kubernetes clusters. If you are using a Red Hat OpenShift cluster, you can replace `kubectl` with `oc`. All the commands are expected to function in a similar fashion.

Configuring and managing S3 object storage using MinIO

In this section, we will create an S3 object storage using MinIO to store artifacts or configuration files created by your applications in Kubernetes. You will learn how to create deployment manifest files, deploy an S3 service, and provide an external IP address for other applications or users to consume the service.

Getting ready

Clone the k8sdevopscookbook/src repository to your workstation to use manifest files under the chapter6 directory, as follows:

```
$ git clone https://github.com/k8sdevopscookbook/src.git
$ cd src/chapter6
```

Make sure you have a Kubernetes cluster ready and kubectl configured so that you can manage the cluster resources.

How to do it...

This section is further divided into the following subsections to make this process easier:

- Creating a deployment YAML manifest
- Creating a MinIO S3 service
- Accessing the MinIO web user interface

Creating a deployment YAML manifest

All Kubernetes resources are created in a declarative way by using YAML manifest files. Let's perform the following steps to create an example file we will use later to deploy an application in Kubernetes:

1. For this recipe, we will use MinIO to create a couple of resources that we can use to understand the file format and later help us deploy the fully functional application. Open the MinIO download website by going to `https://min.io/download#/kubernetes`.

2. On the MinIO website from the list of available download options, click on the **Kubernetes** button and select the **Kubernetes CLI** tab. This page will help us generate the YAML content required for the MinIO application based on our preferences:

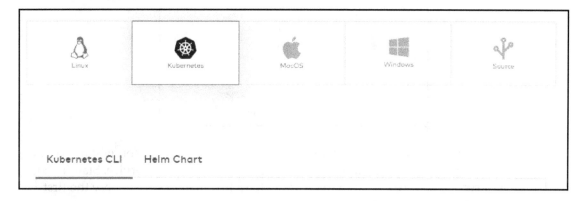

3. Enter your access key and secret key pair. In our example, we used `minio/minio123`. This will be used in place of a username and password when you access your MinIO service. Select **Distributed** as the deployment model and enter 4 for the number of nodes. This option will create a StatefulSet with four replicas. Enter 10 GB as the size. In our example, we'll use the values shown on the following configuration screen:

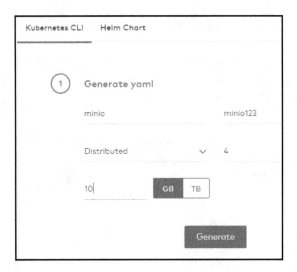

4. Click on the **Generate** button and examine the file's content. You will notice three different resources stored in the YAML manifest, including service, StatefulSet, and second service, which will create a cloud load balancer to expose the first service ports to the external access.
5. Copy the content and save it as `minio.yaml` on your workstation.

Creating a MinIO S3 service

Let's perform the following steps to create the necessary resources to get a functional S3 service using MinIO:

1. Deploy MinIO using the YAML manifest you created in the *Creating a deployment YAML manifest* recipe:

```
$ kubectl apply -f minio.yaml
```

As an alternative method, you can use the sample YAML file saved under the `/src/chapter6/minio` directory in the example repository using the `$ kubectl apply -f minio/minio.yaml` command.

2. Verify StatefulSet. You should see 4 out of 4 replicas deployed, similar to the following output. Note that if you deployed as standalone, you will not have StatefulSets:

```
$ kubectl get statefulsets
NAME   READY AGE
minio 4/4    2m17s
```

Now, you have a MinIO application that's been deployed. In the next recipe, we will learn how to discover its external address to access the service.

Accessing the MinIO web user interface

As part of the deployment process, we have MinIO create a cloud load balancer to expose the service to external access. In this recipe, we will learn how to access the MinIO interface to upload and download files to the S3 backend. To do so, we will perform the following steps:

1. Get the `minio-service` LoadBalancer's external IP using the following command. You will see the exposed service address under the `EXTERNAL-IP` column, similar to the following output:

```
$ kubectl get service
NAME             TYPE          CLUSTER-IP EXTERNAL-IP
PORT(S)    AGE
minio            ClusterIP     None        <none>
9000/TCP 2m49s
minio-service LoadBalancer 10.3.0.4    abc.us-
west-2.elb.amazonaws.com 9000:30345/TCP 2m49s
```

2. As you can see, the output service is exposed via port `9000`. To access the service, we also need to add port `9000` to the end of the address (`http://[externalIP]:9000`) and open the public address of the MinIO service in our browser.

3. You need to have permissions to access the Dashboard. Use the default username of `minio` and the default password of `minio123` we created earlier to log in to the Minio deployment. After you've logged in, you will be able to access the MinIO Browser, as shown in the following screenshot:

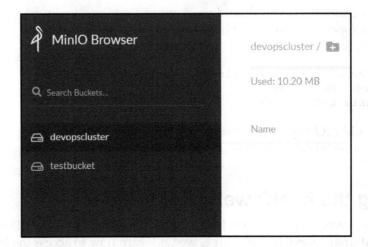

MinIO is compatible with the Amazon S3 cloud storage service and is best suited for storing unstructured data such as photos, log files, and backups. Now that you have access to the MinIO user interface, you can create bucks, upload your files, and access them through S3 APIs, similar to how you would access a standard Amazon S3 service to store your backups. You can learn more about MinIO by going to the *MinIO Documentation* link in the *See also* section.

How it works...

This recipe showed you how to provision a completely Amazon S3 API-compatible service using MinIO deployed on Kubernetes. This service will be used later for disaster recovery and backing up applications running on Kubernetes.

In the *Creating a MinIO S3 service* recipe, in *Step 1*, when we deploy MinIO, it creates a LoadBalancer service at port `9000`. Since we set the number of nodes to `4`, a StatefulSet will be created with four replicas. Each will use the information set under the `volumeClaimTemplates` section to create a PVC. If `storageClassName` is not defined specifically, then the default storage class will be used. As a result, you will see four instance of **PersistentVolumesClaim** (**PVC**) created on the cluster to provide a highly available MinIO service.

See also

- The MinIO documentation,at: `https://docs.min.io/docs/minio-quickstart-guide.html`
- MinIO Operator for Kubernetes at: `https://github.com/minio/minio-operator`
- The MinIO Erasure Code QuickStart Guide at: `https://docs.min.io/docs/minio-erasure-code-quickstart-guide`
- Using MinIO Client, at: `https://docs.min.io/docs/minio-client-quickstart-guide`

Managing Kubernetes Volume Snapshots and restore

In this section, we will create Volume Snapshots from our persistent volumes in Kubernetes. By following this recipe, you will learn how to enable the Volume Snapshot functionality, create snapshot storage classes, and restore from existing Volume Snapshots.

Getting ready

Make sure you have a Kubernetes cluster ready and `kubectl` configured to manage the cluster resources.

Clone the `k8sdevopscookbook/src` repository to your workstation to use the manifest files under the `chapter6` directory, as follows:

```
$ git clone https://github.com/k8sdevopscookbook/src.git
$ cd src/chapter6
```

Make sure the **Container Storage Interface** (**CSI**) driver from your preferred storage vendor is installed on your Kubernetes cluster and has implemented the snapshot functionality. We covered the installation of the AWS EBS, GCP PD, Azure Disk, Rook, and OpenEBS CSI drivers in `Chapter 5`, *Preparing for Stateful Workloads*.

The instructions in this section work similarly with other vendors that support snapshots via CSI. You can find these additional drivers on the Kubernetes CSI documentation site at: `https://kubernetes-csi.github.io/docs/drivers.html`.

How to do it...

This section is further divided into the following subsections to make this process easier:

- Enabling feature gates
- Creating a volume snapshot via CSI
- Restoring a volume from a snapshot via CSI
- Cloning a volume via CSI

Enabling feature gates

Some of the features that will be discussed here may be at different stages (alpha, beta, or GA) at the moment. If you run into an issue, perform the following step:

1. Set the following `feature-gates` flags to `true` for both `kube-apiserver` and `kubelet`:

   ```
   - --feature-gates=VolumeSnapshotDataSource=true
   - --feature-gates=KubeletPluginsWatcher=true
   - --feature-gates=CSINodeInfo=true
   - --feature-gates=CSIDriverRegistry=true
   - --feature-gates=BlockVolume=true
   - --feature-gates=CSIBlockVolume=true
   ```

You can find the latest statuses for features and their states by going to the *Kubernetes Feature Gates* link in the *See also* section.

Creating a volume snapshot via CSI

A volume snapshot is a copy of the state taken from a PVC in the Kubernetes cluster. It is a useful resource for bringing up a stateful application using existing data. Let's perform the following steps to create a volume snapshot using CSI:

1. Create a PVC or select an existing one. In our recipe, we'll use the AWS EBS CSI driver and the `aws-csi-ebs` storage class we created in Chapter 5, *Preparing for Stateful Workloads*, in the *Installing an EBS CSI driver to manage EBS volumes* recipe:

   ```
   $ cat <<EOF | kubectl apply -f -
   apiVersion: v1
   kind: PersistentVolumeClaim
   metadata:
     name: csi-ebs-pvc
   spec:
   ```

```
accessModes:
  - ReadWriteOnce
storageClassName: aws-csi-ebs
resources:
  requests:
    storage: 4Gi
EOF
```

2. Create a pod that will write to the `/data/out.txt` file inside the
   PersistentVolume (PV):

```
$ cat <<EOF | kubectl apply -f -
apiVersion: v1
kind: Pod
metadata:
  name: app
spec:
  containers:
  - name: app
    image: centos
    command: ["/bin/sh"]
    args: ["-c", "while true; do echo $(date -u) >> /data/out.txt;
sleep 5; done"]
    volumeMounts:
    - name: persistent-storage
      mountPath: /data
  volumes:
  - name: persistent-storage
    persistentVolumeClaim:
      claimName: csi-ebs-pvc
EOF
```

3. Create a `VolumeSnapshotClass`. Make sure that the snapshot provider is set to
   your CSI driver name. In this recipe, this is `ebs.csi.aws.com`:

```
$ cat <<EOF | kubectl apply -f -
apiVersion: snapshot.storage.k8s.io/v1alpha1
kind: VolumeSnapshotClass
metadata:
  name: csi-ebs-vsc
snapshotter: ebs.csi.aws.com
EOF
```

4. A PVC must be created using the CSI driver of a storage vendor. In our recipe, we will use the PVC we created in the *Installing EBS CSI driver to manage EBS volumes* recipe. Now, create a `VolumeSnapshot` using the PVC name (`csi-ebs-pvc`) we set in *Step 1*:

```
$ cat <<EOF | kubectl apply -f -
apiVersion: snapshot.storage.k8s.io/v1alpha1
kind: VolumeSnapshot
metadata:
  name: ebs-volume-snapshot
spec:
  snapshotClassName: csi-ebs-vsc
  source:
    name: csi-ebs-pvc
    kind: PersistentVolumeClaim
EOF
```

5. List the Volume Snapshots:

```
$ kubectl get volumesnapshot
NAME AGE
ebs-volume-snapshot 18s
```

6. Validate that the status is `Ready To Use: true` when checking the output of the following command:

```
$ kubectl describe volumesnapshot ebs-volume-snapshot
```

Restoring a volume from a snapshot via CSI

We can create snapshots in an attempt to restore other snapshots. Let's perform the following steps to restore the snapshot we created in the previous recipe:

1. Restore the volume from the snapshot with a PVC using the following command. As you can see, a new PVC named `csi-ebs-pvc-restored` will be created based on the `ebs-volume-snapshot` snapshot:

```
$ cat <<EOF | kubectl apply -f -
apiVersion: v1
kind: PersistentVolumeClaim
metadata:
 name: csi-ebs-pvc-restored
spec:
 accessModes:
 - ReadWriteOnce
 storageClassName: aws-csi-ebs
```

```
    resources:
    requests:
    storage: 4Gi
    dataSource:
    name: ebs-volume-snapshot
    kind: VolumeSnapshot
    apiGroup: snapshot.storage.k8s.io
    EOF
```

2. Create another pod that will continue to write to the `/data/out.txt` file inside the PV. This step will ensure that the volume is still accessible after it's been created:

```
$ cat <<EOF | kubectl apply -f -
apiVersion: v1
kind: Pod
metadata:
  name: newapp
spec:
  containers:
  - name: app
    image: centos
    command: ["/bin/sh"]
    args: ["-c", "while true; do echo $(date -u) >> /data/out.txt;
sleep 5; done"]
    volumeMounts:
    - name: persistent-storage
      mountPath: /data
  volumes:
  - name: persistent-storage
    persistentVolumeClaim:
      claimName: csi-ebs-pvc-restored
    EOF
```

3. Confirm that the `newapp` pod contains the restored data and the timestamps from the *Creating a volume snapshot* recipe:

```
$ kubectl exec -it newapp cat /data/out.txt
```

With this, you've learned how to provision persistent volumes from an existing snapshot. This is a very useful step in a CI/CD pipeline so that you can save time troubleshooting failed pipelines.

Cloning a volume via CSI

While snapshots are a copy of a certain state of PVs, it is not the only way to create a copy of data. CSI also allows new volumes to be created from existing volumes. In this recipe, we will create a PVC using an existing PVC by performing the following steps:

1. Get the list of PVCs. You may have more than one PVC. In this example, we will use the PVC we created in the *Creating a volume snapshot* recipe. You can use another PVC as long as it has been created using the CSI driver that supports `VolumePVCDataSource` APIs:

   ```
   $ kubectl get pvc
   NAME STATUS VOLUME CAPACITY ACCESS MODES STORAGECLASS AGE
   csi-ebs-pvc Bound pvc-574ed379-71e1-4548-b736-7137ab9cfd9d 4Gi RWO
   aws-csi-ebs 23h
   ```

2. Create a PVC using an existing PVC (in this recipe, this is `csi-ebs-pvc`) as the `dataSource`. The data source can be either a `VolumeSnapshot` or PVC. In this example, we used `PersistentVolumeClaim` to clone the data:

   ```
   $ cat <<EOF | kubectl apply -f -
   apiVersion: v1
   kind: PersistentVolumeClaim
   metadata:
       name: clone-of-csi-ebs-pvc
   spec:
     accessModes:
     - ReadWriteOnce
     resources:
       requests:
         storage: 4Gi
     dataSource:
       kind: PersistentVolumeClaim
       name: csi-ebs-pvc
   EOF
   ```

With that, you've learned a simple way of cloning persistent data from an existing data source.

How it works...

This recipe showed you how to create snapshots, bring data back from a snapshot, and how to instantly clone persistent volumes on Kubernetes.

In the *Restoring a volume from a snapshot via CSI* and *Cloning a volume via CSI* recipes, we added a `dataSource` to our PVC that references an existing PVC so that a completely independent, new PVC is created. The resulting PVC can be attached, cloned, snapshotted, or deleted independently if the source is deleted. The main difference is that right after provisioning the PVC, instead of an empty PV, the backend device provisions an exact duplicate of the specified volume.

It's important to note that native cloning support is available for dynamic provisioners using CSI drivers that have already implemented this feature. The CSI project is continuing to evolve and mature, so not every storage vendor provides full CSI capabilities.

See also

- List of Kubernetes CSI drivers, at `https://kubernetes-csi.github.io/docs/drivers.html`
- **Container Storage Interface** (**CSI**) documentation , at `https://kubernetes-csi.github.io`
- The CSI spec, at `https://github.com/container-storage-interface/spec`
- Kubernetes Feature Gates, at `https://kubernetes.io/docs/reference/command-line-tools-reference/feature-gates/`
- Kubernetes Volume Cloning documentation, at `https://kubernetes.io/docs/concepts/storage/volume-pvc-datasource/`
- Kubernetes Volume Snapshots documentation, at `https://kubernetes.io/docs/concepts/storage/volume-snapshots/`

Application backup and recovery using Velero

In this section, we will create disaster recovery backups and migrate Kubernetes applications and their persistent volumes in Kubernetes using VMware Velero (formerly Heptio Ark).

You will learn how to install Velero, create standard and scheduled backups of applications with an S3 target, and restore them back to the Kubernetes clusters.

Getting ready

Make sure you have a Kubernetes cluster ready and `kubectl` configured to manage the cluster resources.

Clone the `k8sdevopscookbook/src` repository to your workstation to use the manifest files under the `chapter6` directory, as follows:

```
$ git clone https://github.com/k8sdevopscookbook/src.git
$ cd src/chapter6
```

This recipe requires an existing stateful workload with presentable data so that we can simulate a disaster and then restore the data. To do this, we will use the `mytestapp` application we created during the *Installing EBS CSI driver to manage EBS volumes* recipe in `Chapter 5`, *Preparing for Stateful Workloads*.

Velero also requires S3-compatible object storage to store the backups. In this recipe, we will use the MinIO S3 target we deployed during the *Configuring and managing S3 object storage using MinIO* recipe for storing our backups.

How to do it...

This section is further divided into the following subsections to make this process easier:

- Installing Velero
- Backing up an application
- Restoring an application
- Creating a scheduled backup
- Taking a backup of an entire namespace
- Viewing backups with MinIO
- Deleting backups and schedules

Installing Velero

Velero is an open source project that's used to make backups, perform disaster recovery, restore, and migrate Kubernetes resources and persistent volumes. In this recipe, we will learn how to deploy Velero in our Kubernetes cluster by following these steps:

1. Download the latest version of Velero:

```
$ wget
https://github.com/vmware-tanzu/velero/releases/download/v1.1.0/vel
ero-v1.1.0-linux-amd64.tar.gz
```

 At the time of writing this book, the latest version of Velero was v1.1.0. Check the Velero repository at https://github.com/vmware-tanzu/ velero/releases and update the link with the latest download link if it's changed since this book's release.

2. Extract the tarball:

```
$ tar -xvzf velero-v1.1.0-linux-amd64.tar.gz
$ sudo mv velero-v1.1.0-linux-amd64/velero /usr/local/bin/
```

3. Confirm that the velero command is executable:

```
$ velero version
Client:
 Version: v1.1.0
 Git commit: a357f21aec6b39a8244dd23e469cc4519f1fe608
<error getting server version: the server could not find the
requested resource (post serverstatusrequests.velero.io)>
```

4. Create the credentials-velero file with the access key and secret key you used in the *Configuring and managing S3 object storage using Minio* recipe:

```
$ cat > credentials-velero <<EOF
[default]
aws_access_key_id = minio
aws_secret_access_key = minio123
EOF
```

5. Update the s3Url with the external IP of your MinIO service and install Velero Server:

```
$ velero install \
    --provider aws \
    --bucket velero \
```

```
--secret-file ./credentials-velero \
--use-restic \
--backup-location-config
region=minio,s3ForcePathStyle="true",s3Url=http://ac76d4a1ac72c4962
99b17573ac4cf2d-512600720.us-west-2.elb.amazonaws.com:9000
```

6. Confirm that the deployment was successful:

```
$ kubectl get deployments -l component=velero --namespace=velero
NAME READY UP-TO-DATE AVAILABLE AGE
velero 1/1 1 1 62s
```

With that, Velero has been configured on your Kubernetes cluster using MinIO as the backup target.

Backing up an application

Let's perform the following steps to take a backup of an application and its volumes using Velero. All the YAML manifest files we create here can be found under the /src/chapter6/velero directory:

1. If you have an application and volumes to back up labeled already, you can skip to *Step 5*. Otherwise, create a namespace and a PVC with the following commands:

   ```
   cat <<EOF | kubectl apply -f -
   apiVersion: v1
   kind: Namespace
   metadata:
     name: backup-example
     labels:
       app: app2backup
   EOF
   ```

2. Create a PVC in the backup-example namespace using your preferred storageClass. In our example this is aws-csi-ebs:

   ```
   cat <<EOF | kubectl apply -f -
   apiVersion: v1
   kind: PersistentVolumeClaim
   metadata:
     name: pvc2backup
     namespace: backup-example
     labels:
       app: app2backup
   spec:
   ```

```
        accessModes:
          - ReadWriteOnce
        storageClassName: aws-csi-ebs
        resources:
          requests:
            storage: 4Gi
    EOF
```

3. Review the `myapp.yaml` file in the `src/chapter6/velero` directory and use it to create a pod that will use the PVC and write to the `/data/out.txt` file inside the pod:

    ```
    $ kubectl apply -f myapp.yaml
    ```

4. Verify that our `myapp` pod writes data to the volume:

    ```
    $ kubectl exec -it myapp cat /data/out.txt -nbackup-example
    Thu Sep 12 23:18:08 UTC 2019
    ```

5. Create a backup for all the objects with the `app=app2backup` label:

    ```
    $ velero backup create myapp-backup --selector app=app2backup
    ```

6. Confirm that the backup phase is completed:

    ```
    $ velero backup describe myapp-backup
    Name: myapp-backup
    Namespace: velero
    Labels: velero.io/storage-location=default
    Annotations: <none>
    Phase: Completed
    . . .
    ```

7. List all the available backups:

    ```
    $ velero backup get
    NAME            STATUS     CREATED                         EXPIRES
    STORAGE LOCATION SELECTOR
    myapp-backup Completed 2019-09-13 05:55:08 +0000 UTC 29d
    default app=app2backup
    ```

With that, you've learned how to create a backup of an application using labels.

Restoring an application

Let's perform the following steps to restore the application from its backup:

1. Delete the application and its PVC to simulate a data loss scenario:

   ```
   $ kubectl delete pvc pvc2backup -nbackup-example
   $ kubectl delete pod myapp -nbackup-example
   ```

2. Restore your application from your previous backup called `myapp-backup`:

   ```
   $ velero restore create --from-backup myapp-backup
   ```

3. Confirm your application is running:

   ```
   $ kubectl get pod -nbackup-example
   NAME   READY STATUS   RESTARTS AGE
   myapp 1/1    Running 0           10m
   ```

4. Confirm that our `myapp` pod writes data to the volume:

   ```
   $ kubectl exec -it myapp cat /data/out.txt -nbackup-example
   ```

With that, you've learned how to restore an application and its volumes from its backup using Velero.

Creating a scheduled backup

Velero supports cron expressions to schedule backup tasks. Let's perform the following steps to schedule backups for our application:

1. Create a scheduled daily backup:

   ```
   $ velero schedule create myapp-daily --schedule="0 0 1 * * ?" --
   selector app=app2backup
   ```

   If you are not familiar with cron expressions, you can create a different schedule using the *Cron expression generator* link in the *See also* section.

    Note that the preceding schedule uses a cron expression. As an alternative, you can use a shorthand expression such as `--schedule="@daily"` or use an online cron maker to create a cron expression.

2. Get a list of the currently scheduled backup jobs:

```
$ velero schedule get
  NAME           STATUS   CREATED                        SCHEDULE
BACKUP TTL LAST BACKUP SELECTOR
  myapp-daily Enabled 2019-09-13 21:38:36 +0000 UTC 0 0 1 * * ?
720h0m0s    2m ago          app=app2backup
```

3. Confirm that a backup has been created by the scheduled backup job:

```
$ velero backup get
  NAME                          STATUS      CREATED
EXPIRES STORAGE LOCATION SELECTOR
myapp-daily-20190913205123 Completed 2019-09-13 20:51:24 +0000 UTC
29d       default app=app2backup
```

With that, you've learned how to create scheduled backups of an application using Velero.

Taking a backup of an entire namespace

When you take backups, you can use different types of selectors or even complete sources in a selected namespace. In this recipe, we will include resources in a namespace by performing the following steps:

1. Take a backup of the entire namespace using the following command. This example includes the `backup-example` namespace. Replace this namespace if needed. The namespace and resources should exist before you can execute the following command:

```
$ velero backup create fullnamespace --include-namespaces backup-example
```

2. If you need to exclude specific resources from the backup, add the `backup: "false"` label to them and run the following command:

```
$ velero backup create fullnamespace --selector 'backup notin (false)'
```

With that, you've learned how to create backups of resources in a given namespace using Velero.

Viewing backups with MinIO

Let's perform the following steps to view the content of the backups on the MinIO interface:

1. Follow the instructions in the *Accessing a MinIO web user interface* recipe and access the MinIO Browser.
2. Click on the `velero` bucket:

3. Open the `backups` directory to find a list of your Velero backups:

4. Click on a backup name to access the content of the backup:

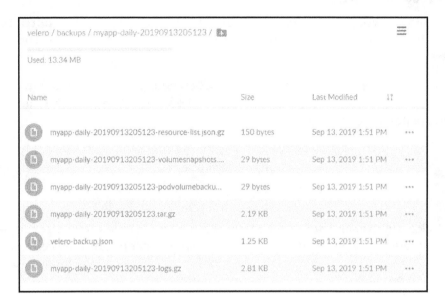

With that, you've learned how to locate and review the content of Velero backups.

Deleting backups and schedules

Velero backups can quickly grow in size if they're not maintained correctly. Let's perform the following steps to remove an existing backup resource and clean up scheduled backups:

1. Delete the existing backup named `myapp-backup`:

   ```
   $ velero backup delete myapp-backup
   ```

2. Delete all existing backups:

   ```
   $ velero backup delete --all
   ```

3. Delete the scheduled backup job named `myapp-daily`:

   ```
   $ velero schedule delete myapp-daily
   ```

How it works...

This recipe showed you how to create disaster recovery backups, restore your application and its data back from an S3 target, and how to create scheduled backup jobs on Kubernetes.

In the *Backing up an application* recipe, in *Step 4*, when you run `velero backup create myapp-backup --selector app=app2backup`, the Velero client calls the Kubernetes API server and creates a backup object.

 You can get a list of **Custom Resource Definitions** (**CRDs**) that have been created by Velero by running the `kubectl get crds |grep velero` command.

Velero's BackupController watches for a new object and when detected, it performs standard validation and processes the backup. Velero's BackupController collects the information to back up by asking resources from the API server. Then, it makes a call to the default storage provider and uploads the backup files.

See also

- The Velero project repository, at `https://github.com/vmware-tanzu/velero/`
- The Velero documentation, at `https://velero.io/docs/master/index.html`
- Velero support matrix, at `https://velero.io/docs/master/supported-providers/`
- Velero podcasts and community articles, at `https://velero.io/resources/`
- Cron expression generator, at `https://www.freeformatter.com/cron-expression-generator-quartz.html`

Application backup and recovery using Kasten

In this section, we will create disaster recovery backups and migrate Kubernetes applications and their persistent volumes in Kubernetes using **Kasten** (**K10**).

You will learn how to install and use K10, create standard and scheduled backups of applications to an S3 target, and restore them back to the Kubernetes clusters.

Getting ready

Make sure you have a Kubernetes cluster ready and `kubectl` and `helm` configured so that you can manage the cluster resources. In this recipe, we will use a three-node Kubernetes cluster on AWS.

This recipe requires an existing stateful workload with presentable data to simulate a disaster. To restore the data, we will use the `mytestapp` application we created in the *Installing EBS CSI Driver to manage EBS volumes* recipe in `Chapter 5`, *Preparing for Stateful Workloads*.

Clone the `k8sdevopscookbook/src` repository to your workstation to use the manifest files under the `chapter6` directory, as follows:

```
$ git clone https://github.com/k8sdevopscookbook/src.git
$ cd src/chapter6
```

K10, by default, comes with a Starter Edition license that allows you to use the software on a cluster with three worker nodes (at most) at no charge. K10 requires a backup target to be configured.

How to do it...

This section is further divided into the following subsections to make this process easier:

- Installing Kasten
- Accessing the Kasten dashboard
- Backing up an application
- Restoring an application

Installing Kasten

Let's perform the following steps to install Kasten as a backup solution in our Kubernetes cluster:

1. Add the K10 helm repository:

```
$ helm repo add kasten https://charts.kasten.io/
```

2. Before we start, let's validate the environment. The following script will execute some pre-installation tests to verify your cluster:

```
$ curl https://docs.kasten.io/tools/k10_preflight.sh | bash
Checking for tools
 --> Found kubectl --> Found helm
Checking access to the Kubernetes context kubernetes-
admin@net39dvo58
 --> Able to access the default Kubernetes namespace
Checking for required Kubernetes version (>= v1.10.0)
 --> Kubernetes version (v1.15.3) meets minimum requirements
Checking if Kubernetes RBAC is enabled
 --> Kubernetes RBAC is enabled
Checking if the Aggregated Layer is enabled
 --> The Kubernetes Aggregated Layer is enabled
Checking if the Kasten Helm repo is present
 --> The Kasten Helm repo was found
Checking for required Helm Tiller version (>= v2.11.0)
 --> Tiller version (v2.14.3) meets minimum requirements
All pre-flight checks succeeded!
```

3. Make sure your preferred storage class is set as the default; otherwise, define it by adding the `-set persistence.storageClass` parameters to the following command. In our example, we are using the `openebs-cstor-default` storage class. Also, add your AWS access key and secret and install K10:

```
$ helm install kasten/k10 --name=k10 --namespace=kasten-io \
--set persistence.storageClass=openebs-cstor-default \
--set persistence.size=20Gi \
--set secrets.awsAccessKeyId="AWS_ACCESS_KEY_ID" \
--set secrets.awsSecretAccessKey="AWS_SECRET_ACCESS_KEY"
```

4. Confirm that the deployment status is DEPLOYED using the following `helm` command:

```
$ helm ls
NAME REVISION UPDATED                     STATUS    CHART      APP
VERSION NAMESPACE
k10  1         Tue Oct 29 07:36:19 2019 DEPLOYED k10-1.1.56 1.1.56
kasten-io
```

All the pods should be deployed in around a minute after this step as Kasten exposes an API based on Kubernetes CRDs. You can either use `kubectl` with the new CRDs (refer to the *Kasten CLI commands* link in the *See also* section) or use the Kasten Dashboard by following the next recipe, that is, the *Accessing the Kasten Dashboard* recipe.

Accessing the Kasten Dashboard

Let's perform the following steps to access the Kasten Dashboard. This is where we will be taking application backups and restoring them:

1. Create port forwarding using the following command. This step will forward the Kasten Dashboard service on port `8000` to your local workstation on port `8080`:

```
$ export KASTENDASH_POD=$(kubectl get pods --namespace kasten-io -l
"service=gateway" -o jsonpath="{.items[0].metadata.name}")
$ kubectl port-forward --namespace kasten-io $KASTENDASH_POD
8080:8000 >> /dev/null &
```

2. On your workstation, open `http://127.0.0.1:8080/k10/#` with your browser:

```
$ firefox http://127.0.0.1:8080/k10/#
```

3. Read and accept the end user license agreement:

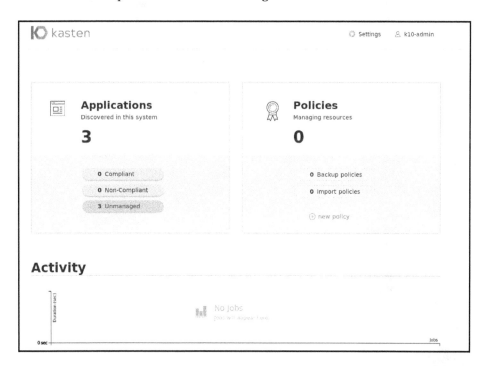

With that, you have accessed the Kasten Dashboard. You can familiarize yourself with it by clicking the main menus and referring to the *Kasten documentation* link in the *See also* section for additional settings if needed.

Backing up an application

Let's perform the following steps to take a backup of our application:

1. If you have an application and persistent volumes associated with the backup labeled already, you can skip to *Step 5*. Otherwise, create a namespace and a PVC using the following example code:

```
$ cat <<EOF | kubectl apply -f -
apiVersion: v1
kind: Namespace
metadata:
 name: backup-example
 labels:
 app: app2backup
EOF
```

2. Create a PVC in the `backup-example` namespace:

```
$ cat <<EOF | kubectl apply -f -
apiVersion: v1
kind: PersistentVolumeClaim
metadata:
  name: pvc2backup
  namespace: backup-example
  labels:
    app: app2backup
spec:
  accessModes:
    - ReadWriteOnce
  storageClassName: openebs-cstor-default
  resources:
    requests:
      storage: 4Gi
EOF
```

3. Create a pod that will use the PVC and write to the /data/out.txt file inside the pod using the sample myapp.yaml manifest under the src/chapter6/kasten directory:

```
$ kubectl apply -f - kasten/myapp.yaml
```

4. Verify that our myapp pod writes data to the volume:

```
$ kubectl exec -it myapp cat /data/out.txt -nbackup-example
Thu Sep 12 23:18:08 UTC 2019
```

5. On the Kasten Dashboard, click on **Unmanaged** applications:

6. In the `backup-example` namespace, click on **Create a policy**:

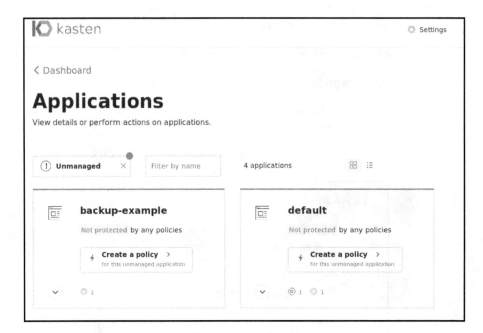

7. Enter a name and select the **Snapshot** action:

8. Select **Daily** as the **Action Frequency**:

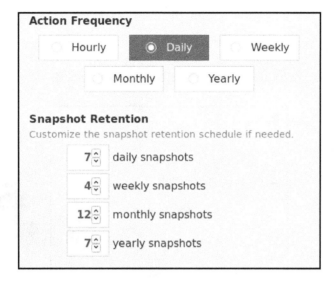

9. Click on **Create Policy**:

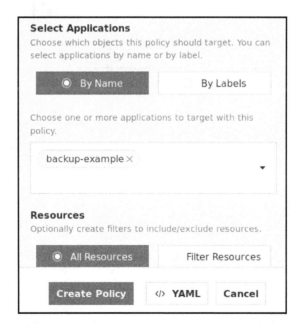

By following these steps, you will have created your first backup using the policy, as well as a schedule for the following backup jobs.

Restoring an application

Let's perform the following steps to restore the application from an existing backup:

1. Under **Applications**, from the list of compliant applications, click the arrow icon next to `backup-example` and select **Restore Application**. If the application was deleted, then the **Removed** option needs to be selected:

2. Select a restore point to recover to:

3. Select `backup-example` and click on **Restore**:

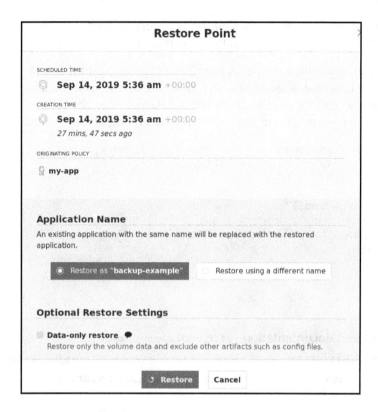

4. Confirm that you want this to be restored:

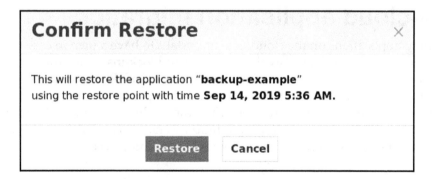

With that, you've learned how to restore an application and its volumes from its backup using Kasten.

How it works...

This recipe showed you how to create disaster recovery backups, restore your application and its data back from an S3 target, and how to create scheduled backups on Kubernetes.

In the *Backing up an application* recipe, in *Step 2*, we created a pod that uses OpenEBS as a storage vendor. In this case, Kasten uses a generic backup method that requires a sidecar to your application that can mount the application data volume. The following is an example that you can add to your pods and deployment when using non-standard storage options:

```
- name: kanister-sidecar
  image: kanisterio/kanister-tools:0.20.0
  command: ["bash", "-c"]
  args:
  - "tail -f /dev/null"
  volumeMounts:
  - name: data
    mountPath: /data
```

See also

- The Kasten documentation , at https://docs.kasten.io/
- Kasten CLI commands, at https://docs.kasten.io/api/cli.html
- More on generic backup and restore using Kanister, at https://docs.kasten.io/kanister/generic.html#generic-kanister

Cross-cloud application migration

When running applications on the cloud, it is important to have a plan in case cloud vendor service outages occur, as well as to avoid possible cloud lock-ins, by abstracting the storage layer using a cloud-native storage solution similar to the OpenEBS management layer that allows you to manage your exposure to each cloud or data center. In this section, we will migrate a cloud-native application from one Kubernetes cluster to another cluster running on a different cloud vendor to simulate a migration scenario. You will learn how to use backups to migrate applications using Kasten and OpenEBS Director.

Getting ready

Make sure you have two Kubernetes clusters ready and `kubectl` configured to manage the cluster resources.

In this recipe, we will use a cluster on AWS that's been deployed and managed by D2iQ `Konvoy` and a cluster that's been deployed using `kops`. As an example, we will migrate an existing `minio` application.

The instructions provided here require an AWS account and an AWS user with a policy that has permission to use the related services. If you don't have one, go to `https://aws.amazon.com/account/` and create one.

How to do it...

This section is further divided into the following subsections to make this process easier:

- Creating an export profile in Kasten
- Exporting a restore point in Kasten
- Creating an import profile in Kasten
- Migrating an application in Kasten
- Importing clusters in OpenEBS Director
- Migrating an application in OpenEBS Director

Creating an export profile in Kasten

First, we will use Kasten and create an export profile to store a remote copy of an example application to be used in the migration scenario. To do this, follow these steps:

1. Under **Settings**, select the **Mobility** tab and click on **New Profile**:

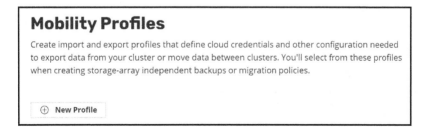

2. To create a destination profile, select **Export**, check the **Enable data portability** box, select Amazon S3, and enter your user credentials.

3. Click on **Validate and Save**:

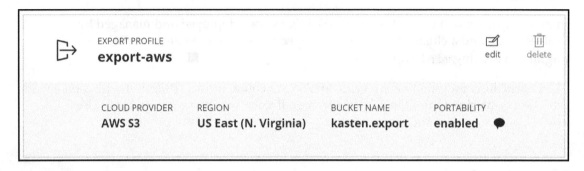

The export profile we created in this recipe will be used later to move data to another cluster.

Exporting a restore point in Kasten

Let's perform the following steps to create an application restore point:

1. Under **Applications**, from the list of compliant applications, click the arrow icon next to **minio** and select **Export Application**.

2. Select a restore point to export:

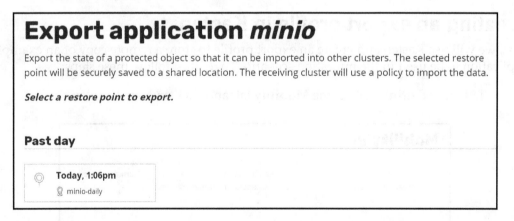

3. Select your export profile and click on **Export**:

4. Confirm the restore.
5. Copy the text block to the clipboard:

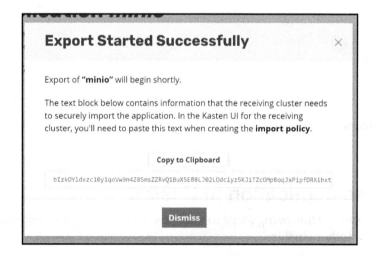

Creating an import profile in Kasten

Let's perform the following steps on our second cluster, which is where we want to migrate our application:

1. Under **Settings**, select the **Mobility** tab and click on **New Profile**:

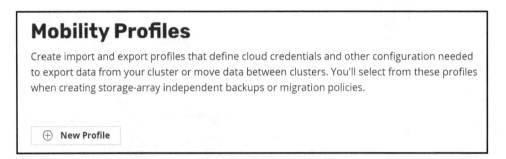

2. To create a destination profile, select **Import**, select **Amazon S3**, and enter your user credentials.
3. Use the bucket name you created for the export profile on the source cluster.
4. Click on **Validate and Save**:

The import profile we created in this recipe will be used later to import data from another cluster.

Migrating an application in Kasten

Finally, let's perform the following steps to use the import profile and migrate an application from another cluster:

1. Under **Policies**, click on **new policies**:

2. Select **Import** and check the **Restore after import** box.
3. Select **Daily** as **Action Frequency** and paste the Config Data text block from the *Exporting a restore point* recipe.
4. Select the import profile you created in the *Creating import profile* recipe:

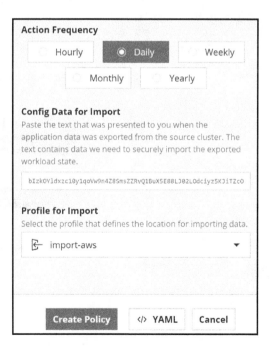

5. Click the **Create Policy** button.

After this step, Kasten will recover the application and its data from the restore point into the new cluster.

Importing clusters into OpenEBS Director

OpenEBS Director Online is a free-to-use **SaaS (Software as a Service)** solution (with the OnPrem option available for Enterprise users) for managing stateful applications in Kubernetes. In addition to its logging and monitoring capabilities, it provides **Data Migration as a Service (DMaaS)**. In this recipe, we will learn how to add our existing clusters to the platform and then perform DMaaS in the following recipe:

1. Go to www.mayadata.io to sign in to your OpenEBS Enterprise Platform at https://portal.mayadata.io/home:

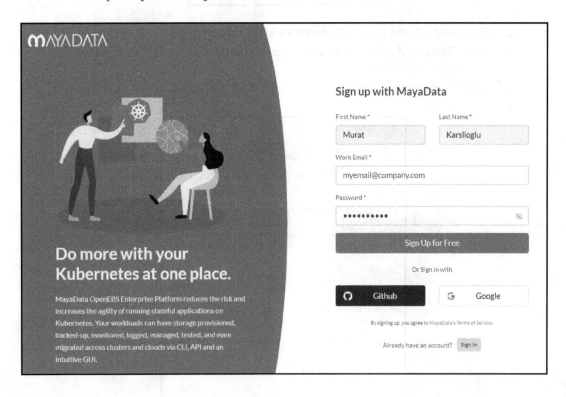

2. Click on the **Connect your Cluster** button:

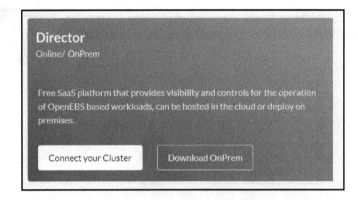

3. Name your project. Here, we used the name GKECluster:

4. Choose your Kubernetes cluster location. Here, we used a cluster on GKE:

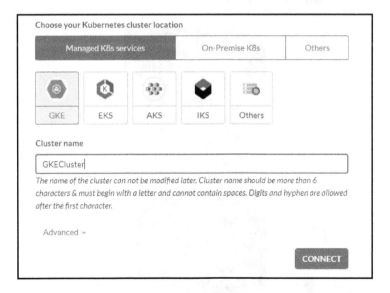

5. Copy and execute the command on your first cluster:

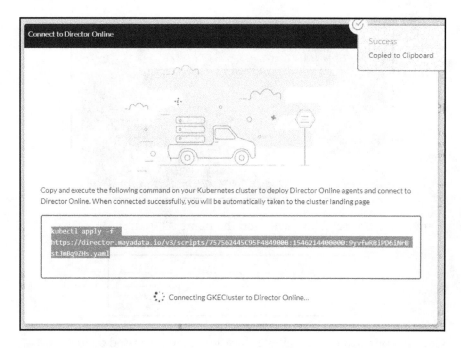

6. From the left-hand menu, click on **Clusters**:

7. On the **Clusters** view, click on **Connect a new Cluster** and repeat *Steps 4* and *5* for the second cluster:

8. Once you are done, you will have both clusters visible on the platform.

Migrating an application in OpenEBS Director

Let's perform data migration (DMaaS) by following these steps:

1. On the **Clusters** view, click on **Free** under the **Subscription** column and start your premium plan evaluation for both clusters:

2. On your source cluster's **Overview** page, click on the workload you want to migrate. In this recipe, we will migrate the MinIO workload:

3. On the **Application** view, select the **DMaaS** tab and click on the **New schedule** button:

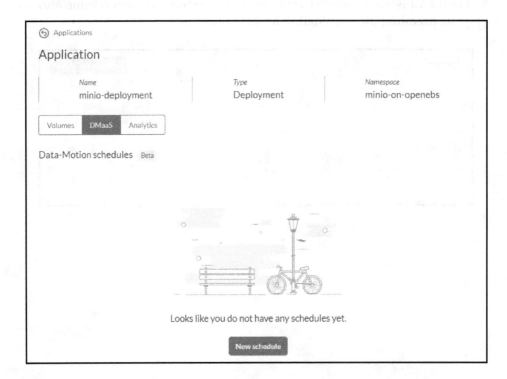

4. On the **New Schedule** view, select **AWS** as an S3 provider and select your credentials and region. Finally, select the backup interval as **Daily** and click on the **Schedule Now** button to create a backup. As an alternative, you can also use GCP or MinIO as an S3 target:

5. From the left-hand menu, select **DMaaS** and click on the **Restore** button next to the schedule you created:

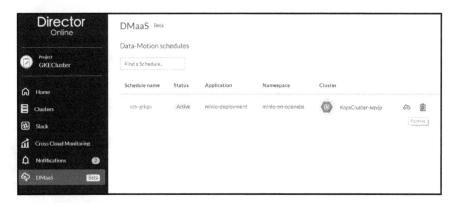

6. Select your target cluster from the list of managed clusters and click on **Start Restore**:

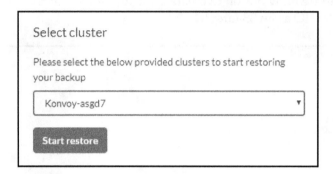

Your workload will be restored to the second cluster.

See also

- OpenEBS Director documentation, at `https://help.mayadata.io/hc/en-us`
- Using OpenEBS Director in Auto DevOps usecase, at `https://youtu.be/AOSUZxUs5BE?t=1210`
- Connecting to OpenEBS Director Online, at `https://docs.openebs.io/docs/next/directoronline.html`

7
Scaling and Upgrading Applications

TERNAIn this chapter, we will discuss the methods and strategies that we can use to dynamically scale containerized services running on Kubernetes to handle the changing traffic needs of our service. After following the recipes in this chapter, you will have the skills needed to create load balancers to distribute traffic to multiple workers and increase bandwidth. You will also know how to handle upgrades in production with minimum downtime.

In this chapter, we will cover the following recipes:

- Scaling applications on Kubernetes
- Assigning applications to nodes with priority
- Creating an external load balancer
- Creating an ingress service and service mesh using Istio
- Creating an ingress service and service mesh using Linkerd
- Auto-healing pods in Kubernetes
- Managing upgrades through blue/green deployments

Technical requirements

The recipes in this chapter assume that you have a functional Kubernetes cluster deployed by following one of the recommended methods described in Chapter 1, *Building Production-Ready Kubernetes Clusters*.

The Kubernetes command-line tool, kubectl, will be used for the rest of the recipes in this chapter since it's the main command-line interface for running commands against Kubernetes clusters. We will also use helm where Helm charts are available to deploy solutions.

Scaling applications on Kubernetes

In this section, we will perform application and cluster scaling tasks. You will learn how to manually and also automatically scale your service capacity up or down in Kubernetes to support dynamic traffic.

Getting ready

Clone the `k8sdevopscookbook/src` repository to your workstation to use the manifest files in the `chapter7` directory, as follows:

```
$ git clone https://github.com/k8sdevopscookbook/src.git
$ cd /src/chapter7/
```

Make sure you have a Kubernetes cluster ready and `kubectl` and `helm` configured to manage the cluster resources.

How to do it...

This section is further divided into the following subsections to make this process easier:

- Validating the installation of Metrics Server
- Manually scaling an application
- Autoscaling applications using Horizontal Pod Autoscaler

Validating the installation of Metrics Server

The *Autoscaling applications using the Horizontal Pod Autoscaler* recipe in this section also requires Metrics Server to be installed on your cluster. Metrics Server is a cluster-wide aggregator for core resource usage data. Follow these steps to validate the installation of Metrics Server:

1. Confirm if you need to install Metrics Server by running the following command:

```
$ kubectl top node
error: metrics not available yet
```

2. If it's been installed correctly, you should see the following node metrics:

```
$ kubectl top nodes
NAME                           CPU(cores)  CPU%  MEMORY(bytes)  MEMORY%
ip-172-20-32-169.ec2.internal  259m        12%   1492Mi         19%
ip-172-20-37-106.ec2.internal  190m        9%    1450Mi         18%
ip-172-20-48-49.ec2.internal   262m        13%   2166Mi         27%
ip-172-20-58-155.ec2.internal  745m        37%   1130Mi         14%
```

If you get an error message stating `metrics not available yet`, then you need to follow the steps provided in the next chapter in the *Adding metrics using the Kubernetes Metrics Server* recipe to install Metrics Server.

Manually scaling an application

When the usage of your application increases, it becomes necessary to scale the application up. Kubernetes is built to handle the orchestration of high-scale workloads.

Let's perform the following steps to understand how to manually scale an application:

1. Change directories to `/src/chapter7/charts/node`, which is where the local clone of the example repository that you created in the *Getting ready* section can be found:

   ```
   $ cd /charts/node/
   ```

2. Install the To-Do application example using the following command. This Helm chart will deploy two pods, including a Node.js service and a MongoDB service:

   ```
   $ helm install . --name my-ch7-app
   ```

3. Get the service IP of `my-ch7-app-node` to connect to the application. The following command will return an external address for the application:

   ```
   $ export SERVICE_IP=$(kubectl get svc --namespace default my-ch7-
   app-node --template "{{ range (index .status.loadBalancer.ingress
   0) }}{{.}}{{ end }}")
   $ echo http://$SERVICE_IP/
   http://mytodoapp.us-east-1.elb.amazonaws.com/
   ```

4. Open the address from *Step 3* in a web browser. You will get a fully functional To-Do application:

5. Check the status of the application using `helm status`. You will see the number of pods that have been deployed as part of the deployment in the `Available` column:

```
$ helm status my-ch7-app
LAST DEPLOYED: Thu Oct 3 00:13:10 2019
NAMESPACE: default
STATUS: DEPLOYED
RESOURCES:
==> v1/Deployment
NAME                     READY UP-TO-DATE AVAILABLE AGE
my-ch7-app-mongodb 1/1   1                1         9m9s
my-ch7-app-node    1/1   1                1         9m9s
. . .
```

6. Scale the node pod to 3 replicas from the current scale of a single replica:

```
$ kubectl scale --replicas 3 deployment/my-ch7-app-node
deployment.extensions/my-ch7-app-node scaled
```

7. Check the status of the application again and confirm that, this time, the number of available replicas is 3 and that the number of `my-ch7-app-node` pods in the `v1/Pod` section has increased to 3:

```
$ helm status my-ch7-app
. . .
RESOURCES:
==> v1/Deployment
NAME READY UP-TO-DATE AVAILABLE AGE
my-ch7-app-mongodb 1/1 1 1 26m
my-ch7-app-node 3/3 3 3 26m
. . .
==> v1/Pod(related)
```

```
NAME READY STATUS RESTARTS AGE
my-ch7-app-mongodb-5499c954b8-1cw27 1/1 Running 0 26m
my-ch7-app-node-d8b94964f-94dsb 1/1 Running 0 91s
my-ch7-app-node-d8b94964f-h9w4l 1/1 Running 3 26m
my-ch7-app-node-d8b94964f-qpm77 1/1 Running 0 91s
```

8. To scale down your application, repeat *Step 5*, but this time with 2 replicas:

```
$ kubectl scale --replicas 2 deployment/my-ch7-app-node
deployment.extensions/my-ch7-app-node scaled
```

With that, you've learned how to scale your application when needed. Of course, your Kubernetes cluster resources should be able to support growing workload capacities as well. You will use this knowledge to test the service healing functionality in the *Auto-healing pods in Kubernetes* recipe.

The next recipe will show you how to autoscale workloads based on actual resource consumption instead of manual steps.

Autoscaling applications using a Horizontal Pod Autoscaler

In this recipe, you will learn how to create a **Horizontal Pod Autoscaler** (HPA) to automate the process of scaling the application we created in the previous recipe. We will also test the HPA with a load generator to simulate a scenario of increased traffic hitting our services. Follow these steps:

1. First, make sure you have the sample To-Do application deployed from the *Manually scaling an application* recipe. When you run the following command, you should get both MongoDB and Node pods listed:

```
$ kubectl get pods | grep my-ch7-app
my-ch7-app-mongodb-5499c954b8-1cw27 1/1 Running 0 4h41m
my-ch7-app-node-d8b94964f-94dsb      1/1 Running 0 4h16m
my-ch7-app-node-d8b94964f-h9w4l      1/1 Running 3 4h41m
```

2. Create an HPA declaratively using the following command. This will automate the process of scaling the application between 1 to 5 replicas when the targetCPUUtilizationPercentage threshold is reached. In our example, the mean of the pods' CPU utilization target is set to 50 percent usage. When the utilization goes over this threshold, your replicas will be increased:

```
cat <<EOF | kubectl apply -f -
apiVersion: autoscaling/v1
```

```
kind: HorizontalPodAutoscaler
metadata:
  name: my-ch7-app-autoscaler
  namespace: default
spec:
  scaleTargetRef:
    apiVersion: apps/v1
    kind: Deployment
    name: my-ch7-app-node
  minReplicas: 1
  maxReplicas: 5
  targetCPUUtilizationPercentage: 50
EOF
```

Although the results may be the same most of the time, a declarative configuration requires an understanding of the Kubernetes object configuration specs and file format. As an alternative, `kubectl` can be used for the imperative management of Kubernetes objects.

 Note that you must have a request set in your deployment to use autoscaling. If you do not have a request for CPU in your deployment, the HPA will deploy but will not work correctly.

You can also create the same `HorizontalPodAutoscaler` imperatively by running the `$ kubectl autoscale deployment my-ch7-app-node --cpu-percent=50 --min=1 --max=5` command.

3. Confirm the number of current replicas and the status of the HPA. When you run the following command, the number of replicas should be `1`:

```
$ kubectl get hpa
NAME                    REFERENCE                   TARGETS
MINPODS MAXPODS REPLICAS AGE
my-ch7-app-autoscaler Deployment/my-ch7-app-node 0%/50%          1
5       1       40s
```

4. Get the service IP of `my-ch7-app-node` so that you can use it in the next step:

```
$ export SERVICE_IP=$(kubectl get svc --namespace default my-ch7-app-node --template "{{ range (index .status.loadBalancer.ingress 0) }}{{.}}{{ end }}")
$ echo http://$SERVICE_IP/
http://mytodoapp.us-east-1.elb.amazonaws.com/
```

5. Start a new Terminal window and create a load generator to test the HPA. Make sure that you replace YOUR_SERVICE_IP in the following code with the actual service IP from the output of *Step 4*. This command will generate traffic to your To-Do application:

```
$ kubectl run -i --tty load-generator --image=busybox /bin/sh

while true; do wget -q -O- YOUR_SERVICE_IP; done
```

6. Wait a few minutes for the Autoscaler to respond to increasing traffic. While the load generator is running on one Terminal, run the following command on a separate Terminal window to monitor the increased CPU utilization. In our example, this is set to 210%:

```
$ kubectl get hpa
NAME                       REFERENCE                    TARGETS
MINPODS MAXPODS REPLICAS AGE
my-ch7-app-autoscaler Deployment/my-ch7-app-node 210%/50%        1
5       1           23m
```

7. Now, check the deployment size and confirm that the deployment has been resized to 5 replicas as a result of the increased workload:

```
$ kubectl get deployment my-ch7-app-node
NAME                 READY UP-TO-DATE AVAILABLE AGE
my-ch7-app-node 5/5    5            5           5h23m
```

8. On the Terminal screen where you run the load generator, press *Ctrl + C* to terminate the load generator. This will stop the traffic coming to your application.

9. Wait a few minutes for the Autoscaler to adjust and then verify the HPA status by running the following command. The current CPU utilization should be lower. In our example, it shows that it went down to 0%:

```
$ kubectl get hpa
NAME                       REFERENCE                    TARGETS MINPODS
MAXPODS REPLICAS AGE
my-ch7-app-autoscaler Deployment/my-ch7-app-node 0%/50%  1        5
1           34m
```

10. Check the deployment size and confirm that the deployment has been scaled down to 1 replica as the result of stopping the traffic generator:

```
$ kubectl get deployment my-ch7-app-node
NAME                 READY UP-TO-DATE AVAILABLE AGE
my-ch7-app-node 1/1    1            1           5h35m
```

In this recipe, you learned how to automate how an application is scaled dynamically based on changing metrics. When applications are scaled up, they are dynamically scheduled on existing worker nodes.

How it works...

This recipe showed you how to manually and automatically scale the number of pods in a deployment dynamically based on the Kubernetes metric.

In this recipe, in *Step 2*, we created an Autoscaler that adjusts the number of replicas between the defined minimum using `minReplicas: 1` and `maxReplicas: 5`. As shown in the following example, the adjustment criteria are triggered by the `targetCPUUtilizationPercentage: 50` metric:

```
spec:
  scaleTargetRef:
    apiVersion: apps/v1
    kind: Deployment
    name: my-ch7-app-node
  minReplicas: 1
  maxReplicas: 5
  targetCPUUtilizationPercentage: 50
```

`targetCPUUtilizationPercentage` was used with the `autoscaling/v1` APIs. You will soon see that `targetCPUUtilizationPercentage` will be replaced with an array called metrics.

To understand the new metrics and custom metrics, run the following command. This will return the manifest we created with V1 APIs into a new manifest using V2 APIs:

```
$ kubectl get hpa.v2beta2.autoscaling my-ch7-app-node -o yaml
```

This enables you to specify additional resource metrics. By default, CPU and memory are the only supported resource metrics. In addition to these resource metrics, v2 APIs enable two other types of metrics, both of which are considered custom metrics: per-pod custom metrics and object metrics. You can read more about this by going to the *Kubernetes HPA documentation* link mentioned in the *See also* section.

See also

- Kubernetes pod Autoscaler using custom metrics: `https://sysdig.com/blog/kubernetes-autoscaler/`
- Kubernetes HPA documentation: `https://kubernetes.io/docs/tasks/run-application/horizontal-pod-autoscale/`
- Declarative Management of Kubernetes Objects Using Configuration Files: `https://kubernetes.io/docs/tasks/manage-kubernetes-objects/declarative-config/`
- Imperative Management of Kubernetes Objects Using Configuration Files: `https://kubernetes.io/docs/tasks/manage-kubernetes-objects/imperative-config/`

Assigning applications to nodes

In this section, we will make sure that pods are not scheduled onto inappropriate nodes. You will learn how to schedule pods into Kubernetes nodes using node selectors, taints, toleration and by setting priorities.

Getting ready

Make sure you have a Kubernetes cluster ready and `kubectl` and `helm` configured to manage the cluster resources.

How to do it...

This section is further divided into the following subsections to make this process easier:

- Labeling nodes
- Assigning pods to nodes using nodeSelector
- Assigning pods to nodes using node and inter-pod affinity

Labeling nodes

Kubernetes labels are used for specifying the important attributes of resources that can be used to apply organizational structures onto system objects. In this recipe, we will learn about the common labels that are used for Kubernetes nodes and apply a custom label to be used when scheduling pods into nodes.

Let's perform the following steps to list some of the default labels that have been assigned to your nodes:

1. List the labels that have been assigned to your nodes. In our example, we will use a kops cluster that's been deployed on AWS EC2, so you will also see the relevant AWS labels, such as availability zones:

```
$ kubectl get nodes --show-labels
NAME                          STATUS ROLES AGE VERSION LABELS
ip-172-20-49-12.ec2.internal  Ready    node  23h v1.14.6
kubernetes.io/arch=amd64,kubernetes.io/instance-type=t3.large,
kubernetes.io/os=linux,failure-domain.beta.kubernetes.io/region=us-
east-1,
failure-domain.beta.kubernetes.io/zone=us-east-1a,
kops.k8s.io/instancegroup=nodes,kubernetes.io/hostname=ip-172-20-49
-12.ec2.internal,
kubernetes.io/role=node,node-role.kubernetes.io/node=
...
```

2. Get the list of the nodes in your cluster. We will use node names to assign labels in the next step:

```
$ kubectl get nodes
NAME                           STATUS  ROLES   AGE  VERSION
ip-172-20-49-12.ec2.internal   Ready   node    23h  v1.14.6
ip-172-20-50-171.ec2.internal  Ready   node    23h  v1.14.6
ip-172-20-58-83.ec2.internal   Ready   node    23h  v1.14.6
ip-172-20-59-8.ec2.internal    Ready   master  23h  v1.14.6
```

3. Label two nodes as production and development. Run the following command using your worker node names from the output of *Step 2*:

```
$ kubectl label nodes ip-172-20-49-12.ec2.internal
environment=production
$ kubectl label nodes ip-172-20-50-171.ec2.internal
environment=production
$ kubectl label nodes ip-172-20-58-83.ec2.internal
environment=development
```

4. Verify that the new labels have been assigned to the nodes. This time, you should see `environment` labels on all the nodes except the node labeled `role=master`:

```
$ kubectl get nodes --show-labels
```

It is recommended to document labels for other people who will use your clusters. While they don't directly imply semantics to the core system, make sure they are still meaningful and relevant to all users.

Assigning pods to nodes using nodeSelector

In this recipe, we will learn how to schedule a pod onto a selected node using the nodeSelector primitive:

1. Create a copy of the Helm chart we used in the *Manually scaling an application* recipe in a new directory called `todo-dev`. We will edit the templates later in order to specify `nodeSelector`:

```
$ cd src/chapter7/charts
$ mkdir todo-dev
$ cp -a node/* todo-dev/
$ cd todo-dev
```

2. Edit the `deployment.yaml` file in the `templates` directory:

```
$ vi templates/deployment.yaml
```

3. Add `nodeSelector:` and `environment: "{{ .Values.environment }}"` right before the `containers:` parameter. This should look as follows:

```
        ...
                mountPath: {{ .Values.persistence.path }}
          {{- end }}
# Start of the addition
        nodeSelector:
          environment: "{{ .Values.environment }}"
# End of the addition
        containers:
          - name: {{ template "node.fullname" . }}

        ...
```

The Helm installation uses templates to generate configuration files. As shown in the preceding example, to simplify how you customize the provided values, `{{expr}}` is used, and these values come from the `values.yaml` file names. The `values.yaml` file contains the default values for a chart.

 Although it may not be practical on large clusters, instead of using `nodeSelector` and labels, you can also schedule a pod on one specific node using the `nodeName` setting. In that case, instead of the `nodeSelector` setting, you add `nodeName: yournodename` to your deployment manifest.

4. Now that we've added the variable, edit the `values.yaml` file. This is where we will set the environment to the `development` label:

   ```
   $ vi values.yaml
   ```

5. Add the `environment: development` line to the end of the files. It should look as follows:

   ```
   . . .
   ## Affinity for pod assignment
   ## Ref:
   https://kubernetes.io/docs/concepts/configuration/assign-pod-node/#
   affinity-and-anti-affinity
   ##
   affinity: {}
   environment: development
   ```

6. Edit the `Chart.yaml` file and change the chart name to its folder name. In this recipe, it's called `todo-dev`. After these changes, the first two lines should look as follows:

   ```
   apiVersion: v1
   name: todo-dev
   . . .
   ```

7. Update the Helm dependencies and build them. The following commands will pull all the dependencies and build the Helm chart:

   ```
   $ helm dep update & helm dep build
   ```

8. Examine the chart for issues. If there are any issues with the chart's files, the linting process will bring them up; otherwise, no failures should be found:

```
$ helm lint .
==> Linting .
Lint OK
1 chart(s) linted, no failures
```

9. Install the To-Do application example using the following command. This Helm chart will deploy two pods, including a Node.js service and a MongoDB service, except this time the nodes are labeled as `environment: development`:

```
$ helm install . --name my-app7-dev --set serviceType=LoadBalancer
```

10. Check that all the pods have been scheduled on the development nodes using the following command. You will find the `my-app7-dev-todo-dev` pod running on the node labeled `environment: development`:

```
$ for n in $(kubectl get nodes -l environment=development --no-
headers | cut -d " " -f1); do kubectl get pods --all-namespaces --
no-headers --field-selector spec.nodeName=${n} ; done
```

With that, you've learned how to schedule workload pods onto selected nodes using the `nodeSelector` primitive.

Assigning pods to nodes using node and inter-pod Affinity

In this recipe, we will learn how to expand the constraints we expressed in the previous recipe, *Assigning pods to labeled nodes using nodeSelector*, using the affinity and anti-affinity features.

Let's use a scenario-based approach to simplify this recipe for different affinity selector options. We will take the previous example, but this time with complicated requirements:

- `todo-prod` must be scheduled on a node with the `environment:production` label and should fail if it can't.
- `todo-prod` should run on a node that is labeled with `failure-domain.beta.kubernetes.io/zone=us-east-1a` or `us-east-1b` but can run anywhere if the label requirement is not satisfied.
- `todo-prod` must run on the same zone as `mongodb`, but should not run in the zone where `todo-dev` is running.

The requirements listed here are only examples in order to represent the use of some affinity definition functionality. This is not the ideal way to configure this specific application. The labels may be completely different in your environment.

The preceding scenario will cover both types of node affinity options (`requiredDuringSchedulingIgnoredDuringExecution` and `preferredDuringSchedulingIgnoredDuringExecution`). You will see these options later in our example. Let's get started:

1. Create a copy of the Helm chart we used in the *Manually scaling an application* recipe to a new directory called `todo-prod`. We will edit the templates later in order to specify `nodeAffinity` rules:

```
$ cd src/chapter7/charts
$ mkdir todo-prod
$ cp -a node/* todo-prod/
$ cd todo-prod
```

2. Edit the `values.yaml` file. To access it, use the following command:

```
$ vi values.yaml
```

3. Replace the last line, `affinity: {}`, with the following code. This change will satisfy the first requirement we defined previously, meaning that a pod can only be placed on a node with an `environment` label and whose value is `production`:

```
## Affinity for pod assignment
## Ref:
https://kubernetes.io/docs/concepts/configuration/assign-pod-node/#
affinity-and-anti-affinity
# affinity: {}
# Start of the affinity addition #1
affinity:
  nodeAffinity:
    requiredDuringSchedulingIgnoredDuringExecution:
      nodeSelectorTerms:
      - matchExpressions:
        - key: environment
          operator: In
          values:
          - production
# End of the affinity addition #1
```

You can also specify more than one `matchExpressions` under the `nodeSelectorTerms`. In this case, the pod can only be scheduled onto a node where all `matchExpressions` are satisfied, which may limit your successful scheduling chances.

Although it may not be practical on large clusters, instead of using `nodeSelector` and labels, you can also schedule a pod on a specific node using the `nodeName` setting. In this case, instead of the `nodeSelector` setting, add `nodeName: yournodename` to your deployment manifest.

4. Now, add the following lines right under the preceding code addition. This addition will satisfy the second requirement we defined, meaning that nodes with a label of `failure-domain.beta.kubernetes.io/zone` and whose value is `us-east-1a` or `us-east-1b` will be preferred:

```
        - production
# End of the affinity addition #1
# Start of the affinity addition #2
    preferredDuringSchedulingIgnoredDuringExecution:
    - weight: 1
      preference:
        matchExpressions:
        - key: failure-domain.beta.kubernetes.io/zone
          operator: In
          values:
          - us-east-1a
          - us-east-1b
# End of the affinity addition #2
```

5. For the third requirement, we will use the inter-pod affinity and anti-affinity functionalities. They allow us to limit which nodes our pod is eligible to be scheduled based on the labels on pods that are already running on the node instead of taking labels on nodes for scheduling. The following podAffinity `requiredDuringSchedulingIgnoredDuringExecution` rule will look for nodes where `app: mongodb` exist and use `failure-domain.beta.kubernetes.io/zone` as a topology key to show us where the pod is allowed to be scheduled:

```
        - us-east-1b
# End of the affinity addition #2
# Start of the affinity addition #3a
    podAffinity:
      requiredDuringSchedulingIgnoredDuringExecution:
      - labelSelector:
          matchExpressions:
```

```
        - key: app
          operator: In
          values:
          - mongodb
        topologyKey: failure-domain.beta.kubernetes.io/zone
# End of the affinity addition #3a
```

6. Add the following lines to complete the requirements. This time, the `podAntiAffinity preferredDuringSchedulingIgnoredDuringExecution` rule will look for nodes where `app: todo-dev` exists and use `failure-domain.beta.kubernetes.io/zone` as a topology key:

```
        topologyKey: failure-domain.beta.kubernetes.io/zone
# End of the affinity addition #3a
# Start of the affinity addition #3b
   podAntiAffinity:
     preferredDuringSchedulingIgnoredDuringExecution:
     - weight: 100
       podAffinityTerm:
         labelSelector:
           matchExpressions:
           - key: app
             operator: In
             values:
             - todo-dev
         topologyKey: failure-domain.beta.kubernetes.io/zone
# End of the affinity addition #3b
```

7. Edit the `Chart.yaml` file and change the chart name to its folder name. In this recipe, it's called `todo-prod`. After making these changes, the first two lines should look as follows:

```
apiVersion: v1
name: todo-prod
...
```

8. Update the Helm dependencies and build them. The following commands will pull all the dependencies and build the Helm chart:

```
$ helm dep update & helm dep build
```

9. Examine the chart for issues. If there are any issues with the chart files, the linting process will bring them up; otherwise, no failures should be found:

```
$ helm lint .
==> Linting .
Lint OK
1 chart(s) linted, no failures
```

10. Install the To-Do application example using the following command. This Helm chart will deploy two pods, including a Node.js service and a MongoDB service, this time following the detailed requirements we defined at the beginning of this recipe:

```
$ helm install . --name my-app7-prod --set serviceType=LoadBalancer
```

11. Check that all the pods that have been scheduled on the nodes are labeled as `environment: production` using the following command. You will find the `my-app7-dev-todo-dev` pod running on the nodes:

```
$ for n in $(kubectl get nodes -l environment=production --no-
headers | cut -d " " -f1); do kubectl get pods --all-namespaces --
no-headers --field-selector spec.nodeName=${n} ; done
```

In this recipe, you learned about advanced pod scheduling practices while using a number of primitives in Kubernetes, including `nodeSelector`, node affinity, and inter-pod affinity. Now, you will be able to configure a set of applications that are co-located in the same defined topology or scheduled in different zones so that you have better **service-level agreement** (**SLA**) times.

How it works...

The recipes in this section showed you how to schedule pods on preferred locations, sometimes based on complex requirements.

In the *Labeling nodes* recipe, in *Step 1*, you can see that some standard labels have been applied to your nodes already. Here is a short explanation of what they mean and where they are used:

- `kubernetes.io/arch`: This comes from the `runtime.GOARCH` parameter and is applied to nodes to identify where to run different architecture container images, such as x86, arm, arm64, ppc64le, and s390x, in a mixed architecture cluster.

- `kubernetes.io/instance-type`: This is only useful if your cluster is deployed on a cloud provider. Instance types tell us a lot about the platform, especially for AI and machine learning workloads where you need to run some pods on instances with GPUs or faster storage options.
- `kubernetes.io/os`: This is applied to nodes and comes from `runtime.GOOS`. It is probably less useful unless you have Linux and Windows nodes in the same cluster.
- `failure-domain.beta.kubernetes.io/region` and `/zone`: This is also more useful if your cluster is deployed on a cloud provider or your infrastructure is spread across a different failure-domain. In a data center, it can be used to define a rack solution so that you can schedule pods on separate racks for higher availability.
- `kops.k8s.io/instancegroup=nodes`: This is the node label that's set to the name of the instance group. It is only used with kops clusters.
- `kubernetes.io/hostname`: Shows the hostname of the worker.
- `kubernetes.io/role`: This shows the role of the worker in the cluster. Some common values include `node` for representing worker nodes and `master`, which shows the node is the master node and is tainted as not schedulable for workloads by default.

In the *Assigning pods to nodes using node and inter-pod affinity* recipe, in *Step 3*, the node affinity rule says that the pod can only be placed on a node with a label whose key is `environment` and whose value is `production`.

In *Step 4*, the `affinity key: value` requirement is preferred (`preferredDuringSchedulingIgnoredDuringExecution`). The `weight` field here can be a value between 1 and 100. For every node that meets these requirements, a Kubernetes scheduler computes a sum. The nodes with the highest total score are preferred.

Another detail that's used here is the `In` parameter. Node Affinity supports the following operators: `In`, `NotIn`, `Exists`, `DoesNotExist`, `Gt`, and `Lt`. You can read more about the operators by looking at the *Scheduler affinities through examples* link mentioned in the *See also* section.

 If selector and affinity rules are not well planned, they can easily block pods getting scheduled on your nodes. Keep in mind that if you have specified both `nodeSelector` and `nodeAffinity` rules, both requirements must be met for the pod to be scheduled on the available nodes.

In *Step 5*, inter-pod affinity is used (`podAffinity`) to satisfy the requirement in PodSpec. In this recipe, `podAffinity` is `requiredDuringSchedulingIgnoredDuringExecution`. Here, `matchExpressions` says that a pod can only run on nodes where `failure-domain.beta.kubernetes.io/zone` matches the nodes where other pods with the `app:mongodb` label are running.

In *Step 6*, the requirement is satisfied with `podAntiAffinity` using `preferredDuringSchedulingIgnoredDuringExecution`.
Here, `matchExpressions` says that a pod can't run on nodes where `failure-domain.beta.kubernetes.io/zone` matches the nodes where other pods with the `app:todo-dev` label are running. The weight is increased by setting it to `100`.

See also

- List of known labels, annotations, and taints: `https://kubernetes.io/docs/reference/kubernetes-api/labels-annotations-taints/`
- Assigning Pods to Nodes in the Kubernetes documentation: `https://kubernetes.io/docs/tasks/configure-pod-container/assign-pods-nodes/`
- More on labels and selectors in the Kubernetes documentation: `https://kubernetes.io/docs/concepts/overview/working-with-objects/labels/`
- Scheduler affinities through examples: `https://banzaicloud.com/blog/k8s-affinities/`
- Node affinity and NodeSelector design document: `https://github.com/kubernetes/community/blob/master/contributors/design-proposals/scheduling/nodeaffinity.md`
- Interpod topological affinity and anti-affinity design document: `https://github.com/kubernetes/community/blob/master/contributors/design-proposals/scheduling/podaffinity.md`

Creating an external load balancer

The load balancer service type is a relatively simple service alternative to ingress that uses a cloud-based external load balancer. The external load balancer service type's support is limited to specific cloud providers but is supported by the most popular cloud providers, including AWS, GCP, Azure, Alibaba Cloud, and OpenStack.

In this section, we will expose our workload ports using a load balancer. We will learn how to create an external GCE/AWS load balancer for clusters on public clouds, as well as for your private cluster using `inlet-operator`.

Getting ready

Make sure you have a Kubernetes cluster ready and `kubectl` and `helm` configured to manage the cluster resources. In this recipe, we are using a cluster that's been deployed on AWS using `kops`, as described in `Chapter 1`, *Building Production-Ready Kubernetes Clusters*, in the *Amazon Web Services* recipe. The same instructions will work on all major cloud providers.

To access the example files, clone the `k8sdevopscookbook/src` repository to your workstation to use the configuration files in the `src/chapter7/lb` directory, as follows:

```
$ git clone https://github.com/k8sdevopscookbook/src.git
$ cd src/chapter7/lb/
```

After you've cloned the examples repository, you can move on to the recipes.

How to do it...

This section is further divided into the following subsections to make this process easier:

- Creating an external cloud load balancer
- Finding the external address of the service

Creating an external cloud load balancer

When you create an application and expose it as a Kubernetes service, you usually need the service to be reachable externally via an IP address or URL. In this recipe, you will learn how to create a load balancer, also referred to as a cloud load balancer.

In the previous chapters, we have seen a couple of examples that used the load balancer service type to expose IP addresses, including the *Configuring and managing S3 object storage using MinIO* and *Application backup and recovery using Kasten* recipes in the previous chapter, as well as the To-Do application that was provided in this chapter in the *Assigning applications to nodes* recipe.

Let's use the MinIO application to learn how to create a load balancer. Follow these steps to create a service and expose it using an external load balancer service:

1. Review the content of the `minio.yaml` file in the examples directory in `src/chapter7/lb` and deploy it using the following command. This will create a StatefulSet and a service where the MinIO port is exposed internally to the cluster via port number `9000`. You can choose to apply the same steps and create a load balancer for your own application. In that case, skip to *Step 2*:

   ```
   $ kubectl apply -f minio.yaml
   ```

2. List the available services on Kubernetes. You will see that the MinIO service shows `ClusterIP` as the service type and `none` under the `EXTERNAL-IP` field:

   ```
   $ kubectl get svc
   NAME         TYPE       CLUSTER-IP   EXTERNAL-IP  PORT(S)   AGE
   kubernetes   ClusterIP  100.64.0.1   <none>       443/TCP   5d
   minio        ClusterIP  None         <none>       9000/TCP  4m
   ```

3. Create a new service with the `TYPE` set to `LoadBalancer`. The following command will expose `port: 9000` of our MinIO application at `targetPort: 9000` using the `TCP` protocol, as shown here:

   ```
   cat <<EOF | kubectl apply -f -
   apiVersion: v1
   kind: Service
   metadata:
     name: minio-service
   spec:
     type: LoadBalancer
     ports:
       - port: 9000
         targetPort: 9000
         protocol: TCP
     selector:
       app: minio
   EOF
   ```

The preceding command will immediately create the `Service` object, but the actual load balancer on the cloud provider side may take 30 seconds to a minute to be completely initialized. Although the object will state that it's ready, it will not function until the load balancer is initialized. This is one of the disadvantages of cloud load balancers compared to ingress controllers, which we will look at in the next recipe, *Creating an ingress service and service mesh using Istio*.

As an alternative to *Step 3*, you can also create the load balancer by using the following command:

```
$ kubectl expose rc example --port=9000 --target-port=9000 --name=minio-
service --type=LoadBalancer
```

Finding the external address of the service

Let's perform the following steps to get the externally reachable address of the service:

1. List the services that use the `LoadBalancer` type. The `EXTERNAL-IP` column will show you the cloud vendor-provided address:

```
$ kubectl get svc |grep LoadBalancer
NAME             TYPE          CLUSTER-IP       EXTERNAL-IP
PORT(S)          AGE
minio-service LoadBalancer 100.69.15.120 containerized.me.us-
east-1.elb.amazonaws.com 9000:30705/TCP 4h39m
```

2. If you are running on a cloud provider service such as AWS, you can also use the following command to get the exact address. You can copy and paste this into a web browser:

```
$ SERVICE_IP=http://$(kubectl get svc minio-service \
-o
jsonpath='{.status.loadBalancer.ingress[0].hostname}:{.spec.ports[]
.targetPort}')
$ echo $SERVICE_IP
```

3. If you are running on a bare-metal server, then you probably won't have a `hostname` entry. As an example, if you are running MetalLB (`https://metallb. universe.tf/`), a load balancer for bare-metal Kubernetes clusters, or SeeSaw (`https://github.com/google/seesaw`), a **Linux Virtual Server** (**LVS**)-based load balancing platform, you need to look for the `ip` entry instead:

```
$ SERVICE_IP=http://$(kubectl get svc minio-service \
-o
jsonpath='{.status.loadBalancer.ingress[0].ip}:{.spec.ports[].targe
```

```
tPort}')
$ echo $SERVICE_IP
```

The preceding command will return a link similar
to `https://containerized.me.us-east-1.elb.amazonaws.com:9000`.

How it works...

This recipe showed you how to quickly create a cloud load balancer to expose your services with an external address.

In the *Creating a cloud load balancer* recipe, in *Step 3*, when a load balancer service is created in Kubernetes, a cloud provider load balancer is created on your behalf without you having to go through the cloud service provider APIs separately. This feature helps you easily manage the creation of load balancers outside of your Kubernetes cluster, but at the same takes a bit of time to complete and requires a separate load balancer for every service, so this might be costly and not very flexible.

To give load balancers flexibility and add more application-level functionality, you can use ingress controllers. Using ingress, traffic routing can be controlled by rules defined in the ingress resource. You will learn more about popular ingress gateways in the next two recipes, *Creating an ingress service and service mesh using Istio* and *Creating an ingress service and service mesh using Linkerd*.

See also

- Kubernetes documentation on the load balancer service type: `https://kubernetes.io/docs/concepts/services-networking/service/#loadbalancer`
- Using a load balancer on Amazon EKS: `https://docs.aws.amazon.com/eks/latest/userguide/load-balancing.html`
- Using a load balancer on AKS: `https://docs.microsoft.com/en-us/azure/aks/load-balancer-standard`
- Using a load balancer on Alibaba Cloud: `https://www.alibabacloud.com/help/doc-detail/53759.htm`
- Load balancer for your private Kubernetes cluster: `https://blog.alexellis.io/ingress-for-your-local-kubernetes-cluster/`

Creating an ingress service and service mesh using Istio

Istio is a popular open source service mesh. In this section, we will get basic Istio service mesh functionality up and running. You will learn how to create a service mesh to secure, connect, and monitor microservices.

Service mesh is a very detailed concept and we don't intend to explain any detailed use cases. Instead, we will focus on getting our service up and running.

Getting ready

Make sure you have a Kubernetes cluster ready and `kubectl` and `helm` configured to manage the cluster resources.

Clone the `https://github.com/istio/istio` repository to your workstation, as follows:

```
$ git clone https://github.com/istio/istio.git
$ cd istio
```

We will use the examples in the preceding repository to install Istio on our Kubernetes cluster.

How to do it...

This section is further divided into the following subsections to make this process easier:

- Installing Istio using Helm
- Verifying the installation
- Creating an ingress gateway

Installing Istio using Helm

Let's perform the following steps to install Istio:

1. Create the Istio CRDs that are required before we can deploy Istio:

   ```
   $ helm install install/kubernetes/helm/istio-init --name istio-init \
   --namespace istio-system
   ```

2. Install Istio with the default configuration. This will deploy the Istio core components, that is, `istio-citadel`, `istio-galley`, `istio-ingressgateway`, `istio-pilot`, `istio-policy`, `istio-sidecar-injector`, and `istio-telemetry`:

   ```
   $ helm install install/kubernetes/helm/istio --name istio \
   --namespace istio-system
   ```

3. Enable automatic sidecar injection by labeling the namespace where you will run your applications. In this recipe, we will be using the `default` namespace:

   ```
   $ kubectl label namespace default istio-injection=enabled
   ```

To be able to get Istio functionality for your application, the pods need to run an Istio sidecar proxy. The preceding command will automatically inject the Istio sidecar. As an alternative, you can find the instructions for manually adding Istio sidecars to your pods using the `istioctl` command in the *Installing the Istio sidecar instructions* link provided in the *See also* section.

Verifying the installation

Let's perform the following steps to confirm that Istio has been installed successfully:

1. Check the number of Istio CRDs that have been created. The following command should return 23, which is the number of CRDs that have been created by Istio:

   ```
   $ kubectl get crds | grep 'istio.io' | wc -l
   23
   ```

2. Run the following command and confirm that the list of Istio core component services have been created:

```
$ kubectl get svc -n istio-system
NAME                   TYPE          CLUSTER-IP      EXTERNAL-IP
PORT(S)                AGE
istio-citadel          ClusterIP     100.66.235.211  <none>
8060/TCP,...           2m10s
istio-galley           ClusterIP     100.69.206.64   <none>
443/TCP,...            2m11s
istio-ingressgateway   LoadBalancer  100.67.29.143   domain.com
15020:31452/TCP,...    2m11s
istio-pilot            ClusterIP     100.70.130.148  <none>
15010/TCP,...          2m11s
istio-policy           ClusterIP     100.64.243.176  <none>
9091/TCP,...           2m11s
istio-sidecar-injector ClusterIP     100.69.244.156  <none>
443/TCP,...            2m10s
istio-telemetry        ClusterIP     100.68.146.30   <none>
9091/TCP,...           2m11s
prometheus             ClusterIP     100.71.172.191  <none>
9090/TCP               2m11s
```

3. Make sure that all the pods listed are in the Running state:

```
$ kubectl get pods -n istio-system
```

4. Confirm the Istio injection enabled namespaces. You should only see istio-injection for the default namespace:

```
$ kubectl get namespace -L istio-injection
NAME             STATUS AGE   ISTIO-INJECTION
default          Active 5d8h  enabled
istio-system     Active 40m
kube-node-lease  Active 5d8h
kube-public      Active 5d8h
kube-system      Active 5d8h
```

You can always enable injection for the other namespaces by adding the istio-injection=enabled label to a namespace.

Creating an ingress gateway

Instead of using a controller to load balance traffic, Istio uses a gateway. Let's perform the following steps to create an Istio ingress gateway for our example application:

1. Review the content of the `minio.yaml` file in the examples directory in `src/chapter7/lb` and deploy it using the following command. This will create a StatefulSet and a service where the MinIO port is exposed internally to the cluster via port number `9000`. You can also choose to apply the same steps and create an ingress gateway for your own application. In that case, skip to *Step 2*:

   ```
   $ kubectl apply -f minio.yaml
   ```

2. Get the ingress IP and ports:

   ```
   $ export INGRESS_HOST=$(kubectl -n istio-system get service istio-
   ingressgateway -o
   jsonpath='{.status.loadBalancer.ingress[0].hostname}')
   $ export INGRESS_PORT=$(kubectl -n istio-system get service istio-
   ingressgateway -o
   jsonpath='{.spec.ports[?(@.name=="http2")].port}')
   $ export SECURE_INGRESS_PORT=$(kubectl -n istio-system get service
   istio-ingressgateway -o
   jsonpath='{.spec.ports[?(@.name=="https")].port}')
   ```

3. Create a new Istio gateway:

   ```
   $ cat <<EOF | kubectl apply -f -
   apiVersion: networking.istio.io/v1alpha3
   kind: Gateway
   metadata:
     name: minio-gateway
   spec:
     selector:
       istio: ingressgateway
     servers:
     - port:
         number: 80
         name: http
         protocol: HTTP
       hosts:
       - "*"
   EOF
   ```

4. Create a new `VirtualService` to forward requests to the MinIO instance via the gateway. This helps specify routing for the gateway and binds the gateway to the `VirtualService`:

```
$ cat <<EOF | kubectl apply -f -
apiVersion: networking.istio.io/v1alpha3
kind: VirtualService
metadata:
 name: minio
spec:
 hosts:
 - "*"
 gateways:
 - minio-gateway.default
 http:
 - match:
 - uri:
 prefix: /
 route:
 - destination:
 port:
 number: 9000
 host: minio
EOF
```

This configuration will expose your services to external access using Istio, and you will have more control over rules.

How it works...

This recipe showed you how to quickly configure the Istio service mesh and use custom Istio resources such as ingress gateway to open a service to external access.

For the service mesh to function correctly, each pod in the mesh needs to run an Envoy sidecar. In the *Installing Istio using Helm* recipe, in *Step 3*, we enabled automatic injection for pods in the `default` namespace so that the pods that are deployed in that namespace will run the Envoy sidecar.

An ingress controller is a reverse-proxy that runs in the Kubernetes cluster and configures routing rules. In the *Creating an ingress gateway* recipe, in *Step 2*, unlike traditional Kubernetes ingress objects, we used Istio CRDs such as Gateway, VirtualService, and DestinationRule to create the ingress.

We created a gateway rule for the ingress Gateway using the `istio:ingressgateway` selector in order to accept HTTP traffic on port number `80`.

In *Step 4*, we created a VirtualService for the MinIO services we wanted to expose. Since the gateway may be in a different namespace, we used `minio-gateway.default` to set the gateway name.

With this, we have exposed our service using HTTP. You can read more about exposing the service using the HTTPS protocol by looking at the link in *See also* section.

There's more...

Although it is very popular, Istio is not the simplest ingress to deal with. We highly recommend that you look at all the options that are available for your use case and consider alternatives. Therefore, it is useful to know how to remove Istio.

Deleting Istio

You can delete Istio by using the following commands:

```
$ helm delete istio
$ helm delete istio-init
```

If you want to completely remove the deleted release records from the Helm records and free the release name to be used later, add the `--purge` parameter to the preceding commands.

See also

- Istio documentation: `https://istio.io/docs/`
- Istio examples: `https://istio.io/docs/examples/bookinfo/`
- Installing the Istio sidecar: `https://istio.io/docs/setup/additional-setup/sidecar-injection/`
- Istio ingress tutorial from Kelsey Hightower: `https://github.com/kelseyhightower/istio-ingress-tutorial`
- Traffic management with Istio: `https://istio.io/docs/tasks/traffic-management/`
- Security with Istio: `https://istio.io/docs/tasks/security/`

- Policy enforcement with Istio: `https://istio.io/docs/tasks/policy-enforcement/`
- Collecting telemetry information with Istio: `https://istio.io/docs/tasks/telemetry/`
- Creating Kubernetes ingress with Cert-Manager: `https://istio.io/docs/tasks/traffic-management/ingress/ingress-certmgr/`

Creating an ingress service and service mesh using Linkerd

In this section, we will get basic Linkerd service mesh up and running. You will learn how to create a service mesh to secure, connect, and monitor microservices.

Service mesh is a very detailed concept in itself and we don't intend to explain any detailed use cases here. Instead, we will focus on getting our service up and running.

Getting ready

Make sure you have a Kubernetes cluster ready and `kubectl` and `helm` configured to manage the cluster resources.

To access the example files for this recipe, clone the `k8sdevopscookbook/src` repository to your workstation to use the configuration files in the `src/chapter7/linkerd` directory, as follows:

```
$ git clone https://github.com/k8sdevopscookbook/src.git
$ cd src/chapter7/linkerd/
```

After you've cloned the preceding repository, you can get started with the recipes.

How to do it...

This section is further divided into the following subsections to make this process easier:

- Installing the Linkerd CLI
- Installing Linkerd
- Verifying a Linkerd deployment
- Viewing the Linkerd metrics

Installing the Linkerd CLI

To interact with Linkerd, you need to install the `linkerd` CLI. Follow these steps:

1. Install the `linkerd` CLI by running the following command:

   ```
   $ curl -sL https://run.linkerd.io/install | sh
   ```

2. Add the `linkerd` CLI to your path:

   ```
   $ export PATH=$PATH:$HOME/.linkerd2/bin
   ```

3. Verify that the `linkerd` CLI has been installed by running the following command. It should show the server as unavailable since we haven't installed it yet:

   ```
   $ linkerd version
   Client version: stable-2.5.0
   Server version: unavailable
   ```

4. Validate that `linkerd` can be installed. This command will check the cluster and point to issues if they exist:

   ```
   $ linkerd check --pre
   Status check results are √
   ```

If the status checks are looking good, you can move on to the next recipe.

Installing Linkerd

Compared to the alternatives, Linkerd is much easier to get started with and manage, so it is my preferred service mesh.

Install the Linkerd control plane using the Linkerd CLI. This command will use the default options and install the linkerd components in the `linkerd` namespace:

```
$ linkerd install | kubectl apply -f -
```

Pulling all the container images may take a minute or so. After that, you can verify the health of the components by following the next recipe, *Verifying a Linkerd deployment*.

Verifying a Linkerd deployment

Verifying Linkerd's deployment is as easy as the installation process.

Run the following command to validate the installation. This will display a long summary of control plane components and APIs and will make sure you are running the latest version:

```
$ linkerd check
...

control-plane-version
---------------------
√ control plane is up-to-date
√ control plane and cli versions match

Status check results are √
```

If the status checks are good, you are ready to test Linkerd with a sample application.

Adding Linkerd to a service

Follow these steps to add Linkerd to our demo application:

1. Change directories to the linkerd folder:

   ```
   $ cd /src/chapter7/linkerd
   ```

2. Deploy the demo application, which uses a mix of gRPC and HTTP calls to service a voting application to the user:

   ```
   $ kubectl apply -f emojivoto.yml
   ```

3. Get the service IP of the demo application. This following command will return the externally accessible address of your application:

   ```
   $ SERVICE_IP=http://$(kubectl get svc web-svc -n emojivoto \
   -o
   jsonpath='{.status.loadBalancer.ingress[0].hostname}:{.spec.ports[]
   .targetPort}')
   $ echo $SERVICE_IP
   ```

4. Open the external address from *Step 3* in a web browser and confirm that the application is functional:

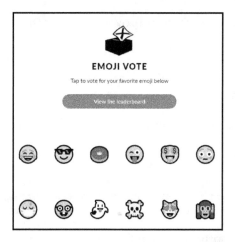

5. Enable automatic sidecar injection by labeling the namespace where you will run your applications. In this recipe, we're using the emojivoto namespace:

    $ kubectl label namespace emojivoto linkerd.io/inject=enabled

You can also manually inject a linkerd sidecar by patching the pods where you run your applications using the
kubectl get -n emojivoto deploy -o yaml | linkerd inject - | kubectl apply -f - command. In this recipe, the emojivoto namespace is used.

There's more...

This section is further divided into the following subsections to make this process easier:

- Accessing the dashboard
- Deleting Linkerd

Accessing the dashboard

We can either use port forwarding or use ingress to access the dashboard. Let's start with the simple way of doing things, that is, by port forwarding to your local system:

1. View the Linkerd dashboard by running the following command:

    $ linkerd dashboard &

2. Visit the following link in your browser to view the dashboard:

    `http://127.0.0.1:50750`

    The preceding commands will set up a port forward from your local system to the `linkerd-web` pod.

If you want to access the dashboard from an external IP, then follow these steps:

1. Download the sample ingress definition:

    ```
    $ wget
    https://raw.githubusercontent.com/k8sdevopscookbook/src/master/chap
    ter7/linkerd/ingress-nginx.yaml
    ```

2. Edit the ingress configuration in the `ingress-nginx.yaml` file in the `src/chapter7/linkerd` directory and change – `host:` `dashboard.example.com` on line 27 to the URL where you want your dashboard to be exposed. Apply the configuration using the following command:

    `$ kubectl apply -f ingress-nginx.yaml`

The preceding example file uses `linkerddashboard.containerized.me` as the dashboard address. It also protects access with basic auth using `admin/admin` credentials. It is highly suggested that you use your own credentials by changing the base64-encoded key pair defined in the `auth` section of the configuration using the `username:password` format.

Deleting Linkerd

To remove the Linkerd control plane, run the following command:

`$ linkerd install --ignore-cluster | kubectl delete -f -`

This command will pull a list of all the configuration files for the Linkerd control plane, including namespaces, service accounts, and CRDs, and remove them.

See also

- Linkerd documentation: `https://linkerd.io/2/overview/`
- Common tasks with Linkerd: `https://linkerd.io/2/tasks/`
- Frequently asked Linkerd questions and answers: `https://linkerd.io/2/faq/`

Auto-healing pods in Kubernetes

Kubernetes has self-healing capabilities at the cluster level. It restarts containers that fail, reschedules pods when nodes die, and even kills containers that don't respond to your user-defined health checks.

In this section, we will perform application and cluster scaling tasks. You will learn how to use liveness and readiness probes to monitor container health and trigger a restart action in case of failures.

Getting ready

Make sure you have a Kubernetes cluster ready and `kubectl` and `helm` configured to manage the cluster resources.

How to do it…

This section is further divided into the following subsections to make this process easier:

- Testing self-healing pods
- Adding liveness probes to pods

Testing self-healing pods

In this recipe, we will manually remove pods in our deployment to show how Kubernetes replaces them. Later, we will learn how to automate this using a user-defined health check. Now, let's test Kubernetes' self-healing for destroyed pods:

1. Create a deployment or StatefulSet with two or more replicas. As an example, we will use the MinIO application we used in the previous chapter, in the *Configuring and managing S3 object storage using MinIO* recipe. This example has four replicas:

```
$ cd src/chapter7/autoheal/minio
$ kubectl apply -f minio.yaml
```

2. List the MinIO pods that were deployed as part of the StatefulSet. You will see four pods:

```
$ kubectl get pods |grep minio
minio-0 1/1 Running 0 4m38ms
minio-1 1/1 Running 0 4m25s
minio-2 1/1 Running 0 4m12s
minio-3 1/1 Running 0 3m48s
```

3. Delete a pod to test Kubernetes' auto-healing functionality and immediately list the pods again. You will see that the terminated pod will be quickly rescheduled and deployed:

```
$ kubectl delete pod minio-0
pod "minio-0" deleted
$ kubectl get pods |grep miniominio-0
minio-0 0/1 ContainerCreating 0 2s
minio-1 1/1 Running           0 8m9s
minio-2 1/1 Running           0 7m56s
minio-3 1/1 Running           0 7m32s
```

With this, you have tested Kubernetes' self-healing after manually destroying a pod in operation. Now, we will learn how to add a health status check to pods to let Kubernetes automatically kill non-responsive pods so that they're restarted.

Adding liveness probes to pods

Kubernetes uses liveness probes to find out when to restart a container. Liveness can be checked by running a liveness probe command inside the container and validating that it returns 0 through TCP socket liveness probes or by sending an HTTP request to a specified path. In that case, if the path returns a success code, then kubelet will consider the container to be healthy. In this recipe, we will learn how to send an HTTP request method to the example application. Let's perform the following steps to add liveness probes:

1. Edit the `minio.yaml` file in the `src/chapter7/autoheal/minio` directory and add the following `livenessProbe` section right under the `volumeMounts` section, before `volumeClaimTemplates`. Your YAML manifest should look similar to the following. This will send an HTTP request to the `/minio/health/live` location every 20 seconds to validate its health:

```
...
        volumeMounts:
        - name: data
          mountPath: /data
```

```
#### Starts here
        livenessProbe:
          httpGet:
            path: /minio/health/live
            port: 9000
          initialDelaySeconds: 120
          periodSeconds: 20
#### Ends here
    # These are converted to volume claims by the controller
    # and mounted at the paths mentioned above.
    volumeClaimTemplates:
```

For liveness probes that use HTTP requests to work, an application needs to expose unauthenticated health check endpoints. In our example, MinIO provides this through the `/minio/health/live` endpoint. If your workload doesn't have a similar endpoint, you may want to use liveness commands inside your pods to verify their health.

2. Deploy the application. It will create four pods:

```
$ kubectl apply -f minio.yaml
```

3. Confirm the liveness probe by describing one of the pods. You will see a `Liveness` description similar to the following:

```
$ kubectl describe pod minio-0
...
    Liveness: http-get http://:9000/minio/health/live delay=120s
timeout=1s period=20s #success=1 #failure=3
...
```

4. To test the liveness probe, we need to edit the `minio.yaml` file again. This time, set the `livenessProbe` port to `8000`, which is where the application will not able to respond to the HTTP request. Repeat *Steps 2* and *3*, redeploy the application, and check the events in the pod description. You will see a `minio failed liveness probe, will be restarted` message in the events:

```
$ kubectl describe pod minio-0
```

5. You can confirm the restarts by listing the pods. You will see that every MinIO pod is restarted multiple times due to it having a failing liveness status:

```
$ kubectl get pods
NAME       READY STATUS   RESTARTS AGE
minio-0 1/1   Running 4         12m
minio-1 1/1   Running 4         12m
minio-2 1/1   Running 3         11m
minio-3 1/1   Running 3         11m
```

In this recipe, you learned how to implement the auto-healing functionality for applications that are running in Kubernetes clusters.

How it works...

This recipe showed you how to use a liveness probe on your applications running on Kubernetes.

In the *Adding liveness probes to pods* recipe, in *Step 1*, we added an HTTP request-based health check.

By adding the StatefulSet path and port, we let kubelet probe the defined endpoints. Here, the `initialDelaySeconds` field tells kubelet that it should wait `120` seconds before the first probe. If your application takes a while to get the endpoints ready, then make sure that you allow enough time before the first probe; otherwise, your pods will be restarted before the endpoints can respond to requests.

In *Step 3*, the `periodSeconds` field specifies that kubelet should perform a liveness probe every `20` seconds. Again, depending on the applications' expected availability, you should set a period that is right for your application.

See also

- Configuring liveness and readiness probes: `https://kubernetes.io/docs/tasks/configure-pod-container/configure-liveness-readiness-startup-probes/`
- Kubernetes Best Practices: Setting up health checks: `https://cloud.google.com/blog/products/gcp/kubernetes-best-practices-setting-up-health-checks-with-readiness-and-liveness-probes`

Managing upgrades through blue/green deployments

The blue-green deployment architecture is a method that's used to reduce downtime by running two identical production environments that can be switched between when needed. These two environments are identified as blue and green. In this section, we will perform rollover application upgrades. You will learn how to roll over a new version of your application with persistent storage by using blue/green deployment in Kubernetes.

Getting ready

Make sure you have a Kubernetes cluster ready and `kubectl` and `helm` configured to manage the cluster resources.

For this recipe, we will need a persistent storage provider to take snapshots from one version of the application and use clones with the other version of the application to keep the persistent volume content. We will use OpenEBS as a persistent storage provider, but you can also use any CSI-compatible storage provider.

Make sure OpenEBS has been configured with the cStor storage engine by following the instructions in `Chapter 5`, *Preparing for Stateful Workloads*, in the *Persistent storage using OpenEBS* recipe.

How to do it...

This section is further divided into the following subsections to make this process easier:

- Creating the blue deployment
- Creating the green deployment
- Switching traffic from blue to green

Creating the blue deployment

There are many traditional workloads that won't work with Kubernetes' way of rolling updates. If your workload needs to deploy a new version and cut over to it immediately, then you may need to perform blue/green deployment instead. Using the blue/green deployment approach, we will label the current production blue. In the next recipe, we will create an identical production environment called green before redirecting the services to green.

Let's perform the following steps to create the first application, which we will call blue:

1. Change directory to where the examples for this recipe are located:

    ```
    $ cd /src/chapter7/bluegreen
    ```

2. Review the content of the `blue-percona.yaml` file and use that to create the blue version of your application:

    ```
    $ kubectl create -f blue-percona.yaml
    pod "blue" created
    persistentvolumeclaim "demo-vol1-claim" created
    ```

3. Review the content of the `percona-svc.yaml` file and use that to create the service. You will see that `selector` in the service is set to `app: blue`. This service will forward all the MySQL traffic to the blue pod:

    ```
    $ kubectl create -f percona-svc.yaml
    ```

4. Get the service IP for `percona`. In our example, the Cluster IP is `10.3.0.75`:

    ```
    $ kubectl get svc percona
    NAME TYPE CLUSTER-IP EXTERNAL-IP PORT(S) AGE
    percona ClusterIP 10.3.0.75 <none> 3306/TCP 1m
    ```

5. Edit the `sql-loadgen.yaml` file and replace the target IP address with your percona service IP. In our example, it is `10.3.0.75`:

    ```
            containers:
          - name: sql-loadgen
            image: openebs/tests-mysql-client
            command: ["/bin/bash"]
            args: ["-c", "timelimit -t 300 sh MySQLLoadGenerate.sh
    10.3.0.75 > /dev/null 2>&1; exit 0"]
            tty: true
    ```

6. Start the load generator by running the `sql-loadgen.yaml` job:

```
$ kubectl create -f sql-loadgen.yaml
```

This job will generate a MySQL load targeting the IP of the service that was forwarded to the Percona workload (currently blue).

Creating the green deployment

Let's perform the following steps to deploy the new version of the application as our green deployment. We will switch the service to green, take a snapshot of blue's persistent volume, and deploy the green workload in a new pod:

1. Let's create a snapshot of the data from the blue application's PVC and use it to deploy the green application:

```
$ kubectl create -f snapshot.yaml
volumesnapshot.volumesnapshot.external-storage.k8s.io "snapshot-
blue" created
```

2. Review the content of the `green-percona.yaml` file and use that to create the green version of your application:

```
$ kubectl create -f green-percona.yaml
pod "green" created
persistentvolumeclaim "demo-snap-vol-claim" created
```

This pod will use a snapshot of the PVC from the blue application as its original PVC.

Switching traffic from blue to green

Let's perform the following steps to switch traffic from blue to the new green deployment:

Edit the service using the following command and replace `blue` with `green`. Service traffic will be forwarded to the pod that is labeled `green`:

```
$ kubectl edit svc percona
```

In this recipe, you have learned how to upgrade your application with a stateful workload using the blue/green deployment strategy.

See also

- Zero Downtime Deployments in Kubernetes with Jenkins: `https://kubernetes.io/blog/2018/04/30/zero-downtime-deployment-kubernetes-jenkins/`
- A Simple Guide to blue/green Deployment: `https://codefresh.io/kubernetes-tutorial/blue-green-deploy/`
- Kubernetes blue-green Deployment Examples: `https://github.com/ContainerSolutions/k8s-deployment-strategies/tree/master/blue-green`

Observability and Monitoring on Kubernetes

8

In this chapter, we will discuss the built-in Kubernetes tools and the popular third-party monitoring options for your containerized DevOps environment. You will learn how to monitor metrics for performance analysis, and also how to monitor and manage the real-time cost of Kubernetes resources.

By the end of this chapter, you should have knowledge of the following:

- Monitoring in Kubernetes
- Inspecting containers
- Monitoring using Amazon CloudWatch
- Monitoring using Google Stackdriver
- Monitoring using Azure Monitor
- Monitoring Kubernetes using Prometheus and Grafana
- Monitoring and performance analysis using Sysdig
- Managing the cost of resources using Kubecost

Technical requirements

The recipes in this chapter assume that you have deployed a functional Kubernetes cluster following one of the recommended methods described in Chapter 1, *Building Production-Ready Kubernetes Clusters*.

Kubernetes' command-line tool, `kubectl`, will be used for the rest of the recipes in this chapter since it's the main command-line interface for running commands against Kubernetes clusters. We will also use Helm where Helm charts are available to deploy solutions.

Monitoring in Kubernetes

In this section, we will configure our Kubernetes cluster to get core metrics, such as CPU and memory. You will learn how to monitor Kubernetes metrics using the built-in Kubernetes tools both in the CLI and on the UI.

Getting ready

Make sure you have a Kubernetes cluster ready and `kubectl` configured to manage the cluster resources.

Clone the `k8sdevopscookbook/src` repository to your workstation to use the manifest files in the `chapter8` directory:

```
$ git clone https://github.com/k8sdevopscookbook/src.git
$ cd /src/chapter8
```

The *Monitoring metrics using Kubernetes Dashboard* recipe requires Kubernetes Dashboard v2.0.0 or later to function. If you want to add metric functionality to the dashboard, make sure that you have Kubernetes Dashboard installed by following the instructions in the *Deploying Kubernetes Dashboard* recipe in `Chapter 1`, *Building Production-Ready Kubernetes Clusters*.

How to do it...

This section is further divided into the following subsections to make the process easier:

- Adding metrics using Kubernetes Metrics Server
- Monitoring metrics using the CLI
- Monitoring metrics using Kubernetes Dashboard
- Monitoring Node Health

Adding metrics using Kubernetes Metrics Server

Getting core system metrics such as CPU and memory not only provides useful information, but is also required by extended Kubernetes functionality such as Horizontal Pod Autoscaling, which we mentioned in Chapter 7, *Scaling and Upgrading Applications*:

1. Clone the Metrics Server repository to your client by running the following command:

   ```
   $ git clone https://github.com/kubernetes-incubator/metrics-
   server.git
   ```

2. Deploy the Metrics Server by applying the manifest in the metrics-server/deploy/1.8+ directory by running the following command:

   ```
   $ kubectl apply -f metrics-server/deploy/1.8+
   ```

This command will create the resources required in the kube-space namespace.

Monitoring metrics using the CLI

As part of the Metrics Server, the Resource Metrics API provides access to CPU and memory resource metrics for pods and nodes. Let's use the Resource Metrics API to access the metrics data from the CLI:

1. First, let's display node resource utilization:

   ```
   $ kubectl top nodes
   NAME                            CPU(cores)  CPU%  MEMORY(bytes)  MEMORY%
   ip-172-20-32-169.ec2.internal   259m        12%   1492Mi         19%
   ip-172-20-37-106.ec2.internal   190m        9%    1450Mi         18%
   ip-172-20-48-49.ec2.internal    262m        13%   2166Mi         27%
   ip-172-20-58-155.ec2.internal   745m        37%   1130Mi         14%
   ```

   The command will return utilized CPU and memory on all your Kubernetes nodes.

   There are a couple of ways to use the metrics information. First of all, at any given time, usage of both CPU and memory should be below your desired threshold, otherwise new nodes need to be added to your cluster to handle services smoothly. Balanced utilization is also important, which means that if the percentage of memory usage is higher than the average percentage of CPU usage, you may need to consider changing your cloud instance type to use better-balanced VM instances.

2. Display pod resource utilization in any namespace. In this example, we are listing the pods in the `openebs` namespace:

```
$ kubectl top pods -n openebs
NAME                                            CPU(cores)
MEMORY(bytes)
maya-apiserver-6ff5bc7bdd-15gmt                 2m          10Mi
openebs-admission-server-76dbdf97d9-swjw9       0m          3Mi
openebs-localpv-provisioner-6777f78966-f6lzp    2m          8Mi
openebs-ndm-operator-797495544c-hblxv           5m          12Mi
openebs-ndm-prvcr                               1m          6Mi
openebs-ndm-qmr66                               1m          6Mi
openebs-ndm-xbc2q                               1m          6Mi
openebs-provisioner-58bbbb8575-jzch2            3m          7Mi
openebs-snapshot-operator-6d7545dc69-b2zr7      4m          15Mi
```

The command should return the utilized CPU and memory on all your pods. Kubernetes features such as Horizontal Pod Scaler can utilize this information to scale your pods.

Monitoring metrics using Kubernetes Dashboard

By default, Kubernetes Dashboard doesn't display detailed metrics unless Kubernetes Metrics Server is installed and the `kubernetes-metrics-scraper` sidecar container is running.

Let's first verify that all the necessary components are running, and then we will see how to access the metrics data from Kubernetes Dashboard:

1. Verify that the `kubernetes-metrics-scraper` pod is running. If not, install Kubernetes Dashboard by following the instructions in the *Deploying the Kubernetes Dashboard* recipe in Chapter 1, *Building Production-Ready Kubernetes Clusters*:

```
$ kubectl get pods -n kubernetes-dashboard
NAME                                        READY STATUS  RESTARTS
AGE
dashboard-metrics-scraper-69fcc6d9df-hhkkw  1/1   Running 0
177m
kubernetes-dashboard-566c79c67d-xqc6h       1/1   Running 0
177m
```

2. On Kubernetes Dashboard, select **Namespaces** and click on the **Overview** menu. This view shows pods in that namespace with their CPU and memory utilization:

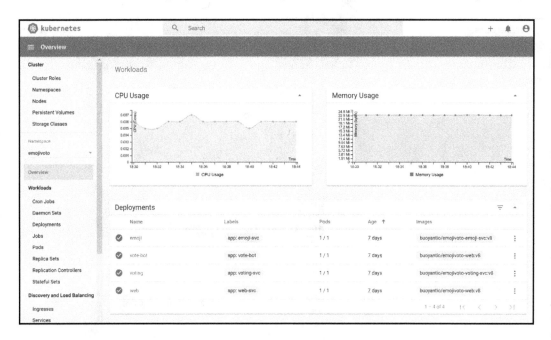

3. On Kubernetes Dashboard, select a namespace and click on **Pods** in the **Overview** menu. This view shows the overall CPU and memory utilization of the workloads within the selected namespace:

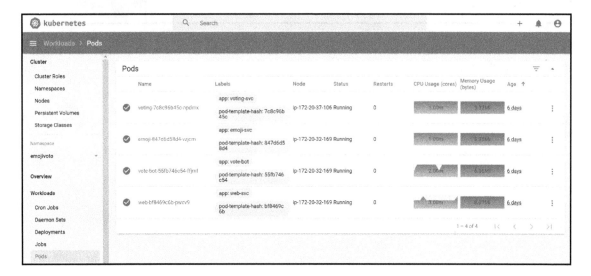

4. Select **Nodes** under the **Cluster** menu. This view shows nodes in the cluster with CPU and memory utilization:

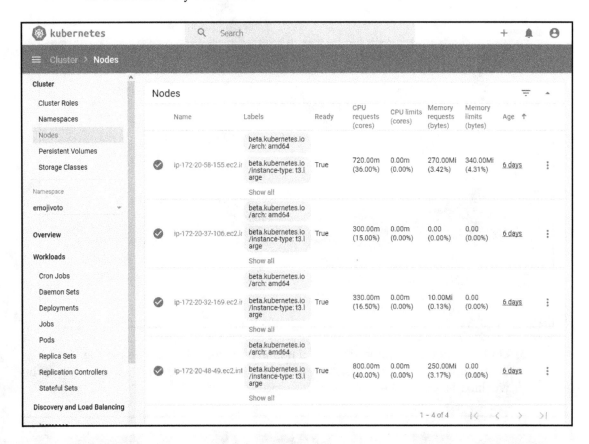

If the requests and limits are set very high, then they can take up more than their expected share of the cluster.

Monitoring node health

In this recipe, we will learn how to create a DaemonSet in the Kubernetes cluster to monitor node health. The node problem detector will collect node problems from daemons and will report them to the API server as NodeCondition and Event:

1. From the `/src/chapter8` folder first, inspect the content of the `node-problem-detector.yaml` file and create the DaemonSet to run the node problem detector:

   ```
   $ cat debug/node-problem-detector.yaml
   $ kubectl apply -f debug/node-problem-detector.yaml
   ```

2. Get a list of the nodes in the cluster. This command will return both worker and master nodes:

   ```
   $ kubectl get nodes
   NAME                          STATUS ROLES  AGE    VERSION
   ip-172-20-32-169.ec2.internal Ready  node   6d23h  v1.14.6
   ip-172-20-37-106.ec2.internal Ready  node   6d23h  v1.14.6
   ip-172-20-48-49.ec2.internal  Ready  master 6d23h  v1.14.6
   ip-172-20-58-155.ec2.internal Ready  node   6d23h  v1.14.6
   ```

3. Describe a node's status by replacing the node name in the following command with one of your node names and running it. In the output, examine the `Conditions` section for error messages. Here's an example of the output:

   ```
   $ kubectl describe node ip-172-20-32-169.ec2.internal | grep -i
   condition -A 20 | grep Ready -B 20
   Conditions:
    Type Status LastHeartbeatTime LastTransitionTime Reason Message
    ---- ------ ----------------- ------------------ ------ -------
    NetworkUnavailable False Sat, 12 Oct 2019 00:06:46 +0000 Sat, 12
   Oct 2019 00:06:46 +0000 RouteCreated RouteController created a
   route
    MemoryPressure False Fri, 18 Oct 2019 23:43:37 +0000 Sat, 12 Oct
   2019 00:06:37 +0000 KubeletHasSufficientMemory kubelet has
   sufficient memory available
    DiskPressure False Fri, 18 Oct 2019 23:43:37 +0000 Sat, 12 Oct
   2019 00:06:37 +0000 KubeletHasNoDiskPressure kubelet has no disk
   pressure
    PIDPressure False Fri, 18 Oct 2019 23:43:37 +0000 Sat, 12 Oct 2019
   00:06:37 +0000 KubeletHasSufficientPID kubelet has sufficient PID
   available
    Ready True Fri, 18 Oct 2019 23:43:37 +0000 Sat, 12 Oct 2019
   00:06:37 +0000 KubeletReady kubelet is posting ready status
   ```

4. Additionally, you can check for `KernelDeadlock`, `MemoryPressure`, and `DiskPressure` conditions by replacing the last part of the command with one of the conditions. Here is an example for `KernelDeadlock`:

```
$ kubectl get node ip-172-20-32-169.ec2.internal -o yaml | grep -B5
KernelDeadlock
  - lastHeartbeatTime: "2019-10-18T23:58:53Z"
  lastTransitionTime: "2019-10-18T23:49:46Z"
  message: kernel has no deadlock
  reason: KernelHasNoDeadlock
  status: "False"
  type: KernelDeadlock
```

The Node Problem Detector can detect unresponsive runtime daemons; hardware issues such as bad CPU, memory, or disk; kernel issues including kernel deadlock conditions; corrupted filesystems; unresponsive runtime daemons; and also infrastructure daemon issues such as NTP service outages.

See also

- Kubernetes Metrics Server Design Document: `https://github.com/kubernetes/ community/blob/master/contributors/design-proposals/instrumentation/ metrics-server.md`
- Configuring and using the monitoring stack in OpenShift Container Platform: `https://access.redhat.com/documentation/en-us/openshift_ container_platform/4.2/html/monitoring/index`
- Krex, a Kubernetes Resource Explorer: `https://github.com/kris-nova/krex`

Inspecting containers

In this section, we will troubleshoot problems related to pods stuck in Pending, ImagePullBackOff, or CrashLoopBackOff states. You will learn how to inspect and debug pods that are having deployment problems in Kubernetes.

Getting ready

Make sure you have a Kubernetes cluster ready and `kubectl` configured to manage the cluster resources.

How to do it...

This section is further divided into the following subsections to make the process easier:

- Inspecting pods in Pending status
- Inspecting pods in ImagePullBackOff status
- Inspecting pods in CrashLoopBackOff status

Inspecting pods in Pending status

When you deploy applications on Kubernetes, it is inevitable that soon or later you will need to get more information on your application. In this recipe, we will learn to inspect common pods problem of pods stuck in Pending status:

1. In the `/src/chapter8` folder, inspect the content of the `mongo-sc.yaml` file and deploy it running the following command. The deployment manifest includes MongoDB Statefulset with three replicas, Service and will get stuck in Pending state due mistake with a parameter and we will inspect it to find the source:

   ```
   $ cat debug/mongo-sc.yaml
   $ kubectl apply -f debug/mongo-sc.yaml
   ```

2. List the pods by running the following command. You will notice that the status is `Pending` for the `mongo-0` pod:

   ```
   $ kubectl get pods
   NAME      READY STATUS   RESTARTS AGE
   mongo-0 0/2   Pending 0          3m
   ```

3. Get additional information on the pods using the `kubectl describe pod` command and look for the `Events` section. In this case, `Warning` is pointing to an unbound `PersistentVolumeClaim`:

   ```
   $ kubectl describe pod mongo-0
   . . .
   Events:
     Type      Reason        Age    From        Message
     ----      ------        ----   ----        -------
     Warning FailedScheduling 2m34s (x34 over 48m) default-scheduler
   pod has unbound immediate PersistentVolumeClaims (repeated 3 times)
   ```

4. Now that we know that we need to look at the PVC status, thanks to the results of the previous step, let's get the list of PVCs in order to inspect the issue. You will see that PVCs are also stuck in the `Pending` state:

```
$ kubectl get pvc
NAME                 STATUS   VOLUME CAPACITY ACCESS MODES STORAGECLASS
AGE
mongo-pvc-mongo-0 Pending                                       storageclass
53m
```

5. Get additional information on the PVCs using the `kubectl describe pvc` command, and look where the events are described. In this case, `Warning` is pointing to a missing storage class named `storageclass`:

```
$ kubectl describe pvc mongo-pvc-mongo-0
...
Events:
  Type     Reason             Age   From           Message
  ----     ------             ----  ----           -------
  Warning ProvisioningFailed 70s   (x33 over 58m) persistentvolume-
controller storageclass.storage.k8s.io "storageclass" not found
```

6. List the storage classes. You will notice that you don't have the storage class named `storageclass`:

```
$ kubectl get sc
NAME                         PROVISIONER AGE
default                      kubernetes.io/aws-ebs 16d
gp2                          kubernetes.io/aws-ebs 16d
openebs-cstor-default (default) openebs.io/provisioner-iscsi 8d
openebs-device               openebs.io/local 15d
openebs-hostpath             openebs.io/local 15d
openebs-jiva-default         openebs.io/provisioner-iscsi 15d
openebs-snapshot-promoter    volumesnapshot.external-
storage.k8s.io/snapshot-promoter 15d
```

7. Now we know that the manifest file we applied in *step 1* used a storage class that does not exist. In this case, you can either create the missing storage class or edit the manifest to include an existing storage class to fix the issue.
   Let's create the missing storage class from an existing default storage class like shown in the example below `gp2`:

```
$ kubectl create -f sc-gp2.yaml
```

8. List the pods by running the following command. You will notice that status is now `Running` for all pods that were previously `Pending` in *step 2*:

```
$ kubectl get pods
NAME      READY STATUS   RESTARTS AGE
mongo-0 2/2   Running 0         2m18s
mongo-1 2/2   Running 0         88s
mongo-2 2/2   Running 0         50s
```

You have successfully learned how to inspect why a pod is pending and fix it.

Inspecting pods in ImagePullBackOff status

Sometimes your manifest files may have a typo in the image name, or the image location may have changed. As a result, when you deploy the application, the container image will not be found and the deployment will get stuck. In this recipe, we will learn how to inspect the common problem of pods becoming stuck in `ImagePullBackOff` status:

1. In the `/src/chapter8` folder, inspect the contents of the `mongo-image.yaml` file and deploy it by running the following command. The deployment manifest includes MongoDB Statefulset with three replicas, Service and will get stuck in ImagePullBackOff state due to typo in the container image name and we will inspect it to find the source:

   ```
   $ cat debug/mongo-image.yaml
   $ kubectl apply -f debug/mongo-image.yaml
   ```

2. List the pods by running the following command. You will notice that the status of the `mongo-0` pod is `ImagePullBackOff`:

   ```
   $ kubectl get pods
   NAME      READY STATUS             RESTARTS AGE
   mongo-0 0/2   ImagePullBackOff 0         32s
   ```

3. Get additional information on the pods using the `kubectl describe pod` command and look for the `Events` section. In this case, `Warning` is pointing to a failure to pull the `mongi` image:

   ```
   $ kubectl describe pod mongo-0
   . . .
   Events:
     Type    Reason         Age            From          Message
     ----    ------         ----           ----          -------
     Warning Failed 25s (x3 over 68s) kubelet,
   ip-172-20-32-169.ec2.internal Error: ErrImagePull
   ```

```
    Warning Failed 25s (x3 over 68s) kubelet,
ip-172-20-32-169.ec2.internal Failed to pull image "mongi": rpc
error: code = Unknown desc = Error response from daemon: pull
access denied for mongi, repository does not exist or may require
'docker login'
    Normal Pulling 25s (x3 over 68s) kubelet,
ip-172-20-32-169.ec2.internal Pulling image "mongi"
    Normal BackOff 14s (x4 over 67s) kubelet,
ip-172-20-32-169.ec2.internal Back-off pulling image "mongi"
    Warning Failed 14s (x4 over 67s) kubelet,
ip-172-20-32-169.ec2.internal Error: ImagePullBackOff
```

4. Now we know that we need to confirm the container image name. The correct name is supposed to be mongo. Let's edit the manifest file, mongo-image.yaml, and change the image name to mongo as follows:

```
...
spec:
terminationGracePeriodSeconds: 10
containers:
- name: mongo
image: mongo
command:
...
```

5. Delete and redeploy the resource by running the following commands:

```
$ kubectl delete -f mongo-image.yaml
$ kubectl apply -f mongo-image.yaml
```

6. List the pods by running the following command. You will notice that the status is now Running for all pods that were previously in ImagePullBackOff status in *step 2*:

```
$ kubectl get pods
NAME      READY STATUS  RESTARTS AGE
mongo-0 2/2   Running 0        4m55s
mongo-1 2/2   Running 0        4m55s
mongo-2 2/2   Running 0        4m55s
```

You have successfully learned to inspect a pod with a status of ImagePullBackOff and troubleshoot it.

Inspecting pods in CrashLoopBackOff status

Inspecting pods in `CrashLoopBackOff` status is fundamentally similar to inspecting Pending pods, but might also require a bit more knowledge of the container workload you are creating. `CrashLoopBackOff` occurs when the application inside the container keeps crashing, the parameters of the pod are configured incorrectly, a liveness probe failed, or an error occurred when deploying on Kubernetes.

In this recipe, we will learn how to inspect the common problem of pods becoming stuck in `CrashLoopBackOff` status:

1. In the `/src/chapter8` folder, inspect the contents of the `mongo-config.yaml` file and deploy it running the following command. The deployment manifest includes a MongoDB statefulset with three replicas, Service and will get stuck in CrashLoopBackOff state due mistake with a missing configuration file and we will inspect it to find the source:

   ```
   $ cat debug/mongo-config.yaml
   $ kubectl apply -f debug/mongo-config.yaml
   ```

2. List the pods by running the following command. You will notice that the status is `CrashLoopBackOff` or `Error` for the `mongo-0` pod:

   ```
   $ kubectl get pods
   NAME READY STATUS RESTARTS AGE
   mongo-0 1/2 CrashLoopBackOff 3 58s
   ```

3. Get additional information on the pods using the `kubectl describe pod` command and look for the `Events` section. In this case, the `Warning` shows that the container has restarted, but it is not pointing to any useful information:

   ```
   $ kubectl describe pod mongo-0
   ...
   Events:
     Type    Reason    Age    From    Message
     ----    ------    ----   ----    -------
   ...
     Normal Pulled 44s (x4 over 89s) kubelet,
   ip-172-20-32-169.ec2.internal Successfully pulled image "mongo"
     Warning BackOff 43s (x5 over 87s) kubelet,
   ip-172-20-32-169.ec2.internal Back-off restarting failed container
   ```

4. When Events from the pods are not useful, you can use the `kubectl logs` command to get additional information from the pod. Check the messages in the pod's logs using the following command. The log message is pointing to a missing file; further inspection of the manifest is needed:

```
$ kubectl logs mongo-0 mongo
/bin/sh: 1: cannot open : No such file
```

5. Inspect and have a closer look at the application manifest file, `mongo-config.yaml`, and you will see that the environmental variable `MYFILE` is missing in this case:

```
...
    spec:
      terminationGracePeriodSeconds: 10
      containers:
        - name: mongo
          image: mongo
          command: ["/bin/sh"]
          args: ["-c", "sed \"s/foo/bar/\" < $MYFILE"]
...
```

6. To fix this issue, you can add a `ConfigMap` to your deployment. Edit the `mongo-config.yaml` file and add the missing file by adding the `MYFILE` parameter with a `ConfigMap` resource to the beginning of the file similar to following:

```
$ cat <<EOF | kubectl apply -f -
apiVersion: v1
kind: ConfigMap
metadata:
  name: app-env
data:
  MYFILE: "/etc/profile"
EOF
```

7. Delete and redeploy the resource by running the following commands:

```
$ kubectl delete -f mongo-image.yaml
$ kubectl apply -f mongo-image.yaml
```

8. List the pods by running the following command. You will notice that the status is now `Running` for all pods that were previously in CrashLoopBackOff status in step 2.

```
$ kubectl get pods
NAME       READY STATUS   RESTARTS AGE
mongo-0 2/2   Running 0          4m15s
mongo-1 2/2   Running 0          4m15s
mongo-2 2/2   Running 0          4m15s
```

You have successfully learned how to inspect a pod's CrashLoopBackOff issue and fix it.

See also

- Debugging init containers: `https://kubernetes.io/docs/tasks/debug-application-cluster/debug-init-containers/`
- Debugging pods and ReplicationControllers `https://kubernetes.io/docs/tasks/debug-application-cluster/debug-pod-replication-controller/`
- Debugging a statefulset: `https://kubernetes.io/docs/tasks/debug-application-cluster/debug-stateful-set/`
- Determining the reason for pod failure: `https://kubernetes.io/docs/tasks/debug-application-cluster/determine-reason-pod-failure/`
- Squash, a debugger for microservices: `https://github.com/solo-io/squash`

Monitoring using Amazon CloudWatch

In this section, we will use Amazon CloudWatch Container Insights to monitor, isolate, and diagnose your containerized applications and microservices environments. As a DevOps or Systems Engineer, you will learn how to use Amazon ECS CloudWatch metrics to monitor service health status and current alarms using automated dashboards that summarize the performance and health of your Amazon EKS clusters by pod, node, namespace, and services.

Getting ready

Clone the `k8sdevopscookbook/src` repository to your workstation to use manifest files in the `chapter8` directory:

```
$ git clone https://github.com/k8sdevopscookbook/src.git
$ cd src/chapter8/
```

Make sure you have an Amazon EKS Kubernetes cluster ready and `kubectl` configured to manage the cluster resources. If you don't already have one you can follow the instructions in *Chapter 1, Building Production-Ready Kubernetes Clusters*, in the *Configuring a Kubernetes cluster on Amazon Web Services* section.

How to do it...

This section is further divided into the following subsections to make the process easier:

- Enabling Webhook authorization mode
- Installing Container Insights Agents for Amazon EKS
- Viewing Container Insights metrics

Enabling Webhook authorization mode

If you have a Kubernetes cluster deployed using the `kops` option running on AWS EC2 instances instead of using Amazon EKS, your kubelet needs to have Webhook authorization mode enabled.

Let's follow these steps:

1. Enable `webhook` authorization mode using the two following flags. The first flag allows a ServiceAccount token to be used to authenticate against the kubelet. The second flag that allows the kubelet to perform an RBAC request and decide if the requesting resource, Amazon CloudWatch in this case, is allowed to access a resource endpoint:

   ```
   --authentication-token-webhook=true
   --authorization-mode=Webhook
   ```

2. You also need to add the necessary policy to the IAM role for your Kubernetes worker nodes. Open the Amazon EC2 console at `https://console.aws.amazon.com/ec2/`.

3. Under **Resources**, click on **Running Instances**:

4. Select one of the worker node instances from the list of and choose the IAM role on the **Description** tab. In our example, **eksctl-adorable-rainbow-157155665-NodeInstanceRole-MOT7WBCOOOHE** is the IAM role:

5. On the **Permissions** tab, click on the **Attach policies** button:

6. Inside the search box, type `CloudWatchAgentServerPolicy` and select the policy:

7. Click on the **Attach Policy** button to attach the policy to your IAM role:

Now you have successfully enabled Webhook authorization mode and added the required policies to the IAM role.

Installing Container Insights Agents for Amazon EKS

In this recipe, we will enable CloudWatch agents to collect cluster metrics from our EKS Kubernetes cluster:

1. Create a namespace called `amazon-cloudwatch` on your cluster using the following command:

```
$ cat <<EOF | kubectl apply -f -
apiVersion: v1
kind: Namespace
metadata:
  name: amazon-cloudwatch
  labels:
    name: amazon-cloudwatch
EOF
```

2. Create a Service account for the CloudWatch agent in the namespace `amazon-cloudwatch` you have created in *step 1*. The following command will also create `cloudwatch-agent-role` ClusterRole and ClusterRoleBinding:

```
$ kubectl apply -f cloudwatch/cwagent-serviceaccount.yaml
```

3. Get the name of your EKS cluster using the `eksctl` command or from the Amazon Container Services dashboard. Here, we will use `eksctl` to get the cluster name. In our example, the cluster name is `adorable-rainbow-1571556654`:

```
$ eksctl get cluster
NAME                          REGION
adorable-rainbow-1571556654   us-west-2
```

4. Create a ConfigMap for the CloudWatch agent. Before you run the following command, replace `"cluster_name": "adorable-rainbow-1571556654"` with the name of your cluster from *step 3*:

```
$ cat <<EOF | kubectl apply -f -
apiVersion: v1
kind: ConfigMap
metadata:
  name: cwagentconfig
  namespace: amazon-cloudwatch
data:
  cwagentconfig.json: |
    {
      "logs": {
```

```
        "metrics_collected": {
          "kubernetes": {
            "cluster_name": "{{cluster_name}}",
            "metrics_collection_interval": 60
          }
        },
        "force_flush_interval": 5
      }
    }
EOF
```

5. Deploy the CloudWatch agent as a DaemonSet. The preceding command will use StatsD, a network daemon that listens for statistics, such as counters and timers, sent over UDP or TCP and sends aggregates to CloudWatch, and also pluggable backend services if they're available:

```
$ kubectl apply -f cloudwatch/cwagent.yaml
```

6. Verify that CloudWatch agent pods are created by running the following command. Since agents run as DaemonSets, you should be able to see one pod per worker node listed. In our example, we have two worker nodes and two agent pods running:

```
$ kubectl get pods -n amazon-cloudwatch
NAME                      READY STATUS   RESTARTS AGE
cloudwatch-agent-dtpxt 1/1   Running 0          67s
cloudwatch-agent-j7frt 1/1   Running 0          67s
```

When complete, the CloudWatch agent will start sending performance log events to the CloudWatch Container Insights service.

Viewing Container Insights metrics

In this recipe, we will learn how to use CloudWatch to monitor node and pod metrics in our Kubernetes cluster:

1. Open the CloudWatch console at `https://console.aws.amazon.com/cloudwatch/`:

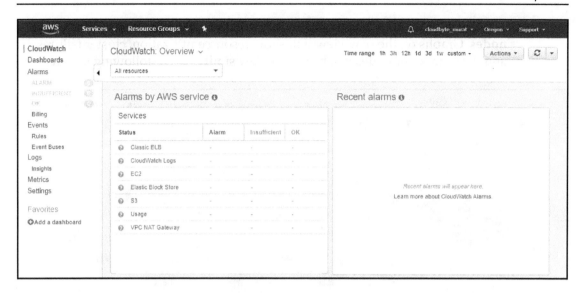

2. Click on the down arrow button next to the **Overview** option and choose
   Container Insights from the list:

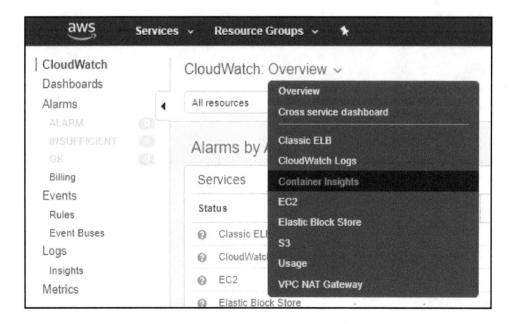

3. To view the EKS node health and statistics, in the top-left corner, switch to **EKS nodes**. Graphs on the new view will show resource utilization, cluster failures, and the number of nodes in a historical view similar to the following screenshot:

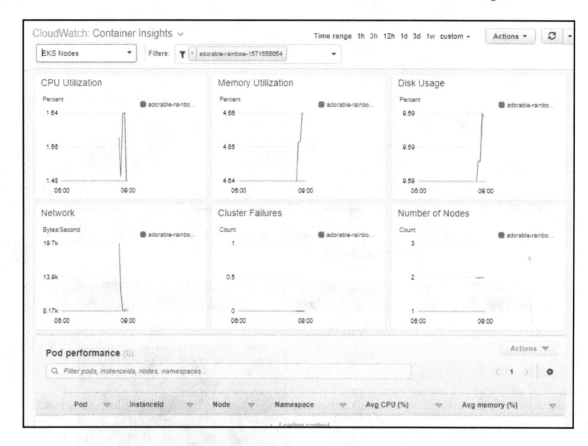

4. To view the container performance statistics, in the top-left corner, switch to **EKS pods**. Graphs on the new view will show the total resource utilization of pods and list of pods with their individual CPU and memory consumption percentages similar to the following screenshot:

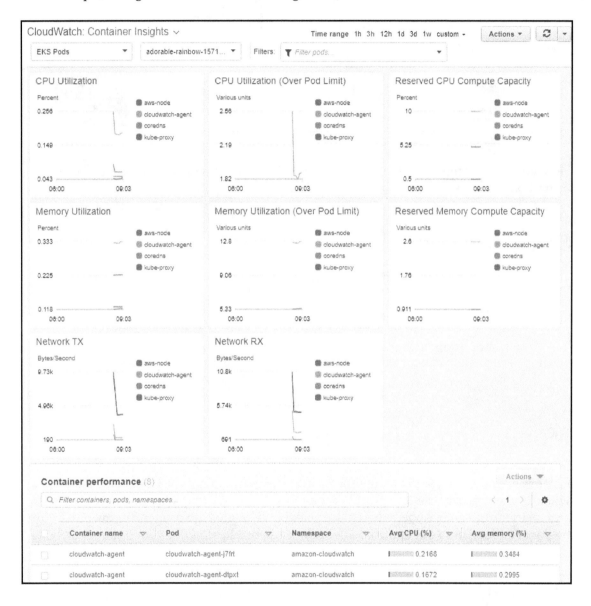

5. To view the detailed logs or AWS X-Ray traces of any resource, select the resource name from the list and click on the **Actions** button. From the drop-down menu, you can choose logs that you would like to review. After you select, logs will open in a new window:

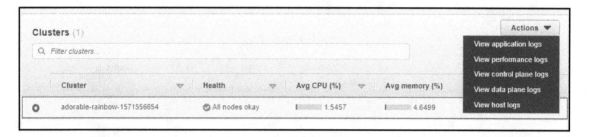

Now you have learned how to monitor node and pod metrics in your Kubernetes cluster using Container Insights.

See also

- Using Container Insights https://docs.aws.amazon.com/AmazonCloudWatch/latest/monitoring/ContainerInsights.html
- Using CloudWatch Anomaly Detection https://docs.aws.amazon.com/AmazonCloudWatch/latest/monitoring/CloudWatch_Anomaly_Detection.html
- List of the metrics collected by Container Insights: https://docs.aws.amazon.com/AmazonCloudWatch/latest/monitoring/Container-Insights-metrics-EKS.html

Monitoring using Google Stackdriver

In this section, we will use Google Stackdriver Kubernetes Engine Monitoring to monitor, isolate, and diagnose your containerized applications and microservices environments. You will learn how to use Stackdriver Kubernetes Engine Monitoring to aggregate logs, events, and metrics from your Kubernetes environment on **Google Kubernetes Engine** (**GKE**) to help you understand your application's behavior in production.

Getting ready

Make sure you have a GKE cluster ready and `kubectl` configured to manage the cluster resources. If you don't already have one, you can follow the instructions in `Chapter 1`, *Building Production-Ready Kubernetes Clusters*, in the *Configuring a Kubernetes cluster on Google Cloud Platform* recipe.

How to do it...

This section is further divided into the following subsections to make the process easier:

- Installing Stackdriver Kubernetes Engine Monitoring support for GKE
- Configuring a workspace on Stackdriver
- Monitoring GKE metrics using Stackdriver

Installing Stackdriver Kubernetes Engine Monitoring support for GKE

Installing Stackdriver monitoring support enables you to easily monitor GKE clusters, debug logs, and analyze your cluster performance using advanced profiling and tracing capabilities. In this recipe, we will enable Stackdriver Kubernetes Engine Monitoring support to collect cluster metrics from our GKE cluster:

1. Open the Google Kubernetes Engine Console at `https://console.cloud.google.com/kubernetes`. On this console, you will see the list of your GKE clusters. In our example, we have only one cluster, and it is called **k8s-devops-cookbook-1**:

2. Click on the little pen-shaped Edit icon next to your cluster:

3. On the cluster configuration page, make sure that **Legacy Stackdriver Logging** and **Legacy Stackdriver Monitoring** are **Disabled** and the **Stackdriver Kubernetes Engine Monitoring** option is set to **Enabled**:

4. Click on the **Save** button to apply changes to your cluster.

Configuring a workspace on Stackdriver

Stackdriver Monitoring helps you to gain deeper insights into your public cloud. Stackdriver's monitoring capabilities include monitoring, logging, tracing, error reporting, and alerting to collect performance and diagnostics data of your public cloud service. Kubernetes monitoring is a small part of the complete solution. In this recipe, you will learn how to configure the Stackdriver workspace after you access it for the first time:

1. Open the Stackdriver Console at `https://app.google.stackdriver.com`. The first time you access the console, you need to add the workspace to the console, otherwise you will see an empty dashboard similar to the following:

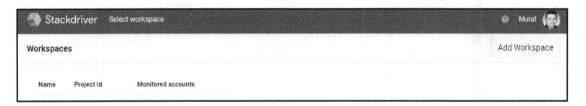

2. Click on the **Add Workspace** button to include your existing workspace. You will be asked for your Google Cloud Platform project name. Click on the empty **Select project** field and select your project from the list. In our example, it's **DevOpsCookBook**. After you select the project, click on the **Create Workspace** button:

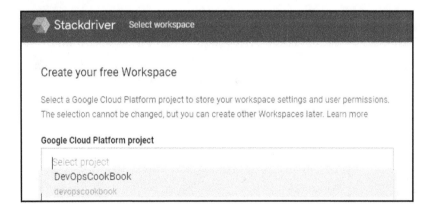

3. Stackdriver also allows you to monitor AWS accounts. For this recipe, we will skip this option. Click **Skip AWS Setup** to move to the next step:

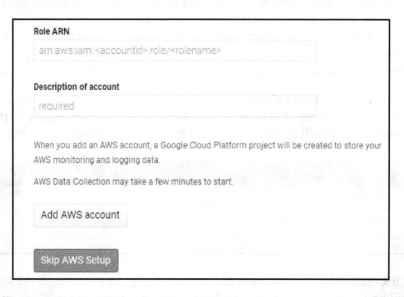

4. In the **Install the Stackdriver Agents** window, click on the **Continue** button.
5. In the **Get Reports by Email** window, select the frequency of reports to be emailed. Select **Weekly reports**. Note that you can always select **No reports** and enable this feature later:

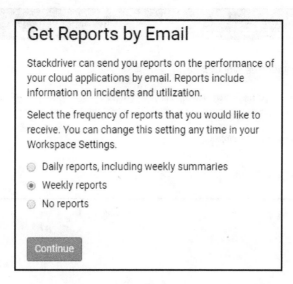

6. Finally, click on the **Launch Monitoring** button to access the Stackdriver console:

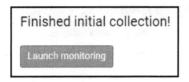

Now you have configured the Stackdriver workspace to collect diagnostics data from your public cloud service.

Monitoring GKE metrics using Stackdriver

Installing Stackdriver monitoring support enables you to easily monitor GKE clusters, debug logs, and analyze your cluster performance using advanced profiling and tracing capabilities. In this recipe, we will enable Stackdriver Kubernetes Engine Monitoring support to collect cluster metrics from our GKE cluster:

1. After following the *Configuring a workspace on Stackdriver* recipe, open the Stackdriver console at `https://app.google.stackdriver.com`:

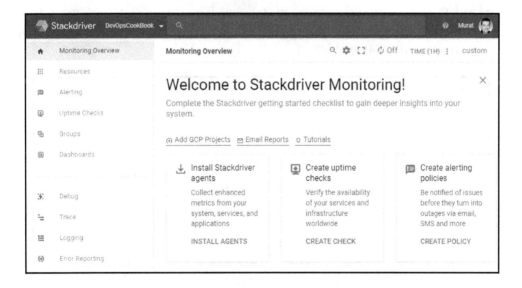

2. From the **Resources** menu, click on the **Kubernetes Engine** option:

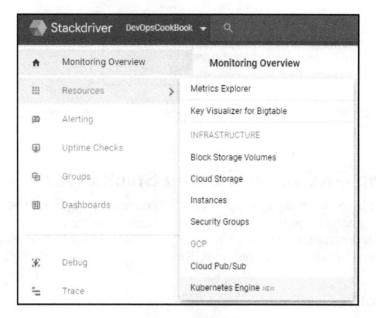

3. The Kubernetes Engine view will show the list of clusters that are Stackdriver Kubernetes Engine Monitoring-enabled. In our example, you can see that we have one cluster available:

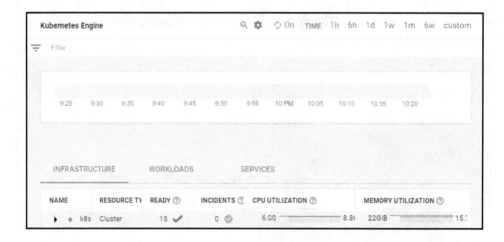

4. On the **Infrastructure** tab, click on the expand icon next to the cluster name. Stackdriver will expand the list with the individual worker nodes. In the **Ready** column, you can see the number of pods deployed and in a ready state in each node. In the **CPU Utilization** column, the value on the left-hand side shows the total available CPUs and the right-hand value shows the current utilization percentage. Similarly, in the **Memory Utilization** column, the value on the left-hand side shows the total available memory (GiB), and the right-hand value shows the current utilization percentage:

5. Click on the expand icon next to a node name, and the list will expand to display the pods deployed on that specific node:

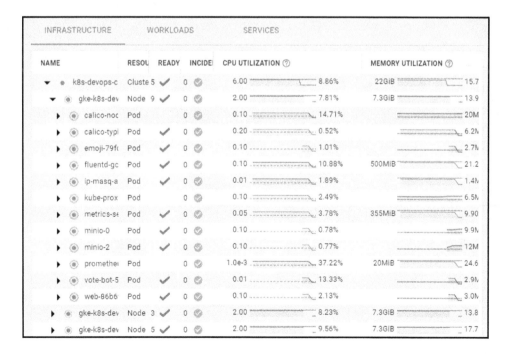

6. Click on one of the pods on your cluster. Stackdriver will show a detailed view of pod metrics, including pod restarts, CPU, memory, storage, and network utilization for the pods. In our example, we can see metrics for the Prometheus pod:

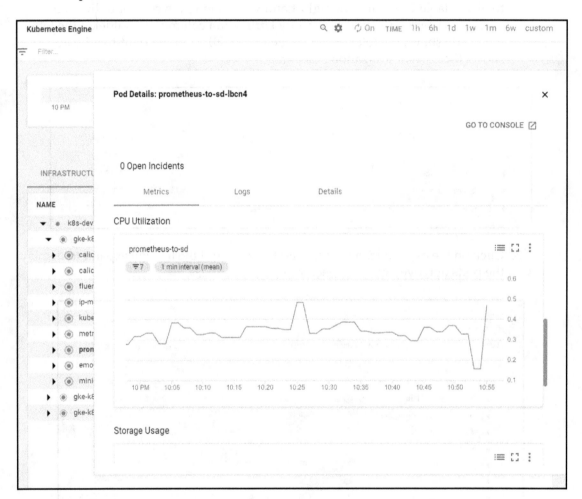

7. Click on the **Logs** tab to switch to the log summary view. This view will only show the most recent logs:

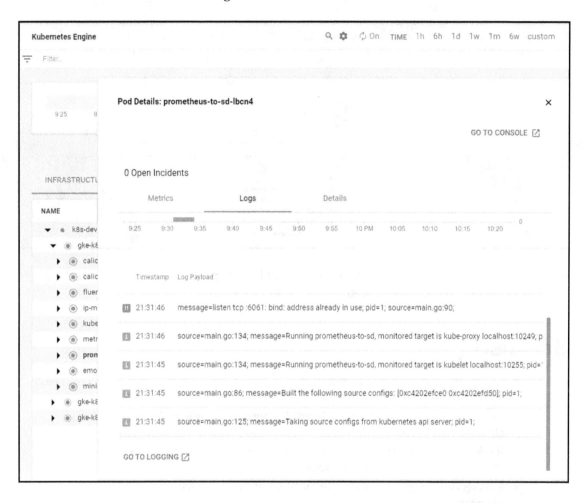

8. Click on the **Go to console** button to open a detailed log view where you can see older logs and use filters to create metrics:

Now you know how to use Stackdriver to monitor health, performance metrics, and logs for GKE clusters and resources deployed on the GKE clusters.

See also

- Google Stackdriver documentation: `https://cloud.google.com/stackdriver/docs/`
- Using Prometheus with Stackdriver Kubernetes Engine Monitoring: `https://cloud.google.com/monitoring/kubernetes-engine/prometheus`
- Stackdriver Prometheus sidecar: `https://github.com/Stackdriver/stackdriver-prometheus-sidecar`
- A collection of technical articles published on Stackdriver by GCP advocates: `https://medium.com/google-cloud/tagged/stackdriver`

Monitoring using Azure Monitor

In this section, we will use Azure Monitor to monitor, isolate, and diagnose your containerized applications and microservices environments. You will learn how to use Azure Monitor to aggregate logs, events, and metrics from your Kubernetes environment on **Azure Kubernetes Service** (**AKS**) to help you understand your application's behavior in production.

Getting ready

Make sure you have an AKS cluster ready and `kubectl` configured to manage the cluster resources. If you don't already have one, you can follow the instructions in `Chapter 1`, *Building Production-Ready Kubernetes Clusters*, in the *Configuring a Kubernetes cluster on Google Cloud Platform* recipe.

How to do it...

This section is further divided into the following subsections to make the process easier:

- Enabling Azure Monitor support for AKS using the CLI
- Monitoring AKS performance metrics using Azure Monitor
- Viewing live logs using Azure Monitor

Enabling Azure Monitor support for AKS using the CLI

Enabling Azure Monitor for AKS clusters gives you performance visibility by collecting memory and processor metrics from controllers, nodes, and containers that are available in Kubernetes through the Kubernetes Metrics API.

In this recipe, we will enable monitoring from AKS Kubernetes clusters to collect metrics and logs through a containerized version of the Log Analytics agent:

1. If you have deployed your AKS cluster following the *Provisioning a managed Kubernetes Cluster on AKS* recipe in Chapter 1, *Building Production-Ready Kubernetes Clusters,* you can use the following command to enable the Azure Monitor for your cluster. Replace the name AKSCluster with your AKS cluster name, and replace the resource group, k8sdevopscookbook, with the Azure resource group name you used when you created your cluster before you run the following command:

```
$ az aks enable-addons -a monitoring \
--name AKSCluster --resource-group k8sdevopscookbook
```

If you are deploying a new cluster, you can add the --enable-addons monitoring parameter to the CLI command to enable Azure Monitor functionality for your AKS cluster during the cluster creation as follows:

```
$ az aks create --resource-group k8sdevopscookbook \
--name AKSCluster \
--node-count 3 \
--service-principal <appId> \
--client-secret <password> \
--enable-addons monitoring \
--generate-ssh-keys
```

When completed, this command will enable Azure Monitor and logs for your AKS cluster.

Monitoring AKS performance metrics using Azure Monitor

Performance metrics of an AKS cluster can be viewed both directly from the AKS cluster management dashboard and also via the Azure Monitor dashboard. In this recipe, we will monitor AKS performance metrics through Azure Monitor:

1. After following the *Enabling Azure Monitor support for AKS using the CLI* recipe, open the Azure portal at https://portal.azure.com and click on the **Kubernetes Service** button to go to the AKS management dashboard:

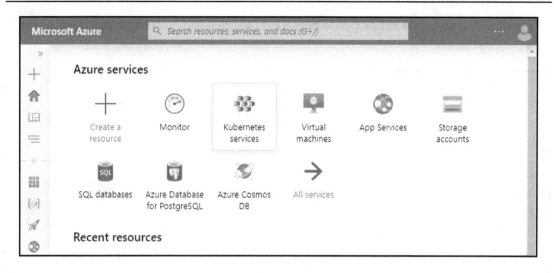

2. On the Kubernetes services view, click on your cluster name. In our example, it is **AKSCluster**:

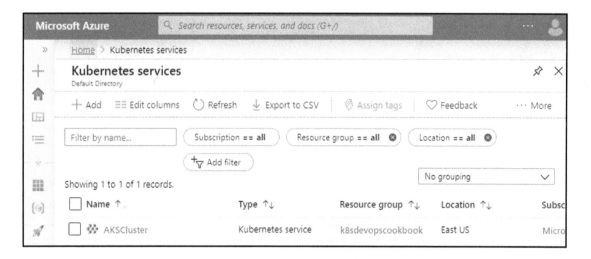

3. Click on the **Monitor Containers** menu to open the Azure Monitor Insights view for your AKS cluster:

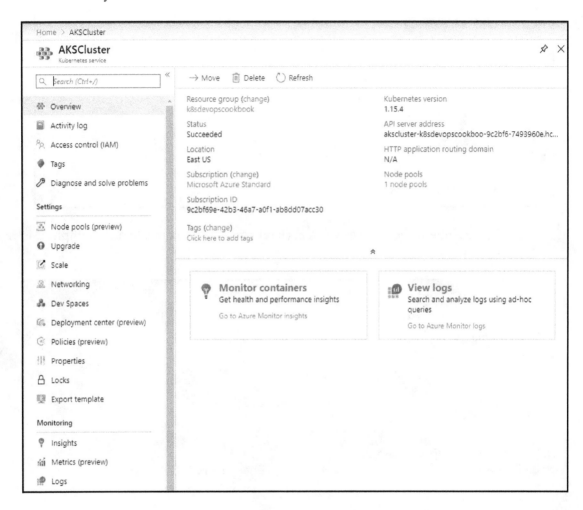

4. Monitoring information about your AKS cluster is organized into five categories: Cluster, Nodes, Controllers, Containers, and Deployments. In this view, on the **Cluster** tab you will be able to see node CPU and memory utilization, AKS node count, and active pod count, like this:

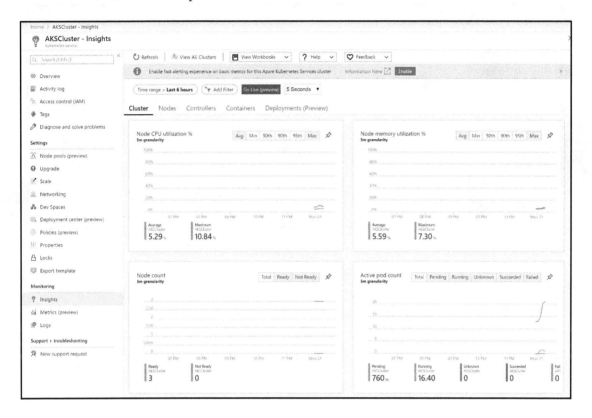

5. Click on the **Nodes** tab to switch to the node performance metrics view. By default, CPU usage data is displayed for the last 6 hours for the 95th percentile. These options can be adjusted using the drop-down menus on the page:

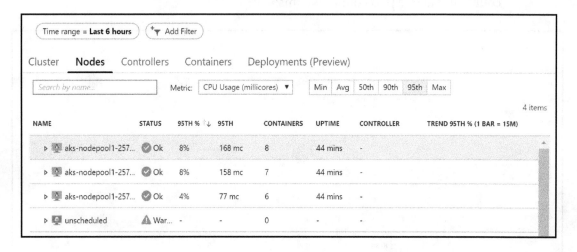

6. Click on the expand icon next to a node name and a list will expand to display the pods and containers inside deployed on that specific node. In this view, CPU utilization of every resource and uptime can be viewed:

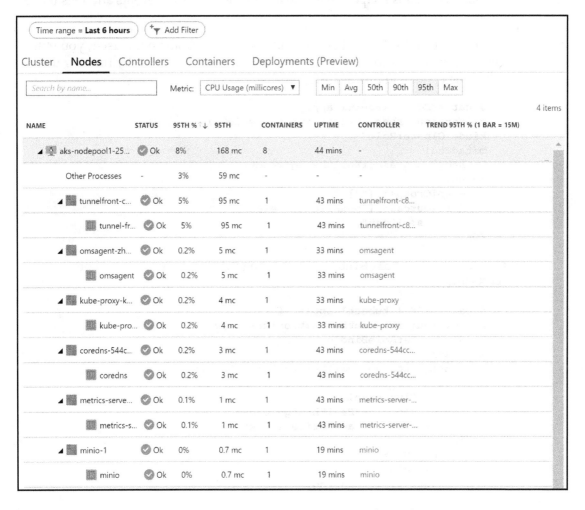

Now you know how to monitor AKS performance metrics through Azure Monitor insights.

Viewing live logs using Azure Monitor

In addition to the performance metrics, Azure Monitor can also help to view logs from the AKS cluster resources. In this recipe, we will learn how to access the events and logs using Azure Monitor:

1. Before you can display pod events and live metrics from your cluster, you will need to apply ClusterRoleBinding. Create a ClusterRole by running the following command on your AKS cluster:

```
$ cat <<EOF | kubectl apply -f -
apiVersion: rbac.authorization.k8s.io/v1
kind: ClusterRole
metadata:
    name: containerHealth-log-reader
rules:
    - apiGroups: [""]
      resources: ["pods/log", "events"]
      verbs: ["get", "list"]
EOF
```

2. Create a ClusterRoleBinding by running the following command on your AKS cluster:

```
$ cat <<EOF | kubectl apply -f -
apiVersion: rbac.authorization.k8s.io/v1
kind: ClusterRoleBinding
metadata:
    name: containerHealth-read-logs-global
roleRef:
    kind: ClusterRole
    name: containerHealth-log-reader
    apiGroup: rbac.authorization.k8s.io
subjects:
    - kind: User
      name: clusterUser
      apiGroup: rbac.authorization.k8s.io
EOF
```

3. Click on the **Monitor Containers** menu to open the Azure Monitor insights view for your AKS cluster.
4. Click on the expand icon next to a node name, and a list will expand displaying the pods and containers deployed on that specific node:

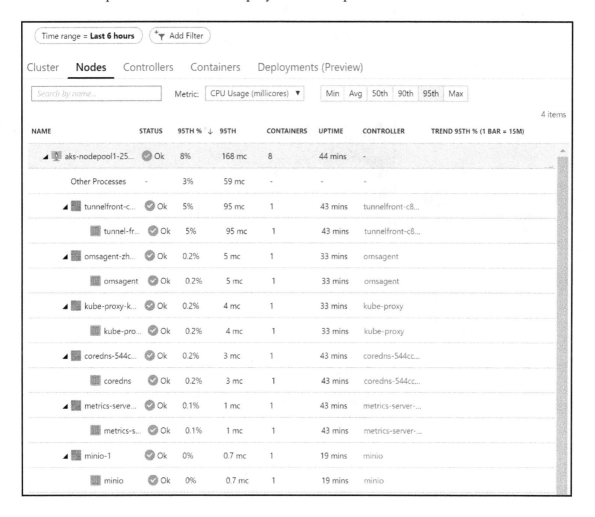

5. Click on one of the pods in your cluster. Insights will show a detailed view of pods metrics on the right-hand panel:

6. On the right-hand pane, click on the **View live data** button. This option will expand the view with live events from the pods and live metrics, as shown in the following screenshot. Events can be used to troubleshoot the pod problems that we discussed in the *Inspecting containers* section of this chapter:

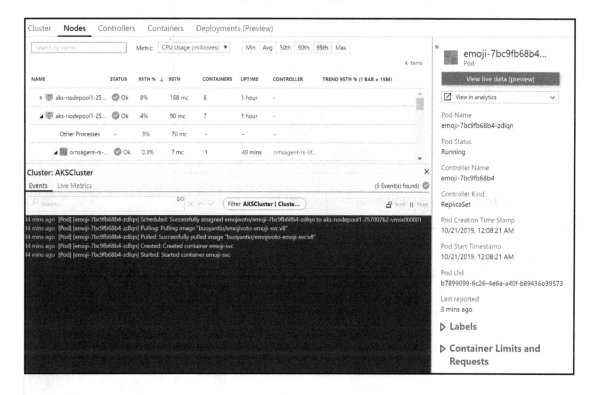

7. The log and event messages you see depend on what resource type is selected in the view. Click on the **View in analytics** button to switch to the **Kubernetes event logs**:

8. In this view, you will be able to see and filter pod events:

9. This time, click on one of the containers inside a pod. Insights will show a detailed view of container information and performance metrics in the right-hand panel:

10. In the right-hand pane, click on the **View in analytics** button to switch to the **View container logs**:

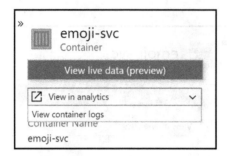

11. In this view, you will be able to see and filter container logs:

Now you know how to use Azure Monitor to monitor health, performance metrics and logs for AKS clusters, and resources deployed on the AKS clusters.

See also

- Azure Monitor for containers documentation: `https://docs.microsoft.com/en-us/azure/azure-monitor/insights/container-insights-overview`
- Using Prometheus with Azure Monitor: `https://azure.microsoft.com/en-us/blog/azure-monitor-for-containers-with-prometheus-now-in-preview/`

Monitoring Kubernetes using Prometheus and Grafana

In this section, we will deploy Prometheus and Grafana on our Kubernetes cluster. You will learn how to monitor a Kubernetes service with Prometheus and use Grafana dashboards to visualize cluster and application metrics.

Getting ready

Clone the `k8sdevopscookbook/src` repository to your workstation to use manifest files in the `chapter8` directory:

```
$ git clone https://github.com/k8sdevopscookbook/src.git
$ cd /src/chapter8
```

Make sure you have a Kubernetes cluster ready and `kubectl` configured to manage the cluster resources.

How to do it...

This section is further divided into the following subsections to make the process easier:

- Deploying Prometheus Operator using Helm charts
- Monitoring metrics using Grafana dashboards
- Adding a Grafana dashboard to monitor applications

Deploying Prometheus using Helm charts

Prometheus is a popular open source solution for event monitoring and alerting. Prometheus records real-time metrics in a time-series database, and it is one of the most popular components of Kubernetes clusters for monitoring. Almost all new managed Kubernetes solutions come with Prometheus installed in some way as part of the cluster deployment. In this recipe, you will learn how to deploy Prometheus on a Kubernetes cluster using Helm charts:

1. Update the Helm repository. This command will fetch up-to-date charts locally from public chart repositories:

```
$ helm repo update
```

2. Deploy Prometheus Operator in the `monitoring` namespace using the `helm install` command. This command will deploy Prometheus along with the Alertmanager, Grafana, the node-exporter and kube-state-metrics addon; basically, a bundle of the components needed to use Prometheus on a Kubernetes cluster:

```
$ helm install stable/prometheus-operator --name prometheus \
    --namespace monitoring
```

3. Verify the status of the pods deployed in the monitoring namespace:

```
$ kubectl get pods -n monitoring
NAME READY STATUS RESTARTS AGE
alertmanager-prometheus-prometheus-oper-alertmanager-0 2/2 Running
0 88s
prometheus-grafana-6c6f7586b6-f9jbr 2/2 Running 0 98s
prometheus-kube-state-metrics-57d6c55b56-wf4mc 1/1 Running 0 98s
prometheus-prometheus-node-exporter-8drg7 1/1 Running 0 98s
prometheus-prometheus-node-exporter-1b715 1/1 Running 0 98s
prometheus-prometheus-node-exporter-vx7w2 1/1 Running 0 98s
prometheus-prometheus-oper-operator-86c9c956dd-88p82 2/2 Running 0
98s
prometheus-prometheus-prometheus-oper-prometheus-0 3/3 Running 1
78s
```

Now you have Prometheus installed with the bundle of components required to operate it on a Kubernetes environment.

Monitoring metrics using Grafana dashboards

Grafana is an open source analytics and monitoring solution. By default, Grafana is used for querying Prometheus. Follow these instructions to expose the included Grafana service instance and access it through your web browser:

1. Get the list of services in the `monitoring` namespace:

```
$ kubectl get svc -n monitoring
NAME                                    TYPE       CLUSTER-IP
EXTERNAL-IP PORT(S)                     AGE
alertmanager-operated                   ClusterIP None
<none>      9093/TCP,9094/TCP,9094/UDP 33m
prometheus-grafana                      ClusterIP 10.0.1.132
<none>      80/TCP                      33m
prometheus-kube-state-metrics           ClusterIP 10.0.69.144
<none>      8080/TCP                    33m
prometheus-operated                     ClusterIP None
```

```
<none>         9090/TCP                         33m
prometheus-prometheus-node-exporter       ClusterIP 10.0.100.183
<none>         9100/TCP                         33m
prometheus-prometheus-oper-alertmanager ClusterIP 10.0.202.140
<none>         9093/TCP                         33m
prometheus-prometheus-oper-operator       ClusterIP 10.0.174.214
<none>         8080/TCP,443/TCP                 33m
prometheus-prometheus-oper-prometheus     ClusterIP 10.0.243.177
<none>         9090/TCP                         33m
```

2. Create a port forwarding to access the Grafana UI using the `kubectl port-forward` command. This command will forward the local port `8000` to port `3000` of a running Grafana pod:

   ```
   $ kubectl port-forward -n monitoring prometheus-grafana 8000:80
   ```

As an alternative, you can patch the `prometheus-grafana` service using the `kubectl edit svc prometheus-grafana -n monitoring` command and change the service type, `ClusterIP`, to `LoadBalancer` to expose the service externally using a cloud load balancer.

3. Go to `http://localhost:8000` (or the External IP, if using LoadBalancer) in your web browser. You should see the Grafana login page:

4. Log in using `admin` as the username and `prom-operator` as the password:

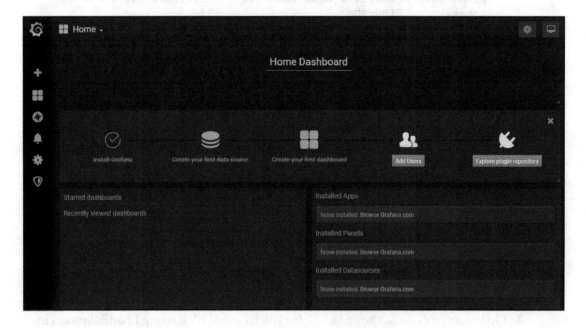

5. Click on the **Home** button in the upper-left corner of the dashboard to list the available built-in dashboards:

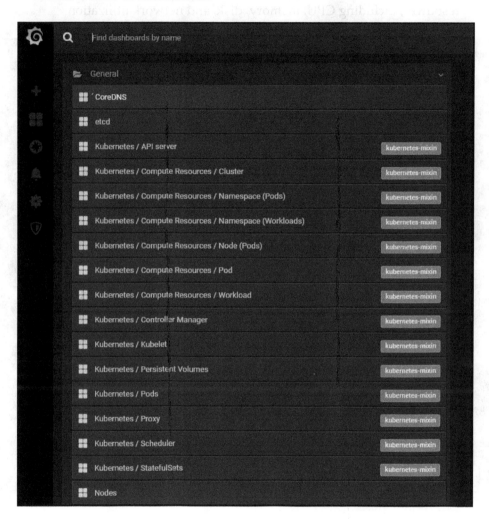

6. As an example, select the **Nodes** dashboard from the list to show Kubernetes nodes metrics. In this view, you will see the graphical representation of node resources, including CPU, memory, disk, and network utilization:

Now you know how to navigate through dashboards in Grafana. You can use Grafana to visualize Kubernetes metrics and other workload metrics that provide metrics for Prometheus by following the next recipe.

Adding a Grafana dashboard to monitor applications

Grafana is used to visualize the metrics stored on Prometheus. It offers dynamic and reusable dashboards with template variables. In this recipe, we will learn how to add a new dashboard from the library of pre-built dashboards to monitor an application deployed on Kubernetes:

1. Every application has different metrics that are relevant to the continuity of the application. First of all, an application needs to expose the metrics to Prometheus (additional info on Writing Prometheus exporters is available in the *See also* section), and Prometheus must be added as a data source to Grafana. For this recipe, we will use the Jenkins we deployed in `Chapter 3`, *Building CI/CD Pipelines*, in the *Setting up a CI/CD pipeline in Jenkins X* recipe.

2. Click on the **Home** button in the top-left corner of the dashboard and click on **Find dashboards on Grafana.com**:

3. In the search field, type `Jenkins`. You will see a couple of Jenkins-specific dashboards:

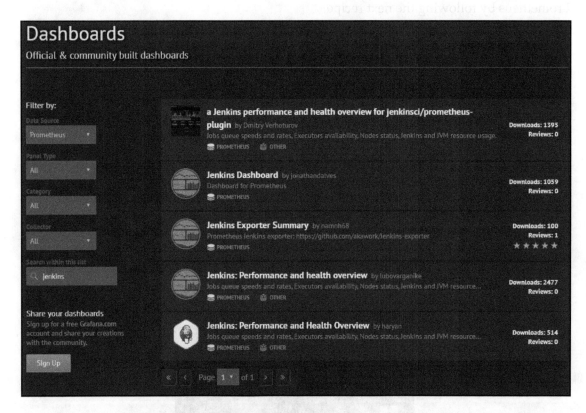

4. Click on **Jenkins: Performance and health overview** and copy the ID to the clipboard. At this point, dashboard ID **306** is all you need to add this pre-built dashboard to your Grafana instance:

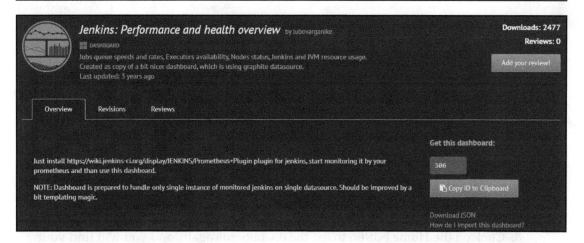

5. If the Dashboard is not enabled, follow the instructions in the **Overview** section.

6. In the Grafana interface, click on **Import dashboard**. Paste the dashboard ID **306** into the **Grafana.com Dashboard** field. Grafana will automatically detect the dashboard and display the details:

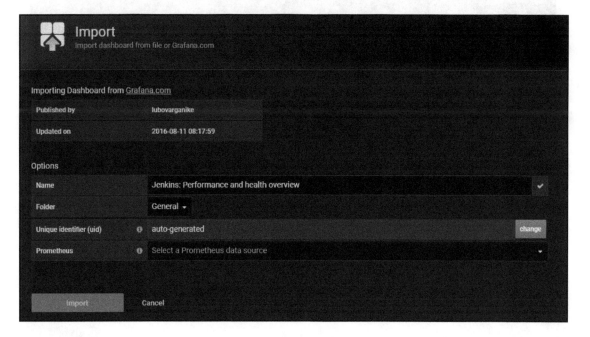

7. Select **Prometheus** as the data source name and click on **Import**:

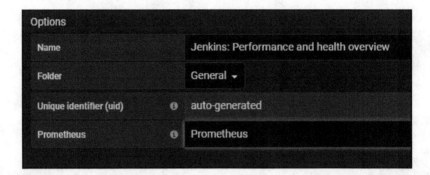

8. Click on the **Home** button to list the dashboards again, and you will find your new dashboard in the most recent dashboards list:

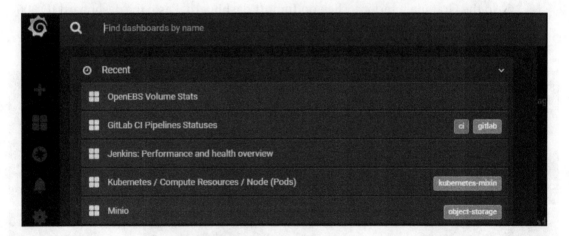

Similarly, you can find a pre-built dashboard on Grafana for the applications we have used in previous chapters such as cloud provider service monitoring (AWS, GCP, Azure, Alibaba), GitLab CI, Minio, OpenEBS, and many additional Kubernetes cluster metrics.

See also

- Prometheus documentation: `https://prometheus.io/docs/introduction/overview/`
- Writing Prometheus exporters: `https://prometheus.io/docs/instrumenting/writing_exporters/`
- GitHub repository for Prometheus-Operator: `https://github.com/coreos/prometheus-operator`
- Grafana documentation: `https://grafana.com/docs/`
- Grafana community dashboards: `https://grafana.com/grafana/dashboards`
- Grafana plugins: `https://grafana.com/grafana/plugins`
- Enabling the Jenkins Prometheus plugin: `https://wiki.jenkins.io/display/JENKINS/Prometheus+Plugin`
- Adding Stackdriver as a data source: `https://grafana.com/grafana/plugins/stackdriver`
- Adding Azure Monitor as a data source: `https://grafana.com/grafana/plugins/grafana-azure-monitor-datasource`
- Prometheus alternatives:
    - DataDog: `https://www.datadoghq.com`
    - New Relic: `https://newrelic.com`
    - Open Falcon: `http://open-falcon.org`

Monitoring and performance analysis using Sysdig

In this section, we will use Sysdig Monitor to monitor and simplify Kubernetes troubleshooting. You will learn how to install Sysdig Monitor and extend Prometheus functionality to meet more advanced enterprise needs.

Getting ready

All operations mentioned here require a Sysdig account. If you don't have one, go to `https://sysdig.com/sign-up/` and create a trial or full account.

For this recipe, we need to have a Kubernetes cluster ready and the Kubernetes command-line tools `kubectl` and `helm` installed to manage the cluster resources.

How to do it...

This section is further divided into the following subsections to make the process easier:

- Installing the Sysdig agent
- Analyzing application performance

Installing the Sysdig agent

Sysdig Monitor is a tool for monitoring and troubleshooting applications available as part of the Sysdig Cloud Native Visibility and Security Platform. In this recipe, you will learn to deploy Sysdig Monitor and leverage Prometheus metrics:

1. If you don't have your Sysdig Monitor access key ready, go to your **Account Settings** at `https://app.sysdigcloud.com/#/settings/agentInstallation` and retrieve your access key:

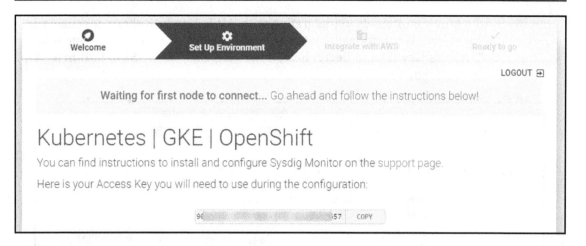

2. Install the Sysdig agent using the Helm chart after replacing `YourAccessKey` in the following command with your Sysdig Monitor access key from *step 1*. This command will install the Sysdig agent required for Sysdig Monitor and Sysdig Secure onto all your Kubernetes worker nodes in your cluster as a DaemonSet:

```
$ helm install --name sysdig-agent --set
sysdig.accessKey=YourAccessKey, \
sysdig.settings.tags='linux:ubuntu, dept:dev,local:ca' \
--set sysdig.settings.k8s_cluster_name='my_cluster' stable/sysdig
```

3. Once the Sysdig agent is installed, the nodes will be detected by Sysdig Monitor. In this view, all the nodes should be detected. In our example, we have four nodes detected. Click on the **Go to Next Step** button to continue:

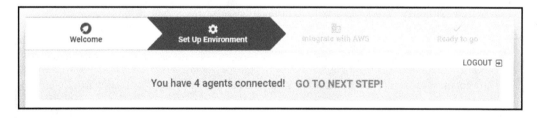

4. Sysdig Monitor offers deep integration with AWS. If your Kubernetes cluster is deployed on AWS, optionally, you can enable the integration by entering your AWS **Access Key ID** and **Secret** here; otherwise, click on the **Skip** button to skip the AWS integration:

○ Welcome	✿ Set Up Environment	▦ Integrate with AWS	Ready to go

LOGOUT ⏻

Integrate with AWS

Sysdig Monitor offers deep integration with AWS, allowing you to monitor services such as EC2, ELB and RDS within Sysdig Monitor, and also pull your tags and other AWS metadata.

To enable the integration, you just need to provide Sysdig Monitor with read-only access to your account. See here for specific instructions on how to generate the necessary keys.

Access Key ID: ••••••••••••••••••••••••••••••••••••••

Secret Access Key: ••••••••••••••••••••••••••••••••••••••

CloudWatch Integration Status

Disabled ◖● Enabled

Note: Once you provide the necessary keys, CloudWatch integration will be enabled by default. When this feature is enabled, Sysdig Monitor will poll the CloudWatch API every 5 minutes, which will generate a small additional charge from AWS (see Amazon CloudWatch Pricing).

You're not using a cloud provider? Don't worry, Sysdig Monitor will still work well for your infrastructure.

BACK   SKIP   NEXT

5. Click on **Let's Get Started** to explore Sysdig Monitor:

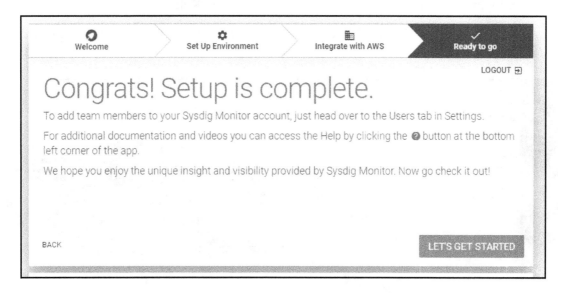

Now you know how to deploy Sysdig Monitor and leverage Prometheus metrics.

Analyzing application performance

Latency, traffic, errors, and saturation are considered Golden Signals by Google SRE teams.

Let's follow these instructions to learn how to navigate through the Sysdig Monitor interface to find the Golden Signals for your application on Kubernetes:

1. Log in to your Sysdig Cloud-Native Visibility and Security Platform dashboard at `https://app.sysdigcloud.com`:

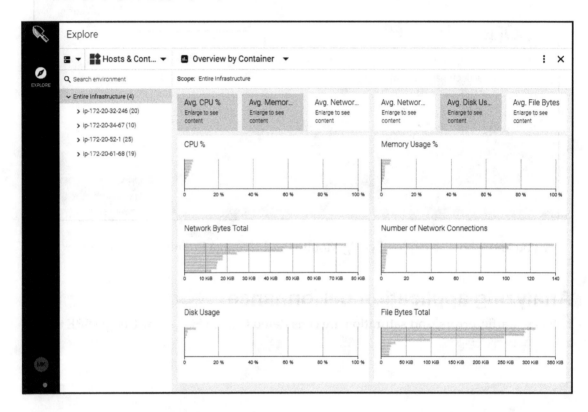

2. Resources are automatically grouped in the **Hosts & Containers** group. Click on the groups dropdown and select **Deployments and pods**:

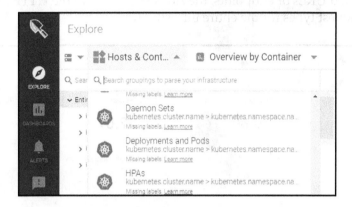

3. Click on the dashboard and metrics dropdown and select the **HTTP** dashboard under **Default Dashboards | Applications**:

4. Sysdig can identify and decode application protocols such as HTTP and give you detailed metrics. In this view, you can see the number of requests, the most requested URLs or endpoints, the slowest URLs, and the HTTP response codes and request types for the entire infrastructure:

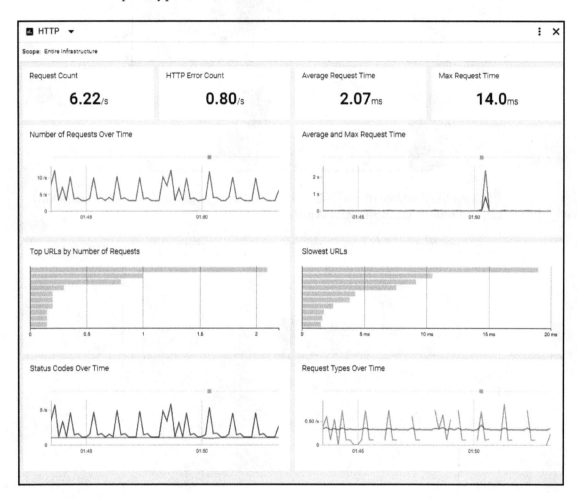

5. As an example of performance troubleshooting, move your mouse over the **Slowest URLs** graph to identify problems and applications with slow response times. In our example, we see a slow response time of 48 ms from the Kubecost Prometheus server we deployed earlier:

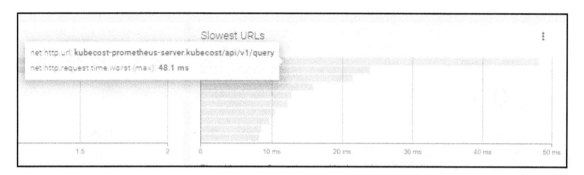

Now you have basic knowledge about how to navigate through Sysdig dashboards. Sysdig provides deep tracing capabilities that can be used when monitoring more than one container. We will learn more about Sysdig's security features and anomaly detection usage in Chapter 9, *Securing Applications and Clusters*. You can find the additional use cases in the *Sysdig examples* link in the *See also* section.

See also

- Sysdig Falco – Behavioral activity monitoring tool: `https://github.com/draios/oss-falco`
- Sysdig Inspect – Container troubleshooting and security investigation tool: `https://github.com/draios/sysdig-inspect`
- Monitoring distributed systems (Golden Signals): `https://landing.google.com/sre/sre-book/chapters/monitoring-distributed-systems/`
- Sysdig examples: `https://github.com/draios/sysdig/wiki/sysdig-examples`

Managing the cost of resources using Kubecost

In this section, we will install and configure the open source Kubecost project, which gives you cost-related visibility into your Kubernetes resources. You will learn how to monitor resource costs to reduce spending and potentially prevent resource-based outages.

Getting ready

This recipe requires a functional Kubernetes cluster deployed on AWS or GCP. Currently, other cloud providers are not supported.

Before you can execute the commands in the following recipes, you need to have `kubectl` and `helm` installed. You can find the instructions to install Helm in Chapter 2, *Operating Applications on Kubernetes*, in the *Deploying workloads using Helm charts* section.

How to do it...

This section is further divided into the following subsections to ease the process:

- Installing Kubecost
- Accessing Kubecost dashboard
- Monitoring Kubernetes resource cost allocation

Installing Kubecost

Kubecost creates Kubernetes resource-granular models of current and historical Kubernetes spending. These models can be used to provide monitoring of resource allocations and cost transparency in Kubernetes environments that support multiple applications, teams, and departments. In this recipe, we will take a look at the basic steps to get Kubecost up and running:

1. Add the Kubecost chart repository to the local Helm repository list:

   ```
   $ helm repo add kubecost https://kubecost.github.io/cost-analyzer/
   ```

2. Install Kubecost into the `kubecost` namespace using the `Helm install` command:

   ```
   $ helm install kubecost/cost-analyzer --namespace kubecost --name
   kubecost --set kubecostToken="dGVzdEB0ZXN0LmNvbQ==xm343yadf98"
   ```

3. Verify that all pods are running. As you can see, this project also deploys its own instances of Prometheus and Grafana:

   ```
   $ kubectl get pods -nkubecost
   NAME READY STATUS RESTARTS AGE
   cost-analyzer-checks-1571781600-6mhwh 0/1 Completed 0 7m1s
   kubecost-cost-analyzer-54bc969689-8rznl 3/3 Running 0 9m7s
   ```

```
kubecost-grafana-844d4b9844-dkdvn 3/3 Running 0 9m7s
kubecost-prometheus-alertmanager-85bbbd6b7b-fpmqr 2/2 Running 0
9m7s
kubecost-prometheus-kube-state-metrics-857c5d4b4f-gxmgj 1/1 Running
0 9m7s
kubecost-prometheus-node-exporter-6bsp2 1/1 Running 0 9m7s
kubecost-prometheus-node-exporter-jtw2h 1/1 Running 0 9m7s
kubecost-prometheus-node-exporter-k69fh 1/1 Running 0 9m7s
kubecost-prometheus-pushgateway-7689458dc9-rx5jj 1/1 Running 0 9m7s
kubecost-prometheus-server-7b8b759d74-vww8c 2/2 Running 0 9m7s
```

If you have an existing Prometheus deployment, `node-exporter` pods may get stuck in Pending mode. In that case, you need to use different ports for Kubecost to be deployed; otherwise, pods will not be able to get the requested pod ports.

Now you have the Kubecost cost analyzer installed with a bundle of components required to operate it in a Kubernetes environment.

Accessing the Kubecost dashboard

Let's follow these instructions to access the Kubecost dashboard where you can monitor your Kubernetes resources and their costs in real time:

1. Get the list of the services in the `kubecost` namespace:

```
$ kubectl get svc -nkubecost
NAME TYPE CLUSTER-IP EXTERNAL-IP PORT(S) AGE
kubecost-cost-analyzer ClusterIP 100.65.53.41 <none>
9001/TCP,9003/TCP,9090/TCP 13m
kubecost-grafana ClusterIP 100.69.52.23 <none> 80/TCP 13m
kubecost-prometheus-alertmanager ClusterIP 100.71.217.248 <none>
80/TCP 13m
kubecost-prometheus-kube-state-metrics ClusterIP None <none> 80/TCP
13m
kubecost-prometheus-node-exporter ClusterIP None <none> 9100/TCP
13m
kubecost-prometheus-pushgateway ClusterIP 100.69.137.163 <none>
9091/TCP 13m
kubecost-prometheus-server ClusterIP 100.64.7.82 <none> 80/TCP 13m
```

2. Create a port forwarding to access the Kubecost UI using the `kubectl port-forward` command. This command will forward the local port 9090 to the Kubecost cost analyzer pod:

   ```
   $ kubectl port-forward --namespace kubecost deployment/kubecost-cost-analyzer 9090
   ```

As an alternative, you can patch the `kubecost-cost-analyzer` service using the `kubectl edit svc kubecost-cost-analyzer -nkubecost` command and change the service type `ClusterIP` to `LoadBalancer` to expose the service externally using a cloud load balancer.

3. Open the address `http://localhost:9090` (or the External IP, if using LoadBalancer) in your web browser. You should see the Kubecost login page:

4. The dashboard can be expanded by adding additional Kubecost endpoints into one and used to monitor multiple clusters from a single dashboard. If you have more than one cluster, click on the add new cluster icon and add your endpoint URLs from the other clusters:

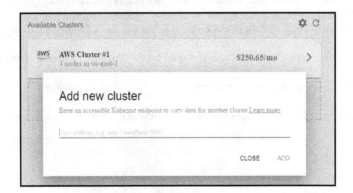

Monitoring Kubernetes resource cost allocation

Let's follow these instructions to learn how to monitor Kubernetes-related cloud spending and find possible saving recommendations using Kubecost:

1. Access your Kubecost dashboard by following the previous recipe, *Accessing the Kubecost dashboard*. Click on your cluster name on the dashboard to access the detailed summary. This view will show the monthly cost and cluster efficiency in terms of idle resources:

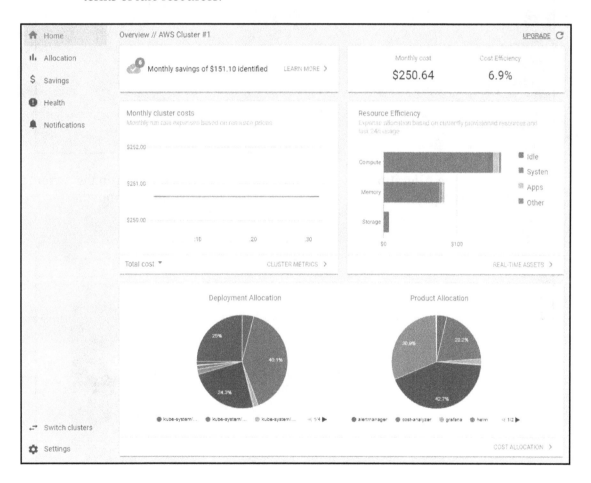

2. Click on the **Real-time assets** button. This view shows the real-time costs associated with the current cloud provider. In our example, it is one master, three worker Kubernetes clusters deployed on an AWS cluster using `kops`, each showing around $60 billed since they were created:

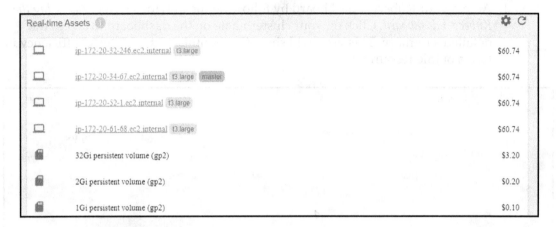

3. Click on the **Allocations** menu. This view shows cumulative costs in the current namespaces. You can apply range filters to get the daily, weekly, monthly, or custom-range cost of the resource in the selected namespace:

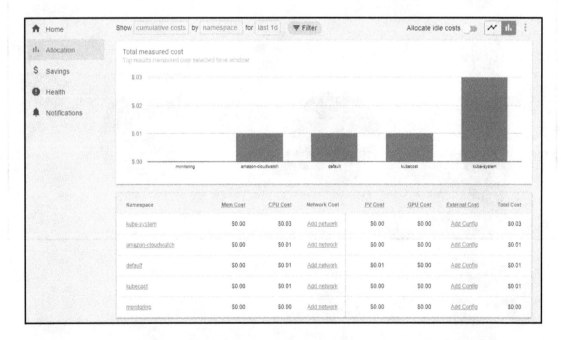

4. Click on the **Savings** menu. Information in this menu is very important, and points to possible optimization steps you can take. As an example, the following view shows that we have two underutilized nodes (utilization is below 60%) that can provide savings if we scale down our cluster. In this case, we can drain the nodes and scale down the cluster. Click on each saving category to learn more about the actions you can take to achieve the saving rate displayed here:

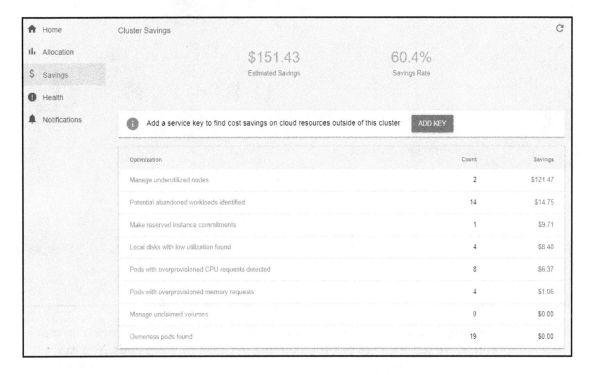

5. Click on the **Health** menu. This view shows the assessment of reliability and cluster health risks:

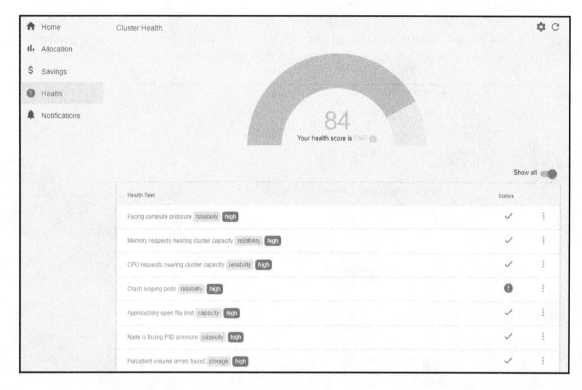

6. Disable the **Show all** option to list problems that require your attention. In our example, we see one high priority pointing to **Crash looping pods**. You can follow the instructions from the *Inspecting containers* section in this chapter to further identify the issues:

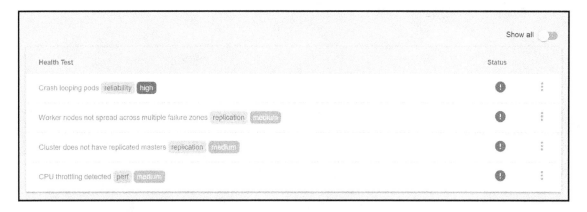

7. Click on the **Notifications** menu. From this menu, you can specify how to handle notifications. If you have a Slack channel, you can click on the **ADD** button here to forward notifications to it; otherwise, an email notification is available as an option:

Now you have the knowledge to monitor project costs and a better understanding of what actions to take to increase the return on the investment of your DevOps environment.

See also

- Kubecost documentation: `http://docs.kubecost.com/`
- Deploying Kubecost as a pod only: `https://github.com/kubecost/cost-model/blob/master/deploying-as-a-pod.md`

Securing Applications and Clusters

9

00000000000000In this chapter, we will discuss the fundamental steps of reducing the attack surface and securing Kubernetes clusters before we go live from test to production. We will talk about security auditing, building DevSecOps into CI/CD pipelines, detecting metrics for performance analysis, and how to securely manage secrets and credentials.

In this chapter, we will cover the following recipes:

- Using RBAC to harden cluster security
- Configuring Pod Security Policies
- Using Kubernetes CIS Benchmark for security auditing
- Building DevSecOps into the pipeline using Aqua Security
- Monitoring suspicious application activities using Falco
- Securing credentials using HashiCorp Vault

Technical requirements

The recipes in this chapter require that you have a functional Kubernetes cluster deployed by following one of the recommended methods described in `Chapter 1`, *Building Production-Ready Kubernetes Clusters*.

The Kubernetes command-line tool, `kubectl`, will be used for the rest of the recipes in this chapter since it's the main command-line interface for running commands against Kubernetes clusters. We will also use `helm` where Helm charts are available to deploy solutions.

Using RBAC to harden cluster security

In a complex system such as Kubernetes, authorization mechanisms are used to set who is allowed to make what changes to the cluster resources and manipulate them. **Role-based access control** (**RBAC**) is a mechanism that's highly integrated into Kubernetes that grants users and applications granular access to Kubernetes APIs.

As good practice, you should use the Node and RBAC authorizers together with the `NodeRestriction` admission plugin.

In this section, we will cover getting RBAC enabled and creating Roles and RoleBindings to grant applications and users access to the cluster resources.

Getting ready

Make sure you have an RBAC-enabled Kubernetes cluster ready (since Kubernetes 1.6, RBAC is enabled by default) and that `kubectl` and `helm` have been configured so that you can manage the cluster resources. Creating private keys will also require that you have the `openssl` tool before you attempt to create keys for users.

Clone the `k8sdevopscookbook/src` repository to your workstation to use the manifest files IN the `chapter9` directory, as follows:

```
$ git clone https://github.com/k8sdevopscookbook/src.git
$ cd src/chapter9/rbac
```

RBAC is enabled by default starting with Kubernetes 1.6. If it is disabled for any reason, start the API server with `--authorization-mode=RBAC` to enable RBAC.

How to do it...

This section is further divided into the following subsections to make this process easier:

- Viewing the default Roles
- Creating user accounts
- Creating Roles and RoleBindings
- Testing the RBAC rules

Viewing the default Roles

RBAC is a core component of the Kubernetes cluster that allows us to create and grant roles to objects and control access to resources within the cluster. This recipe will help you understand the content of roles and role bindings.

Let's perform the following steps to view the default roles and role bindings in our cluster:

1. View the default cluster roles using the following command. You will see a long mixed list of `system:`, `system:controller:`, and a few other prefixed `roles`. `system:*` roles are used by the infrastructure, `system:controller` roles are used by a Kubernetes controller manager, which is a control loop that watches the shared state of the cluster. In general, they are both good to know about when you need to troubleshoot permission issues, but they're not something we will be using very often:

   ```
   $ kubectl get clusterroles
   $ kubectl get clusterrolebindings
   ```

2. View one of the system roles owned by Kubernetes to understand their purpose and limits. In the following example, we're looking at `system:node`, which defines the permission for kubelets. In the output in Rules, `apiGroups:` indicates the core API group, `resources` indicates the Kubernetes resource type, and `verbs` indicates the API actions allowed on the role:

   ```
   $ kubectl get clusterroles system:node -oyaml
   ```

3. Let's view the default user-facing roles since they are the ones we are more interested in. The roles that don't have the `system:` prefix are intended to be user-facing roles. The following command will only list the non-system: prefix roles. The main roles that are intended to be granted within a specific namespace using RoleBindings are the `admin`, `edit`, and `view` roles:

   ```
   $ kubectl get clusterroles | grep -v '^system'
   NAME AGE
   admin 8d #gives read-write access
    to all resources
   cluster-admin 8d #super-user, gives read-write access
    to all resources
   edit 8d #allows create/update/delete on resources except RBAC
   permissions
   kops:dns-controller 8d
   kube-dns-autoscaler 8d
   view 8d #read-only access to resources
   ```

4. Now, review the default cluster binding, that is, `cluster-admin`, using the following command. You will see that this binding gives the `system:masters` group cluster-wide superuser permissions with the `cluster-admin` role:

```
$ kubectl get clusterrolebindings/cluster-admin -o yaml
apiVersion: rbac.authorization.k8s.io/v1
kind: ClusterRoleBinding
metadata:
...
roleRef:
  apiGroup: rbac.authorization.k8s.io
  kind: ClusterRole
  name: cluster-admin
subjects:
- apiGroup: rbac.authorization.k8s.io
  kind: Group
  name: system:masters
```

Since the Kubernetes 1.6 release, RBAC is enabled by default and new users can be created and start with no permissions until permissions are assigned by an admin user to a specific resource. Now, you know about the available default roles.

In the following recipes, you will learn how to create new Roles and RoleBindings and grant accounts the permissions that they need.

Creating user accounts

As explained in the Kubernetes docs, Kubernetes doesn't have objects to represent normal user accounts. Therefore, they need to be managed externally (check the *Kubernetes Authentication* documentation in the *See also* section for more details). This recipe will show you how to create and manage user accounts using private keys.

Let's perform the following steps to create a user account:

1. Create a private key for the example user. In our example, the key file is `user3445.key`:

```
$ openssl genrsa -out user3445.key 2048
```

2. Create a **certificate sign request** (CSR) called `user3445.csr` using the private key we created in *Step 1*. Set the username (`/CN`) and group name (`/O`) in the `-subj` parameter. In the following example, the username is `john.geek`, while the group is `development`:

```
$ openssl req -new -key user3445.key \
-out user3445.csr \
-subj "/CN=john.geek/O=development"
```

3. To use the built-in signer, you need to locate the cluster-signing certificates for your cluster. By default, the `ca.crt` and `ca.key` files should be in the `/etc/kubernetes/pki/` directory.If you are using kops to deploy, your cluster signing keys can be downloaded from `s3://$BUCKET_NAME/$KOPS_CLUSTER_NAME/pki/private/ca/*.key` and `s3://$BUCKET_NAME/$KOPS_CLUSTER_NAME/pki/issued/ca/*.crt`. Once you've located the keys, change the `CERT_LOCATION` mentioned in the following code to the current location of the files and generate the final signed certificate:

```
$ openssl x509 -req -in user3445.csr \
-CA CERT_LOCATION/ca.crt \
-CAkey CERT_LOCATION/ca.key \
-CAcreateserial -out user3445.crt \
-days 500
```

4. If all the files have been located, the command in *Step 3* should return an output similar to the following:

```
Signature ok
subject=CN = john.geek, O = development
Getting CA Private Key
```

Before we move on, make sure you store the signed keys in a safe directory. As an industry best practice, using a secrets engine or Vault storage is recommended. You will learn more about Vault storage later in this chapter IN the *Securing credentials using HashiCorp Vault* recipe.

5. Create a new context using the new user credentials:

```
$ kubectl config set-credentials user3445 --client-
certificate=user3445.crt --client-key=user3445.key
$ kubectl config set-context user3445-context --cluster=local --
namespace=secureapp --user=user3445
```

6. List the existing context using the following comment. You will see that the new `user3445-context` has been created:

```
$ kubectl config get-contexts
CURRENT NAME                           CLUSTER AUTHINFO NAMESPACE
*        service-account-context local    kubecfg
         user3445-context            local    user3445 secureapp
```

7. Now, try to list the pods using the new user context. You will get an access denied error since the new user doesn't have any roles and new users don't come with any roles assigned to them by default:

```
$ kubectl --context=user3445-context get pods
Error from server (Forbidden): pods is forbidden: User "john.geek"
cannot list resource "pods" in API group "" in the namespace
"secureapps"
```

8. Optionally, you can `base64` encode all three files (`user3445.crt`, `user3445.csr`, and `user3445.key`) using the `openssl base64 -in <infile> -out <outfile>` command and distribute the populated `config-user3445.yml` file to your developers. An example file can be found in this book's GitHub repository in the `src/chapter9/rbac` directory. There are many ways to distribute user credentials. Review the example using your text editor:

```
$ cat config-user3445.yaml
```

With that, you've learned how to create new users. Next, you will create roles and assign them to the user.

Creating Roles and RoleBindings

Roles and RolesBindings are always used in a defined namespace, meaning that the permissions can only be granted for the resources that are in the same namespace as the Roles and the RoleBindings themselves compared to the ClusterRoles and ClusterRoleBindings that are used to grant permissions to cluster-wide resources such as nodes.

Let's perform the following steps to create an example Role and RoleBinding in our cluster:

1. First, create a namespace where we will create the Role and RoleBinding. In our example, the namespace is `secureapp`:

```
$ kubectl create ns secureapp
```

2. Create a role using the following rules. This role basically allows all operations to be performed on deployments, replica sets, and pods for the `deployer` role in the `secureapp` namespace we created in *Step 1*. Note that any permissions that are granted are only additive and there are no deny rules:

```
$ cat <<EOF | kubectl apply -f -
apiVersion: rbac.authorization.k8s.io/v1
kind: Role
metadata:
  namespace: secureapp
  name: deployer
rules:
- apiGroups: ["", "extensions", "apps"]
  resources: ["deployments", "replicasets", "pods"]
  verbs: ["get", "list", "watch", "create", "update", "patch",
"delete"]
EOF
```

3. Create a RoleBinding using the `deployer` role and for the username `john.geek` in the `secureapp` namespace. We're doing this since a RoleBinding can only reference a Role that exists in the same namespace:

```
$ cat <<EOF | kubectl apply -f -
kind: RoleBinding
apiVersion: rbac.authorization.k8s.io/v1
metadata:
  name: deployer-binding
  namespace: secureapp
subjects:
- kind: User
  name: john.geek
  apiGroup: ""
roleRef:
  kind: Role
  name: deployer
  apiGroup: ""
EOF
```

With that, you've learned how to create a new Role and grant permissions to a user using RoleBindings.

Testing the RBAC rules

Let's perform the following steps to test the Role and RoleBinding we created earlier:

1. Deploy a test pod in the `secureapp` namespace where the user has access:

```
$ cat <<EOF | kubectl --context=user3445-context apply -f -
apiVersion: v1
kind: Pod
metadata:
  name: busybox
  namespace: secureapp
spec:
  containers:
  - image: busybox
    command:
      - sleep
      - "3600"
    imagePullPolicy: IfNotPresent
    name: busybox
  restartPolicy: Always
EOF
```

List the pods in the new user's context. The same command that failed in the *Creating user accounts* recipe in *Step 7* should now execute successfully:

```
$ kubectl --context=user3445-context get pods
NAME       READY STATUS   RESTARTS AGE
busybox 1/1    Running 1         2m
```

If you try to create the same pod in a different namespace, you will see that the command will fail to execute.

How it works...

This recipe showed you how to create new users in Kubernetes and quickly create Roles and RoleBindings to grant permission to user accounts on Kubernetes.

Kubernetes clusters have two types of users:

- **User accounts**: User accounts are normal users that are managed externally.
- **Service accounts**: Service accounts are the users who are associated with the Kubernetes services and are managed by the Kubernetes API with its own resources.

You can read more about service accounts by looking at the *Managing service accounts* link in the *See also* section.

In the *Creating Roles and RoleBindings* recipe, in *Step 1*, we created a Role named `deployer`. Then, in *Step 2*, we granted the rules associated with the deployer Role to the user account `john.geek`.

RBAC uses the `rbac.authorization.k8s.io` API to make authorization decisions. This allows admins to dynamically configure policies using the Kubernetes APIs. If you wanted to use the existing Roles and give someone cluster-wide superuser permission, you could use the `cluster-admin` ClusterRole with a ClusterRoleBinding instead. ClusterRoles don't have namespace limits and can execute commands in any namespace with the granted permissions. Overall, you should be careful while assigning the `cluster-admin` ClusterRole to users. ClusterRoles can be also limited to namespaces, similar to Roles if they are used with RoleBindings to grant permissions instead.

See also

- RBAC Authorization in Kubernetes documentation: `https://kubernetes.io/docs/reference/access-authn-authz/rbac/#rolebinding-and-clusterrolebinding`
- More on the default roles and role bindings: `https://kubernetes.io/docs/reference/access-authn-authz/rbac/#default-roles-and-role-bindings`
- Autogenerating RBAC policies based on Kubernetes audit logs: `https://github.com/liggitt/audit2rbac`
- Kubernetes Authentication: `https://kubernetes.io/docs/reference/access-authn-authz/authentication/`
- Managing Service Accounts: `https://kubernetes.io/docs/reference/access-authn-authz/service-accounts-admin/`
- The kubectl-bindrole tool for finding Kubernetes Roles bound to a specified ServiceAccount: `https://github.com/Ladicle/kubectl-bindrole`

Configuring Pod Security Policies

Pod Security Policies (PSP) are used on Kubernetes clusters to enable granular authorization of pod creation and to control security aspects of pods. PodSecurityPolicy objects define the conditions for a pod to be accepted into the cluster and run as expected.

In this section, we will cover the recreation and configuration of PSPs on Kubernetes.

Getting ready

Make sure you have an RBAC-enabled Kubernetes cluster ready (since Kubernetes 1.6, RBAC is enabled by default) and `kubectl` and `helm` configured to manage the cluster resources.

Clone the `k8sdevopscookbook/src` repository to your workstation to use the manifest files in the `chapter9` directory, as follows:

```
$ git clone https://github.com/k8sdevopscookbook/src.git
$ cd src/chapter9/psp
```

Verify if PodSecurityPolicy needs to be enabled on your cluster by running the `kubectl get psp` command. If you get a message stating `the server doesn't have a resource type "podSecurityPolicies".`, then PSP needs to be enabled on your cluster.

How to do it...

This section is further divided into the following subsections to make this process easier:

- Enabling PSPs on EKS
- Enabling PSPs on GKE
- Enabling PSPs on AKS
- Creating a restricted PSPs

Enabling PSPs on EKS

As a best practice, PSPs should not be enabled before you create your own policies. This recipe will take you through how to enable PSP on Amazon EKS and how to review default policies.

Let's perform the following steps:

1. Deploy Kubernetes version 1.13 or higher. PSP will be enabled by default. The default configuration comes with a non-disruptive policy named `eks.privileged` that has no restrictions. View the default policy with the following command:

```
$ kubectl get psp eks.privileged
NAME            PRIV CAPS SELINUX   RUNASUSER FSGROUP   SUPGROUP
```

```
READONLYROOTFS VOLUMES
eks.privileged true *      RunAsAny RunAsAny   RunAsAny RunAsAny false
*
```

2. Describe the policy to see its full details, as follows:

   ```
   $ kubectl describe psp eks.privileged
   ```

3. To review, restore, or delete the default PSP, use the YAML manifest in the example repository in `src/chapter9/psp` named `eks-privileged-psp.yaml`.

Enabling PSPs on GKE

As a best practice, PSPs should not be enabled before you create your own policies. This recipe will take you through how to enable PSP on **Google Kubernetes Engine** (**GKE**) and how to review default policies.

Let's perform the following steps:

1. You can enable PSP on the cluster you deployed by following the instructions given in `Chapter 1`, *Building Production-Ready Kubernetes Clusters*, in the *Provisioning a managed Kubernetes cluster on GKE* recipe by running the following command. Replace `k8s-devops-cookbook-1` with your own cluster name:

   ```
   $ gcloud beta container clusters update k8s-devops-cookbook-1 --
   enable-pod-security-policy
   ```

2. The default configuration comes with a non-disruptive policy named `gce.privileged` that has no restrictions and couple of other policies. View the default policies with the following command:

   ```
   $ kubectl get psp
   NAME                             PRIV  CAPS SELINUX   RUNASUSER FSGROUP
   SUPGROUP READONLYROOTFS VOLUMES
   gce.event-exporter               false        RunAsAny RunAsAny  RunAsAny
   RunAsAny false          hostPath,secret
   gce.fluentd-gcp                  false        RunAsAny RunAsAny  RunAsAny
   RunAsAny false          configMap,hostPath,secret
   gce.persistent-volume-binder false        RunAsAny RunAsAny  RunAsAny
   RunAsAny false          nfs,secret,projected
   gce.privileged                   true  *     RunAsAny RunAsAny  RunAsAny
   RunAsAny false          *
   gce.unprivileged-addon           false
   SETPCAP,MKNOD,AUDIT_WRITE,CHOWN,NET_RAW,DAC_OVERRIDE,FOWNER,FSETID,
   ```

```
KILL,SETGID,SETUID,NET_BIND_SERVICE,SYS_CHROOT,SETFCAP RunAsAny
RunAsAny RunAsAny RunAsAny false
emptyDir,configMap,secret,projected
```

3. Describe the policy to see its full details, as follows:

```
$ kubectl describe psp gce.privileged
```

4. To review, restore, or delete the default PSP, use the YAML manifest in the example repository in `src/chapter9/psp` named `gce-privileged-psp.yaml`.

Enabling PodSecurityPolicy on AKS

As a best practice, PodSecurityPolicy should not be enabled before you create your own policies. This recipe will take you through how to enable PSP on **Azure Kubernetes Service (AKS)** and how to review default policies.

Let's perform the following steps:

1. You can enable PSP on the cluster you have deployed by following the instructions given in `Chapter 1` *Building Production-Ready Kubernetes Clusters*, in the *Provisioning a managed Kubernetes cluster on AKS* recipe by running the following command. Replace `k8sdevopscookbook` with your own resource group and `AKSCluster` with your cluster name:

```
$ az aks create --resource-group k8sdevopscookbook \
--name AKSCluster \
--enable-pod-security-policy
```

2. he default configuration comes with a non-disruptive policy named `privileged` that has no restrictions. View the default policy with the following command:

```
$ kubectl get psp
NAME PRIV CAPS SELINUX RUNASUSER FSGROUP SUPGROUP READONLYROOTFS
VOLUMES
privileged true * RunAsAny RunAsAny RunAsAny RunAsAny false *
configMap,emptyDir,projected,secret,downwardAPI,persistentVolumeCla
im
```

3. Describe the policy to see its full details, as follows:

```
$ kubectl describe psp privileged
```

4. To review, restore, or delete the default PSP, use the YAML manifest in the example repository in `src/chapter9/psp` named `aks-privileged-psp.yaml`.

Creating a restricted PSPs

As a security best practice, it is recommended to restrict containers in pods from running with root user privileges to limit any possible risks. When running in privileged mode, processes that run inside the container have the same privileges and access as the processes outside the container, which can raise the risk of some management capabilities being accessed by attackers.

Let's perform the following steps to create a root access restricted PodSecurityPolicy:

1. Deploy a new restricted `PodSecurityPolicy`:

```
$ cat <<EOF | kubectl apply -f -
apiVersion: extensions/v1beta1
kind: PodSecurityPolicy
metadata:
  name: restricted-psp
spec:
  privileged: false
  runAsUser:
    rule: MustRunAsNonRoot
  seLinux:
    rule: RunAsAny
  fsGroup:
    rule: RunAsAny
  supplementalGroups:
    rule: RunAsAny
  volumes:
  - '*'
EOF
```

2. Confirm that the policy has been created. You will notice that the RUNASUSER column shows MustRunAsNonRoot, which indicates that using root privileges is not allowed:

```
$ kubectl get psp restricted-psp
NAME                 PRIV  CAPS       SELINUX   RUNASUSER          FSGROUP
SUPGROUP READONLYROOTFS  VOLUMES
restricted-psp false                  RunAsAny MustRunAsNonRoot RunAsAny
RunAsAny false                *
```

3. Verify the PSP by running a pod that requires root access. The deployment will fail and show a message stating `container has runAsNonRoot and image will run as root`, as shown in the following code:

```
$ kubectl run --image=mariadb:10.4.8 mariadb --port=3306 --
env="MYSQL_ROOT_PASSWORD=my-secret-pw"
$ kubectl get pods
NAME                        READY  STATUS
RESTARTS AGE
mariadb-5584b4f9d8-q6whd 0/1     container has runAsNonRoot and image
will run as root 0          46s
```

With that, you've learned how to create a root access restricted PodSecurityPolicy.

There's more...

This section is further divided into the following subsections to make this process easier:

- Restricting pods to access certain volume types
- Using Kubernetes PSPs advisor

Restricting pods to access certain volume types

As part of the PodSecurityPolicy rule, you may want to limit the use of a specific type of volume. In this recipe, you will learn how to restricts containers to volume types.

Let's perform the following steps to create a PodSecurityPolicy:

1. Create a new restricted `PodSecurityPolicy`. This policy limits the type of volume to `nfs` only:

```
$ cat <<EOF | kubectl apply -f -
kind: PodSecurityPolicy
metadata:
  name: restricted-vol-psp
spec:
  privileged: false
  runAsUser:
    rule: RunAsAny
  seLinux:
    rule: RunAsAny
  fsGroup:
    rule: RunAsAny
  supplementalGroups:
```

```
    rule: RunAsAny
  volumes:
  - 'nfs'
EOF
```

2. Verify the policy by deploying an application that requires persistent storage. Here, we will use the MinIO example from previous chapters. The deployment should fail with a message stating `persistentVolumeClaim volumes are not allowed to be used`:

```
$ kubectl create -f \
https://raw.githubusercontent.com/k8sdevopscookbook/src/master/chap
ter6/minio/minio.yaml
```

3. Delete both the PSPs and the deployment:

```
$ kubectl delete psp restricted-vol-psp
$ kubectl delete -f \
https://raw.githubusercontent.com/k8sdevopscookbook/src/master/chap
ter6/minio/minio.yaml
```

4. The recommended set of allowed volumes for new PSPs are `configMap`, `downwardAPI`, `emptyDir`, `persistentVolumeClaim`, `secret`, and `projected`. You can find the complete list of volume types by going to the *Type of volumes supported* link in the *See also* section. Create a new restricted PodSecurityPolicy using the following content. This policy limits the type of volume to `persistentVolumeClaim` only:

```
$ cat <<EOF | kubectl apply -f -
kind: PodSecurityPolicy
metadata:
  name: permit-pvc-psp
spec:
  privileged: false
  runAsUser:
    rule: RunAsAny
  seLinux:
    rule: RunAsAny
  fsGroup:
    rule: RunAsAny
  supplementalGroups:
    rule: RunAsAny
  volumes:
  - 'persistentVolumeClaim'
EOF
```

5. Repeat *Step 2* to deploy the application. This time, `persistentVolumeClaim` creation will be allowed and the PVC that was requested by the pod will be created.

Using Kubernetes PodSecurityPolicy advisor

Kubernetes PodSecurityPolicy Advisor is a simple tool from Sysdig that's used to enforce best security practices in Kubernetes. `kube-psp-advisor` scans the existing security context of Kubernetes resources and generates the PSPs for the resources in the cluster to remove unnecessary privileges.

Let's perform the following steps to enable `kube-psp-advisor` on our cluster:

1. Clone the repository and build the project using the following command:

```
$ git clone https://github.com/sysdiglabs/kube-psp-advisor
$ cd kube-psp-advisor && make build
```

2. Run the scan process by executing the binary. If you want to limit the scan to a namespace, you can specify it by adding the `--namespace=` parameter to the command, similar to what can be seen in the following code. If you don't do this, it will scan the whole cluster. After doing this, a `PodSecurityPolicy` will be generated:

```
$ ./kube-psp-advisor --namespace=secureapp > psp-advisor.yaml
```

3. Review the content of the `psp-advisor.yaml` file and apply the generated PSP:

```
$ cat psp-advisor.yaml
$ kubectl apply -f psp-advisor.yaml
```

With that, you've learned how to generate a PSP in a simpler way to reduce the unnecessary permissions that may increase the attack surface.

See also

- Kubernetes documentation – PodSecurityPolicy: https://kubernetes.io/docs/concepts/policy/pod-security-policy/
- Type of volumes supported: https://kubernetes.io/docs/concepts/storage/volumes/#types-of-volumes

Using Kubernetes CIS Benchmark for security auditing

Kubernetes CIS Benchmarks are the security configuration best practices that are accepted by industry experts. The CIS Benchmark guide can be download as a PDF file from the **Center for Internet Security (CIS)** website at `https://www.cisecurity.org/`. `kube-bench` is an application that automates documented checks.

In this section, we will cover the installation and use of the open source `kube-bench` tool to run Kubernetes CIS Benchmarks for security auditing of Kubernetes clusters.

Getting ready

For this recipe, we need to have a Kubernetes cluster ready and the Kubernetes command-line tool `kubectl` installed.

Clone the `k8sdevopscookbook/src` repository to your workstation to use the manifest files in the `chapter9` directory, as follows:

```
$ git clone https://github.com/k8sdevopscookbook/src.git
$ cd src/chapter9/cis
```

Some of the tests target Kubernetes nodes and can only be executed on fully self-managed clusters where you have control over the master nodes. Therefore, managed clusters such as EKS, GKE, AKS, and so on will not be able to execute all the tests and require different job descriptions or parameters to execute the tests. These will be mentioned when necessary.

How to do it...

This section is further divided into the following subsections to make this process easier:

- Running kube-bench on Kubernetes
- Running kube-bench on managed Kubernetes services
- Running kube-bench on OpenShift
- Running kube-hunter

Running kube-bench on Kubernetes

The CIS Benchmark has tests for both master and worker nodes. Therefore, the full scope of the test can only be completed on self-managed clusters where you have control over the master nodes. In this recipe, you will learn how to run kube-bench directly on the master and worker nodes.

Let's perform the following steps to run the CIS recommended tests:

1. Download and install the `kube-bench` command-line interface on one of your master nodes and one of your worker nodes:

```
$ curl --silent --location
"https://github.com/aquasecurity/kube-bench/releases/download/v0.1.
0/kube-bench_0.1.0_linux_amd64.tar.gz" | tar xz -C /tmp
$ sudo mv /tmp/kube-bench /usr/local/bin
```

2. SSH into your Kubernetes master node and run the following command. It will quickly return the result of the test with an explanation and a list of additional manual tests that are recommended to be run after. Here, you can see that 31 checks passed and 36 tests failed:

```
$ kube-bench master
...
== Summary ==
31 checks PASS
36 checks FAIL
24 checks WARN
1 checks INFO
```

3. To save the results, use the following command. After the test is complete, move the `kube-bench-master.txt` file to your localhost for further review:

```
$ kube-bench master > kube-bench-master.txt
```

4. Review the content of the `kube-bench-master.txt` file. You will see the status of the checks from the CIS Benchmark for the Kubernetes guide, similar to the following:

```
[INFO] 1 Master Node Security Configuration
[INFO] 1.1 API Server
[PASS] 1.1.1 Ensure that the --anonymous-auth argument is set to
false (Not Scored)
[FAIL] 1.1.2 Ensure that the --basic-auth-file argument is not set
(Scored)
[PASS] 1.1.3 Ensure that the --insecure-allow-any-token argument is
```

```
not set (Not Scored)
[PASS] 1.1.4 Ensure that the --kubelet-https argument is set to
true (Scored)
[FAIL] 1.1.5 Ensure that the --insecure-bind-address argument is
not set (Scored)
[FAIL] 1.1.6 Ensure that the --insecure-port argument is set to 0
(Scored)
[PASS] 1.1.7 Ensure that the --secure-port argument is not set to 0
(Scored)
[FAIL] 1.1.8 Ensure that the --profiling argument is set to false
(Scored)
[FAIL] 1.1.9 Ensure that the --repair-malformed-updates argument is
set to false (Scored)
[PASS] 1.1.10 Ensure that the admission control plugin AlwaysAdmit
is not set (Scored)
...
```

Tests are split into categories that have been suggested in the CIS Benchmark guidelines, such as API Server, Scheduler, Controller Manager, Configuration Manager, etcd, General Security Primitives, and PodSecurityPolicies.

5. Follow the methods suggested in the *Remediations* section of the report to fix the failed issues and rerun the test to confirm that the correction has been made. You can see some of the remediations that were suggested by the preceding report here:

```
== Remediations ==
1.1.2 Follow the documentation and configure alternate mechanisms
for authentication. Then,
edit the API server pod specification file
/etc/kubernetes/manifests/kube-apiserver.manifest
on the master node and remove the --basic-auth-file=<filename>
parameter.

1.1.5 Edit the API server pod specification file
/etc/kubernetes/manifests/kube-apiserver.manife$
on the master node and remove the --insecure-bind-address
parameter.

1.1.6 Edit the API server pod specification file
/etc/kubernetes/manifests/kube-apiserver.manife$
apiserver.yaml on the master node and set the below parameter.
--insecure-port=0

1.1.8 Edit the API server pod specification file
/etc/kubernetes/manifests/kube-apiserver.manife$
on the master node and set the below parameter.
```

```
--profiling=false

1.2.1 Edit the Scheduler pod specification file
/etc/kubernetes/manifests/kube-scheduler.manifest
file on the master node and set the below parameter.
--profiling=false
...
```

6. Let's take one of the issues from the preceding list. `1.2.1` suggests that we disable the profiling API endpoint. The reason for this is that highly sensitive system information can be uncovered by profiling data and the amount of data and load that's created by profiling your cluster could be put out of service (denial-of-service attack) by this feature. Edit the `kube-scheduler.manifest` file and add `--profiling=false` right after the `kube-schedule` command, as shown in the following code:

```
...
spec:
  containers:
  - command:
    - /bin/sh
    - -c
    - mkfifo /tmp/pipe; (tee -a /var/log/kube-scheduler.log <
/tmp/pipe & ) ; exec
        /usr/local/bin/kube-scheduler --profiling=False --
kubeconfig=/var/lib/kube-scheduler/kubeconfig
        --leader-elect=true --v=2 > /tmp/pipe 2>&1
...
```

7. Run the test again and confirm that the issue on `1.2.1` has been corrected. Here, you can see that the number of passed tests has increased from `31` to `32`. One more check has been cleared:

```
$ kube-bench master
...
== Summary ==
32 checks PASS
35 checks FAIL
24 checks WARN
1 checks INFO
```

8. Run the test on the worker nodes by using the following command:

```
$ kube-bench node
...
== Summary ==
9 checks PASS
```

```
12 checks FAIL
2 checks WARN
1 checks INFO
```

9. To save the results, use the following command. After the test has completed, move the `kube-bench-worker.txt` file to your localhost for further review:

```
$ kube-bench node > kube-bench-worker.txt
```

10. Review the content of the `kube-bench-worker.txt` file. You will see the status of the checks from the CIS Benchmark for the Kubernetes guide, similar to the following:

```
[INFO] 2 Worker Node Security Configuration
[INFO] 2.1 Kubelet
[PASS] 2.1.1 Ensure that the --anonymous-auth argument is set to
false (Scored)
[FAIL] 2.1.2 Ensure that the --authorization-mode argument is not
set to AlwaysAllow (Scored)
[PASS] 2.1.3 Ensure that the --client-ca-file argument is set as
appropriate (Scored)
...
```

Similarly, follow all the remediations until you've cleared all the failed tests on the master and worker nodes.

Running kube-bench on managed Kubernetes services

The difference between managed Kubernetes services such as EKS, GKE, AKS, and so on is that you can't run the checks on the master. Instead, you have to either only follow the worker checks from the previous recipe or run a Kubernetes job to validate your environment. In this recipe, you will learn how to run kube-bench on managed Kubernetes service-based nodes and also in cases where you don't have direct SSH access to the nodes.

Let's perform the following steps to run the CIS recommended tests:

1. For this recipe, we will use EKS as our Kubernetes service, but you can change the Kubernetes and container registry services to other cloud providers if you wish. First, create an ECR repository where we will host the kube-bench image:

```
$ aws ecr create-repository --repository-name
k8sdevopscookbook/kube-bench --image-tag-mutability MUTABLE
```

2. Clone the `kube-bench` repository to your localhost:

```
$ git clone https://github.com/aquasecurity/kube-bench.git
```

3. Log in to your **Elastic Container Registry** (**ECR**) account. You need to be authenticated before you can push images to the registry:

```
$ $(aws ecr get-login --no-include-email --region us-west-2)
```

4. Build the kube-bench image by running the following command:

```
$ docker build -t k8sdevopscookbook/kube-bench
```

5. Replace `<AWS_ACCT_NUMBER>` with your AWS account number and execute it to push it to the ECR repository. The first command will create a tag, while the second command will push the image:

```
$ docker tag k8sdevopscookbook/kube-bench:latest
<AWS_ACCT_NUMBER>.dkr.ecr.us-west-2.amazonaws.com/k8s/kube-
bench:latest
# docker push <AWS_ACCT_NUMBER>.dkr.ecr.us-
west-2.amazonaws.com/k8s/kube-bench:latest
```

6. Edit the `job-eks.yaml` file and replace the image name on line 12 with the URI of the image you pushed in *Step 5*. It should look similar to the following, except you should use your AWS account number in the image URI:

```
apiVersion: batch/v1
kind: Job
metadata:
  name: kube-bench
spec:
  template:
    spec:
      hostPID: true
      containers:
      - name: kube-bench
        # Push the image to your ECR and then refer to it here
        image: 316621595343.dkr.ecr.us-
west-2.amazonaws.com/k8sdevopscookbook/kube-bench:latest
...
```

7. Run the job using the following command. It will be executed and completed shortly:

```
$ kubectl apply -f job-eks.yaml
```

8. List the kube-bench pods that were created in your cluster. It should show `Completed` as the status, similar to the following example:

```
$ kubectl get pods |grep kube-bench
kube-bench-7lxzn 0/1 Completed 0 5m
```

9. Replace the pod name with the output of the previous command and view the pod logs to retrieve the `kube-bench` results. In our example, the pod name is `kube-bench-7lxzn`:

```
$ kubectl logs kube-bench-7lxzn
```

Now, you can run kube-bench on any managed Kubernetes cluster. After you get the logs, follow all the remediation suggestions until you clear the failed tests on the worker nodes.

Running kube-bench on OpenShift

OpenShift has different command-line tools, so if we run the default test jobs, we won't be able to gather the required information on our cluster unless specified. In this recipe, you will learn how to run `kube-bench` on OpenShift.

Let's perform the following steps to run the CIS recommended tests:

1. SSH into your OpenShift master node and run the following command using `--version ocp-3.10` or `ocp-3.11` based on your OpenShift version. Currently, only 3.10 and 3.11 are supported:

```
$ kube-bench master --version ocp-3.11
```

2. To save the results, use the following command. After the test has been completed, move the `kube-bench-master.txt` file to your localhost for further review:

```
$ kube-bench master --version ocp-3.11 > kube-bench-master.txt
```

3. SSH into your OpenShift worker node and repeat the first two steps of this recipe, but this time using the `node` parameter for the OpenShift version you are running. In our example, this is OCP 3.11:

```
$ kube-bench node --version ocp-3.11 > kube-bench-node.txt
```

Follow the *Running kube-bench on Kubernetes* recipe's instructions to patch security issues with the suggested remediations.

How it works...

This recipe showed you how to quickly run CIS Kubernetes Benchmarks on your cluster using kube-bench.

In the *Running kube-bench on Kubernetes* recipe, in *step 1*, after you executed the checks, kube-bench accessed the configuration files that were kept in the following directories: `/var/lib/etcd`, `/var/lib/kubelet`, `/etc/systemd`, `/etc/kubernetes`, and `/usr/bin`. Therefore, the user who runs the checks needs to provide root/sudo access to all the config files.

If the configuration files can't be found in their default directories, the checks will fail. The most common issue is the missing `kubectl` binary in the `/usr/bin` directory. kubectl is used to detect the Kubernetes version. You can skip this directory by specifying the Kubernetes version using `--version` as part of the command, similar to the following:

```
$ kube-bench master --version 1.14
```

Step 1 will return four different states. The `PASS` and `FAIL` states are self-explanatory as they indicate whether the tests were run successfully or failed. `WARN` indicates that the test requires manual validation, which means it requires attention. Finally, `INFO` means that no further action is required.

See also

- CIS Kubernetes Benchmarks: `https://www.cisecurity.org/benchmark/kubernetes/`
- kube-bench repository: `https://github.com/aquasecurity/kube-bench`
- How to customize the default configuration: `https://github.com/aquasecurity/kube-bench/blob/master/docs/README.md#configuration-and-variables`
- Automating compliance checking for Kubernetes-based applications: `https://github.com/cds-snc/security-goals`
- Hardening Kubernetes from Scratch: `https://github.com/hardening-kubernetes/from-scratch`
- CNCF Blog on 9 Kubernetes Security Best Practices Everyone Must Follow: `https://www.cncf.io/blog/2019/01/14/9-kubernetes-security-best-practices-everyone-must-follow/`
- Hardening Guide for Rancher `https://rancher.com/docs/rancher/v2.x/en/security/hardening-2.2/`

- Must-have Kubernetes security audit tools:
  - Kube-bench: `https://github.com/aquasecurity/kube-bench`
  - Kube-hunter: `https://kube-hunter.aquasec.com/`
  - Kubeaudit: `https://github.com/Shopify/kubeaudit`
  - Kubesec:`https://github.com/controlplaneio/kubesec`
  - Open Policy Agent:`https://www.openpolicyagent.org/`
  - K8Guard: `https://k8guard.github.io/`

Building DevSecOps into the pipeline using Aqua Security

The **Shift Left** approach to DevOps Security is becoming increasingly popular, which means that security must be built into the process and pipeline. One of the biggest problems with shortened pipelines is that they often leave little room for proper security checks. Due to this, another approach called **deploy changes as quickly as possible** was introduced, which is key to the success of DevOps.

In this section, we will cover automating vulnerability checks in container images using Aqua Security to reduce the application attack surface.

Getting ready

Make sure you have an existing CI/CD pipeline configured using your preferred CI/CD tool. If not, follow the instructions in `Chapter 3`, *Building CI/CD Pipelines*, to configure GitLab or CircleCI.

Clone the `k8sdevopscookbook/src` repository to your workstation to use the manifest files in the `chapter9` directory, as follows:

```
$ git clone https://github.com/k8sdevopscookbook/src.git
$ cd src/chapter9
```

Make sure you have a Kubernetes cluster ready and `kubectl` configured to manage the cluster resources.

How to do it...

This section will show you how to integrate Aqua with your CI/CD platform. This section is further divided into the following subsections to make this process easier:

- Scanning images using Aqua Security Trivy
- Building vulnerability scanning into GitLab
- Building vulnerability scanning into CircleCI

Scanning images using Trivy

Trivy is an open source container scanning tool that's used to identify container vulnerabilities. It is one of the simplest and most accurate scanning tools in the market. In this recipe, we will learn how to install and scan container images using Trivy.

Let's perform the following steps to run Trivy:

1. Get the latest Trivy release number and keep it in a variable:

```
$ VERSION=$(curl --silent
"https://api.github.com/repos/aquasecurity/trivy/releases/latest" |
\
grep '"tag_name":' | \
sed -E 's/.*"v([^"]+)".*/\1/')
```

   Download and install the `trivy` command-line interface:

```
$ curl --silent --location
"https://github.com/aquasecurity/trivy/releases/download/v${VERSION
}/trivy_${VERSION}_Linux-64bit.tar.gz" | tar xz -C /tmp
$ sudo mv /trivy /usr/local/bin
```

3. Verify that `trivy` is functional by running the following command. It will return its current version:

```
$ trivy --version
trivy version 0.1.7
```

4. Execute `trivy` checks by replacing the container image name with your target image. In our example, we scanned the `postgres:12.0` image from the Docker Hub repository:

```
$ trivy postgres:12.0
2019-11-12T04:08:02.013Z INFO Updating vulnerability database...
2019-11-12T04:08:07.088Z INFO Detecting Debian vulnerabilities...
```

```
postgres:12.0 (debian 10.1)
===========================
Total: 164 (UNKNOWN: 1, LOW: 26, MEDIUM: 122, HIGH: 14, CRITICAL:
1)
. . .
```

5. The test summary will show the number of vulnerabilities that have been detected and will include a detailed list of vulnerabilities, along with their IDs and an explanation of each of them:

```
+-----------+-----------------+----------+----------+-----------+-----
--+
| LIBRARY   | V ID            | SEVERITY | INST VER | FIXED VER |
TITLE|
+-----------+-----------------+----------+----------+-----------+-----
--+
| apt       | CVE-2011-3374 | LOW      | 1.8.2    |           |
|
+-----------+-----------------+          +----------+-----------+-----
--+
| bash      | TEMP-0841856  |          | 5.0-4    |           |
|
+-----------+-----------------+          +----------+-----------+-----
--+
| coreutils | CVE-2016-2781 |          | 8.30-3   |           |
|
+           +-----------------+          +          +-----------+-----
--+
|           | CVE-2017-18018|          |          |           |
|
+-----------+-----------------+----------+----------+-----------+-----
--+
| file      | CVE-2019-18218| HIGH     | 1:5.35-4 | 1:5.35-4+d|
file:|
. . .
```

With that, you've learned how to quickly scan your container images. Trivy supports a variety of container base images (CentOS, Ubuntu, Alpine, Distorless, and so on) and natively supports container registries such as Docker Hub, Amazon ECR, and Google Container Registry GCR. Trivy is completely suitable for CI. In the next two recipes, you will learn how you can add Trivy into CI pipelines.

Building vulnerability scanning into GitLab

With GitLab Auto DevOps, the container scanning job uses CoreOS Clair to analyze Docker images for vulnerabilities. However, it is not a complete database of all security issues for Alpine-based images. Aqua Trivy has nearly double the number of vulnerabilities and is more suitable for CI. For a detailed comparison, please refer to the *Trivy Comparison* link in the *See also* section. This recipe will take you through adding a test stage to a GitLab CI pipeline.

Let's perform the following steps to add Trivy vulnerability checks in GitLab:

1. Edit the CI/CD pipeline configuration `.gitlab-ci.yml` file in your project:

   ```
   $ vim .gitlab-ci.yml
   ```

2. Add a new stage to your pipeline and define the stage. You can find an example in the `src/chapter9/devsecops` directory. In our example, we're using the `vulTest` stage name:

   ```
   stages:
     - build
     - vulTest
     - staging
     - production
   #Add the Step 3 here
   ```

3. Add the new stage, that is, `vulTest`. When you define a new stage, you specify a stage name parent key. In our example, the parent key is `trivy`. The commands in the `before_script` section will download the `trivy` binaries:

   ```
   trivy:
     stage: vulTest
     image: docker:stable-git
     before_script:
       - docker build -t trivy-ci-test:${CI_COMMIT_REF_NAME} .
       - export VERSION=$(curl --silent
   "https://api.github.com/repos/aquasecurity/trivy/releases/latest" |
   grep '"tag_name":' | sed -E 's/.*"v([^"]+)".*/\1/')
       - wget
   https://github.com/aquasecurity/trivy/releases/download/v${VERSION}
   /trivy_${VERSION}_Linux-64bit.tar.gz
       - tar zxvf trivy_${VERSION}_Linux-64bit.tar.gz
     variables:
       DOCKER_DRIVER: overlay2
     allow_failure: true
     services:
   ```

```
    - docker:stable-dind
#Add the Step 4 here
```

4. Finally, review and add the Trivy scan script and complete the `vulTest` stage. The following script will return `--exit-code 1` for the critical severity vulnerabilities, as shown here:

```
script:
    - ./trivy --exit-code 0 --severity HIGH --no-progress --auto-
refresh trivy-ci-test:${CI_COMMIT_REF_NAME}
    - ./trivy --exit-code 1 --severity CRITICAL --no-progress --
auto-refresh trivy-ci-test:${CI_COMMIT_REF_NAME}
    cache:
      directories:
        - $HOME/.cache/trivy
```

Now, you can run your pipeline and the new stage will be included in your pipeline. The pipeline will fail if a critical vulnerability is detected. If you don't want the stage to fail your pipeline, you can also specify `--exit-code 0` for critical vulnerabilities.

Building vulnerability scanning into CircleCI

CircleCI uses Orbs to wrap predefined examples to speed up your project configurations. Currently, Trivy doesn't have a CircleCI Orb, but it is still easy to configure Trivy with CircleCI. This recipe will take you through adding a test stage to the CircleCI pipeline.

Let's perform the following steps to add Trivy vulnerability checks in CircleCI:

1. Edit the CircleCI configuration file located in our project repository in `.circleci/config.yml`. You can find our example in the `src/chapter9/devsecops` directory:

```
$ vim .circleci/config.yml
```

2. Start by adding the job and the image. In this recipe, the job name is `build`:

```
jobs:
  build:
    docker:
      - image: docker:18.09-git
#Add the Step 3 here
```

3. Start adding the steps to build your image. The `checkout` step will checkout the project from its code repository. Since our job will require docker commands, add `setup_remote_docker`. When this step is executed, a remote environment will be created and your current primary container will be configured appropriately:

```
steps:
    - checkout
    - setup_remote_docker
    - restore_cache:
        key: vulnerability-db
    - run:
        name: Build image
        command: docker build -t trivy-ci-test:${CIRCLE_SHA1} .
#Add the Step 4 here
```

4. Add the necessary step to install Trivy:

```
    - run:
        name: Install trivy
        command: |
          apk add --update curl
          VERSION=$(
              curl --silent
"https://api.github.com/repos/aquasecurity/trivy/releases/latest" | \
              grep '"tag_name":' | \
              sed -E 's/.*"v([^"]+)".*/\1/'
          )

          wget
https://github.com/aquasecurity/trivy/releases/download/v${VERSION}
/trivy_${VERSION}_Linux-64bit.tar.gz
          tar zxvf trivy_${VERSION}_Linux-64bit.tar.gz
          mv trivy /usr/local/bin
#Add the Step 5 here
```

5. Add the step that will scan a local image with Trivy. Modify the `trivy` parameters and preferred exit codes as needed. Here, `trivy` only checks for critical vulnerabilities (`--severity CRITICAL`) and fails if a vulnerability is found (`--exit-code 1`). It suppresses the progress bar (`--no-progress`) and refreshes the database automatically when updating its version (`--auto-refresh`):

```
    - run:
        name: Scan the local image with trivy
```

```
        command: trivy --exit-code 1 --severity CRITICAL --no-
progress --auto-refresh trivy-ci-test:${CIRCLE_SHA1}
      - save_cache:
          key: vulnerability-db
          paths:
            - $HOME/.cache/trivy
#Add the Step 6 here
```

6. Finally, update the workflows to trigger the vulnerability scan:

```
workflows:
 version: 2
 release:
 jobs:
 - build
```

Now, you can run your pipeline in CircleCI and the new stage will be included in your pipeline.

See also

- Aqua Security Trivy Comparison: https://github.com/aquasecurity/trivy#comparison-with-other-scanners
- Aqua Security Trivy CI examples: https://github.com/aquasecurity/trivy#comparison-with-other-scanners
- Aqua Security Trivy Alternatives for image vulnerability testing:
    - Aqua Security Microscanner: https://github.com/aquasecurity/microscanner
    - Clair: https://github.com/coreos/clair
    - Docker Hub: https://beta.docs.docker.com/v17.12/docker-cloud/builds/image-scan/
    - GCR: https://cloud.google.com/container-registry/docs/container-analysis
    - Layered Insight: https://layeredinsight.com/
    - NeuVector: https://neuvector.com/vulnerability-scanning/
    - Sysdig Secure: https://sysdig.com/products/secure/
    - Quay: https://coreos.com/quay-enterprise/docs/latest/security-scanning.html
    - Twistlock: https://www.twistlock.com/platform/vulnerability-management-tools/

Monitoring suspicious application activities using Falco

Falco is a cloud-native runtime security toolset. Falco gains deep insight into system behavior through its runtime rule engine. It is used to detect intrusions and abnormalities in applications, containers, hosts, and the Kubernetes orchestrator.

In this section, we will cover the installation and basic usage of Falco on Kubernetes.

Getting ready

Clone the `k8sdevopscookbook/src` repository to your workstation to use the manifest files in the `chapter9` directory, as follows:

```
$ git clone https://github.com/k8sdevopscookbook/src.git
$ cd src/chapter9
```

Make sure you have a Kubernetes cluster ready and `kubectl` and `helm` configured to manage the cluster resources.

How to do it...

This section will show you how to configure and run Falco. This section is further divided into the following subsections to make this process easier:

- Installing Falco on Kubernetes
- Detecting anomalies using Falco
- Defining custom rules

Installing Falco on Kubernetes

Falco can be installed in various ways, including directly on Linux hosts by deploying Falco as a DaemonSet or by using Helm. This recipe will show you how to install Falco as a DaemonSet.

Let's perform the following steps to get Falco deployed on our cluster:

1. Clone the Falco repository into your current working directory:

```
$ git clone https://github.com/falcosecurity/falco.git
$ cd falco/integrations/k8s-using-daemonset/k8s-with-rbac
```

2. Create a Service Account for Falco. The following command will also create the ClusterRole and ClusterRoleBinding for it:

```
$ kubectl create -f falco-account.yaml
```

3. Create a service using the following command from the cloned repository location:

```
$ kubectl create -f falco-service.yaml
```

4. Create a `config` directory and copy the deployment configuration file and rule files in the `config` directory. We will need to edit these later:

```
$ mkdir config
$ cp ../../../falco.yaml config/
$ cp ../../../rules/falco_rules.* config/
$ cp ../../../rules/k8s_audit_rules.yaml config/
```

5. Create a ConfigMap using the config files in the `config/` directory. Later, the DaemonSet will make the configuration available to Falco pods using the ConfigMap:

```
$ kubectl create configmap falco-config --from-file=config
```

6. Finally, deploy Falco using the following command:

```
$ kubectl create -f falco-daemonset-configmap.yaml
```

7. Verify that the DaemonSet pods have been successfully created. You should see one pod per schedulable worker node on the cluster. In our example, we used a Kubernetes cluster with four worker nodes:

```
$ kubectl get pods | grep falco-daemonset
falco-daemonset-94p8w 1/1 Running 0 2m34s
falco-daemonset-c49v5 1/1 Running 0 2m34s
falco-daemonset-htrxw 1/1 Running 0 2m34s
falco-daemonset-kwms5 1/1 Running 0 2m34s
```

With that, Falco has been deployed and started monitoring behavioral activity to detect anomalous activities in our applications on our nodes.

Detecting anomalies using Falco

Falco detects a variety of suspicious behavior. In this recipe, we will produce some activities that would be suspicious on a normal production cluster.

Let's perform the following steps to produce activities that would trigger a syscall event drop:

1. First, we need to review the full rules before we test some of the behaviors. Falco has two rules files. The default rules are located at `/etc/falco/falco_rules.yaml`, while the local rules file is located at `/etc/falco/falco_rules.local.yaml`. Your custom rules and modifications should be in the `falco_rules.local.yaml` file:

   ```
   $ cat config/falco_rules.yaml
   $ cat config/falco_rules.local.yaml
   ```

2. You will see a long list of default rules and macros. Some of them are as follows:

   ```
   - rule: Disallowed SSH Connection
   - rule: Launch Disallowed Container
   - rule: Contact K8S API Server From Container
   - rule: Unexpected K8s NodePort Connection
   - rule: Launch Suspicious Network Tool in Container
   - rule: Create Symlink Over Sensitive Files
   - rule: Detect crypto miners using the Stratum protocol
   ```

3. Let's test that Falco is working by getting a bash shell into one of the Falco pods and view the logs afterward. List the Falco pods:

   ```
   $ kubectl get pods | grep falco-daemonset
   falco-daemonset-94p8w 1/1 Running 0 2m34s
   falco-daemonset-c49v5 1/1 Running 0 2m34s
   falco-daemonset-htrxw 1/1 Running 0 2m34s
   falco-daemonset-kwms5 1/1 Running 0 2m34s
   ```

4. Get bash shell access to one of the Falco pods from the output of the preceding command and view the logs:

   ```
   $ kubectl exec -it falco-daemonset-94p8w bash
   $ kubectl logs falco-daemonset-94p8w
   ```

5. In the logs, you will see that Falco detects our shell access to the pods:

```
{"output":"00:58:23.798345403: Notice A shell was spawned in a
container with an attached terminal (user=root k8s.ns=default
k8s.pod=falco-daemonset-94p8w container=0fcbc74d1b4c shell=bash
parent=docker-runc cmdline=bash terminal=34816
container_id=0fcbc74d1b4c image=falcosecurity/falco) k8s.ns=default
k8s.pod=falco-daemonset-94p8w container=0fcbc74d1b4c k8s.ns=default
k8s.pod=falco-daemonset-94p8w
container=0fcbc74d1b4c","priority":"Notice","rule":"Terminal shell
in container","time":"2019-11-13T00:58:23.783345403Z",
"output_fields":
{"container.id":"0fcbc74d1b4c","container.image.repository":"falcos
ecurity/falco","evt.time":1573606703798345403,"k8s.ns.name":"defaul
t","k8s.pod.name":"falco-
daemonset-94p8w","proc.cmdline":"bash","proc.name":"bash","proc.pna
me":"docker-runc","proc.tty":34816,"user.name":"root"}}
```

With that, you've learned how to use Falco to detect anomalies and suspicious behavior.

Defining custom rules

Falco rules can be extended by adding our own rules. In this recipe, we will deploy a simple application and create a new rule to detect a malicious application accessing our database.

Perform the following steps to create an application and define custom rules for Falco:

1. Change to the `src/chapter9/falco` directory, which is where our examples are located:

   ```
   $ cd src/chapter9/falco
   ```

2. Create a new `falcotest` namespace:

   ```
   $ kubectl create ns falcotest
   ```

3. Review the YAML manifest and deploy them using the following commands. These commands will create a MySQL pod, web application, a client that we will use to ping the application, and its services:

   ```
   $ kubectl create -f mysql.yaml
   $ kubectl create -f ping.yaml
   $ kubectl create -f client.yaml
   ```

4. Now, use the client pod with the default credentials of bob/foobar to send a ping to our application. As expected, we will be able to authenticate and complete the task successfully:

```
$ kubectl exec client -n falcotest -- curl -F "s=OK" -F "user=bob"
-F "passwd=foobar" -F "ipaddr=localhost" -X POST
http://ping/ping.php
```

5. Edit the falco_rules.local.yaml file:

```
$ vim config/falco_rules.local.yaml
```

6. Add the following rule to the end of the file and save it:

```
  - rule: Unauthorized process
    desc: There is a running process not described in the base
template
    condition: spawned_process and container and
k8s.ns.name=falcotest and k8s.deployment.name=ping and not
proc.name in (apache2, sh, ping)
    output: Unauthorized process (%proc.cmdline) running in
(%container.id)
    priority: ERROR
    tags: [process]
```

7. Update the ConfigMap that's being used for the DaemonSet and delete the pods to get a new configuration by running the following command:

```
$ kubectl delete -f falco-daemonset-configmap.yaml
$ kubectl create configmap falco-config --from-file=config --dry-
run --save-config -o yaml | kubectl apply -f -
$ kubectl apply -f falco-daemonset-configmap.yaml
```

8. We will execute a SQL injection attack and access the file where our MySQL credentials are stored. Our new custom rule should be able to detect it:

```
$ kubectl exec client -n falcotest -- curl -F "s=OK" -F "user=bad"
-F "passwd=wrongpasswd' OR 'a'='a" -F "ipaddr=localhost; cat
/var/www/html/ping.php" -X POST http://ping/ping.php
```

9. The preceding command will return the content of the PHP file. You will be able to find the MySQL credentials there:

```
3 packets transmitted, 3 received, 0% packet loss, time 2044ms
rtt min/avg/max/mdev = 0.028/0.035/0.045/0.007 ms
<?php
$link = mysqli_connect("mysql", "root", "foobar", "employees");
?>
```

10. List the Falco pods:

```
$ kubectl get pods | grep falco-daemonset
falco-daemonset-5785b 1/1 Running 0 9m52s
falco-daemonset-brjs7 1/1 Running 0 9m52s
falco-daemonset-mqcjq 1/1 Running 0 9m52s
falco-daemonset-pdx45 1/1 Running 0 9m52s
```

11. View the logs from a Falco pod:

```
$ kubectl exec -it falco-daemonset-94p8w bash
$ kubectl logs falco-daemonset-94p8w
```

12. In the logs, you will see that Falco detects our shell access to the pods:

```
05:41:59.9275580001: Error Unauthorized process (cat
/var/www/html/ping.php) running in (5f1b6d304f99) k8s.ns=falcotest
k8s.pod=ping-74dbb488b6-6hwp6 container=5f1b6d304f99
```

With that, you know how to add custom rules using Kubernetes metadata such as `k8s.ns.name` and `k8s.deployment.name`. You can also use other filters. This is described in more detail in the *Supported filters* link in *See also* section.

How it works...

This recipe showed you how to detect anomalies based on the predefined and custom rules of your applications when they're running on Kubernetes.

In the *Installing Falco on Kubernetes* recipe, in *Step 5,* we created a ConfigMap to be used by the Falco pods. Falco has two types of rules files.

In Step 6, when we created the DaemonSet, all the default rules are provided through the `falco_rules.yaml` file in the ConfigMap.These are placed in `/etc/falco/falco_rules.yaml` inside the pods, while the local rules file `, falco_rules.local.yaml,` can be found at `/etc/falco/falco_rules.local.yaml`.

The default rules file contains rules for many common anomalies and threats. All pieces of customization must be added to the `falco_rules.local.yaml` file, which we did in the *Defining custom rules* recipe.

In the *Defining custom rules* recipe, in *Step 6,* we created a custom rule file containing the `rules` element. The Falco rule file is a YAML file that uses three kinds of elements: `rules`, `macros`, and `lists`.

The rules define certain conditions to send alerts about them. A rule is a file that contains at least the following keys:

- `rule`: The name of the rule
- `condition`: An expression that's applied to events to check if they match the rule
- `desc`: Detailed description of what the rule is used for
- `output`: The message that is displayed to the user
- `priority`: Either emergency, alert, critical, error, warning, notice, informational, or debug

You can find out more about these rules by going to the *Understanding Falco Rules* link that's provided in the *See also* section.

See also

- Falco documentation: `https://falco.org/docs/`
- Falco repository and integration examples: `https://github.com/falcosecurity/falco`
- Understanding Falco
  Rules: `https://falco.org/dochttps://falco.org/docs/rules/s/rules/`
- Comparing Falco with other tools: `https://sysdig.com/blog/selinux-seccomp-falco-technical-discussion/`
- Supported filters: `https://github.com/draios/sysdig/wiki/Sysdig-User-Guide#all-supported-filters`

Securing credentials using HashiCorp Vault

HashiCorp Vault is a popular tool for securely storing and accessing secrets such as credentials, API keys, and certificates. Vault provides secure secret storage, on-demand dynamic secrets, data encryption, and support for secret revocation.

In this section, we will cover the installation and basic use case of accessing and storing secrets for Kubernetes.

Getting ready

Clone the `k8sdevopscookbook/src` repository to your workstation to use the manifest files in the `chapter9` directory, as follows:

```
$ git clone https://github.com/k8sdevopscookbook/src.git
$ cd src/chapter9
```

Make sure you have a Kubernetes cluster ready and `kubectl` and `helm` configured to manage the cluster resources.

How to do it...

This section is further divided into the following subsections to make this process easier:

- Installing Vault on Kubernetes
- Accessing the Vault UI
- Storing credentials on Vault

Installing Vault on Kubernetes

This recipe will show you how to get a Vault service on Kubernetes. Let's perform the following steps to get Vault installed using Helm charts:

1. Clone the chart repository:

```
$ git clone https://github.com/hashicorp/vault-helm.git
$ cd vault-helm
```

2. Check out the latest stable release:

```
$ git checkout v$(curl --silent
"https://api.github.com/repos/hashicorp/vault-helm/releases/latest"
| \
grep '"tag_name":' | \
sed -E 's/.*"v([^"]+)".*/\1/')
```

3. If you would like to install a highly available Vault, skip to *Step 4*; otherwise, install the standalone version using the Helm chart parameters shown here:

```
$ helm install --name vault --namespace vault ./
```

4. To deploy a highly available version that uses an HA storage backend such as Consul, use the following Helm chart parameters. This will deploy Vault using a StatefulSet with three replicas:

```
$ helm install --name vault --namespace vault --
set='server.ha.enabled=true' ./
```

5. Verify the status of the pods. You will notice that the pods aren't ready since the readiness probe requires Vault to be initialized first:

```
$ $ kubectl get pods -nvault
NAME                                     READY STATUS   RESTARTS AGE
vault-0                                  0/1   Running  0        83s
vault-agent-injector-5fb898d6cd-rct82 1/1   Running  0        84s
```

6. Check the initialization status. It should be `false`:

```
$ kubectl exec -it vault-0 -nvault -- vault status
Key                 Value
---                 -----
Seal Type           shamir
Initialized         false
Sealed              true
Total Shares        0
Threshold           0
Unseal Progress 0/0
Unseal Nonce        n/a
Version             n/a
HA Enabled          false
```

7. Initialize the Vault instance. The following command will return an unseal key and root token:

```
$ kubectl exec -it vault-0 -nvault -- vault operator init -n 1 -t 1

Unseal Key 1: lhLeU6SRdUNQgfpWAqWknwSxns1tfWP57iZQbbYtFSE=
Initial Root Token: s.CzcefEkOYmCt70fGSbHgSZ14
Vault initialized with 1 key shares and a key threshold of 1.
Please securely
distribute the key shares printed above. When the Vault is re-
sealed,
restarted, or stopped, you must supply at least 1 of these keys to
unseal it
before it can start servicing requests.
```

8. Unseal Vault using the unseal key from the output of the following command:

```
$ kubectl exec -it vault-0 -nvault -- vault operator unseal
lhLeU6SRdUNQgfpWAqWknwSxns1tfWP57iZQbbYtFSE=
Key            Value
---            -----
Seal Type      shamir
Initialized    true
Sealed         false
Total Shares   1
Threshold      1
Version        1.3.1
Cluster Name   vault-cluster-6970c528
Cluster ID     dd88cca8-20bb-326c-acb3-2d924bb1805c
HA Enabled     false
```

9. Verify the pod's status. You will see that the readiness probe has been validated and that the pod is ready:

```
$ kubectl get pods -nvault
NAME                                    READY STATUS  RESTARTS AGE
vault-0                                 1/1   Running 0        6m29s
vault-agent-injector-5fb898d6cd-rct82 1/1   Running 0        6m30s
```

Vault is ready to be used after it is initialized. Now, you know how to get Vault running on Kubernetes.

Accessing the Vault UI

By default, the Vault UI is enabled when using a Helm chart installation. Let's perform the following steps to access the Vault UI:

1. Since access to Vault is a security concern, it is not recommended to expose it with a service. Use port-forwarding to access the Vault UI using the following command:

```
$ kubectl port-forward vault-0 -nvault 8200:8200
```

2. Once forwarding is complete, you can access the UI
    at `http://localhost:8200`:

Now, you have access to the web UI. Take the Vault Web UI tour to familiarize yourself
with its functionality.

Storing credentials on Vault

This recipe will show you how to use Vault in Kubernetes and retrieve secrets from Vault.

Let's perform the following steps to enable the Kubernetes authentication method in Vault:

1. Log in to Vault using your token:

   ```
   $ vault login <root-token-here>
   ```

2. Write a secret to Vault:

   ```
   $ vault write secret/foo value=bar
   Success! Data written to: secret/foo
   $ vault read secret/foo
   Key                Value
   ---                -----
   refresh_interval   768h
   value              bar
   ```

3. Let's configure Vault's Kubernetes authentication backend. First, create a ServiceAccount:

   ```
   $ kubectl -n vault create serviceaccount vault-k8s
   ```

4. Create a RoleBinding for the `vault-k8s` ServiceAccount:

   ```
   $ cat <<EOF | kubectl apply -f -
   apiVersion: rbac.authorization.k8s.io/v1beta1
   kind: ClusterRoleBinding
   metadata:
     name: role-tokenreview-binding
     namespace: default
   roleRef:
     apiGroup: rbac.authorization.k8s.io
     kind: ClusterRole
     name: system:auth-delegator
   subjects:
   - kind: ServiceAccount
     name: vault-k8s
     namespace: default
   EOF
   ```

5. Get the token:

```
$ SECRET_NAME=$(kubectl -n vault get serviceaccount vault-k8s -o
jsonpath={.secrets[0].name})
$ ACCOUNT_TOKEN=$(kubectl -n vault get secret ${SECRET_NAME} -o
jsonpath={.data.token} | base64 --decode; echo)
$ export VAULT_SA_NAME=$(kubectl get sa -n vault vault-k8s -o
jsonpath="{.secrets[*].name}")
$ export SA_CA_CRT=$(kubectl get secret $VAULT_SA_NAME -n vault -o
jsonpath={.data.'ca\.crt'} | base64 --decode; echo)
```

6. Enable the Kubernetes auth backend in the vault:

```
$ vault auth enable kubernetes
$ vault write auth/kubernetes/config
kubernetes_host="https://MASTER_IP:6443"
kubernetes_ca_cert="$SA_CA_CRT"
token_reviewer_jwt=$TR_ACCOUNT_TOKEN
```

7. Create a new policy called `vault-policy` from the example repository using the `policy.hcl`: file:

```
$ vault write sys/policy/vault-policy policy=@policy.hcl
```

8. Next, create a Role for the ServiceAccount:

```
$ vault write auth/kubernetes/role/demo-role \
bound_service_account_names=vault-coreos-test \
bound_service_account_namespaces=default \
policies=demo-policy \
ttl=1h
```

9. Authenticate with the Role by running the following command:

```
$ DEFAULT_ACCOUNT_TOKEN=$(kubectl get secret $VAULT_SA_NAME -n
vault -o jsonpath={.data.token} | base64 — decode; echo )
```

10. Log in to the Vault with the token by running the following command:

```
$ vault write auth/kubernetes/login role=demo-role
jwt=${DEFAULT_ACCOUNT_TOKEN}
```

11. Create a secret at the `secret/demo` path:

```
$ vault write secret/demo/foo value=bar
```

With that, you've learned how to create a Kubernetes auth backend with Vault and use Vault to store Kubernetes secrets.

See also

- Hashicorp Vault documentation: `https://www.vaultproject.io/docs/`
- Hashicorp Vault repository: `https://github.com/hashicorp/vault-helm`
- Hands-on with Vault on Kubernetes: `https://github.com/hashicorp/hands-on-with-vault-on-kubernetes`

10 Logging with Kubernetes

In this chapter, we will discuss cluster logging for Kubernetes clusters. We will talk about setting up a cluster to ingest logs, as well as how to view them using both self-managed and hosted solutions.

In this chapter, we will cover the following recipes:

- Accessing Kubernetes logs locally
- Accessing application-specific logs
- Building centralized logging in Kubernetes using the EFK stack
- Logging with Kubernetes using Google Stackdriver
- Using a managed Kubernetes logging service
- Logging for your Jenkins CI/CD environment

Technical requirements

The recipes in this chapter expect you to have a functional Kubernetes cluster deployed by following one of the recommended methods described in Chapter 1, *Building Production-Ready Kubernetes Clusters*.

The *Logging for your Jenkins CI/CD environment* recipe in this chapter expects you to have a functional Jenkins server with an existing CI pipeline created by following one of the recommended methods described in Chapter 3, *Building CI/CD Pipelines*.

The Kubernetes command-line tool kubectl will be used for the rest of the recipes in this chapter since it's the main command-line interface for running commands against Kubernetes clusters. We will also use helm where Helm charts are available in order to deploy solutions.

Accessing Kubernetes logs locally

In Kubernetes, logs can be used for debugging and monitoring activities to a certain level. Basic logging can be used to detect configuration problems, but for cluster-level logging, an external backend is required to store and query logs. Cluster-level logging will be covered in the *Building centralized logging in Kubernetes using the EFK stack* and *Logging Kubernetes using Google Stackdriver* recipes.

In this section, we will learn how to access basic logs based on the options that are available in Kubernetes.

Getting ready

Clone the `k8sdevopscookbook/src` repository to your workstation to use the manifest files in the `chapter10` directory, as follows:

```
$ git clone https://github.com/k8sdevopscookbook/src.git
$ cd src/chapter10
```

Make sure you have a Kubernetes cluster ready and `kubectl` and `helm` configured to manage the cluster resources.

How to do it...

This section is further divided into the following subsections to make this process easier:

- Accessing logs through Kubernetes
- Debugging services locally using Telepresence

Accessing logs through Kubernetes

This recipe will take you through how to access Kubernetes logs and debug services locally.

Let's perform the following steps to view logs by using the various options that are available in Kubernetes:

1. Get the list of pods running in the `kube-system` namespace. The pods running in this namespace, especially `kube-apiserver`, `kube-controller-manager`, `kube-dns`, and `kube-scheduler`, play a critical role in the Kubernetes control plane:

```
$ kubectl get pods -n kube-system
NAME                                              READY STATUS   RST
AGE
dns-controller-6577fb57f7-hx9wz                   1/1   Running 0
16d
etcd-manager-events-ip-172-20-8-2.ec2.internal    1/1   Running 0
16d
etcd-manager-main-ip-172-20-8-2.ec2.internal      1/1   Running 0
16d
kube-apiserver-ip-172-20-8-2.ec2.internal         1/1   Running 2
16d
kube-controller-manager-ip-172-20-8-2.ec2.int...  1/1   Running 0
16d
kube-dns-66d58c65d5-mw6n5                         3/3   Running 0
16d
kube-dns-66d58c65d5-rntmj                         3/3   Running 0
16d
kube-dns-autoscaler-6567f59ccb-c9rmv              1/1   Running 0
16d
kube-proxy-ip-172-20-32-123.ec2.internal          1/1   Running 0
16d
kube-proxy-ip-172-20-38-218.ec2.internal          1/1   Running 1
16d
kube-proxy-ip-172-20-45-93.ec2.internal           1/1   Running 0
16d
kube-scheduler-ip-172-20-58-244.ec2.internal      1/1   Running 0
3d6h
```

2. View the logs from a pod with a single container in the `kube-system` namespace. In this example, this pod is `kube-apiserver`. Replace the pod's name and repeat this for the other pods as needed:

```
$ kubectl logs kube-apiserver-ip-172-20-58-244.ec2.internal -n
kube-system
. . .
E1112 08:11:05.662027 1 authentication.go:65] Unable to
authenticate the request due to an error: [invalid bearer token,
Token has been invalidated]
I1112 09:09:39.448428 1 log.go:172] http: TLS handshake error from
```

```
124.84.242.10:49016: tls: first record does not look like a TLS
handshake
I1112 09:30:00.726871 1 trace.go:81] Trace[76921086]:
"GuaranteedUpdate etcd3: *coordination.Lease" (started: 2019-11-12
09:30:00.177607414 +0000 UTC m=+1250671.527180434) (total time:
549.223921ms):
```

As shown in the preceding output, you can find the time, source, and a short explanation of the event in the logs.

> The output of the logs can become long, though most of the time all you need is the last few events in the logs. If you don't want to get all the logs since you only need the last few events in the log, you can add `-tail` to the end of the command, along with the number of lines you want to look at. For example, `kubectl logs <podname> -n <namespace> -tail 10` would return the last 10 lines. Change the number as needed to limit the output.

3. Pods can contain multiple containers. When you list the pods, the numbers under the `Ready` column show the number of containers inside the pod. Let's view a specific container log from a pod with multiple containers in the `kube-system` namespace. Here, the pod we're looking at is called `kube-dns`. Replace the pod's name and repeat this for any other pods with multiple containers:

```
$ kubectl -n kube-system logs kube-dns-66d58c65d5-mw6n5
Error from server (BadRequest): a container name must be specified
for pod kube-dns-66d58c65d5-mw6n5, choose one of: [kubedns dnsmasq
sidecar]
$ kubectl -n kube-system logs kube-dns-66d58c65d5-mw6n5 kubedns
```

4. To view the logs after a specific time, use the `--since-time` parameter with a date, similar to what can be seen in the following code. You can either use an absolute time or request a duration. Only the logs after the specified time or within the duration will be displayed:

```
$ kubectl -n kube-system logs kube-dns-66d58c65d5-mw6n5 kubedns --
since-time="2019-11-14T04:59:40.417Z"
...
I1114 05:09:13.309614 1 dns.go:601] Could not find endpoints for
service "minio" in namespace "default". DNS records will be created
once endpoints show up.
```

5. Instead of pod names, you can also view logs by label. Here, we're listing pods using the `k8s-app=kube-dns` label. Since the pod contains multiple containers, we can use the `-c kubedns` parameter to set the target container:

```
$ kubectl -n kube-system logs -l k8s-app=kube-dns -c kubedns
```

6. If the container has crashed or restarted, we can use the `-p` flag to retrieve logs from a previous instantiation of a container, as follows:

```
$ kubectl -n kube-system logs -l k8s-app=kube-dns -c kubedns -p
```

Now you know how to access pod logs through Kubernetes.

Debugging services locally using Telepresence

When a build fails in your CI pipeline or a service running in a staging cluster contains a bug, you may need to run the service locally to troubleshoot it properly. However, applications depend on other applications and services on the cluster; for example, a database. Telepresence helps you run your code locally, as a normal local process, and then forwards requests to the Kubernetes cluster. This recipe will show you how to debug services locally while running a local Kubernetes cluster.

Let's perform the following steps to view logs through the various options that are available in Kubernetes:

1. On **OSX**, install the Telepresence binary using the following command:

```
$ brew cask install osxfuse
$ brew install datawire/blackbird/telepresence
```

On **Windows**, use Ubuntu on the **Windows Subsystem for Linux (WSL)**. Then, on **Ubuntu**, download and install the Telepresence binary using the following command:

```
$ curl -s
https://packagecloud.io/install/repositories/datawireio/tel
epresence/script.deb.sh | sudo bash
$ sudo apt install --no-install-recommends telepresence
```

2. Now, create a deployment of your application. Here, we're using a `hello-world` example:

```
$ kubectl run hello-world --image=datawire/hello-world --port=8000
```

3. Expose the service using an external `LoadBalancer` and get the service IP:

```
$ kubectl expose deployment hello-world --type=LoadBalancer --
name=hello-world
$ kubectl get service hello-world
NAME           TYPE          CLUSTER-IP      EXTERNAL-IP
PORT(S)        AGE
hello-world LoadBalancer 100.71.246.234 a643ea7bc0f0311ea.us-
east-1.elb.amazonaws.com 8000:30744/TCP 8s
```

4. To be able to query the address, store the address in a variable using the following command:

```
$ export HELLOWORLD=http://$(kubectl get svc hello-world -o
jsonpath='{.status.loadBalancer.ingress[0].hostname}'):8000
```

5. Send a query to the service. This will return a `Hello, world!` message similar to the following:

```
$ curl $HELLOWORLD/
Hello, world!
```

6. Next, we will create a local web service and replace the Kubernetes service `hello-world` message with the local web server service. First, create a directory and a file to be shared using the HTTP server:

```
$ mkdir /tmp/local-test && cd /tmp/local-test
$ echo "hello this server runs locally on my laptop" > index.html
```

7. Create a web server and expose the service through port `8000` using the following command:

```
$ telepresence --swap-deployment hello-world --expose 8000 \
--run python3 -m http.server 8000 &

...

T: Forwarding remote port 8000 to local port 8000.
T: Guessing that Services IP range is 100.64.0.0/13. Services
started after this point will be inaccessible if are outside
T: this range; restart telepresence if you can't access a new
Service.
T: Setup complete. Launching your command.
Serving HTTP on 0.0.0.0 port 8000 (http://0.0.0.0:8000/) ...
```

The preceding command will start a proxy using the `vpn-tcp` method. Other methods can be found in the *Full list of Telepresence methods* link in the *See also* section.

 When a service is exposed over the network, remember that your computer is exposed to all the risks of running a web server. When you expose a web service using the commands described here, make sure that you don't have any important files in the `/tmp/local-test` directory that you don't want to expose externally.

8. Send a query to the service. You will see that queries to the `hello-world` Service will be forwarded to your local web server:

    ```
    $ curl $HELLOWORLD/
    hello this server runs locally on my laptop
    ```

9. To end the local service, use the `fg` command to bring the background Telepresence job in the current shell environment into the foreground. Then, use the *Ctrl + C* keys to exit it.

How it works...

In this recipe, you learned how to access logs and debug service problems locally.

In the *Debugging services locally using Telepresence* recipe, in *Step 7*, we ran the `telepresence --swap-deployment` command to replace the service with a local web service.

Telepresence functions by building a two-way network proxy. The `--swap-deployment` flag is used to define the pod that will be replaced with a proxy pod on the cluster. Telepresence starts a `vpn-tcp` process to send all requests to the locally exposed port, that is, `8000`. The `--run python3 -m http.server 8000 &` flag tells Telepresence to run an `http.server` using Python 3 in the background via port `8000`.

In the same recipe, in *Step 9*, the `fg` command is used to move the background service to the foreground. When you exit the service, the old pod will be restored. You can learn about how Telepresence functions by looking at the *How Telepresence works* link in the *See also* section.

See also

- `kubectl` log commands: https://kubernetes.io/docs/reference/generated/kubectl/kubectl-commands#logs
- Telepresence source code repository: https://github.com/telepresenceio/telepresence
- Full list of Telepresence methods: https://telepresence.io/reference/methods.html
- How Telepresence works: https://www.telepresence.io/discussion/how-it-works
- How to use volume access support with Telepresence: https://telepresence.io/howto/volumes.html

Accessing application-specific logs

In Kubernetes, pod and deployment logs that are related to how pods and containers are scheduled can be accessed through the `kubectl logs` command, but not all application logs and commands are exposed through Kubernetes APIs. Getting access to these logs and shell commands inside a container may be required.

In this section, we will learn how to access a container shell, extract logs, and update binaries for troubleshooting.

Getting ready

Clone the `k8sdevopscookbook/src` repository to your workstation to use the manifest files under the `chapter10` directory, as follows:

```
$ git clone https://github.com/k8sdevopscookbook/src.git
$ cd src/chapter10
```

Make sure you have a Kubernetes cluster ready and `kubectl` configured to manage the cluster resources.

How to do it...

This section is further divided into the following subsections to make this process easier:

- Getting shell access in a container
- Accessing PostgreSQL logs inside a container

Getting shell access in a container

Let's perform the following steps to create a deployment with multiple containers and get a shell into running containers:

1. In this recipe, we will deploy PostgreSQL on OpenEBS persistent volumes to demonstrate shell access. Change the directory to the example files directory in `src/chapter10/postgres`, which is where all the YAML manifest for this recipe are stored. Create a `ConfigMap` with a database name and credentials similar to the following or review them and use the `cm-postgres.yaml` file:

```
$ cd postgres
$ cat <<EOF | kubectl apply -f -
apiVersion: v1
kind: ConfigMap
metadata:
 name: postgres-config
 labels:
 app: postgres
data:
 POSTGRES_DB: postgresdb
 POSTGRES_USER: testuser
 POSTGRES_PASSWORD: testpassword123
EOF
```

2. Create the service for `postgres`:

```
$ cat <<EOF | kubectl apply -f -
apiVersion: v1
kind: Service
metadata:
  name: postgres
  labels:
    app: postgres
spec:
  type: NodePort
  ports:
   - port: 5432
```

```
    selector:
      app: postgres
  EOF
```

3. Review the `postgres.yaml` file and apply it to create the PostgreSQL StatefulSet. We can use this to deploy the pods and to auto-create the PV/PVC:

```
$ kubectl apply -f postgres.yaml
```

4. Get the pods with the `postgres` label:

```
$ kubectl get pods -l app=postgres
NAME READY STATUS RESTARTS AGE
postgres-0 1/1 Running 0 7m5s
postgres-1 1/1 Running 0 6m58s
```

5. Get a shell into the `postgres-0` container:

```
$ kubectl exec -it postgres-0 -- /bin/bash
```

The preceding command will get you shell access to the running container.

Accessing PostgreSQL logs inside a container

Let's perform the following steps to get the logs from the application running inside a container:

1. While you are in a shell, connect to the PostgreSQL database named `postgresdb` using the username `testuser`. You will see the PostgreSQL prompt, as follows:

```
$ psql --username testuser postgresdb
psql (12.1 (Debian 12.1-1.pgdg100+1))
Type "help" for help.
```

2. While on the PostgreSQL prompt, use the following command to create a table and add some data to it:

```
CREATE TABLE test (
    id int GENERATED BY DEFAULT AS IDENTITY PRIMARY KEY,
    a int NOT NULL,
    created_at timestamptz NOT NULL DEFAULT CURRENT_TIMESTAMP
);
INSERT INTO test (a) SELECT * FROM generate_series(-1, -1000, -1);
```

3. Get the log's configuration details from `postgresql.conf`. You will see that the logs are stored in the `/var/log/postgresql` directory:

   ```
   $ cat /var/lib/postgresql/data/postgresql.conf |grep log
   ```

4. List and access the logs in the `/var/log/postgresql` directory:

   ```
   $ ls /var/log/postgresql
   ```

5. Optionally, while you're inside the container, you can create a backup of our example `postgresdb` database in the `tmp` directory using the following command:

   ```
   $ pg_dump --username testuser postgresdb > /tmp/backup.sql
   ```

With that, you have learned how to get shell access into a container and how to access the locally stored logs and files inside the container.

Building centralized logging in Kubernetes using the EFK stack

As described in the the *Accessing Kubernetes logs locally* section, basic logging can be used to detect configuration problems, but for cluster-level logging, an external backend is required to store and query logs. A cluster-level logging stack can help you quickly sort through and analyze the high volume of production log data that's produced by your application in the Kubernetes cluster. One of the most popular centralized logging solutions in the Kubernetes ecosystem is the **Elasticsearch, Logstash, and Kibana** (ELK) stack.

In the ELK stack, Logstash is used as the log collector. Logstash uses slightly more memory than Fluent Bit, which is a low-footprint version of Fluentd. Therefore, in this recipe, we will use the **Elasticsearch, Fluent-bit, and Kibana** (EFK) stack. If you have an application that has Logstash dependencies, you can always replace Fluentd/Fluent Bit with Logstash.

In this section, we will learn how to build a cluster-level logging system using the EFK stack to manage Kubernetes logs.

Getting ready

Clone the `k8sdevopscookbook/src` repository to your workstation to use the manifest files in the `chapter10` directory, as follows:

```
$ git clone https://github.com/k8sdevopscookbook/src.git
$ cd src/chapter10
```

Make sure you have a Kubernetes cluster ready and `kubectl` and `helm` configured to manage the cluster resources.

How to do it...

This section will show you how to configure an EFK stack on your Kubernetes cluster. This section is further divided into the following subsections to make this process easier:

- Deploying Elasticsearch Operator
- Requesting an Elasticsearch endpoint
- Deploying Kibana
- Aggregating logs with Fluent Bit
- Accessing Kubernetes logs on Kibana

Deploying Elasticsearch Operator

Elasticsearch is a highly scalable open source full-text search and analytics engine. Elasticsearch allows you to store, search, and analyze big volumes of data quickly. In this recipe, we will use it to store Kubernetes logs.

Let's perform the following steps to get **Elastic Cloud on Kubernetes (ECK)** deployed:

1. Deploy Elasticsearch Operator and its CRDs using the following command:

```
$ kubectl apply -f
https://download.elastic.co/downloads/eck/1.0.0/all-in-one.yaml
```

2. Elasticsearch Operator will create its own **CustomResourceDefinition** (**CRD**). We will use this CRD later to deploy and manage Elasticsearch instances on Kubernetes. List the new CRDs using the following command:

```
$ kubectl get crds |grep elastic.co
apmservers.apm.k8s.elastic.co                2019-11-25T07:52:16Z
elasticsearches.elasticsearch.k8s.elastic.co 2019-11-25T07:52:17Z
kibanas.kibana.k8s.elastic.co                2019-11-25T07:52:17Z
```

3. Create a new namespace called `logging`:

```
$ kubectl create ns logging
```

4. Create Elasticsearch using the default parameters in the `logging` namespace using the following command:

```
$ cat <<EOF | kubectl apply -f -
apiVersion: elasticsearch.k8s.elastic.co/v1beta1
kind: Elasticsearch
metadata:
 name: elasticsearch
 namespace: logging
spec:
 version: 7.4.2
 nodeSets:
 - name: default
 count: 3
 config:
 node.master: true
 node.data: true
 node.ingest: true
 node.store.allow_mmap: false
EOF
```

5. Get the status of the Elasticsearch nodes:

```
$ kubectl get elasticsearch -n logging
NAME HEALTH NODES VERSION PHASE AGE
elasticsearch green 3 7.4.2 Ready 86s
```

6. You can also confirm the pod's status in the logging namespace using the following command:

```
$ kubectl get pods -n logging
NAME                         READY STATUS  RESTARTS AGE
elasticsearch-es-default-0 1/1   Running 0        2m24s
elasticsearch-es-default-1 1/1   Running 0        2m24s
elasticsearch-es-default-2 1/1   Running 0        2m24s
```

A three-node Elasticsearch cluster will be created. By default, the nodes we created here are all of the following types: master-eligible, data, and ingest. As your Elasticsearch cluster grows, it is recommended to create dedicated master-eligible, data, and ingest nodes.

Requesting the Elasticsearch endpoint

When an Elasticsearch cluster is created, a default user password is generated and stored in a Kubernetes secret. You will need the full credentials to request the Elasticsearch endpoint.

Let's perform the following steps to request Elasticsearch access:

1. Get the password that was generated for the default `elastic` user:

```
$ PASSWORD=$(kubectl get secret elasticsearch-es-elastic-user \
-n logging -o=jsonpath='{.data.elastic}' | base64 --decode)
```

2. Request the Elasticsearch endpoint address:

```
$ curl -u "elastic:$PASSWORD" -k
"https://elasticsearch-es-http:9200"
{
   "name" : "elasticsearch-es-default-2",
   "cluster_name" : "elasticsearch",
   "cluster_uuid" : "E_ATzAz8Th6oMvd4D_QocA",
   "version" : {...},
   "tagline" : "You Know, for Search"
}
```

If you are accessing the Kubernetes cluster remotely, you can create a port-forwarding service and use localhost, similar to what can be seen in the following code:

```
$ kubectl port-forward service/quickstart-es-http 9200
$ curl -u "elastic:$PASSWORD" -k "https://localhost:9200"
```

Now, we have access to our three-node small Elasticsearch cluster that we deployed on Kubernetes. Next, we need to deploy Kibana to complete the stack.

Deploying Kibana

Kibana is an open source data visualization dashboard that lets you visualize your Elasticsearch data.

Let's perform the following steps to get Kibana deployed:

1. Create a Kibana instance associated with the Elasticsearch cluster we created previously:

```
$ cat <<EOF | kubectl apply -f -
apiVersion: kibana.k8s.elastic.co/v1beta1
kind: Kibana
metadata:
  name: mykibana
  namespace: logging
spec:
  version: 7.4.2
  count: 1
  elasticsearchRef:
    name: elasticsearch
EOF
```

2. Get the status of the Kibana node:

```
$ kubectl get elasticsearch -n logging
NAME      HEALTH NODES VERSION AGE
mykibana green  1      7.4.2   2m27s
```

3. You can also confirm the pod's status in the logging namespace using the following command:

```
$ kubectl get pods -n logging
NAME                         READY STATUS  RESTARTS AGE
elasticsearch-es-default-0   1/1   Running 0        37m
elasticsearch-es-default-1   1/1   Running 0        37m
elasticsearch-es-default-2   1/1   Running 0        37m
mykibana-kb-7864bfdb45-261pq 1/1   Running 0        3m36s
```

With that, you have both Elasticsearch and Kibana nodes deployed. Next, we will deploy fluent-bit to forward container logs to our Elasticsearch deployment.

Aggregating logs with Fluent Bit

Let's perform the following steps to get fluent-bit deployed:

1. Get the password for the default `elastic` user:

```
$ kubectl get secret elasticsearch-es-elastic-user \
-n logging -o=jsonpath='{.data.elastic}' | base64 --decode; echo
```

2. Copy the output of *Step 1* and edit the `fluent-bit-values.yaml` file in the `/src/chapter10/efk` directory. Replace the `http_passwd` value with the output of *Step 1* and save the file:

```
backend:
  type: es
  es:
    host: elasticsearch-es-http
    port: 9200
    http_user: elastic
    http_passwd: m2zr9fz49zqbkbpksprf4r76
    # Optional TLS encryption to ElasticSearch instance
    tls: "on"
    tls_verify: "off"
```

3. Deploy fluent-bit using the Helm chart:

```
$ helm install stable/fluent-bit --name=fluent-bit --
namespace=logging -f fluent-bit-values.yaml
```

4. Confirm the pod's status in the `logging` namespace using the following command:

```
$ kubectl get pods -n logging
NAME                           READY STATUS  RESTARTS AGE
elasticsearch-es-default-0     1/1   Running 0        158m
elasticsearch-es-default-1     1/1   Running 0        158m
elasticsearch-es-default-2     1/1   Running 0        158m
fluent-bit-249ct               1/1   Running 0        2m11s
fluent-bit-4nb9k               1/1   Running 0        2m11s
fluent-bit-fqtz9               1/1   Running 0        2m11s
fluent-bit-lg9hn               1/1   Running 0        2m11s
mykibana-kb-5596b888b5-qv8wn   1/1   Running 0        115m
```

With that, you have deployed all the components of the EFK stack. Next, we will connect to the Kibana dashboard.

Accessing Kubernetes logs on Kibana

Let's perform the following steps to connect to the Kibana dashboard:

1. Confirm that the Kibana service has been created. By default, a `ClusterIP` service will be created:

```
$ kubectl get service mykibana-kb-http -n logging
```

2. Before we connect to the dashboard, get the password for the default `elastic` user:

```
$ kubectl get secret elasticsearch-es-elastic-user \
-n logging -o=jsonpath='{.data.elastic}' | base64 --decode; echo
```

3. Create a port-forwarding service to access the Kibana dashboard from your workstation:

```
$ kubectl port-forward service/mykibana-kb-http 5601
```

4. Open the Kibana dashboard at `https://localhost:5601` in your browser. Enter `elastic` as the username and the password from the output of *Step 2*:

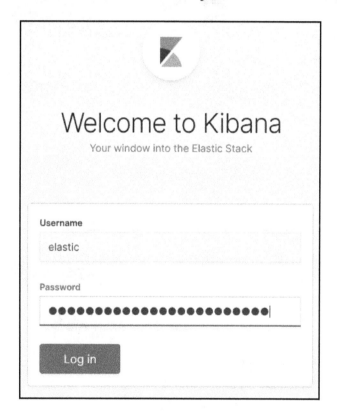

5. On the home page, click on the **Connect to your Elasticsarch index** button, as shown in the following screenshot:

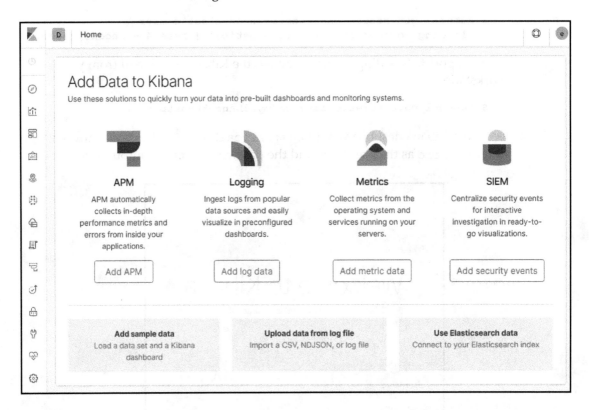

6. Kibana will search for Elasticsearch index patterns. Define the index pattern that matches your results. In our example, we used `kubernetes_cluster-*`. Click on **Next step** to continue:

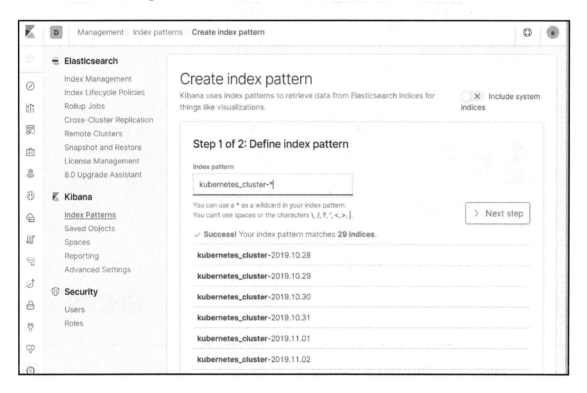

7. Specify **Time Filter field name** as @timestamp and click on the **Create index pattern** button, as shown in the following screenshot:

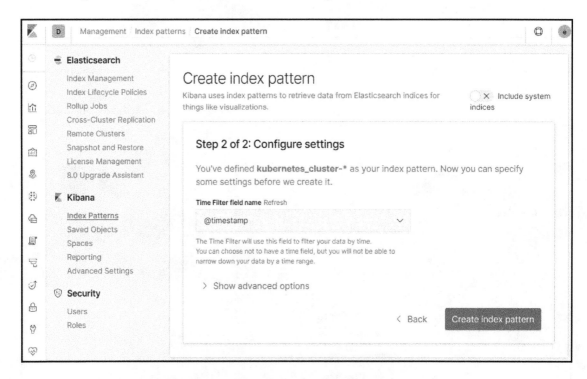

8. Click on the **Discover** menu. It is the first icon from the top:

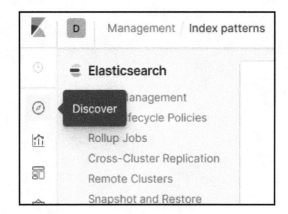

9. On the **Discover** page, use the search field to look for keywords and filters:

10. If the keyword you are looking for can't be found in the current time frame, you need to change the date range by clicking on the calendar icon next to the search field and clicking on the **Apply** button after the new range has been selected:

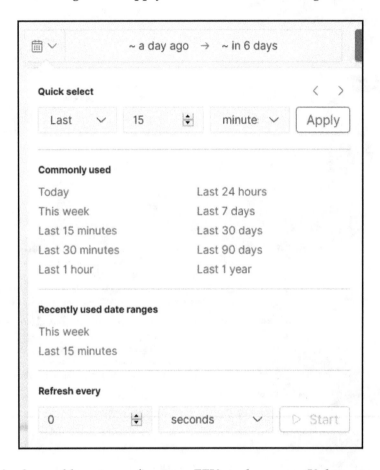

With that, you've learned how to configure an EFK stack on your Kubernetes cluster in order to manage and visualize cluster-wide logs.

See also

- **Elastic Cloud on Kubernetes (ECK)**: `https://github.com/elastic/cloud-on-k8s`
- Deployment instructions on Red Hat OpenShift: `https://www.elastic.co/guide/en/cloud-on-k8s/0.9/k8s-openshift.html`

- Elasticsearch Service documentation: `https://www.elastic.co/guide/en/cloud/current/index.html`
- Introduction to Kibana: `https://www.elastic.co/guide/en/kibana/7.4/introduction.html#introduction`
- Fluentd documentation: `https://docs.fluentd.org/`
- Fluent Bit documentation: `https://docs.fluentbit.io/manual/`
- Rancher Elastic Stack Kubernetes Helm Charts: `https://github.com/rancher/charts/tree/master/charts/efk/v7.3.0`
- Kudo Elastic Operator: `https://github.com/kudobuilder/operators/tree/master/repository/elastic`

Logging Kubernetes using Google Stackdriver

In this section, we will use Google Stackdriver Kubernetes Engine Monitoring to monitor, isolate, and diagnose our containerized applications and microservices environments. You will learn how to use Stackdriver Kubernetes Engine Monitoring to aggregate logs, events, and metrics from your Kubernetes environment on GKE to help you understand your application's behavior in production.

Getting ready

Make sure you have a **Google Kubernetes Engine (GKE)** cluster ready and `kubectl` configured to manage the cluster resources. If you don't have one, you can follow the instructions in `Chapter 1`, *Building Production-Ready Kubernetes Clusters*, in the *Configuring a Kubernetes cluster on Google Cloud Platform* recipe.

How to do it...

This section is further divided into the following subsections to make this process easier:

- Installing Stackdriver Kubernetes Engine Monitoring support for GKE
- Configuring a workspace on Stackdriver
- Viewing GKE logs using Stackdriver

Installing Stackdriver Kubernetes Engine Monitoring support for GKE

Installing Stackdriver Monitoring support allows you to easily monitor GKE clusters, debug logs, and analyze your cluster's performance using advanced profiling and tracing capabilities. In this recipe, we will enable Stackdriver Kubernetes Engine Monitoring support to collect cluster metrics from our GKE cluster. Follow these steps:

1. Open the Google Kubernetes Engine Console at `https://console.cloud.google.com/kubernetes`. On this console, you will see a list of your GKE clusters. Here, we have one cluster called `k8s-devops-cookbook-1`:

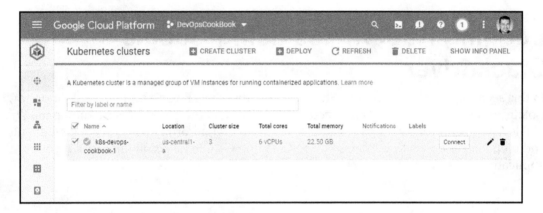

2. Click on the little pen-shaped **Edit** icon next to your cluster:

3. On the cluster configuration page, make sure that **Legacy Stackdriver Logging** and **Legacy Stackdriver Monitoring** are **Disabled** and that the **Stackdriver Kubernetes Engine Monitoring** option is set to **Enabled**:

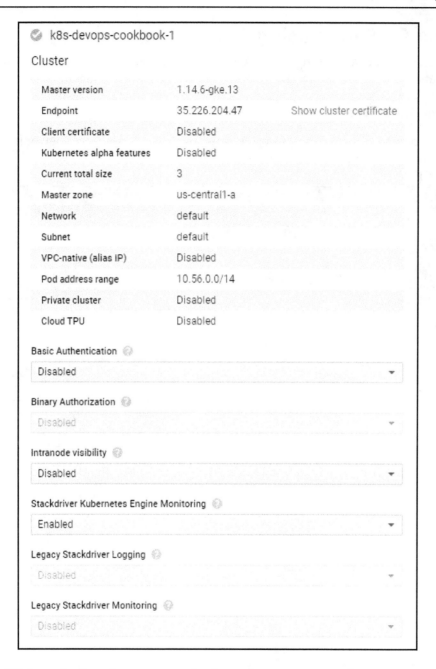

4. Click on the **Save** button to apply these changes to your cluster.

Viewing GKE logs using Stackdriver

Enabling Stackdriver Monitoring support allows you to easily monitor GKE clusters, debug logs, and analyze your cluster performance using advanced profiling and tracing capabilities. In this recipe, we will learn how to access the logs of our Kubernetes cluster on GKE. Follow these steps:

1. From the Google Cloud Console, open the Stackdriver Logs Viewer by going to `https://console.cloud.google.com/logs/viewer`:

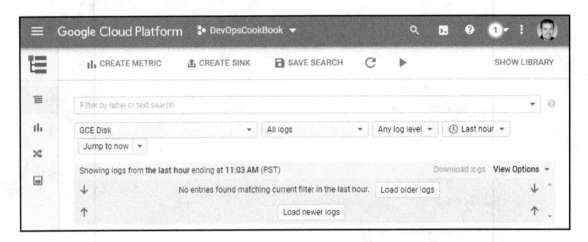

2. From the **Resources** menu, click on the **Kubernetes Container** option:

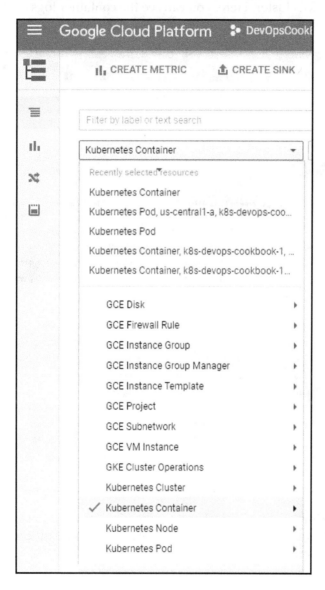

3. The Stackdriver Logging view will show a list of logs for your container in the selected GKE cluster. Here, you can see the container logs for the last 7 days being displayed:

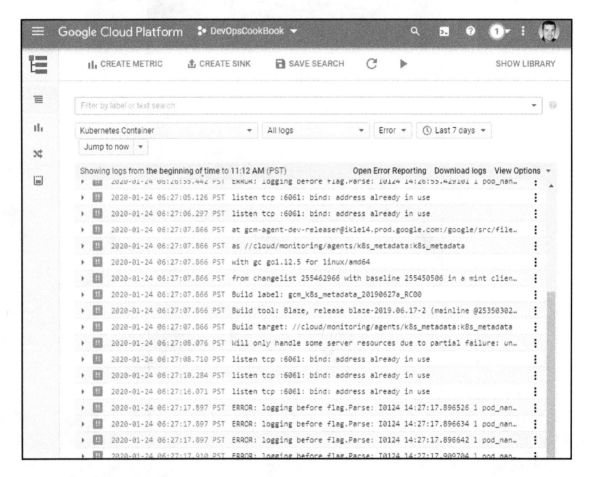

4. Filter the log level to **Critical** and set the time frame to the **Last 24 hours** to view the most recent critical container logs. An example result can be seen in the following screenshot:

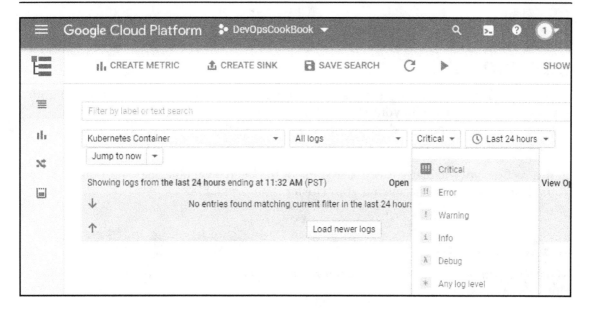

With that, you know how to use Stackdriver to view logs for GKE clusters and resources, such as containers that have been deployed on the GKE clusters.

See also

- Google Stackdriver Logging documentation: https://cloud.google.com/logging/docs
- Basic query example for Stackdriver: https://cloud.google.com/logging/docs/view/basic-queries
- QuickStart using logging tools: https://cloud.google.com/logging/docs/quickstart-sdk
- Stackdriver Logs Router Overview: https://cloud.google.com/logging/docs/routing/overview

Using a managed Kubernetes logging service

Running an EFK stack to store and maintain Kubernetes logs in your cluster is useful until something goes wrong with your cluster. It is recommended that you keep your log management system and production cluster separate so that you have access in case of cluster failure.

In this section, we will learn how to use some of the freely available SaaS solutions to keep your cluster logs accessible, even if your cluster is not available.

Getting ready

Make sure you have a Kubernetes cluster ready and `kubectl` configured to manage the cluster resources.

How to do it...

This section is further divided into the following subsections to make this process easier:

- Adding clusters to Director Online
- Accessing logs using Director Online

Connecting clusters to Director Online

OpenEBS Director provides a freely managed EFK stack as a SaaS solution so that you can store and manage your Kubernetes cluster logs. In this recipe, we will add our Kubernetes cluster to the Director SaaS platform to store our logs in the cloud:

1. Go to `www.mayadata.io` to sign in to your OpenEBS Enterprise Platform at `https://portal.mayadata.io/home`:

2. Click on the **Connect your Cluster** button:

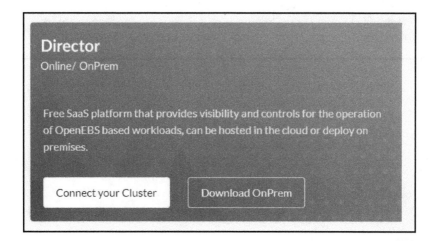

3. From the main menu, select **Clusters** and click on the **Connect a new Cluster** button.

4. Choose your Kubernetes cluster location and name your project. Here, we've used an **AWS** cluster and set `AWSCluster` as our cluster name:

5. Copy and execute the command on your first cluster:

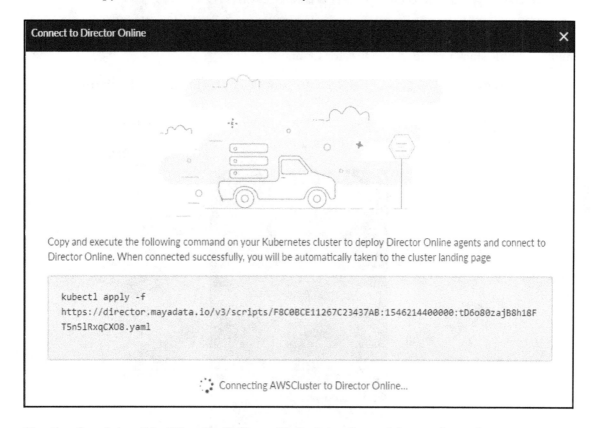

Shortly after doing this, Director Online will deploy a fluentd forwarder and aggregator on your cluster to collect logs on its platform.

Accessing logs using Director Online

OpenEBS Director's free plan stores cluster logs for up to 1 week. Additional storage is provided with the premium plan. In this recipe, we will learn how to access logs using the managed EFK stack provided by Director Online:

1. Go to www.mayadata.io to sign in to your OpenEBS Enterprise Platform at https://portal.mayadata.io/home.

2. From the home menu, select **Clusters** and select your active cluster.

3. From the left-hand menu, click on **Logs**:

4. A Logs view will open on the Kibana Discover dashboard. Here, you can use search for and filter the functionalities of Elasticsearch and Kibana to manage your Kubernetes logs:

With that, you've learned how to simply keep logs accessible using managed Kubernetes logging solutions. You can use Director Online on multiple clusters and manage logs from a single interface.

Logging for your Jenkins CI/CD environment

CI/CD pipelines can generate a great amount of metadata every day in busy build environments. Elasticsearch is the perfect platform for feeding this kind of data from Jenkins.

In this section, we will learn how to enable and access the logs of our Jenkins instance and analyze team efficiency.

Getting ready

All the operations mentioned in this recipe require a fully functional Jenkins deployment, as described in `Chapter 3`, *Building CI/CD Pipelines*, in the *Setting up a CI/CD pipeline in Jenkins X* section.

Clone the `k8sdevopscookbook/src` repository to your workstation to use the manifest files in the `chapter10` directory:

```
$ git clone https://github.com/k8sdevopscookbook/src.git
$ cd src/chapter10
```

Make sure you have a Kubernetes cluster, Jenkins X, and an EFK stack ready and that `kubectl` has been configured so that you can manage the cluster resources.

How to do it...

This section will show you how to feed Jenkins logs to Elasticsearch. This section is further divided into the following subsections to make this process easier:

- Installing the Fluentd plugin
- Streaming Jenkins logs to Elasticsearch using Fluentd

Installing the Fluentd plugin

Fluentd is part of the EFK Stack, along with Elasticsearch and Kibana. It is an open source data collector for building a unified logging layer. This recipe will show you how to install the Fluentd plugin for Jenkins, which will forward the Jenkins logs to your Fluentd logger.

Let's perform the following steps to install the Fluentd plugin on Jenkins:

1. Access your Jenkins service dashboard and click on the **Manage Jenkins** menu:

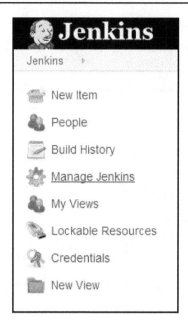

2. In the **Manage Jenkins** menu, click on the **Manage Plugins** button:

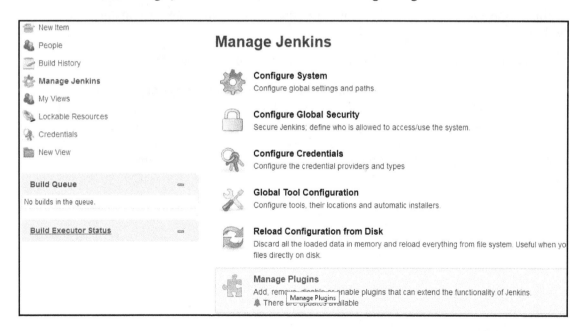

3. Click on the **Available** tab and search for `fluentd` in the **Filter** field. The result should look similar to the following. Click on the **Install without restart** button to install the Fluentd plugin:

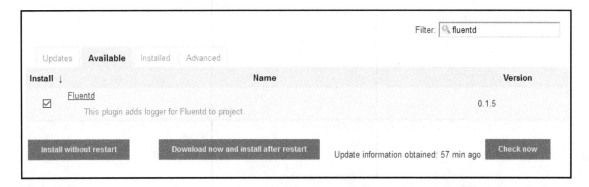

The Fluentd plugin will be installed without the need to restart the Jenkins instance.

Streaming Jenkins logs to Elasticsearch using Fluentd

In this recipe, we will learn how to configure the Fluentd plugin that we installed on Jenkins.

Let's perform the following steps to feed Jenkins logs to Elasticsearch:

1. In the **Manage Jenkins** menu, click on the **Configure System** button.
2. Scroll through the settings. Under the **Logger for Fluentd** settings, enter a logger name. The logger name is used as a prefix for Fluentd. In the **Host** field, enter the Service name of your Fluentd service and the exposed port number. In our example, in our Kubernetes cluster, we used the stable/fluentd Helm chart to install Fluentd. The service name is `fluentd`. This is exposed via port `24220`. Save the changes:

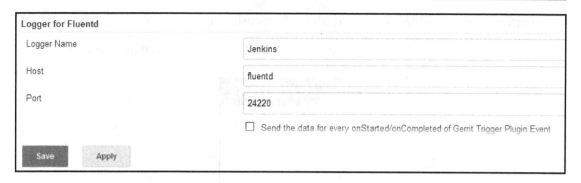

3. Select a job under the pipeline configuration.
4. Click on the **Add post-build action** button and select the **Send to Fluentd** option from the drop-down menu.

Now, the Fluentd plugin will push the logs to Elasticsearch through the log collector.

There's more...

If you are using the ELK stack instead of Fluentd in the EFK stack, then follow the recipes given here. This section is further divided into the following subsections to make this process easier:

- Installing the Logstash plugin
- Streaming Jenkins logs to Elasticsearch using Logstash

Installing the Logstash plugin

Logstash is part of the Elastic Stack, along with Beats, Elasticsearch, and Kibana. It is an open source data collection engine with real-time pipelining capabilities. In this recipe, you will learn how to install the Logstash plugin for Jenkins.

Let's perform the following steps to install the Logstash plugin for Jenkins:

1. Access your Jenkins service dashboard and click on the **Manage Jenkins** menu:

2. In the **Manage Jenkins** menu, click on the **Manage Plugins** button:

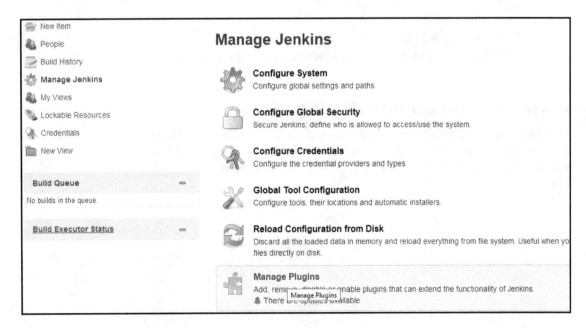

3. Click on the **Available** tab and search for `logstash` in the **Filter** field. The result should look similar to the following. Click on the **Install without restart** button to install the Logstash plugin:

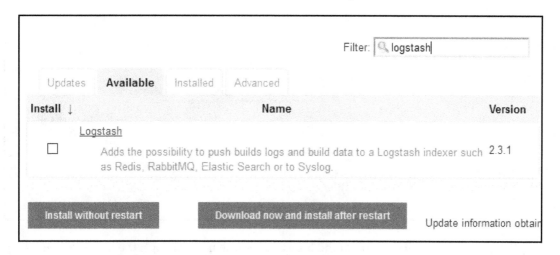

The Logstash plugin will be installed without you needing to restart your Jenkins instance.

Streaming Jenkins logs to Elasticsearch using Logstash

In this recipe, we will show you how to configure the Logstash plugin that you installed on Jenkins previously.

Let's perform the following steps to feed Jenkins logs to Elasticsearch:

1. In the **Manage Jenkins** menu, click on the **Configure System** button.
2. Scroll through the settings. Under the Logstash settings, check the **Enable sending logs to an Indexer** checkbox. When this setting is enabled, it will open four new fields.

3. In the URI field, enter the service name, followed by the indexer name; for example, `http://elasticsearch-es-http:9200/logstash/jenkins`. Enter your `elastic` username and password and save the changes:

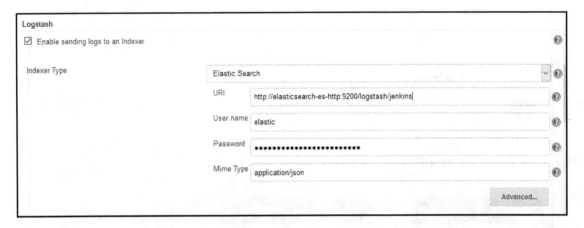

Now, the Logstash plugin will push the logs to Elasticsearch through the log collector.

See also

- Jenkins Logstash plugin documentation: `https://wiki.jenkins.io/display/JENKINS/Logstash+Plugin`
- Jenkins FluentD plugin documentation: `https://github.com/jenkinsci/fluentd-plugin`
- Debug logging in Jenkins: `https://wiki.jenkins.io/display/JENKINS/Logging`

Other Books You May Enjoy

If you enjoyed this book, you may be interested in these other books by Packt:

Hands-On Microservices with Kubernetes

Gigi Sayfan

ISBN: 978-1-78980-546-8

- Understand the synergy between Kubernetes and microservices
- Create a complete CI/CD pipeline for your microservices on Kubernetes
- Develop microservices on Kubernetes with the Go kit framework using best practices
- Manage and monitor your system using Kubernetes and open source tools
- Expose your services through REST and gRPC APIs
- Implement and deploy serverless functions as a service
- Externalize authentication, authorization, and traffic shaping using a service mesh
- Run a Kubernetes cluster in the cloud on Google Kubernetes Engine

Hands-On Kubernetes on Azure
Shivakumar Gopalakrishnan, Gunther Lenz

ISBN: 978-1-78953-610-2

- Use the Kubernetes dashboard to review clusters and deployed applications
- Find out the benefits and limitations, and how to avoid potential problems while using AKS
- Understand the implementation of Microsoft toolchains such as Visual Studio Code and Git
- Implement simple and advanced AKS solutions
- Ensure automated scalability and high reliability of your applications with Microsoft AKS
- Apply kubectl commands to monitor applications

Leave a review - let other readers know what you think

Please share your thoughts on this book with others by leaving a review on the site that you bought it from. If you purchased the book from Amazon, please leave us an honest review on this book's Amazon page. This is vital so that other potential readers can see and use your unbiased opinion to make purchasing decisions, we can understand what our customers think about our products, and our authors can see your feedback on the title that they have worked with Packt to create. It will only take a few minutes of your time, but is valuable to other potential customers, our authors, and Packt. Thank you!

Index

A

Adobe Experience Manager (AEM) 226
AKS clusters
    accessing 27
    changes, deploying 174, 176, 178
AKS performance metrics
    monitoring, with Azure Monitor 416, 419, 421
AKS, on GitHub
    reference link 29
Alibaba Cloud account
    reference link 30
Alibaba Cloud
    highly available Kubernetes cluster, provisioning
        on 32
    Kubernetes cluster, configuring on 30, 35
Alibaba Container Service clusters
    accessing 34, 35
Aliyun 30
Aliyun Web Console
    URL 33
Amazon CloudWatch
    using, for monitoring 395
Amazon EBS volumes
    managing, in Kubernetes 242
Amazon EKS FAQ
    reference link 19
Amazon EKS Management Console
    used, for provisioning EKS Cluster 16
Amazon Elastic Compute Cloud (Amazon EC2)
    about 8
    Kubernetes cluster. provisioning on 10, 12
Amazon Elastic Container Service for Kubernetes
    (Amazon EKS)
    about 8
    Container Insights Agents, installing for 399, 400
    managed Kubernetes cluster, provisioning on 12

Amazon Web Services (AWS)
    CI/CD pipeline, setting up 140, 153
    Kubernetes cluster, configuring on 8, 13
    reference link 154
anomalies
    detecting, Falco used 490, 491
Ansible module, for working with Kubernetes
    reference link 52
Ansible playbook
    used, for provisioning Kubernetes cluster 50
Ansible
    installing 50
    used, for configuring Kubernetes cluster 49, 50
anti-patterns
    detecting, with SonarQube 218, 219, 232
Apache Kafka Operator
    installing, KUDO used 83
    installing, KUDU used 83
application status
    checking 107
application-specific logs
    accessing 510, 511
application
    backing up 310, 311, 320, 321, 322, 323
    backing up, Kasten used 316, 317, 326
    backing up, Velero used 307, 308, 316
    deleting, with Helm 77
    deploying, Kubernetes operators used 81, 82
    importing 92
    importing, as pipeline 106, 107
    incremental rollouts, to production 124, 126
    installing, Helm charts used 73, 74
    migrating, in Kasten 330, 331, 332
    migrating, in OpenEBS Director 335, 336, 337,
        338
    operating, Kubernetes operators used 81, 82
    promoting, to production 108

recovering, Kasten used 316, 317, 326
recovering, Velero used 307, 308, 316
restoring 312, 324, 325
rolling back, Helm used 76
rollout, to production 164, 166
searching, in Helm repositories 74, 75
upgrading, with Helm 75, 76
applications, scaling on Kubernetes
  about 340
  HPA, using 343, 345, 346
  manually 341, 342
  Metrics Server installation, validating 340
Aqua Security Trivy CI
  examples, reference link 487
Aqua Security Trivy Comparison
  reference link 487
Aqua Security
  used, for building DevSecOps into pipeline 481,
  482
Auto DevOps
  enabling 117, 118
  used, for creating pipeline 123, 124
auto-healing pods
  in Kubernetes 373
  liveness probes, adding to pods 374, 376
autogenerated self-signed certificates
  using 99
AWS account
  reference link 8
AWS CodeBuild
  used, for building project 145, 148, 149
AWS CodeCommit code repository
  creating 141, 142, 144
AWS CodeDeploy deployment
  creating 150
AWS CodePipeline
  used, for building pipeline 150, 152
AWS Command Line Interface (CLI) 9
AWS Command Reference S3 Create Bucket API
  reference link 19
AWS EBS CSI driver documentation
  reference link 253
AWS EBS CSI driver repository
  reference link 253, 271
AWS EBS volume types

reference link 252
AWS Fargate product
  reference link 19
AWS Global Infrastructure Map
  reference link 19
AWS Shell
  using 14
Azure DevOps documentation
  reference link 179
Azure DevOps
  about 169
  CI/CD pipeline, setting up 168, 178
  reference link 168
Azure Disk CSI driver
  installing 269, 270, 271
Azure Disk persistent volumes
  deleting 268
Azure Disk storage classes
  creating 265, 266
  used, for creating dynamic PVs 267, 268
Azure Disk volume types
  managing, in Kubernetes 264
  reference link 271
Azure Kubernetes Service (AKS)
  about 264, 415, 468
  managed Kubernetes cluster, provisioning on 27
  PodSecurityPolicy, enabling on 468
Azure Monitor for containers documentation
  reference link 428
Azure Monitor support, for AKS
  enabling, with CLI 415
Azure Monitor, as datasource
  reference link 439
Azure Monitor
  used, for monitoring AKS performance metrics
  416, 419, 421
  used, for viewing live logs 422, 425, 428
  using, for monitoring 415
Azure Pipelines documentation
  reference link 179
Azure Pipelines
  configuring 170, 171, 173

B

backups and schedules
  deleting 315
Blue deployment
  creating 378, 379
  traffic, switching to Green deployment 379
  upgrades, managing through 377
bugs
  detecting, with SonarQube 218, 219, 232

C

canary deployment strategy, for Kubernetes
  deployments
  reference link 179
Center for Internet Security (CIS)
  about 473
  URL 473
Central Registration Depository (CRD) 189
centralized logging
  building, in Kubernetes with EFK stack 513
Ceph block storage class
  creating 274
  used, for creating dynamic PVs 276
Ceph cluster's health
  verifying 273, 274
Ceph cluster
  creating 273
Ceph provider
  installing, with Rook 272
certificate sign request (CSR) 461
Chaos Charts, for Kubernetes
  reference link 198
Chaos Charts
  using, for Kubernetes 191, 192, 193
Chaos Engineering
  automating, with Gremlin 198
chaos experiment logs
  viewing 196, 197
chaos experiment results
  reviewing 195, 196
Chaoskube project
  reference link 198
chart template
  reference link 81

Chart.yaml file
  reference link 81
ChartMuseum 79
CI/CD pipeline
  creating, in CircleCI 130, 131, 134
  creating, in GitLab 111, 112, 126
  creating, in Jenkins X 104, 110
  setting up, on Amazon Web Services 140, 153
  setting up, on Azure DevOps 168, 178
  setting up, with GitHub Actions 135
  setting up, with Spinnaker on Google Cloud Build
    154, 155
CI/CD services
  service account, configuring 156
CI/CD, on Google Cloud Quickstarts
  reference link 168
CircleCI
  CI/CD pipeline, creating 130, 131, 134
  overview 131
  reference link 134
  URL 131
  vulnerability scanning, building into 485, 486,
    487
CIS Kubernetes Benchmarks
  reference link 480
CLI
  used, for enabling Azure Monitor support for AKS
    416
  used, for monitoring metrics 383, 384
Cloud Source Repositories
  reference link 168
CloudWatch Anomaly Detection
  reference link 404
cluster configuration
  editing 16
cluster conformance
  validating 91
clusters
  connecting, to Director Online 532
  deleting 16, 25, 29, 49
  deploying, with custom network configuration 24
  importing 40, 41
CNCF certified Kubernetes installers
  reference link 20
Codacy badge

adding, to repository 217, 218
Codacy
  documentation, reference link 218
  URL 211
code review, with Codacy
  automating 210
command-line tools
  installing, to configure Alibaba cloud services 31, 32
  installing, to configure AWS services 9
  installing, to configure Azure services 26
  installing, to configure GCP services 21
commits and PRs
  reviewing 213, 214, 215
compliance checking, for Kubernetes-based applications
  reference link 480
configuration options
  reference link 101
Container Insights Agents
  installing, for Amazon EKS 399, 400
Container Insights metrics
  reference link 404
  viewing 400, 402, 403, 404
Container Insights
  reference link 404
Container Storage Interface (CSI)
  about 242, 301
  reference link 307
  volume snapshot, creating through 302, 303, 304
  volume, restoring from snapshot via 304, 305
containers
  inspecting 388
  PostgreSQL logs, accessing 512, 513
  shell access, obtaining 511, 512
CPU attack
  creating, against Kubernetes worker 201, 203, 204, 205
CrashLoopBackOff status
  pods, inspecting in 393, 394, 395
credentials, on Vault
  storing 499, 500
credentials
  securing, HashiCorp Vault used 494, 495

cross-cloud application
  migrating 326, 327
Crunchy Data PostgreSQL Operator
  reference link 86
CSI spec
  reference link 307
custom metrics
  reference link 347
custom network configuration
  used, for deploying cluster 24
Custom Resource Definitions (CRDs) 316, 515
custom rules
  defining 491, 492, 493

D

Data Migration as a Service (DMaaS) 332
DataDog
  reference link 439
default Roles
  viewing 459, 460
default storage class
  changing 244, 245, 255, 256, 257
  changing, to ZRS 266
deploy changes as quickly as possible approach 481
deployment YAML manifest
  creating 297, 298
Deployment
  creating 58, 59
  deleting 63
  editing 60, 61
  rolling back 62
  verifying 59, 60
development
  base, creating for 67, 70
DevSecOps
  building, into pipeline Aqua Security used 481, 482
Director Online
  clusters, connecting to 532
  used, for accessing 536
disaster recovery (DR) 295
Docker build workflow
  creating 137
Docker Registry

images, building 138
images, publishing 138
Dynamic Application Security Testing (DAST) 111
dynamic NFS PVs
   creating, with OpenEBS NFS provisioner storage
     class 290
   creating, with Rook NFS operator storage class
     289, 290
dynamic persistent volumes
   creating, with GCE PD storage classes 259
dynamic PVs
   creating, with Ceph block storage class 276
   creating, with OpenEBS storage class 284

E

EBS CSI driver
   installing, to manage EBS volumes 250, 251,
     252
EBS persistent volumes
   deleting 248, 249
EBS storage classes
   creating 243, 244
   used, for creating persistent volumes 246, 247
EBS volumes
   managing, to install EBS CSI driver 250, 251,
     252
   used, for persistent storage 245
EKS Cluster
   provisioning, with Amazon EKS Management
     Console 16
Elastic Cloud on Kubernetes (ECK)
   about 514
   reference link 524
Elastic Container Registry (ECR) 140, 478
Elastichsearh, Fluent-bit, and Kibana (EFK) stack
   about 513
   used, for building centralized logging in
     Kubernetes 513
Elasticsearch endpoint
   requesting 516
Elasticsearch Operator
   deploying 514, 516
Elasticsearch, Logstash, and Kibana (ELK) stack
   513
ephemeral storage

used, for creating persistent volumes 279, 280
event-driven automation
   building, with StackStorm 182
events
   configuring, to trigger pipeline 157
export profile
   creating, in Kasten 327, 328
external load balancer
   creating 357, 361
   external address of service, finding 360
   external cloud load balancer, creating 358, 360

F

Falco
   installing, on Kubernetes 488, 489
   used, for detecting anomalies 490, 491
   used, for monitoring suspicious application
     activities 488
feature gates
   enabling 302
Fluent Bit
   used, for aggregating logs 517
Fluentd
   used, for streaming Jenkins logs to Elasticsearch
     540
FOSSA badge
   adding, to project 238, 239
FOSSA
   projects, adding 234, 235, 236
   used, for detecting license compliance issues
     233

G

GCE PD CSI driver repository
   reference link 264
GCE PD persistent volumes
   deleting 260
GCE PD storage classes
   used, for creating dynamic persistent volumes
     259
GCE PD types
   reference link 264
GCE PD volumes
   managing, in Kubernetes 253, 263
   used, for persistent storage 257, 258

GCE persistent disk storage class
  creating 254, 255
GCP account
  reference link 20
GCP Compute PD CSI driver
  installing, to manage PD volumes 261, 262
GCP documentation
  reference link 25
GitHub Actions
  reference link 140
  used, for setting up CI/CD pipeline 135
GitHub repository, for Prometheus-Operator
  reference link 439
GitHub
  project, importing 114, 116
GitLab cloud-native Helm chart documentation
  URL 101
GitLab Community Edition
  installation link 101
GitLab dashboard
  connecting 96
GitLab Operator
  enabling 100
  reference link 101
GitLab user
  creating 96, 97
GitLab Web IDE 127
GitLab
  CI/CD pipeline, creating 111, 112, 126
  deleting 100
  installing, Helm used 95
  life cycle, deploying 94, 98
  life cycle, managing 94, 98
  reference link 130
  upgrading 97, 98
  using, for monitoring environments 128, 129
  vulnerability scanning, building into 484, 485
GKE clusters
  accessing 22
GKE logs
  viewing, with Stackdriver 528, 530
GKE metrics
  monitoring, with Stackdriver 409, 413
GKE on-prem installation
  reference link 25

Google Cloud Build
  CI/CD pipeline, setting up with Spinnaker 154, 155
  project, building 161, 162, 163
Google Cloud Platform (GCP)
  about 20, 87, 253
  Kubernetes cluster, configuring on 20, 23
Google Cloud Shell
  using 23
Google Cloud Source code repository
  creating 159, 160
Google Compute Engine (GCE) 20
Google Kubernetes Engine (GKE)
  about 20, 253, 467
  managed Kubernetes cluster, provisioning on 22
  PodSecurityPolicy, enabling on 467, 468
  Stackdriver Kubernetes Engine Monitoring
    support, installing 526, 527
  Stackdriver Kubernetes Engine Monitoring
    support, installing for 405, 406
Google Stackdriver
  used, for logging Kubernetes 525
  using, for monitoring 404
gossip-based cluster
  using 15
Grafana community dashboards
  reference link 439
Grafana dashboards
  adding, to monitor applications 435, 437, 439
  used, for monitoring metrics 430, 433, 434
Grafana plugins
  reference link 439
Grafana
  reference link 439
  used, for monitoring Kubernetes 429
Green deployment
  creating 379
  upgrades, managing through 377
Gremlin credentials
  setting up 199, 200
Gremlin
  Chaos Engineering, automating with 198
  deleting, from cluster 209, 210
  documentation, reference link 210
  installing, on Kubernetes 200

reference link 198
URL 202

H

Hashicorp Vault documentation
  URL 501
Hashicorp Vault repository
  URL 501
HashiCorp Vault
  used, for securing credentials 494, 495
Helm 2.x
  installing 72, 73
Helm chart
  building 79, 80
Helm charts
  hosting methods, reference link 81
  used, for deploying Prometheus 429
  used, for deploying Spinnaker 158, 159
  used, for deploying workloads 71, 72, 80
  used, for installing application 73, 74
Helm repositories
  adding 77, 78, 79
  application, searching in 74, 75
Helm
  documentation, reference link 81
  used, for deleting application 77
  used, for installing GitLab 95
  used, for installing SonarQube 219
  used, for Istio installation 363
  used, for rolling back application 76
  used, for upgrading application 75, 76
High Availability (HA) 182
highly available Kubernetes cluster
  provisioning, on Alibaba Cloud 32
Horizontal Pod Autoscaler (HPA)
  used, for autoscaling applications 343, 345, 346
host volume
  bind mounting 43

I

Identity and Access Management (IAM) 149
ImagePullBackOff status
  pods, inspecting in 391, 392
images
  building, to Docker Registry 138

publishing, to Docker Registry 138
import profile
  creating, in Kasten 330
ingress service
  creating, Linkerd used 368
  creating, with Istio 362
init containers, debugging
  reference link 395
installation issues
  troubleshooting 52, 53
iSCSI client prerequisites
  installing 278
issues
  viewing, by category 215, 216
Istio Operator
  reference link 86
Istio
  deleting 367
  ingress gateway, creating 365, 366, 367
  installation, verifying 363, 364
  installing, Helm used 363
  reference link 367
  used, for creating ingress service 362
  used, for creating service mesh 362

J

Jenkins CI/CD environment
  Fluentd plugin, installing 538, 540
  Jenkins logs, streaming to Elasticsearch with
    Fluentd 540
  Jenkins logs, streaming to to Elasticsearch with
    Logstash 543
  logging for 537
  Logstash plugin, installing 541, 543
Jenkins Pipeline Console
  connecting 105, 106
Jenkins Prometheus plugin
  reference link 439
Jenkins X application
  upgrading 93
Jenkins X CLI
  commands and explanation, reference link 94
  installing 87
Jenkins X components
  verifying 89, 90

Jenkins X Kubernetes cluster
  creating 88, 89
  deleting 93
Jenkins X tutorials
  URL 94
Jenkins X
  CI/CD pipeline, creating 104, 110
  life cycle, deploying 86, 87, 91
  life cycle, managing 86, 87, 91
  reference link 94
  repository and binaries, reference link 94
Jenkins
  reference link 94
JX release site
  URL 87

K

K3s
  reference link 45
K9s
  reference link 55
Kafka Operators
  reference link 86
Kasten CLI commands
  reference link 326
Kasten Dashboard
  accessing 319, 320
Kasten
  application, migrating in 330, 331, 332
  documentation, reference link 326
  export profile, creating in 327, 328
  import profile, creating in 330
  installing 317, 318
  restore point, exporting in 328, 329
  used, for backing up application 316, 317, 326
  used, for recovering application 316, 317, 326
Kibana
  deploying 516, 517
  Kubernetes logs, accessing 518, 520, 522, 524
Konvoy
  reference link 20
kops
  installing, to provision Kubernetes cluster 10
  reference link 19
Krex

reference link 388
kube-bench
  reference link 480
  running, on Kubernetes 474, 476, 477
  running, on managed Kubernetes services 477,
    478, 479
  running, on OpenShift 479
KubeAdm
  reference link 20
Kubecost dashboard
  accessing 449, 450
Kubecost
  installing 448
  reference link 455
  used, for managing resource cost 447
kubectl cheat sheet
  reference link 55
kubectl command
  reference link 55
KubeOne
  reference link 20
Kubernetes Authentication
  reference link 465
Kubernetes CIS Benchmark
  using, for security auditing 473, 480
Kubernetes cluster integration
  enabling 119, 120, 121, 122
Kubernetes clusters
  accessing 51
  changes, deploying on EKS 132, 133
  configuring, on Alibaba Cloud 30, 36
  configuring, on Amazon Web Services 8, 13
  configuring, on Google Cloud Platform 20, 23
  configuring, on Microsoft Azure 25, 28
  configuring, with Ansible 49, 50
  configuring, with Rancher 37
  deploying 39, 40
  managing, with Rancher 37
  provisioning, on Amazon EC2 10, 12
  provisioning, with Ansible playbook 50
  switching 90
  users, types 464
  version, validating 65
Kubernetes CSI
  reference link 301

Kubernetes CSI drivers
  list, reference link 307
Kubernetes Dashboard
  deploying 17, 19
  used, for monitoring metrics 384, 385, 386
  viewing 29
Kubernetes Feature Gates
  reference link 307
Kubernetes logging conventions
  reference link 54
Kubernetes logs
  accessing 504, 509
  accessing, on Kibana 518, 520, 522, 524
Kubernetes manifests guide
  authoring, reference link 64
Kubernetes Metrics Server Design Document
  reference link 388
Kubernetes Metrics Server
  used, for adding metrics 383
Kubernetes nodes
  Rancher, running on 44
Kubernetes objects, declarative management
  reference link 64
Kubernetes operators
  examples, reference link 52
  list, reference link 85
  reference link 85
  used, for deploying application 81, 82
  used, for operating application 81, 82
Kubernetes PodSecurityPolicy advisor
  using 472
Kubernetes resource cost allocation
  monitoring 451, 452, 454
Kubernetes resources
  generating, from YAML files 65, 66
Kubernetes restore
  managing 301, 302, 306
Kubernetes Universal Declarative Operator (KUDO)
  about 82
  installing 82, 83
  reference link 85
  used, for installing Apache Kafka Operator 83
Kubernetes Volume Cloning
  documentation, reference link 307
Kubernetes Volume Snapshots

documentation, reference link 307
  managing 301, 302
Kubernetes volume snapshots
  managing 306
Kubernetes worker
  CPU attack, creating against 201, 203, 204,
    205
  node shutdown attack, creating against 205,
    206, 207
Kubernetes YAML validator
  reference link 64
Kubernetes
  about 30
  Amazon EBS volumes, managing 242
  applications, scaling 340
  auto-healing pods 373
  Azure Disk volumes, managing 264
  centralized logging, building with EFK stack 513
  Chaos Charts, using 191, 192, 193
  Falco, installing on 488, 489
  GCE PD volumes, managing 253, 263
  Gremlin, installing on 200
  kube-bench, running on 474, 476, 477
  logging, with Google Stackdriver 525
  logs, accessing through 504, 505, 506
  monitoring 382
  monitoring, with Grafana 429
  monitoring, with Prometheus 429
  NFS for shared storage, setting up 286
  Vault, installing on 495, 496, 497
KubeSpray
  reference link 20
KUDO kubectl plugin
  installing 82, 83
Kustomize concepts
  reference link 71
Kustomize
  examples, reference link 71
  used, for deploying workloads 64, 71

L

Lambda function, example for EKS deployment
  reference link 154
license compliance issues
  detecting, with FOSSA 233

licensing issues
  triaging 236, 238
Linkerd
  adding, to service 370, 371
  CLI, installing 369
  dashboard, accessing 371
  deleting 372
  deployment, verifying 370
  installing 369
  reference link 372
  used, for creating ingress service 368
  used, for creating service mesh 368
linter, for YAML files
  reference link 64
Linux Virtual Server (LVS) 360
Litmus documentation
  reference link 198
Litmus framework
  used, for automating tests 189, 190
Litmus Operator
  installing 190
live logs
  viewing, with Azure Monitor 422, 425, 428
log levels
  setting 54
logs
  accessing, through Kubernetes 504, 505, 506
  accessing, with Director Online 536
  aggregating, with Fluent Bit 517
Logstash
  used, for streaming Jenkins logs 543

M

Managed Kubernetes 30
managed Kubernetes cluster
  provisioning, on AKS 27
  provisioning, on Amazon EKS 12
  provisioning, on GKE 22
managed Kubernetes logging service
  using 532
marketplace plugins
  adding 230, 231
MetalLB
  reference link 360
metrics

adding, with Kubernetes Metrics Server 383
monitoring, with CLI 383, 384
monitoring, with Grafana dashboards 430, 432, 434
monitoring, with Kubernetes Dashboard 384, 385, 386
Microsoft AKS FAQ
  reference link 29
Microsoft Azure
  Kubernetes cluster, configuring on 25, 28
MinIO documentation
  reference link 301
MinIO Erasure Code QuickStart Guide
  reference link 301
MinIO Operator, for Kubernetes
  reference link 301
MinIO S3 service
  creating 298, 299
MinIO web user interface
  accessing 299, 300
MinIO
  used, for configuring object storage 296, 300
  used, for managing object storage 296, 300
  used, for viewing backups 314, 315
monitoring stack, OpenShift Container Platform
  reference link 388
monitoring
  in Kubernetes 382
  with Amazon CloudWatch 395
  with Azure Monitor 415
  with Google Stackdriver 404
  with Sysdig 440
Multi-AZ Kubernetes 30

N

namespace
  backup, creating 313
New Relic
  reference link 439
Nexus 91
NFS for shared storage
  setting up, on Kubernetes 286
NFS prerequisites
  installing 287
NFS provider

installing, with Rook NFS operator 287, 289
NFS provisioner
  installing, with OpenEBS 290
Node and InterPod Affinity
  used, for assigning pods to nodes 351, 354, 355
  working 355, 357
node health
  monitoring 387, 388
node shutdown attack
  creating, against Kubernetes worker 205, 206, 207
nodes
  applications, assigning 347
  labeling 348
  pods, assigning with Node and InterPod Affinity 351, 353, 355
  pods, assigning with nodeSelector 349, 350, 351
nodeSelector
  used, for assigning pods to nodes 349, 351

O

object storage
  configuring, MinIO used 296, 300
  managing, MinIO used 296, 300
Open Falcon
  reference link 439
OpenEBS Director Online
  connecting, reference link 338
OpenEBS Director, using in Auto DevOps usecase
  reference link 338
OpenEBS Director
  application, migrating in 335, 336, 337, 338
  clusters, importing into 332, 333, 334, 335
  reference link 338
OpenEBS NFS provisioner storage class
  used, for creating dynamic NFS PVs 290
OpenEBS provisioning, read-write-many PVCs
  reference link 291
OpenEBS storage class
  creating 282, 283
  used, for creating dynamic PVs 284
OpenEBS
  installing 279
  reference link 286

used, for configuring persistent storage 277, 285
  used, for installing NFS provisioner 290
  used, for managing persistent storage 277, 285
OpenShift binaries
  downloading 46
OpenShift cluster
  accessing 47
  provisioning 46, 47
OpenShift Container Platform 4.3 Documentation
  reference link 49
OpenShift
  kube-bench, running on 479
Operator Lifecycle Manager (OLM)
  installing 84

P

Pending status
  pods, inspecting in 389, 390, 391
performance analysis
  with Sysdig 440
persistent storage
  configuring, with OpenEBS 277, 285
  configuring, with Rook 271
  EBS volumes, using 245
  managing, with OpenEBS 277, 285
  managing, with Rook 271
Persistent Volume Claim (PVC) 244, 300
persistent volumes
  creating, with EBS storage classes 246, 247
  creating, with ephemeral storage 279, 280
  in pending state 292, 293
pipeline
  building, with AWS CodePipeline 150, 152
  creating, with Auto DevOps 123, 124
  creating, with QuickStart application 109
pod deletion chaos experiment
  creating 193, 194, 195
pod failure, reason
  reference link 395
Pod Security Policies (PSP)
  configuring 465, 466
  enabling, on AKS 468
  enabling, on EKS 466
  enabling, on GKE 467, 468
  reference link 472

pods and ReplicationControllers, debugging
  reference link 395
pods
  inspecting, in CrashLoopBackOff status 393,
    394, 395
  inspecting, in ImagePullBackOff status 391, 392
  inspecting, in Pending status 389, 390, 391
  restricting, to access certain volume types 470,
    472
PostgreSQL logs
  accessing, inside container 512, 513
production Deployment
  base, creating for 67, 70
Programming Mistake Detector (PMD) 226
Project Dashboard
  accessing 211, 212
project
  adding 227, 228
  building, with AWS CodeBuild 145, 148, 149
  building, with Google Cloud Build 161, 162, 163
  creating, with templates 112, 113
  importing, from GitHub 114, 116
  quality, reviewing 229, 230
Prometheus exporters
  reference link 439
Prometheus, with Azure Monitor
  reference link 428
Prometheus, with Stackdriver Kubernetes Engine
    Monitoring
  reference link 414
Prometheus
  deploying, with Helm charts 429
  reference link 439
  used, for monitoring Kubernetes 429
Pull Request (PR) 91, 217
Pumba project
  reference link 198
PV deletion
  terminating 293
PVC deletion
  terminating 293
Python client
  reference link 189

Q

quality profiles
  enabling 224, 226, 227
QuickStart application
  used, for creating pipeline 109

R

Rancher 2.x Documentation
  reference link 45
Rancher Kubernetes Engine (RKE) 37
Rancher server
  installing 38
Rancher
  about 37
  clusters, using 42
  Kubernetes clusters, configuring 37, 43
  Kubernetes clusters, managing 37, 43
  node providers, enabling 42
  running, on Kubernetes nodes 44
RBAC Authorization, in Kubernetes Documentation
  reference link 465
RBAC policies
  autogenerating, reference link 465
RBAC rules
  testing 464
ReadWriteMany (RWX) 286
Red Hat OpenShift
  configuring 45, 48
Red Hat Operator SDK, used for building
    Kubernetes Operators
  list, reference link 85
Red Hat Package Manager/Debian (RPM/Deb)
  182
Resource Orchestration Service (ROS) 32
restricted PSP
  creating 469, 470
Rio
  reference link 45
Role-based access control (RBAC)
  using, to harden cluster security 458, 465
Roles and RoleBindings
  creating 462, 463
Rook documentation
  reference link 277

Rook NFS operator documentation
  reference link 291
Rook NFS operator storage class
  used, for creating dynamic NFS PVs 289, 290
Rook NFS operator
  used, for installing NFS provider 287, 289
Rook
  Ceph provider, installing 272
  used, for configuring persistent storage 271
  used, for managing persistent storage 271

S

S3 bucket
  regions, using for 15
scenario-based attacks
  running 208, 209
scheduled backup
  creating 312, 313
SeeSaw
  reference link 360
self-healing pods
  testing 373, 374
Serverless Kubernetes 30
service account
  configuring, for CI/CD services 156
service mesh
  creating, Linkerd used 368
  creating, with Istio 362
service-level agreement (SLA) 355
services
  debugging, with Telepresence 507, 509
shell access
  obtaining, in container 511, 512
SonarQube Community
  reference link 233
SonarQube Dashboard
  accessing 220, 221, 222
SonarQube extension, for Azure DevOps
  reference link 233
SonarQube Scanner, for Ant
  reference link 233
SonarQube Scanner, for Maven
  reference link 233
SonarQube Scanner, for MSBuild
  reference link 233

SonarQube
  deleting, from cluster 232
  documentation, reference link 232
  installing, Helm used 219
  used, for detecting anti-patterns 218, 219, 232
  used, for detecting bugs 218, 219, 232
SonarScanner, for Jenkins
  reference link 232
Spin CLI
  configuring 155
  installing 155
Spinnaker pipeline
  configuring 164
Spinnaker
  deploying, with Helm charts 158, 159
  used, for setting up CI/CD pipeline on Google
    Cloud Build 154, 155
Squash
  reference link 395
st2 CLI
  using 185, 186
Stackdriver Kubernetes Engine Monitoring support
  installing, for GKE 405, 406, 526, 527
Stackdriver Prometheus sidecar
  reference link 414
Stackdriver, as data source
  reference link 439
Stackdriver
  reference link 414
  used, for monitoring GKE metrics 409, 413
  used, for viewing GKE logs 528, 530
  workspace, configuring on 407, 409
StackStorm CLI
  reference link 189
StackStorm documentation
  reference link 189
StackStorm rule
  defining 186, 187, 188
  deploying 188, 189
StackStorm UI
  accessing 183, 184, 185
StackStorm
  event-driven automation, building with 182
  examples, reference link 189
  installing 182, 183

statefulset, debugging
   reference link 395
Static Application Security Testing (SAST) 111
storage issues
   troubleshooting 291
storage pools
   creating 281, 282
suspicious application activities
   monitoring, Falco used 488
Sysdig agent
   installing 440, 442
Sysdig examples
   reference link 447
Sysdig Falco
   reference link 447
Sysdig Inspect
   reference link 447
Sysdig Monitor 440
Sysdig
   application performance, analyzing 444, 445,
   446, 447
   using, for monitoring 440
   using, for performance analysis 440

T

Telepresence
   used, for debugging services 507, 509
templates
   used, for creating project 112, 113
tests
   automating, with Litmus framework 189, 190
Trivy
   used, for scanning image 482, 483

U

user accounts
   creating 460, 461, 462
user and tokens
   creating 222, 223, 224
user volumes
   keeping persistent 44

V

Vault UI
   accessing 497, 498

Vault
   installing, on Kubernetes 495, 496, 497
Velero project repository
   reference link 316
Velero
   installing 309, 310
   used, for backing up application 307, 308, 316
   used, for recovering application 307, 308
   used, for restoring application 316
visual guide, on troubleshooting Kubernetes
   deployments
   reference link 55
volume snapshot
   creating, through CSI 302, 303, 304
volume, via CSI
   cloning 306
volumes
   restoring, from snapshot via CSI 304, 305
   types, reference link 472
vulnerability scanning
   building, into CircleCI 485, 486, 487
   building, into GitLab 484, 485

W

Webhook authorization mode
   enabling 396, 397, 398
wildcard certificate
   using 99
Windows Subsystem for Linux (WSL) 507
workflow file
   creating 135, 136
workflow status badge
   adding 139
Workloads Dashboard
   viewing 25
workloads
   deploying, Helm charts used 71, 72, 80
   deploying, Kustomize used 64, 71
   deploying, YAML files used 58, 63
workspace
   configuring, on Stackdriver 407, 408

Y

YAML files
   Kubernetes resources, generating from 65, 66

Yet Another Markup Language (YAML) files
    about 58
    used, for deploying workloads 58, 63

Z

Zalando PostgreSQL Operator
    installing 84, 85
    reference link 86

www.ingramcontent.com/pod-product-compliance
Lightning Source LLC
Chambersburg PA
CBHW060636060326
40690CB00020B/4421